AFRICA REMEMBERED

AFRICA REMEMBERED

Narratives by West Africans
from the Era of the Slave Trade

Edited by

Philip D. Curtin

Johns Hopkins University

WAVELAND

PRESS, INC.

Long Grove, Illinois

For information about this book, contact:
Waveland Press, Inc.
4180 IL Route 83, Suite 101
Long Grove, IL 60047-9580
(847) 634-0081
info@waveland.com
www.waveland.com

Cover illustration by Leo and Diane Dillon.

PREFACE

The personal narratives collected in this volume have been chosen to illustrate the African side of the Atlantic slave trade. They are therefore limited to accounts by Africans (with one exception), to the eighteenth and nineteenth centuries, and to West Africa between Senegal and Nigeria. The book's objective is to make historical sources more widely available, and this implies that the texts should be reprinted in a form as unabridged as possible. In fact, only two of the narratives represent selections from a larger whole: Chapter 2 is limited to the African portions of Olaudah Equiano's two-volume work, while Chapter 3 consists of ten representative letters selected from Philip Quaque's correspondence addressed to the Society for the Propagation of the Gospel. While most of the narratives have been printed in the past, they are not well known; but the chief justification for the present form of publication is to present them in the context of their time and place. Therefore, each is introduced and annotated by a specialist in the history or culture of its own particular region.

African personal and place names are found with widely inconsistent spellings, and this volume is inevitably caught in the pattern. While authorities like *Webster's Geographical Dictionary* have been followed in most cases, the spellings preferred by the editors of individual chapters sometimes appear. African political and religious titles have been italicized throughout.

The general editor wishes to express his gratitude for the cordial cooperation of the contributors. On their behalf as well as his own he wishes to express gratitude for the financial assistance of the Carnegie Corporation of New York, through the Program in Comparative Tropical History at the University of Wisconsin. His own contributions were also supported in part by the Research Committee of the Graduate School from special funds voted by the State Legislature of Wisconsin.

P. D. C.

Dakar, Senegal

CONTENTS

ILLUSTRATIONS

MAPS

Maps by the University of Wisconsin Cartographic Laboratory.

AFRICA REMEMBERED

GENERAL INTRODUCTION

The Atlantic slave trade was one of the greatest intercontinental migrations of world history, surpassed only by the European exodus of the nineteenth century. Today, about one-third of all people of African descent live outside of Africa—a proportion only slightly less than the equivalent one-half of all "Europeans" living outside of Europe. Yet the historical record of the slave trade remains curiously uneven. The public campaigns against it during the nineteenth century drew attention to the horrors of the trade, rather than to its mechanisms. More recent historians have examined the mechanisms, but usually only those of the European-dominated, maritime segment from the coast of Africa to the New World.

These failings of historiography are not entirely a matter of documentary survival, though European records are far more detailed for the European than for the African sectors of the trade. Records, even records left by the Europeans, do throw a good deal of light on the African trade routes and on the institutions that brought slaves to the coast for sale. Other sources are constantly being discovered in the form of local written records, oral traditions, and personal narratives.[1] But all of these sources were necessarily neglected by historians until recent years. Scattered references were unclear or hard to interpret without a thorough knowledge of African history, and

1. See, for example, D. Forde (ed.), *Efik Traders of Old Calabar* (London, 1956), containing the diary of Entera Duke, an eighteenth-century African slave trader.

3

concentrated research into the history of Africa has only begun in the last two decades.

The documents collected in this volume all mirror the West African slave trade from the non-European viewpoint. No collection of this kind, however, could fully represent the African aspects of the slave trade. The very nature of the trade made it unlikely that many slaves could either write or preserve detailed personal narratives of their experiences. The enslaved were necessarily non-Western in culture. Only a small minority were literate (usually in Arabic), and even they had little opportunity to produce a diary or journal. Reminiscences are more common, but they have survived only through unusual combinations of luck, European interest, and extraordinary ability on the part of the narrator himself. They are generally either the work of the fortunate few who managed to escape from slavery and obtain a Western education, or else a secondhand account as told to a European reporter.[2]

The nature of European curiosity has itself given a peculiar bias to the body of surviving narratives. In the eighteenth century, the romantic view of the noble savage aroused the European interest in Africans—if they were thought to have had high status in their own so-

2. In addition to the accounts reprinted below, see "Autobiography of Omar ibn Said, Slave in North Carolina, 1831," *American Historical Review*, 30:787–95 (1924); John W. Barber (ed.), *A History of the Amistad Captives* . . . (New Haven, 1840); Ottobah Cugoano, *Thoughts and Sentiments on the Evil and Wicked Traffic of Slavery and Commerce of the Human Species* (London, 1787); Theodore Dwight, "On the Sereculeh Nation, in Nigritia," *American Annals of Education and Instruction*, 5:451–56 (1835); T. Dwight, "The Condition and Character of Negroes in Africa," *Methodist Quarterly Review*, 46:71–90 (January 1864); T. H. Gallaudet, *A Statement with Regard to the Moorish Prince, Abduhl Rahhahman* (New York, 1826); [J. A. U. Gronniosaw], *Wondrous Grace Display'd in the Life and Conversion of James Albert Ukawsaw Gronniosaw* (Leeds, 1785), other editions of which had differing titles; Menèzes de Drumond, "Lettres sur l'Afrique ancienne et moderne," *Journal des voyages*, 32:190–224 (December 1826); Mary Prince, *The History of Mary Price, A West Indian Slave, Related by Herself, with a Supplement by the Editor, to Which Is Added the Narrative of Asa-Asa, a Captured African* (London, 1831); V. Smith, *A Narrative of the Life and Adventures of Venture, A Native of Africa, but Resident above Sixty Years in the United States of America, related by Himself* (New London, 1835); J. Washington, "Some Account of Mohammedu Sisei, A Mandingo of Nyani-Maru on the Gambia," *Journal of the Royal Geographical Society*, 8:448–54 (1838). The introduction of S. W. Koelle, *Polyglotta Africana* (London, 1854), contains brief records of some 179 cases of enslavement, which have been analyzed by P. E. Hair, "The Enslavement of Koelle's Informants," *Journal of African History*, 6:193–203 (1965). Narratives of experience in slavery, especially in the United States, are much more common. See the discussion and bibliography of Charles H. Nichols, *Many Thousand Gone: The Ex-Slaves' Account of Their Bondage and Freedom* (Leyden, 1963).

cieties. Later, in the nineteenth century, the romantic interest in Africa was replaced by the humanitarian concern of the anti-slave-trade movement. Both motives, however, prompted Europeans not only to record slave narratives, but also to manufacture them out of whole cloth. In all, European writers probably have set down more fictitious accounts of Africans in the slave trade than the whole body of genuine narratives.

The eighteenth-century fashion was touched off in part by the noble-savage literature going back to Mrs. Behn's *Oroonoko* (1688), and in part by the appearance of African "kings" at the courts of France and England. The best-known of these was "Prince Aniaba," from Assini on the present-day Ivory Coast. He was not merely received at the French court: he was baptized by Bossuet himself, with Louis XIV acting as godfather. In England, Ayuba Suleiman of Bondu, whose narrative is included in the present collection, was received at court with similar notoriety in the 1730's. The fact that Aniaba was something of an impostor, or that Ayuba was not really from the social class the English imagined, hardly mattered. Their visits struck the literary imagination, and they were soon followed by a body of frankly fictional accounts of the adventures of similar African notables. These *romans africains,* as the type was called in France, began to flourish in the middle of the eighteenth century. At first they were only faintly African—merely early romantic novels dressed up with exotic nomenclature, or labeled, as in one case, *traduite du monomotapien.*[3]

In time, however, some truth came to be mixed with the fiction. A fictionalized story of Aniaba appeared in the anonymous novel, *Histoire de Louis Anniaba, roi d'Essénie en Afrique* (1740).[4] In addition to the genuine account of Ayuba's travels, published in 1734, elements of the story were taken over and attached to the person of another visitor from Africa. The result was a new anonymous novel, *The Royal African: or Memoirs of the Young Prince of Annamaboe* (probably 1749).[5] At the furthest remove into the world of reality, Baron Roger's *Kélédor, histoire africaine,* of 1829,

3. R. Mercier, *L'Afrique noire dans la littérature française: Les premières images (17ᵉ–18ᵉ siècles)* (Dakar, 1962), pp. 29–30, 91–93, 128, 147–48, 186–92; H. Fairchild, *The Noble Savage: A Study in Romantic Naturalism* (New York, 1928); W. Sypher, *Guinea's Captive Kings* (Chapel Hill, N.C., 1942).

4. Mercier, *L'Afrique noire,* esp. p. 30.

5. W. Sypher, "The African Prince in London," *Journal of the History of Ideas,* 2:237–47 (1941), pp. 239–44.

used the vehicle of fiction to carry the results of his own ethnographic and historical research in Senegal. In this case, the accuracy of the African background measured up to the best European standards of scholarship. Even some of the dialogue between historical characters was lifted straight from Wolof oral tradition.

As fiction moved closer to fact, false narratives began to appear, representing fiction *as* fact. Both the attackers and the defenders of the slave trade depended heavily on the evidence of European slave traders. But the evidence of the slaves themselves would be still more effective in the antislavery cause. Some genuine narratives were published for this reason, but antislavery writers also invented slave narratives in the style of the *romans africains* and passed them off as the real thing. Not all of these are easily distinguished from the occasionally garbled reporting of genuine African accounts—as the introductions to the accounts that follow will show. Others, however, reported the African scene with an inaccuracy rivaling the earliest of the *romans africains*. *The Life and Adventures of Zamba, an African Negro King; and his Experiences of Slavery in South Carolina, written by Himself*[6] is one of the more blatant forgeries. The protagonist supposedly came from the banks of the Congo, but his name (Zamba or Samba) is the ordinary name for a second-born son in Senegal, some two thousand miles away. His childhood sweetheart was called Zillah—exotic enough, but clearly Biblical and not Kikongo. In addition, the author talks about white men as *bukras*, a Jamaican word, all but unknown in the southern United States, and derived from either Efik or Ibo, languages spoken in present-day eastern Nigeria.[7]

Still another pious hoax in the antislavery cause was *A Narrative of the Travels etc. of John Ismael Agustus James, An African of the Mandingo Tribe, who was Captured, sold into Slavery, and subsequently liberated by a Benevolent English Gentlemen.*[8] In this case, the narrator claimed to be from a Mandingo village near the coast of present-day Ghana (where no Mandingo village ever existed), and to have been captured by a raiding party of Europeans (at a period when Europeans purchased slaves, rather than capturing them). In point of accuracy, Roger's admittedly fictional *Kélédor* is far more truthful than either Zamba or James. Thus the genuine slave narra-

6. Edited by Peter Nielson (London, 1847).
7. Personal communication from Professor Frederick Cassidy, University of Wisconsin.
8. Truro, England, 1836.

tives were produced in competition with pious forgeries and fictional accounts.

They also suffer from defects that might be expected of this kind of record. Only two of the present collection were composed by the narrator himself in an African language: Ali Eisami dictated his Kanuri account to a Western linguist, while Abū Bakr al-Ṣiddīq wrote at least one version of his narrative in Arabic. The others are partly childhood memories of the fortunate few who managed to escape from slavery and to become literate in a Western language—like Olaudah Equiano, Samuel Crowther, and Joseph Wright. But some are accounts received by a Western amanuensis and published by him—as in the case of Ayuba Suleiman, Ṣāliḥ Bilāli, Osifekunde, and Wargee. Only the letters of Philip Quaque were a report of events as they happened, and in the words of the narrator himself.

Highly various circumstances of composition make the collection equally various in form of presentation, literary quality, and accuracy. As sources for history, the narratives suffer especially from two failings that are inseparable from the circumstances that led to their preservation. With the exception of Quaque's letters and Wargee's account of his travels, they are recollections of the more or less distant past—often memories of childhood, recorded after years or decades. As such, they suffer from all the possible weaknesses of human memory. In addition, many were recorded, and no doubt edited, by a Western writer who passed them through the filter of differing cultures and imperfect knowledge of a common language. Errors of transmission are therefore to be expected in accounts such as those by Ayuba Suleiman and Osifekunde. But even the Westernized narrators who wrote in English were writing for a European audience, and they took the audience into account in deciding what to tell and what to omit. Thus, even Equiano, Crowther, and Wright were subject to a kind of self-imposed censorship as they sought to explain themselves and their past to aliens of limited background.

All of these narratives nevertheless have certain redeeming features. Many are the earliest written records of the authors' homelands. All three of the Yoruba narrators (Osifekunde, Joseph Wright, and Samuel Crowther) refer to a period earlier than any detailed Western record of Yoruba. Others, while they are not the sole written source for their time and place, constitute significant additions to what is otherwise known. Ayuba Suleiman, for example,

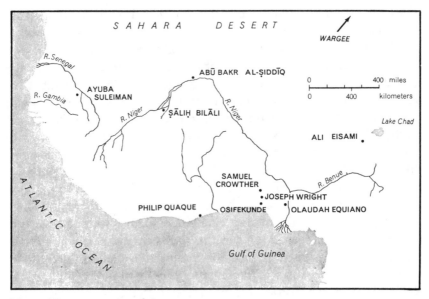

Map 1. Home countries of the narrators.

provides the earliest record of Bondu by a Bonduke. In spite of relatively abundant Arabic documentation for the region of the middle Niger, Abū Bakr al-Ṣiddīq, Ṣāliḥ Bilāli, and Wargee all add to our knowledge of the state of society there on the eve of the nineteenth-century religious revolutions.

Even the fact that several of these authors were partly Westernized is a source of interest as well as a source of possible distortion. Modernization under Western influence is a major theme in modern African history. Accidents of survival have preserved narratives by some notable individuals, representatives of the earliest generations of the modernizing élite that has since remade Africa. Philip Quaque was the first African ordained in the Church of England. Joseph Wright was the first African ordained as a Methodist clergyman. Samuel Crowther was the first African to become an Anglican bishop. All three were men of unusual ability, and their narratives gain a special importance because of their authors' later roles in history. None of the three described his times or his youth from a vantage point completely within an African culture, but all three illustrate possible points of view by Africans midway between two ways of life. While these three narratives lack the qualities of a candid and introspective autobiography, such as we might like, they nevertheless present some insights that are virtually impossible to find in any other source.

That is, indeed, the strength of the collection as a whole. It may add something to our knowledge of West African history, but its greatest interest is in another direction: these narratives are among the very few personal recollections of men who were enslaved and shipped from the coast of Africa (as all but Philip Quaque and Wargee were). They give us some notion of the feelings and attitudes of many millions whose feelings and attitudes are unrecorded. Imperfect as the sample may be, it is the only view we can recover of the slave trade as seen by the slaves themselves.

PART I

*African
Travellers
of the
Eighteenth
Century*

The three eighteenth-century narratives included here share certain characteristics of the period, even though they represent widely differing parts of West Africa. Ayuba Suleiman, Olaudah Equiano, and Philip Quaque cover a geographic range stretching from Senegal to the lower Niger Valley, and the span of their lives overlapped for only a few decades in the middle of the century. Their lives were also extremely diverse, representing a Pulo cleric, a Christian missionary, and an ex-slave who made his way to a position of modest attainment in Great Britain. But all three belonged to the era of the *romans africains,* with all this implied in the form of European romantic interest in things African. It was also a period before the rise of pseudo-scientific racism, and before the rise of an important European demand for the abolition of the Atlantic slave trade. At this time, dealings on the African coast were a partnership between African sellers and European buyers of slaves; and it was a more equal partnership than it was to be in the nineteenth century, when European military power could make itself predominant on the African coast.

It was thus a time when some Africans found their way to Europe as free men, even though the vast majority of those who left Africa departed for lifelong slavery in the Americas. There were, indeed, more free Africans in Europe than Europeans in the lightly manned trading posts of tropical Africa. Ayuba, Equiano, and Quaque all belonged at some time in their lives to this body of African expatriates, and in each case the period of residence in Europe was the factor that made it possible for them to leave a narrative of their experience in Africa. Each of these travellers also is broadly representative of one of the three principal ways in which Africans reached Europe—and of the diversity of reception that was common to each.

The largest group of Africans in Europe came by way of the West Indies, often in the company of their masters and still in a condition of servitude. Others arrived as crew members aboard ships in the Africa trade, recruited on the coast to help fill out the ranks after European sailors had died of disease or had deserted. They usually intended to return to Africa on a later voyage, but many were stranded in Europe and found their way into the lower ranks of European society. Those who came as servants often remained servants, even if they managed to become freemen. Africans were already associated with the status of colonial slavery, which made it difficult for them to escape from the working class, even if they had the skill or ability to do so.[1] A few, however, managed to obtain some education. Olaudah Equiano was one of these. His autobiography in two volumes covers the whole progress from childhood near the Niger, to slavery in the West Indies, then through many travels to the position of a barber and occasional domestic servant in London. It is unique among works of its kinds in the detail it supplies about the background in Africa, but it was not alone among autobiographical accounts of similar Afro-Englishmen of his time. Ignatius Sancho also made a name for himself as a literary man, and his publishers identified him as an African. In fact, he was brought to England from the West Indies as a child, and his culture was completely Western.[2] Other Afro-English writers touched on their African origins, but only in passing.[3]

1. See Shelby T. McCloy, *The Negro in France* (Lexington, Ky., 1961); Great Britain, Privy Council, *Report of the Lords of the Committee of Council for . . . Trade and Foreign Plantations . . . Concerning the Present State of Trade to Africa, and Particularly the Trade in Slaves . . .* (London, 1789), Part I; J. J. Hecht, *Continental and Colonial Servants in Eighteenth Century England* (Northampton, Mass., 1954).

2. See I. Sancho, *Letters of the Late Ignatius Sancho, An African* (2 vols., London, 1783).

3. See Ottobah Cugoano, *Thoughts and Sentiments on the Evil and Wicked Traffic of Slavery and Commerce of the Human Species* (London, 1787); [J. A. U. Gronniosaw], *Wonderous Grace Display'd in the Life and Conversion of James Albert Ukawsaw Gronniosaw* (Leeds, 1785).

In addition to the working-class Africans, another group came direct from Africa as the protégés of European slave traders. They were often the sons or relatives of African merchants, who sent them to pick up a smattering of literacy in Western languages and a knowledge of the broader commercial world with which they would have to deal. These Africans travelled on the slave ships by way of the West Indies, but they travelled as guests, often under the temporary guardianship of a European merchant. After a period of education in France, Holland, or Britain, they returned to their fathers' business on the coast. Philip Quaque is a representative of this group, even though he came under missionary, rather than commercial, sponsorship. As with Equiano, he was merely one among many similar figures, but he happened to leave a more significant account of Africa than the rest. The most successful in European intellectual circles, however, was Anton Wilhelm Amo, another Gold Coaster, who came to Europe in 1707 at the age of four. His education was thus completely European, and he made a distinguished academic career at a series of German universities. He always identified himself as an African, and he ultimately returned to the Gold Coast sometime between 1740 and 1758; but his published work consists of Latin treatises on logic, psychology, and history. The only apparent mark of his African origins was his occasional defense of African culture against European prejudice.[4]

A third, and much smaller, group, represented by Ayuba Suleiman, consisted of Africans who were able to move in European court circles and who sought to play a diplomatic role in the relations between Africa and Europe. Southern Europe had seen a number of diplomatic visitors from Africa in the fifteenth and sixteenth centuries. In the seventeenth century they began to reach northern Europe as well. One of the earliest was Matteo Lopez, royal interpreter to Kpoyizoun, the king of Ardra (in present-day Dahomey). He was presented at the court of Louis XIV in 1670 and was lionized briefly

4. N. Lochner, "Anton Wilhelm Amo: A Ghana Scholar in Eighteenth Century Germany," *Transactions of the Historical Society of Ghana*, 3:169–79 (1958). Still another African in European university circles as a theology student was J. E. J. Capitein, who actually defended the thesis that slavery per se is not contrary to Christian doctrine. See J. E. J. Capitein, *Dissertatio politico-theologica, de servitute, libertati christianae non contraria* (Leyden, 1742); R. Mercier, *L'Afrique noire dans la littérature française: Les premières images (17ᵉ–18ᵉ siècles)* (Dakar, 1962), p. 86.

by the French aristocracy, but the projected treaty of alliance between France and Ardra was never ratified.[5]

He was followed a few years later by Aniaba from the Ivory Coast, who came on the recommendation of Dominican missionaries stationed in Assini. Aniaba succeeded in passing himself off as the son of the reigning king, though in fact he was only the favorite slave of an important courtier. He stayed in France from 1687 to 1701, serving as an officer in the French cavalry. When he did return to Africa, he went with a French military expedition, hoping to seize Assini and turn it into a Christian kingdom with himself as king.[6] The expedition failed, but his effort to manipulate the European authorities for his own advantage, while they in turn tried to manipulate him for theirs, was to be echoed some thirty years later in the career of Ayuba Suleiman.

5. R. Cornevin, *Histoire du Dahomey* (Paris, 1962), p. 250; Mercier, *L'Afrique noire*, p. 29.

6. McCloy, *The Negro in France*, p. 15; Mercier, *L'Afrique noire*, pp. 29–30. In 1716–23, another and more famous African, Gannibal, Pushkin's great-grandfather, spent a period of training in France, including service in the French army (Vladimir Nabokov, "Pushkin and Gannibal," *Encounter*, 19:11–26 (July 1962).

CHAPTER 1

AYUBA SULEIMAN DIALLO OF BONDU

Philip D. Curtin

Ayuba Suleiman Diallo of Bondu, known to the Europeans as Job ben Solomon, was probably the best known of the early African travellers to Europe. The story of his life and adventures as told to Thomas Bluett was published in 1734, and Ayuba's narrative was reprinted many times in both French and English. The story in outline has the classic elements of many later works on the theme of the noble savage. Here was a man of high station, reputedly the son of the high priest of Bondu, far away in the interior of Africa. He was captured by enemies during a commercial venture to the Gambia in 1731, sold as a slave to Maryland, and put to work growing tobacco. After an attempted escape, he was rescued from slavery by Bluett, who discovered his education and recognized his quality. With the assistance of English gentlemen, he was emancipated, taken to England, presented at the British court, and finally helped to return to his proper station in life, and to his home in Africa. Both Bluett and Francis Moore, who knew Ayuba on the Gambia, described him as having all the qualities the eighteenth century expected to find in one of nature's noblemen.

So much for the literary rendering. The real Ayuba Suleiman is a good deal more obscure, and the account of his life is somewhat garbled by his historians. Nevertheless, some of the mist can be dissipated by other evidence, and the picture that emerges is that of an eighteenth-century Muslim African merchant, tolerably well informed about his own country and its neighbors, and caught up in the maze of complex political and economic rivalries surrounding the slave trade of the Senegambia. His account helps to fill out a historical framework otherwise based on French reports from the upper Senegal and oral traditions recorded in the nineteenth centuy.

Unlike most regions of West Africa, the Senegambia was not normally a significant source of slaves. The Europeans who had been trading on that coast since the fifteenth century went there for gum arabic, gold, hides, ivory, and beeswax—plus small numbers of slaves derived from the Wolof states south of the Senegal mouth and from the petty Malinke kingdoms scattered along either side of the Gambia. The products that determined commercial strategy before the eighteenth century were gold and gum, and the key to commercial geography was the pair of parallel and navigable rivers leading into the interior.

Inter-European rivalries of the seventeenth century had shaken out by the eighteenth century into a relatively stable situation. The French normally dominated the trade of the Senegal. The English normally dominated that of the Gambia. Dutch ships, however, still traded from time to time along the open coasts, especially the Mauritanian coast to the north of the Senegal. Portuguese, who had once dominated the European trade from both rivers, were now relegated to coastal trade and especially to the region south of the Gambia.

This distribution of strategic advantage gave the French traders a special position in the gum trade. The gum tree (*Acacia senegal*) grows wild in the steppe country between the Sahara proper and the well-watered savanna of the Western Sudan. The most accessible supplies were those to the north of the Senegal, where nomadic Moors had long been accustomed to gather gum and prepare it for shipment. By the early eighteenth century this source was responsible for the greater part of the gum entering world trade, and gum was essential to the growing European textile industry. With their domination of the water-borne trade of the Senegal, the French were able to monopolize the supplies of gum from the trading posts along the river, though they were forced to compete with other European merchants at the ports scattered along the Mauritanian coast between the Senegal and Cape Blanc.

Gold exports tended to be less valuable than gum, but Europeans were especially susceptible to the lure of gold. Both the French and the English regarded the Senegambia as potentially of the greatest

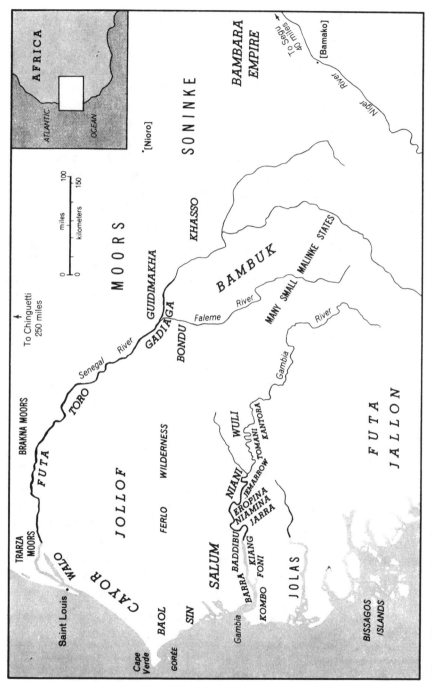

Map 2. The Senegambia and its hinterland, *ca.* 1735.

importance—if only they could find a secure route to the gold deposits, establish their control, and increase production. Most of the gold exports by way of the Senegambia originated in Bambuk and from alluvial workings along the Faleme River, though some may have come from farther east in Bure. They were therefore accessible along either of the two rivers, and both European nations had been jockeying for position in an on-and-off manner for many decades. The English had sent several expeditions as far as Barrakunda Falls in 1618–22. Others went farther in 1661–62, 1681, and 1723–27, but no significant changes in the pattern of trade seem to have resulted.[1] The English traded regularly as far as Barrakunda Falls, but no higher. By the 1730's, the French appeared to be closer to success. They had established a pattern of regular annual voyages up the Senegal to Gadiaga in 1685, and these continued with only occasional periods of lapse. At the end of the seventeenth century, the French established a fortified post near the town of Daramané, and in 1714 they returned and established Fort Saint Joseph at Tambucané. In 1725 and again in 1730, French travellers from the fort actually penetrated into Bambuk, and by 1734 their upriver establishment included some forty-four Europeans.[2]

But the English commercial position was not so unfavorable for inland trade as these facts may indicate. Ayuba, after all, came from a region only a few days' walk from the French post in Gadiaga, but he was captured while trading on the Gambia, several hundred miles from home. In fact, the Senegal was an unhandy and expensive river for commerce. Ocean-going ships were usually unable to cross the bar into the river itself, and even smaller craft could only reach Gadiaga in high water (from July to November). Even then, the current was swift and the boats often had to be poled or pulled upstream from the shore. By contrast, tides in the Gambia carried as far as Barrakunda Falls in low water, and ocean-going ships could reach points about 120 miles from the mouth in any season. In practice, they rarely went farther, but African traders like Ayuba often found it worth while to travel overland in order to deal with English super-

1. J. M. Gray, *History of the Gambia* (London, 1940), pp. 18, 21–26, 72–74, and 184–85.

2. Michel Jajolet de la Courbe, *Premier voyage du Sieur de La Courbe fait à la coste d'Afrique en 1685* (Paris, 1913), p. iii; Jean Baptiste Labat, *Nouvelle Rélation de l'Afrique occidentale* (4 vols., Paris, 1728), 4:30; A. Delcourt, *La France et les établissements française au Sénégal entre 1713 et 1763* (Dakar, 1952), pp. 153–57.

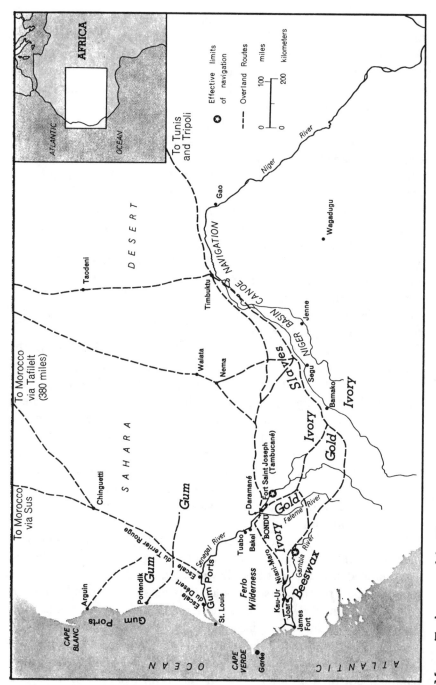

Map. 3. Trade routes of the Western Sudan.

cargoes at tidewater, rather than passing their goods through the hands of Senegalese middlemen who made the annual voyage from Saint Louis to Gadiaga.

The Senegambian trade was thus highly competitive between the French-dominated and the English-dominated routes to the interior. It was also competitive within the French or British sector. Both governments had tried in the past to establish national monopolies in the hands of chartered companies, but this policy had long since failed. French companies with varying privileges had operated on the Senegal since 1664, but each in turn was sold or liquidated after a few years. In 1719, the newly chartered Compagnie des Indes took on a monopoly privilege for the French trade between Cape Blanc and Sierra Leone, but the company preferred not to engage in the trans-Atlantic trade on its own account. Instead, it sold African products to private French shipping firms, which paid a license fee for the privilege of infringing the company's monopoly; and in later years it received a government subsidy in return for maintaining trading posts. On the English side, the Royal African Company, founded in 1671, had failed by the end of the century. It too kept in business on the Gambia by allowing private shippers to buy from its local agents or from African merchants. Unlike its French counterpart, it did engage in some trans-Atlantic trade on its own account, and in the 1730's it was already receiving a government subsidy. But the position of both companies was one of having lost most of their advantage in the Atlantic trade. Their commercial future, if they were to have any, would have to be found in their position as suppliers of African goods for sale on the coast. The decade of the 1730's was, indeed, the most successful in the whole history of the Royal African Company's commerce on the Gambia, as its factors pushed aggressively for an ever-widening circle of influence.

It was precisely this commercial effort that gave Ayuba Suleiman Diallo his opportunity to escape from slavery. His home in Bondu had a crucial strategic position. It was the neighboring country to the south of the French posts in Gadiaga. It also commanded the overland route from the Gambia to the Bambuk gold fields. Gadiaga at this time was reduced to relative insignificance. Bambuk itself was a congeries of small Malinke principalities, city-states, and independent walled villages. The French might easily have penetrated into Bambuk, but their position could hardly have been secure if Bondu were on friendly terms with the Royal African Company. In addition, western Bondu bordered on the still-untapped source of gum in the Ferlo wilderness. Ayuba's appearance in Maryland, and later in England, was therefore calculated to arouse more practical sentiments than mere romantic sympathy for a man of high station, fallen into slavery in a foreign land.

But Ayuba's actual position in Bondu[3] remains something of a puzzle. By his own account, he was born about 1701 to a family of Fulbe Muslim clerics, migrants from Futa Toro in the time of his grandfather some fifty years earlier (or about 1680). The pattern of Fulbe movement southeastward from Futa Toro was typical of this period. The Tukulor state, or Futa Toro, was then (as now) a relatively dense band of population along the middle portion of the Senegal which is watered by the annual flood. Groups of seminomadic Fulbe had been in the habit of drifting away from the Senegal Valley for several centuries, as their transhumant pastoralism led them off in search of better grazing lands. Other *hal pularen* also travelled

3. Nomenclature in the Senegambia is shifting, contradictory, and completely unstandardized. Bluett, for example, gives "Boonda," where the modern French spelling is "Bondou" and the modern English spelling is "Bondu." But the actual pronunciation is closer to Bluett's version, or still more to the older French spelling, "Boundou," with equal stress on the two syllables.

The confusion in proper names is complicated by the presence of the same families in both the English-speaking Gambia and the French-speaking Senegal. Thus, the Diallo family of Senegal will be called Jallow in the Gambia—and with identical pronunciation. Other unlikely ways of getting at the same sound are Diop and Jobe, N'Diaye and N'Jie, Cissé and Seesay. Place names here and below will follow those most commonly found on modern maps. Personal names will be given in a somewhat Anglicized version of the French spellings—that is, with French *ou* rendered as *u* and without an accent on the letter *e*, though it should be pronounced like the French *é*. The French convention of an apostrophe after an initial *n* has also been dropped, since the missing vowel sound comes before, not after, the consonant *n*.

Ayuba's ethnic identity presents another kind of problem. His people call themselves *hal pularen* (speakers of the Pular language). But they are most often called *Toucouleur* in Senegalese French, and *Fula* in the Gambia. Farther afield, they would be called *Fulani* in Nigerian English, which has adopted the Hausa word for them. Usage is further complicated by a distinction sometimes made in ethnographic literature between *Toucouleur* or *Tukulor*, thought to be sedentary farmers, and *Peubl* or *Fula*, sometimes used solely for those whose material culture is dominated by cattle-keeping. In Bondu, however, *Toucouleur* is merely the French word used for *hal pularen* as a whole, though this is not standard among all Pular-speaking peoples. Indeed, the language itself is called *Fulfulde* in Nigeria and the Cameroons.

To avoid confusion in the present volume, the term *Fulbe* (sing. *Pulo*) will be adopted for the whole people, whether sedentary or pastoral, eastern or western—since this is the most general term used by the people themselves.

widely in the Western Sudan as merchants and Muslim clerics, until they had established Fulbe communities as far east as Nigeria. These parallel movements were, in time, to have revolutionary consequences for the whole of the Western Sudan.

In the more immediate situation of the late seventeenth century, *hal pularen* were encroaching on their neighbors closer to home, especially on the Malinke- and Soninke-speaking territories south of the Senegal and upstream from Futa Toro proper. A greater Gadiaga had once dominated the Senegal-Faleme confluence and the territory around it, including what later became Bondu, Guidimakha, Bambuk, and Khasso, as well as the reduced Gadiaga of the eighteenth century. Political weakness combined with population pressures in Futa Toro encouraged Fulbe or Tukulor from the middle Senegal to establish colonies and sometimes new states of their own. Most of these migrants were lost to the political control of Futa Toro, but new towns founded within or near the home country were often put under the local government of the original founder and his descendants in the male line, so long as they remained politically loyal.

Ayuba's family were clearly among the body of migrants to Bondu who continued to maintain political relations with the *satigis* (or rulers) of Futa Toro. The *Satigi* Bubakar in Ayuba's account was Bubakar Sawa Lamu, sometimes called Bubakar Tabakali, whose reign has been put (on other evidence) at about 1640–73,[4] close enough to Ayuba's estimate of the date of his grandfather's migration. (The genealogy given in Table 1, based on the chronicle of Siré Abbas Soh,[5] shows the probable relationship between Bubakar and the other

4. M. Delafosse and H. Gaden, "Chroniques du Fouta Sénégalais," *Revue du Monde Musulman*, 24:1–144 and 25:165–235 (1913), esp. 25:222.

5. Delafosse and Gaden, "Fouta Sénégalais," esp. 24:24–32. It is, however, difficult to make a perfect identification between the individual Ayuba names and the traditions of Futa Toro. Differing traditions of Futa Toro also disagree, particularly for periods of dynastic struggle, since one king-list will remember as legitimate some rulers whom others regard as mere usurpers.

The confusion is increased by Fulbe personal nomenclature. Each individual received a "Christian" name (*indé*), such as Ayuba. This was followed by one or two additional names, indicating descent; and the whole series ended with the *yettodé*, the clan or family name (Diallo, in Ayuba's case). All the individuals on the genealogical table would bear the Denianke *yettodé*, Ba. Confusion comes from two sources. First, the *indé* was normally chosen from a limited number borne in the past by eminent members of the family. Thus Samba, Bubakar, and Geladio recur frequently. Second, the pre-Islamic Futa Toro had been matrilineal, while the Islamic tradition was patrilineal. The mixture of the two left the possibility of having two alternate sets of descent names between the *indé* and

TABLE I

Abbreviated genealogy of the Denianke dynasty of Futa Toro, early eighteenth century

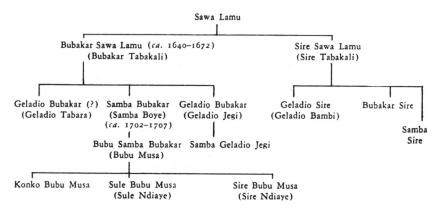

members of the Denianke dynasty to whom Ayuba refers.) But Bluett created an element of uncertainty by mistaking the country of Bondu for a town of the same name. It is uncertain whether Ayuba intended to say that his grandfather, Ibrahima Diallo, was founder of a new town, or founder of Bondu itself as a new province under the suzerainty of the *satigis* of Futa Toro.

The general tenor of Ayuba's account suggests the second alternative, but it is impossible to be certain. At the least, it can be said that the Diallo family were Muslim clerics who held some kind of political authority. But no external evidence mentions a Diallo family as rulers over Bondu as a whole, nor does Ayuba's own career suggest that of a man being prepared to succeed to such a high office. He was clearly on a commercial venture to the Gambia at the time of his capture, and his entourage was small. This and the breadth of his earlier travels suggest that he himself belonged to the world of commerce

---

the *yettodé,* one indicating descent on the father's side and the other indicating descent on the mother's side. Thus, Bubakar was son of Sawa, the son of Lamu. But Bubakar was also known as Bubakar Tabakali, Tabakali being his mother's *indé.* See A. Leriche, "Anthroponymie Toucouleur," *Bulletin de l'I.F.A.N.,* 18:169–88 (1956); H. Gaden, "Du nom chez les Toucouleurs et Peuls Islamisés du Fouta Sénégalais," *Revue d'Ethnographie et de Sociologie,* 3:50–56 (1912). Transliteration in the genealogy, as elsewhere in this chapter, approximates Fulbe usage, even of Arabic names—thus Bubakar, rather than the Arabic Abū Bakr.

(whatever his father's position). The level of his knowledge of Arabic also points to the kind of education that might be expected of a *diula,* or travelling merchant, rather than that of an important Islamic scholar.[6]

The traditional political history of Bondu also runs counter to the Diallo claims. The region that became Bondu was lightly populated in the seventeenth century, and it was claimed by Gadiaga (though it may well have been claimed by Futa Toro as well). The dominant traditions hold that the new kingdom of Bondu was founded by Malik Si,[7] a religious leader from Futa Toro who played much the same role that Ayuba assigns to Ibrahima Diallo, his own grandfather. But Malik Si is supposed to have obtained his authority and a cession of territory from the *tunka* of Tuabo, one of the rulers of Gadiaga. He then settled the land with relatives and followers from Futa Toro, and with other immigrants from as far away as the Wolof states in the west and the region of Nioro to the northeast. This much fits the pattern of welcome to strangers, which Ayuba reports as well.

These traditions also emphasize Malik Si's religious leadership, and the fact that he gained Bondu without a conquest. Instead, Malik Si had such religious prestige that the *tunka* wanted the spiritual advantages of having such a man as a neighbor. Authorities differ as to the precise date of the foundation of Bondu, since they

6. See reproduction (facing p. 52) of a letter from Ayuba Suleiman to Sir Hans Sloane, 8 December 1734, from Sloane Papers, Ad. MSS 4053, British Museum. The script is the Maghribi script usual in the Western Sudan, and it is accurately learned. The language, on the other hand, is either ungrammatical or lifted from the Koran by whole phrases. The author was clearly neither familiar with spoken Arabic nor grounded in classical written Arabic to the level of such well-known Sudanese authors as Mahmud Kati and Abderrahman al-Sa'di (personal communication from Mohammed Alwan and William A. Brown).

7. Anne Raffenel, *Nouveau voyage au pays des nègres* (2 vols., Paris, 1856), 2:269–70; Djibril Ly, "Coutumes et contes des Toucouleurs du Fouta Toro," *Bulletin du Comité des études historiques et scientifique de l'A.O.F.* (cited hereafter as *Bulletin CEHSAOF*), 21(2):304–26 (April-June 1938), pp. 312, 316–17; Charles Monteil, *Les Khassonké* (Paris, 1915), pp. 12–22; Félix Brigaud, *Histoire traditionelle du Sénégal* (Saint Louis du Sénégal, 1962); M. G. Adam, *Légendes historiques du Pays de Nioro (sahel)* (Paris, 1904); A. Bonnel de Mezières, "Les Diakanké de Banisraila et du Bondou méridional (Sénégal), annoté par R. Mauny," *Notes africaines*, 41:20–24 (January 1949), p. 23; A. Rançon, "Le Boundou," *Bulletin de la Société de Géographie de Bordeaux*, 17(new ser.):433–63, 465–84, 497–548, 561–91, 593–647 (1894), esp. p. 480; Abdoulaye Kane, "Histoire et origine des familles du Fouta-Toro," *Bulletin CEHSAOF*, 1: 325–43 (1916), p. 341.

place Malik Si's death at various times between 1680[8] and 1720,[9] but the traditions of the dynasty (the Sisibe) suggest that he died in 1699.[10] Thus even the timing of Sisibe claims to the foundation of Bondu is similar to that of the Diallo. The similarity continues in the combination of religious leadership and secular rule. Ayuba's father and grandfather bore the title of *alfa,* clearly religious but of variable meaning in the Western Sudan. The Sisibe, on the other hand, took the religious title of *eliman.*[11] Its religious connotations and the fact that the Sisibe owed no allegiance to the *satigis* of Futa Toro are of some importance, since they imply that Bondu was the earliest of the series of religiously oriented states to be founded by Fulbe in many parts of West Africa—a forerunner of the religious revolution in Futa Jallon and of the jihad in Futa Toro itself toward the end of the eighteenth century.

The conflict between tradition and Ayuba's account immediately raises the question whether he was lying, or whether Bluett simply misunderstood him. Both are possible, but the subsequent history of Bondu can be squared to a degree with Ayuba's claims for his own family. The second ruler in the Sisibe line was Bubu Malik Si, who is chiefly remembered for conquests to the south, incorporating a number of small Malinke states in the process. The enmity between the Fulbe and the Malinke on the Gambia, as reported by Ayuba, was apparently a reflection of these wars. Bubu Malik's reign can be

8. J. S. Trimmingham, *A History of Islam in West Africa* (London, 1962), p. 173.

9. P. Marty, *Études sénégalaises* (Paris, *ca.* 1926), p. 104.

10. Rançon, "Le Boundou," p. 480.

11. Derived from the Arabic, *al-Imām* (leader of prayer at a mosque). The precise history of the evolution of this religious office into a political office is uncertain. It is generally believed that the lesser title, *eliman,* and the greater *almami,* are of similar derivation (J. S. Trimmingham, *Islam in West Africa* [Oxford, 1959], p. 69; *History of Islam,* p. 167). An alternate derivation, however, traces *almami* to the Arabic *al-imām al-mu'minin* (leader of the faithful), or perhaps even to *amir al-mu'minin* (commander of the faithful), the more traditional Islamic title (M. Bayol, "La France au Fouta-Djalon," *Revue des Deux-Mondes,* 54:902–32 [15 December 1882], p. 907). Rulers of Bondu bore the title *eliman* from the time of Malik Si to about 1764, when they changed to *almami* (Rançon, "Le Boundou," pp. 479, 501). *Almami* was also chosen toward the end of the eighteenth century as the title for the successful religious revolutionary leaders in Futa Toro and Futa Jallon, while in nineteenth-century Futa Toro *eliman* was kept in use as one of a number of titles borne by leaders subordinate to the *almami* (Jules Rémy, *La Sénégambie* [n.p., *ca.* 1883], "Fouta Sénégalais," p. 8). Usuman (or 'Uthmān) dan Fodio, leader of the Fulbe jihad in northern Nigeria is thought to be the first of the religious revolutionaries to take the full Arabic title of *al-amir al-mu'minin* (Trimmingham, *History of Islam,* p. 168).

taken to have begun about 1699, and differing calculations for traditional reign lengths indicate that it ended in either 1718, 1720, or 1727.[12] Whatever the date, Bubu Malik's death marked the beginning of an interregnum during which the Sisibe lost control over the central government, and the central government lost control over the provinces. Ultimate power appears to have slipped to the level of the walled towns and villages, which ran their own affairs and kept whatever peace they could over the surrounding countryside. If Ayuba Suleiman left Bondu during this period of decentralization, Suleiman, his father, may well have been the ruler of a town, or even a pretender to central control, and he may have owed some form of allegiance to the *satigi* of Futa Toro. If so, Ayuba is partly excused for his failure to mention the Sisibe.

The phase of governmental breakdown was ended by a son of Bubu Malik, Maka Bubu Malik Si or Maka Jiba, who gathered Fulbe supporters in Futa Toro and reconquered Bondu in a war that combined dynastic quarrels with a struggle between localism and central power. Ayuba reports that between 1731 and 1735, while he was overseas, a war took place in Bondu which was disastrous to the country and to his family fortunes as well. Chronological calculations from the reign-lengths of traditional history support the identification of these wars as Maka Jiba's war of reconquest, since the most reliable estimates place Maka Jiba's accession to power in 1728 or 1731.[13]

If this speculative reconstruction is accurate, it exonerates Ayuba from the suspicion that he intentionally deceived his friends in England. It also explains why the Gambia officials of the Royal African Company continued to work with him after his return from England. They showed no sign of believing that Ayuba's story was a fabrication, and they were certainly in a position to know about the major political changes in Bondu.

These same officials had good reason to be concerned about poli-

12. These traditions record the name of each ruler and the length of his reign. The calculations are those made by Rançon, in "Le Boundou," pp. 480–82, or based on the traditional data supplied by Kane, "Histoire du Fouta-Toro," p. 341, and Adam, *Légendes de Nioro,* p. 55. Marty, *Études sénégalaises,* p. 104, places the reign of Bubu Malik Si in 1720–47, which is certainly too late.

13. Rançon's estimate, in "Le Boundou," p. 483, is 1728. The date 1731 is calculated from traditional data supplied by Kane, "Histoire du Fouta-Toro," p. 341.

tics in Bondu during the 1720's and 1730's. The commercial position of the French and British alike was in process of drastic alteration by events in distant parts of Africa. Far off to the east, on the upper Niger around Segu, Marmari Kulubari (ruled *ca.* 1712–55) began to establish an important new Bambara kingdom.[14] Prisoners of war were the inevitable by-product of successful empire building, and they were an item of commerce. Some were sold to other regions in the Western Sudan, and some to Morocco, but they also began to flow along the trade routes toward the European posts on the Senegal and Gambia. This new situation of the 1720's and 1730's was in sharp contrast to that of the later seventeenth century, when the offerings of Senegambian slaves were small and prices were high. The English, for example, had exported only 106 slaves in 1679–80, and the Royal African Company later made it a point not to buy slaves there, except as needed to encourage caravans to come down from the interior with other goods. French exports from the Senegal ran at only about a hundred slaves a year during the 1680's.[15] By the early 1730's, however, the slave trade from the Gambia reached about 2,000 in a peak year, while the Compagnie des Indes sold an annual average of 975 slaves from the Senegal in the period 1732–40.[16] These higher figures were not enough to make the Senegambia rival the Niger Delta or Angola as a source of

14. Some authorities formerly put the reign of Marmari Kulubari in the seventeenth century, but evidence from Saharan chronicles supports the chronology indicated. See Louis Tauxier, *Histoire des Bambara* (Paris, 1942), pp. 69–78.

15. K. G. Davies, *The Royal African Company* (London, 1957), pp. 219 and 236; Abdoulaye Ly, *La Compagnie de Sénégal* (Paris, 1958), pp. 283–84. It is probably no mere accident that the peak of the Senegambian slave trade happened to coincide with the reign of Marmari Kulubari in Segu. French estimates from the 1750's to the 1780's put the level of the Senegalese slave trade at about 2,000 annually. By the 1790's, however, the flow of slaves was much reduced in the French sector on account of the war with England, and the English traders on the Gambia noted a sharp decrease during the 1780's. By the mid-1790's, exports from the Gambia by all nations were estimated to be less than 1,000 slaves per year, and Senegal exports had fallen even lower (Pierre Cultru, *Les origines de l'Afrique occidentale: Histoire du Sénégal du xve siècle à 1870* [Paris, 1910], pp. 245–76; evidence of Captain Heatley in *Report of the Lords of the Committee of Council for . . . Trade and Foreign Plantations . . . Concerning the Present State of Trade to Africa, and Particularly the Trade in Slaves . . .* [London, 1789], Part I; Mungo Park, *Travels in the Interior Districts of Africa* [new ed., 2 vols., London, 1816–17], 1:36).

16. Francis Moore, *Travels into the Inland Parts of Africa . . .* (London, 1738), p. 41; Delcourt, *Établissements français*, p. 398.

slaves, but the middle decades of the eighteenth century were those in which the Senegambian slave trade reached its peak of importance. This surge in the slave trade was one factor intensifying the Franco-British trade rivalry on the two rivers.

It also helped to heighten the importance of Bondu. The French, with their posts in Gadiaga, might have expected the bulk of the new slave trade to fall into their hands. But caravans moving from Segu toward the Atlantic had a choice of routes and trading partners, creating a commercial strategy similar to that of the gold trade from Bambuk. Caravans could stop in Gadiaga and trade with the French, or they could go another 200 miles overland and deal with the English on the middle Gambia. Normally, the cost of transportation down some 350 miles of the Senegal should have been cheaper than a 200-mile overland march, but political considerations also entered. The overland route had to pass through Bondu, and the Senegal River route had to pass through Futa Toro. If either kingdom were relatively stable, friendly to passing merchants, and moderate in the rate of tolls charged for passage, it might well divert the trade in its own direction. Political instability, high tolls, or anarchy would have the opposite effect.

Futa Toro was in an especially delicate position. Through the whole of its history before the twentieth century it faced a nomad problem. The well-watered Senegal Valley had some characteristics of an oasis surrounded by semiarid steppe, occupiable only by scattered nomads. When the *hal pularen* were strong, they could dominate both banks of the river and defend the country against nomadic incursions. When they were weak, the northern bank often had to be given up to Trarza Moors north of the Senegal mouth, or to the Brakna north of Futa Toro itself. Nomadic raids then often crossed to the south of the river. This was the situation during the first half of the eighteenth century, and it tended to weaken the naturally strong position of the French, to favor the English, and to favor the route through Bondu.

Political weakness on the middle Senegal was connected with political changes far to the north. Morocco had a long tradition of sporadic political relations with the Western Sudan. These entered a new phase in 1672, when 'Ali ibn Haidar, a political refugee from dynastic wars in Morocco, raised an army in the Niger Valley and attempted a counterinvasion across the desert toward his home country. The plan failed, but the new *sultan,* Moulay Ismaïl (1672-

1727), took over the Negro army and transformed it into a standing army on the Turkish model of a Mamluq or Janissary force—a slave army recruited outside the country, responsible only to the ruler, but endowed by virtue of its military power with an important voice in politics.[17]

Partly because his military support was recruited in the Western Sudan, Moulay Ismaïl began to intervene actively in Sudanese affairs; and his interest turned from the old Moroccan concern with the Niger bend to a new interest in the Senegal Valley, reached from a Moroccan base at Chinguetti, some 330 miles to the north of the river. In the early eighteenth century, Moulay Ismaïl worked especially closely with 'Ali Chendura (1702–27), *emir* of the Trarza Moors. With Moroccan help, 'Ali Chendura made the Trarza dominant over the steppe and desert near the coast, and he brought the whole area under the nominal suzerainty of Morocco.

While Moroccan armies might cross the desert, Moroccan authority was more difficult to establish. Instead of founding a Moroccan empire on the fringe of the Western Sudan, the Moroccan contingents became a semi-independent force and a cause of disturbance all along the Senegal. From 1718 into the 1730's, they established an informal protectorate over the Tukulor kingdom, making and unmaking *satigis* at pleasure. (Thomas Pellow, an English adventurer in Moroccan service, has left a first-hand account of one raid of about 1730, in which his forces captured a French ship on the Senegal.[18]) As a result, the French Company reduced its efforts to penetrate into Bambuk and kept whatever strength it could muster for endless diplomacy with the Moroccans, the Trarza, and Futa Toro, in order to keep open the river trade.[19]

17. See Maurice Delafosse, "Les débuts des troupes noires au Maroc," *Hésperis*, 3:1–12 (1923); C.-A. Julien, *Histoire de l'Afrique du nord* (2d ed., 2 vols., Paris, 1952), 2:224–30.

18. F. de la Chapelle, "Esquisse d'une histoire du Sahara occidental," *Hésperis*, 11: 35–95 (1930), pp. 80–81; Ahmed Ennasiri Esslaoui [es-Slawi], "Kitab Elistiqsa," *Archives Marocaines*, 9 and 10 (Paris, 1906), 9:76–77; T. Pellow, *The Adventure of Thomas Pellow, of Penryn, Mariner*, ed. Robert Brown (London, 1890 [first published 1740]), pp. 195–96 and 201–2; P. Marty, *L'Emirat des Trarzas* (Paris, 1919), pp. 68–75; A. Leriche, "Notes sur les classes sociales et sur quelques tribus de Mauritanie," *Bulletin de l'I.F.A.N.*, 17(ser. B): 173–203 (1955), pp. 180–81; Delcourt, *Établissements français*, pp. 153–57.

19. See Delcourt, *Établissements français*, pp. 139–75. It is also possible, though not now demonstrable, that Moroccan pressure, beginning as far back as the 1670's, was the instrument pressure behind Fulbe population movements that led to the settlement and foundation of Bondu.

It was in this strategic setting that Ayuba returned in 1734 from his splendid reception in England. It is clear that the Royal African Company intended to use his friendship as a commercial entry into Bondu, partly for the sake of keeping open the flow of slaves, partly for access to the gold fields of Bambuk, and partly in hope of opening a gum trade with Ferlo.[20] He left the Gambia for Bondu late in 1735, accompanied by Thomas Hull, nephew of the governor of James Island. Hull's journal was skimpy (and, unfortunately, not available to the present editor), but the Company continued to be encouraged by what it learned from its first direct contact with Bondu. Early in 1736, Ayuba and Thomas Hull again set out from the Gambia into the interior, and this time Hull had orders to cross Bondu and proceed into Bambuk.[21] The Company also began giving wide publicity to the prospects of gum trade in Ferlo and gold beyond the upper Gambia. One of Ayuba's letters to Sir Hans Sloane was released to the Royal Society and widely reprinted in the English and colonial press.[22]

In 1737, the Royal African Company recruited Melchoir De Jaspas, an Armenian who knew Arabic and happened to be in London. He and James Anderson were sent from England with the mission of following up whatever advantage Ayuba's connections might bring. They were instructed first to go together to Bondu, after which Anderson would return to one of the higher posts on the Gambia, there to expedite trade, while De Jaspas remained in Bondu and made further explorations.[23]

20. Gray, *Gambia*, p. 210; Royal African Company to Richard Hull, Charles Orfeur, and Hugh Hamilton, 4 July 1734, Treasury Papers, Public Record Office, London (hereafter abbreviated T.) 70/55; Court of Assistants to Richard Hull *et al.*, 13 January 1736/37, T. 70/55. The gum forests of Ferlo ultimately became an important source of gum, but only very much later; see P. Bellouard, "La gomme arabique en A.O.F.," *Bois et forêts des tropiques*, 1(9):3–18 (1947).

21. Job the Son of Solomon to Mr. Smith, Yanimerow [Niani-Maro], 27 January 1735/36, quoted in Elizabeth Donnan, *Documents Illustrative of the History of the Slave Trade to America* (4 vols., Washington, 1930–35), 2:456–57; Gray, *Gambia*, pp. 210–11; Court of Assistants to Richard Hull *et al.*, 19 May 1737, T. 50/55. There is also evidence from the French side that Ayuba actually crossed Bondu and Bambuk, since he was captured by the French in December 1736 and held briefly at Fort Saint Joseph for acting as an English agent and for having introduced an Englishman into Bondu (J. Machat, *Documents sur les établissements français et l'Afrique occidentale au xviii° siècle* [Paris, 1906], p. 46).

22. See, for example, *Boston Weekly News-Letter*, 6–13 January 1737; *Virginia Gazette*, 28 January 1737.

23. Court of Assistants to Richard Hull *et al.*, 19 May 1737, T. 50/55.

The project rapidly collapsed. Anderson died. Part of Ayuba's original stock of presents from England was lost in a fire at the Company's warehouse in Yamyamcunda on the Gambia. Some of the rest was lost in the shipwreck of a French sloop taking them around from the Gambia to the Senegal for shipment by river to Gadiaga.[24] In addition, De Jaspas hit it off badly with the officials at James Island. He waited, or was kept waiting, for a year. Then he left the Company's service briefly in 1738, but he finally managed to reach Bondu in the company of "Lahamin Jay," or Lamine Ndiaye, Ayuba's servant and companion in slavery, who was now freed and returned to Africa as a favor to his former masters. De Jaspas remained in Bondu and its neighborhood from 1738 to 1740, but no detailed account of his journey is known.

The record of Ayuba's further transactions with the Company becomes more and more sketchy with the decade of the 1740's and a general decline of the Company's fortunes. Ayuba took De Jaspas inland to Bondu at least once more, and De Jaspas also made an overland journey from the Gambia to Cacheu in Guiné in 1744; but the next year he was killed, along with Governor Charles Orfeur, in a quarrel with the people of Barra, the north-bank kingdom opposite James Island. Meanwhile, Ayuba continued to visit the Gambia from time to time. He applied at one point for Company assistance in visiting England for a second time, but the London office discouraged any such attempt. At his final mention in the Company's records, Ayuba was involved in a complicated palaver over two slaves and a pawned watch he claimed were owing to him.[25]

Though Ayuba maintained some kind of contact with the British on the Gambia until his death in 1773,[26] the Royal African Company itself died in 1751–52 and was replaced by the Company of Merchants Trading to Africa. The final, and failing, years of the old Company were no time for pursuing trade in the far interior, but the dream of a forward movement from the Gambia remained a minor thread in British strategic thought about West Africa for more than

24. This was, at least, the official explanation. The Company's officials suspected the French of embezzlement of the cargo entrusted to them. By the same token, the loss of Ayuba's goods by fire may not have been as great as they reported. See Court of Assistants to Richard Hull et al., 19 May 1737, T. 50/55.

25. Royal African Company to Charles Orfeur et al., 26 March 1741; Chief Agents to Royal African Company, 11 October 1746, T. 70/56.

26. John Nicholas, Literary Anecdotes of the Eighteenth Century (6 vols., London, 1812), 6:90–91.

a century. Bondu itself grew comparatively wealthy on the profits of passing caravans, until it was devastated in the 1850's by the wars of a new religious revolution.

THE CAPTURE AND TRAVELS
OF AYUBA SULEIMAN IBRAHIMA

The most comprehensive account of Job's capture and travels is that written down by Thomas Bluett and published in 1734 under the title *Some Memoirs of the Life of Job, the Son of Solomon the High Priest of Boonda in Africa; Who was a Slave about two Years in Maryland; and afterwards being brought to England, was set free, and sent to his native Land in the Year 1734* (London, Richard Ford, 1734). The extract printed here is from pages 9 to 53 of the original, without omissions or changes other than modernization of the typography.

INTRODUCTION

Having had occasion to inform myself of many considerable and curious circumstances of the life of Job, the African priest, in a more exact and particular manner than the generality of his acquaintance in England could do; I was desired by himself, a little before his departure, to draw up an account of him agreeable to the information he had given me at different times, and to the truth of the facts, which I had either been a witness to, or personally concerned in upon his account. I have been solicited also by several gentlemen, who were benefactors to Job, to publish what I knew of him: and I am of opinion such an account is pretty generally wanted; at least it cannot but be agreeable to those persons, who were pleased to do kind offices to this stranger, merely from a principle of humanity, before any particular account of him could be had. Therefore I have at length resolved to communicate to the world such particulars of the life and character of this African gentleman, as I think will be most useful and entertaining; intending to advance nothing as fact, but what I either knew to be such, or have had from Job's own mouth, whose veracity I have no reason to doubt of.

Pursuant to this resolution, I shall not trouble my reader with any very long and particular detail of the geography, history, or rarities of that country of Africa which Job belongs to; nor shall I meddle any farther with these matters, in the present account, than to relate such observations concerning them, as Job himself made to me in conversation; being either not generally known or so curious as to bear a repetition here, consistently with the design of these memoirs. However, I shall endeavour to make the whole as agreeable as the nature of the subject, and the limits of this pamphlet will allow; and therefore, without any farther preface, shall proceed to the thing proposed.

SECTION I

Job's countrymen, like the Eastern people and some others, use to design themselves by the names of their ancestors, and in their appellations mention their progenitors several degrees backward; tho' they also have sirnames for distinguishing their particular families, much after the same manner as in England. Job's name, in his own country, is Hyuba, Boon Salumena, Boon Hibrahema; i.e., Job, the son of Solomon, the son of Abraham. The sirname of his family is Jallo [Diallo].[27]

Job, who is now about 31 or 32 years of age, was born at a town called Boonda [Bondu][28] in the county of Galumbo (in our maps

27. The modern version of the Pular name would be Ayuba Suleiman Ibrahima Diallo, and Ayuba's Arabic signature would be transliterated as Ayūb ibn Sulaymān Jāl. The *yettodé,* or surname, of Diallo is in fact the name of one of the four major divisions of the Fulbe people. Ayuba's mother was Tanomata, the first wife of Suleiman (Nicholas, *Literary Anecdotes,* 6:90–91). His name as a slave was Simon, but he discarded this in favor of Job, the English equivalent of Ayuba.

28. The phrase "a town called Boonda" might mean a town in Bondu, or it might refer to the capital of the country, following a construction that was fairly common in the Western Sudan. For example, Abū Bakr al-Ṣiddīq (see Chap. 5) refers to Birnin Gazargamo, then the capital of Bornu, in an Arabic phrase translated as "the city of Bornu." In the same way, the phrase actually used by Ayuba in talking with Bluett may well have been something like "the city of Bondu," meaning its capital. It is more likely, however, that Bluett simply made a mistake. The capital at this period shifted from place to place with the movements of the ruler (Brigaud, *Histoire traditionelle du Sénégal,* p. 218; Rançon, "Le Boundou," pp. 433–63).

Catumbo)[29] in the kingdom of Futa[30] in Africa; which lies on both sides the River Senegal, and on the south side reaches as far as the River Gambia. These two rivers, Job assured me, run pretty near parallel to one another, and never meet, contrary to the position they have in most of our maps.[31] The eastern boundary of the kingdom of Futa or Senega is the great lake, called in our maps Lacus Guarde. The extent of it, towards the north, is not so certain. The chief city or town of it is Tombut; over against which, on the other side of the river, is Boonda, the place of Job's nativity.[32]

About fifty years ago Hibrahim, the grandfather of Job, founded the town of Boonda, in the reign of Bubaker, [33] then King of Futa, and was, by his permission, sole Lord Proprietor and Governor of it, and at the same time High Priest, or *Alpha;*[34] so that he had a power to make what laws and regulations he thought proper for the increase and good government of his new city.[35] Among other institu-

29. Galumbo and Catumbo are variants of Galam, or, more correctly, Ngalam or Gadiaga.

30. Fulbe kingdoms were often prefaced by Futa—as Futa Toro, Futa Jallon, and sometimes Futa Bondu. In this case, it appears to refer to Futa Toro and Bondu together. The *satigis* of Futa Toro may have claimed jurisdiction as far as the Gambia, but there is no evidence of their having more than a vague claim to suzerainty over the Ferlo wilderness or over Gadiaga, and this only at certain periods.

31. In the eighteenth century the Niger River, which was known to Europeans only in its upper reaches and only through Arab reports, was believed to flow from east to west across the Western Sudan, dividing into two branches which emptied into the Atlantic as the Senegal and the Gambia. It was not until the nineteenth century that Europeans recognized the intricate system of waterways flowing into the Gulf of Guinea between the Bights of Benin and Biafra as the delta of the Niger.

32. Bluett's reporting is confused by a little knowledge. Eighteenth-century Europeans knew Timbuktu as Tombut, mainly through the sixteenth-century account by Leo Africanus. Bluett was evidently trying to bring Ayuba's account into line with Leo Africanus. Thus, when Ayuba reported that the eastern boundary of Bondu was water—and it was, in fact, the Faleme River—Bluett translated this information to conform to seventeenth- and eighteenth-century maps of Africa, which showed Lacus Guarde about where Lake Débo now is, along the course of the Niger in Mali. In the same way, Ayuba reported the country of Bambuk across the Faleme from Bondu, but Bluett warped the information to make Bambuk appear as the city of Tombut.

33. The Denianke *satigi* of Futa Toro, Bubakar Sawa Lamu (*ca.* 1640–73).

34. *Alfa,* usually meaning simply a learned man, derived from the Arabic *al-fāqih,* a person learned in law.

35. The suggestion that Ayuba's town (or even the state of Bondu) was founded by authority of the *satigi* of Futa Toro runs counter to the dominant Sisibe tradition that Bondu was founded by Malik Si with the authority of the *tunka* of Tuabo. It is, however, far from impossible that population movements into the sparsely settled Bondu of the late

tions, one was, that no person who flies thither for protection shall be made a slave. This privilege is in force there to this day, and is extended to all in general, that can read and know God, as they express it; and it has contributed much to the peopling of the place, which is now very large and flourishing. Some time after the settlement of this town Hibrahim died; and, as the priesthood is hereditary there, Salumen his son, the father of Job, became High Priest.[36] About the same time Bubaker the King dying, his brother Gelazi [Geladio], who was next heir, succeeded him.[37] Gelazi had a son,

---

seventeenth century could have been sponsored by several neighboring rulers who had claims to the territory. One variant tradition given in 1941 by Sada Abdul Si (a descendant of the Sisibe dynasty and canton chief of Koussan since 1917) reported that the Sisibe themselves came to Bondu under Tukulor authority, though not that of the *satigis* (Bonnel de Mezières, "Les Diakanké," p. 23).

36. In present-day Bondu, the principal Islamic office in each village or town is that of Imam of the Mosque (Pular: *eliman*), who leads the Friday prayers. This office is frequently passed from father to son, just as the equivalent secular office of village head is also passed from father to son. The situation Ayuba describes, of having the two offices combined in a single person, is sometimes found today, though it is uncommon.

His information, however, provides a clue for the tentative identification of Ayuba's town. The largest concentration in present-day Bondu of people bearing the name Diallo is the town of Marsa, about fifteen miles southeast of Bakel. While village headship and the imamate of the mosque are not always held by the same individual, they often have been in the past; and both offices are hereditary in the Diallo family—the only instance in present-day Bondu where this is the case. Furthermore, the village still has an unusually strong Islamic religious tradition. While village traditions do not remember Ayuba by name (since they preserve only the names of the family head in each generation), the most prominent member of the family in recent times was Suleiman Diallo, village head and imam of the mosque in the 1850's. The customary practices of personal nomenclature suggest that one or more people named Suleiman Diallo had been prominent in the family during the more distant past. Possibly Ayuba's father, Suleiman, was one of them (personal communication from Mamadou Diallo, Imam of the Mosque, Marsa, and from other notables of Marsa).

This evidence at least creates a presumption that Ayuba came from Marsa, and the fact that the Diallo of present-day Bondu are mainly found in the region between Gabou and Kidira creates an even stronger presumption that he must at least have come from the northeastern part of Bondu. But people of Ayuba's social group, the Muslim clerics with mercantile interests, were easily mobile. He may have lived in a number of different places.

37. According to the local version of Islamic law, inheritance of the kingship was supposed to pass to the oldest member of the ruling family. In practice, this meant that it passed to the oldest living brother of the deceased monarch until no brothers remained, rather than passing directly to the sons of any of them. But pre-Islamic Futa Toro had been matrilineal. A male child inherited from his maternal uncle, not from his father. This had left a mark on Tukulor kinship patterns. As late as the twentieth century, a man's

named Sambo [Samba], whom he put under the care of Salumen, Job's father, to learn the Koran and Arabick language. Job was at this time also with his father, was companion to Sambo, and studied along with him. Sambo, upon the death of Gelazi, was made King of Futa,[38] and reigns there at present. When Job was fifteen years old, he assisted his father as *Emaum*,[39] or sub-priest. About this age he

---

children were thought of as especially closely related to those of his sister. These cross-cousins were known as *dendirabe,* and marriage between *dendirabe* of the opposite sex was especially favored. The advantage in the case of inheritance is obvious. Property and heritable office could be passed to a man's descendants by both Islamic law and matrilineal succession (Henri Gaden, *Proverbes et maximes peuls et toucouleurs, traduits, expliqués, et annotés* [Paris, 1931], pp. 17–19). The Denianke of the late seventeenth and early eighteenth century played a similar game in seeking the office of *satigi* for their sons by arranging marriages that would reinforce the claim in Islamic law with a second, matrilineal claim (Labat, *Nouvelle Rélation,* 2:197–98).

The order of succession, however, was very confused in Futa Toro during the early eighteenth century. French reports make it clear that the intervention of Trarza and Morrocan forces made for brief reigns with many pretenders appearing, who might or might not be recognized in later tradition. King-lists therefore disagree with one another, and none of them takes account of repeated returns to power by a single ruler. It is clear, however, that Bubakar Tabakali was succeeded by his brother, as Ayuba's account says— but the brother in question was Sire Tabakali, not Geladio (see Table 1, above). Geladio Jegi came to the throne much later, being deposed in 1718 and dying shortly afterward (Delcourt, *Établissements français*, p. 155).

38. According to one tradition, Samba Geladio Jegi was an adolescent when his father died (F. V. Equilbecq, *Contes indigènes de l'ouest africain français* [3 vols., Paris, 1913–16], 2:4). Since Ayuba would have been about seventeen in 1718, he and Samba Geladio Jegi were very nearly the same age, helping to confirm the identification of Ayuba's Samba with the traditional figure of Samba Geladio Jegi. But Samba was not universally recognized as king, though he fought for many years as a pretender to the satigiship and achieved some control of the country briefly in 1735. In 1737, he signed a treaty with the French official in charge of Fort Saint Joseph in Gadiaga, by which he was to secure French help against the reigning *satigi,* Konko Bubu Musa (for text of the treaty, see Delcourt, *Établissements français*, pp. 412–13). His literary fame, however, was far greater than his achievements. Ironically enough, Ayuba's report that Samba was a great king in Africa may well have led to the popularity of Sambo as a name for Afro-Americans (A. P. Middleton, "The Strange Story of Job Ben Solomon," *William and Mary Quarterly,* 5[3rd ser.]:342 [1948]). Within Africa, his long struggles against Konko Bubu Musa were turned into legend and then into epic poetry. In the end, he came to be the best remembered in the Western Sudan of all the Denianke dynasty. For various versions of the legend of Samba Geladio Jegi, see Siré Abbas Soh, in Delafosse and Gaden, "Fouta Sénégalais," pp. 31–32; Raffenel, *Nouveau voyage,* 2:320–44; Equilbecq, *Contes indigènes,* 2:3–42; L. J. B. Bérenger-Féraud, *Recueil des contes populaires de la Sénégambie* (Paris, 1885), pp. 39–49; Lanrezac, "Légendes soudanaises," *Revue économique française,* 5:607–19 (October 1907), pp. 615–19; Franz de Zeltner, *Contes du Sénégal et du Niger* (Paris, 1913), pp.151–57.

39. *Imam,* leader of prayer at the mosque.

married the daughter of the Alpha of Tombut,[40] who was then only eleven years old. By her he had a son (when she was thirteen years old) called Abdolah; and after that two more sons, called Hibrahim and Sambo. About two years before his captivity he married a second wife, daughter of the Alpha of Tomga;[41] by whom he has a daughter named Fatima, after the daughter of their prophet Mahommed. Both these wives, with their children, were alive when he came from home.

SECTION II

In February, 1730, Job's father hearing of an English ship at Gambia River, sent him, with two servants to attend him, to sell two Negroes, and to buy paper, and some other necessaries; but desired him not to venture over the river, because the country of the Mandingoes,[42] who are enemies to the people of Futa, lies on the other side. Job not agreeing with Captain Pike (who commanded the ship, lying then at Gambia,[43] in the service of Captain Henry Hunt, brother to Mr. William Hunt, merchant, in Little Tower-street, London) sent back the two servants to acquaint his father with it, and to let him know that he intended to go farther. Accordingly having agreed with another man, named Loumein Yoas,[44] who understood the Mandingoe language, to go with him as his interpreter, he crossed the River Gambia, and disposed of his Negroes for some cows. As he was returning home, he stopped for some refreshment at the house of an old acquaintance; and the weather being hot, he

40. Unlikely to be Tombut, or Timbuktu, some 600 miles away. Should be understood as "an *alfa* from Bambuk."

41. Damga, the southeasternmost part of the Tukulor kingdom bordering on Bondu and Gadiaga.

42. Mandingo or Mandinka sometimes refers to all of the Mande-speaking peoples, and sometimes more narrowly to the Malinke. Malinke actually lived on both banks of the lower Gambia.

43. Pike's ship was at Joar, near the present-day town Kau-Ur, about 110 miles upstream from the mouth of the Gambia and 200 miles from Bondu.

44. He appears later in the correspondence of the Royal African Company as Lahmin Jay (Lamine Ndiaye). Ndiaye is a Wolof name, but the Ndiaye family, of Jollof origin, had already established themselves as the dominant family in Bakel. The concern Ayuba showed later in securing his return from slavery in America suggests that Lamine was not a casual acquaintance in the Gambia, but one of the Ndiaye family of Bakel.

hung up his arms in the house, while he refreshed himself. Those arms were very valuable; consisting of a gold-hilted sword, a gold knife, which they wear by their side, and a rich quiver of arrows, which King Sambo had made him a present of. It happened that a company of the Mandingoes, who live upon plunder, passing by at that time, and observing him unarmed, rushed in, to the number of seven or eight at once, at a back door, and pinioned Job, before he could get to his arms, together with his interpreter, who is a slave in Maryland still.⁴⁵ They then shaved their heads and beards, which Job and his man resented as the highest indignity; tho' the Mandingoes meant no more by it, than to make them appear like Slaves taken in war. On the 27th of February, 1730, they carried them to Captain Pike at Gambia, who purchased them; and on the first of March they were put on board. Soon after Job found means to acquaint Captain Pike that he was the same person that came to trade with him a few days before, and after what manner he had been taken. Upon this Captain Pike gave him leave to redeem himself and his man; and Job sent to an acquaintance of his father's, near Gambia, who promised to send to Job's father, to inform him of what had happened, that he might take some course to have him set at liberty. But it being a fortnight's journey between that friend's house and his father's, and the ship sailing in about a week after,⁴⁶ Job was brought with the rest of the slaves to Annapolis in Maryland, and delivered to Mr. Vachell Denton, factor to Mr. Hunt, before mentioned. Job heard since, by vessels that came from Gambia, that his father sent down several slaves, a little after Captain Pike sailed, in order to procure his redemption; and that Sambo, King of Futa, had made war upon the

45. Ayuba and Lamine were captured in Jarra, the kingdom midway between Kiang and Niamina. Lamine was ransomed and returned to Africa in 1738.

46. Francis Moore, at James Island farther down the Gambia, gave this account in his journal of 11 April 1731: "Soon after came down the *Arabella*, Captain Pyke, a separate trader, from Joar, loaded with slaves; and having stay'd a day or two at James Fort, sail'd for Maryland, having among his compliment of slaves one man call'd Job Ben Solomen, of the Pholey [Fulbe] race, and son of the high-priest of Bundo in Foota, a place about ten days journey from Gillyfree [Jufureh, on the north bank of the Gambia, opposite James Island]; who was travelling on the south side of this river, with a servant, and about twenty or thirty head of cattle, which induced the King of a country a little way inland, between Tancrowall [near present-day Janna-Kunda] and the Yamina [Niamina, opposite Joar], not only to seize his cattle, but also his person and man, and sold them both to Captain Pyke, as he was trading at Joar. He would have been redeemed by the Pholeys, but was carried out of the river before they had notice of his being a slave" (Moore, *Travels*, p. 69).

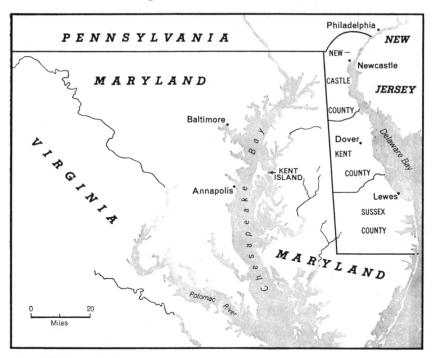

Map 4. Chesapeake Bay, *ca.* 1731.

Mandingoes, and cut off great numbers of them, upon account of the injury they had done to his schoolfellow.

Mr. Vachell Denton sold Job to one Mr. Tolsey in Kent Island in Maryland,[47] who put him to work in making tobacco; but he was soon convinced that Job had never been used to such labour. He every day showed more and more uneasiness under this exercise, and at last grew sick, being no way able to bear it; so that his master was obliged to find easier work for him, and therefore put him to tend the cattle. Job would often leave the cattle, and withdraw into the woods to pray; but a white boy frequently watched him, and whilst he was at his devotion would mock him, and throw dirt in his face. This very much disturbed Job, and added considerably to his other misfortunes; all which were increased by his ignorance of the English language, which prevented his complaining, or telling his case to any person about him. Grown in some measure desperate, by reason of

47. The largest island in Chesapeake Bay, at its closest point about seven miles east of Annapolis. The eastern approaches to the Chesapeake Bay Bridge now cross the island.

his present hardships, he resolved to travel at a venture; thinking he might possibly be taken up by some master, who would use him better, or otherwise meet with some lucky accident, to divert or abate his grief. Accordingly, he travelled thro' the woods, till he came to the County of Kent,[48] upon Delaware Bay, now esteemed part of Pensilvania; altho' it is properly a part of Maryland, and belongs to my Lord Baltimore. There is a law in force, throughout the colonies of Virginia, Maryland, Pensilvania, etc. as far as Boston in New England, viz. that any Negroe, or white servant who is not known in the county, or has no pass, may be secured by any person, and kept in the common goal [*sic*], till the master of such servant shall fetch him.[49] Therefore Job being able to give no account of himself, was put in prison there.

This happened about the beginning of June, 1731, when I, who was attending the courts there,[50] and had heard of Job, went with several gentlemen to the goaler's [*sic*] house, being a tavern, and desired to see him. He was brought into the tavern to us, but could not speak one word of English. Upon our talking and making signs to him, he wrote a line or two before us, and when he read it, pronounced the words Allah and Mahommed; by which, and his refusing a glass of wine we offered him, we perceived he was a Mahometan, but could not imagine of what country he was, or how he got thither; for by his affable carriage, and the easy composure of his countenance, we could perceive he was no common slave.

When Job had been some time confined, an old Negroe man, who lived in that neighbourhood, and could speak the Jalloff[51] language, which Job also understood, went to him, and conversed with him. By this Negroe the keeper was informed to whom Job belonged, and

48. Now Kent County, Delaware. In the eighteenth century, Kent, Sussex, and New Castle counties were in dispute between the rival proprietors of Pennsylvania and Maryland. They now form the separate State of Delaware, but at that time they were in the effective possession of Pennsylvania. Ayuba's escape therefore took him across the narrow channel separating Kent Island from the mainland of Queen Annes County, Maryland, then eastward across that county and across the colonial boundary into the Penns' jurisdiction, a distance of some thirty or forty miles in all.

49. This Pennsylvania legislation, passed in 1725–26, carried the penalty of ten lashes on the bare back for any slave found away from his master's house after nine at night, or more than ten miles from his master's property at any time, without written permission (E. R. Turner, *The Negro in Pennsylvania* [Washington, 1911], pp. 31–32).

50. Dover, Delaware, then, as now, the county seat of Kent County.

51. Wolof, a language related to Ayuba's native Pular.

what was the cause of his leaving his master. The keeper thereupon wrote to his master, who soon after fetched him home, and was much kinder to him than before; allowing him a place to pray in, and some other conveniencies, in order to make his slavery as easy as possible. Yet slavery and confinement was by no means agreeable to Job, who had never been used to it; he therefore wrote a letter in Arabick to his father, acquainting him with his misfortunes, hoping he might yet find means to redeem him. This letter he sent to Mr. Vachell Denton, desiring it might be sent to Africa by Captain Pike; but he being gone to England, Mr. Denton sent the letter inclosed to Mr. Hunt, in order to be sent to Africa by Captain Pike from England; but Captain Pike had sailed for Africa before the letter came to Mr. Hunt, who therefore kept it in his own hands, till he should have a proper opportunity of sending it. It happened that this letter was seen by James Oglethorpe, Esq.;[52] who, according to his usual goodness and generosity, took compassion on Job, and gave his bond to Mr. Hunt for the payment of a certain sum, upon the delivery of Job here in England. Mr. Hunt upon this sent to Mr. Denton, who purchased him again of his master for the same money which Mr. Denton had formerly received for him; his master being very willing to part with him, as finding him no ways fit for his business.

He lived some time with Mr. Denton at Annapolis, before any ship could stir out, upon account of the ice that lay in all the rivers of Maryland at that time. In this interval he became acquainted with the Reverend Mr. Henderson,[53] a gentleman of great learning, minister of Annapolis, and commissary to the Bishop of London, who gave Job the character of a person of great piety and learning; and

52. James Edward Oglethorpe (1696–1785), M. P., 1722–54; founder of the colony of Georgia in 1732; director of the Royal African Company, 1730–32, and its deputy governor for a time in 1732. Oglethorpe was a philanthropist as well as a colonial promoter, and slavery was initially forbidden in Georgia; see A. A. Ettinger, *James Edward Oglethorpe, Imperial Idealist* (Oxford, 1936).

53. Jacob Henderson (d. 1751), born in Glenary, Ireland; ordained in the Church of England, 1710; served for a time as a missionary in Dover, Delaware, for the Society for the Propagation of the Gospel; resigned from S.P.G.; became the first clergyman in Annapolis, Maryland, and later (1715–23) Commissary to the Bishop of London for the Western Shore of Maryland; Commissary for the whole of Maryland in 1729–34 (Nelson W. Richtmyer, *Maryland's Established Church* [Baltimore, 1956], pp. 188–89). The connection between Henderson and Vachell Denton, the slave dealer, was evidently through the Church, since Denton was a vestryman at St. Anne's, Annapolis, where Henderson had once been rector (Ethan Allen, *Historical Notices of St. Ann's Parish, Ann Arundel County, Maryland* [Baltimore, 1857], p. 125).

indeed his good nature and affability gained him many friends besides in that place.

In March, 1733, he set sail in the *William,* Captain George Uriel Commander; in which ship I was also a passenger. The character which the Captain and I had of him at Annapolis, induced us to teach him as much of the English language as we could, he being then able to speak but few words of it, and those hardly intelligible. This we set about as soon as we were out at sea, and in about a fortnight's time taught him all his letters, and to spell almost any single syllable, when distinctly pronounced to him; but Job and myself falling sick, we were hindered from making any greater progress at that time. However, by the time that we arrived in England, which was the latter end of April, 1733, he had learned so much of our language, that he was able to understand most of what we said in common conversation; and we that were used to his manner of speaking, could make shift to understand him tolerably well.

During the voyage, he was very constant in his devotions; which he never omitted, on any pretence, notwithstanding we had exceeding bad weather all the time we were at sea. We often permitted him to kill our fresh stock, that he might eat of it himself; for he eats no flesh, unless he has killed the animal with his own hands, or knows that it has been killed by some Mussulman. He has no scruple about fish; but won't touch a bit of pork, it being expressly forbidden by their law. By his good nature and affability he gained the good will of all the sailors, who (not to mention other kind offices) all the way up the channel showed him the head lands and remarkable places; the names of which Job wrote down carefully, together with the accounts that were given him about them. His reason for so doing, he told me, was, that if he met with any Englishman in his country, he might by these marks be able to convince him that he had been in England.

On our arrival in England, we heard that Mr. Oglethorpe was gone to Georgia, and that Mr. Hunt had provided a lodging for Job at Limehouse. After I had visited my friends in the country, I went up on purpose to see Job. He was very sorrowful, and told me, that Mr. Hunt had been applied to by some persons to sell him, who pretended they would send him home; but he feared they would either sell him again as a slave, or if they sent him home would expect an unreasonable ransom for him. I took him to London with me, and waited on Mr. Hunt, to desire leave to carry him to Cheshunt in Hartfordshire; which Mr. Hunt complyed with. He told me he had been applyed to, as Job had suggested, but did not intend to part with him without his own consent; but as Mr. Oglethorpe was out of England, if any of Job's friends would pay the money, he would accept of it, provided they would undertake to send him home safely to his own country. I also obtained his promise that he would not dispose of him till he heard farther from me.

Job, while he was at Cheshunt, had the honour to be sent for by most of the gentry of that place, who were mightily pleased with his company, and concerned for his misfortunes. They made him several handsome presents, and proposed that a subscription should be made for the payment of the money to Mr. Hunt. The night before we set out for London from Cheshunt, a footman belonging to Samuel Holden, Esq.; brought a letter to Job, which was, I think, directed to Sir Byby Lake.[54] The letter was delivered at the African House;[55] upon which the House was pleased to order that Mr. Hunt should bring in a bill of the whole charges which he had been at about Job, and be there paid; which was accordingly done, and the sum amounted to fifty-nine pounds, six shillings, and eleven pence half-penny. This sum being paid, Mr. Oglethorpe's bond was delivered up to the Company. Job's fears were now over, with respect to his being sold again as a slave; yet he could not be persuaded but that he must pay an extravagant ransom, when he got home. I confess, I doubted much of the success of a subscription, the sum being great, and Job's acquaintance in England being so small; therefore, to ease Job's mind, I spoke to a gentleman about the affair, who has all along been Job's friend in a very remarkable manner. This gentleman was so far from discouraging the thing, that he began the subscription himself with a handsome sum, and promised his further assistance at a dead lift. Not to be tedious: several friends, both in London and in the country, gave in their charitable contributions very readily; yet the sum was so large, that the subscription was about twenty pounds short of it; but that generous and worthy gentleman before mentioned, was pleased to make up the defect, and the whole sum was compleated.

I went (being desired) to propose the matter to the African Company; who, after having heard what I had to say, showed me the or-

54. Sub-Governor of the Royal African Company.
55. In the City of London, headquarters of the Royal African Company.

ders that the House had made; which were, that Job should be accommodated at the African House at the Company's expence, till one of the Company's ships should go to Gambia, in which he should be sent back to his friends without any ransom. The Company then asked me, if they could do any thing more to make Job easy; and upon my desire, they ordered, that Mr. Oglethorpe's bond should be cancelled, which was presently done, and that Job should have his freedom in form, which he received handsomely engrossed, with the Company's seal affixed; after which the full sum of the whole charges (viz. fifty-nine pounds, six shillings, and eleven pence half-penny) was paid in to their clerk, as was before proposed.

Job's mind being now perfectly easy, and being himself more known, he went chearfully among his friends to several places, both in town and country. One day being at Sir Hans Sloan's,[56] he expressed his great desire to see the Royal Family. Sir Hans promised to get him introduced, when he had clothes proper to go in. Job knew how kind a friend he had to apply to upon occasion; and he was soon cloathed in a rich silk dress, made up after his own country fashion, and introduced to their Majesties, and the rest of the Royal Family. Her Majesty was pleased to present him with a rich gold watch; and the same day he had the honour to dine with his Grace the Duke of Mountague,[57] and some others of the nobility, who were pleased to make him a handsome present after dinner. His Grace, after that, was pleased to take Job often into the country with him, and show him the tools that are necessary for tilling the ground, both in gardens and fields, and made his servants show him how to use them; and afterwards his Grace furnished Job with all sorts of such instruments, and several other rich presents, which he ordered to be carefully done up in chests, and put on board for his use. 'Tis not possible for me to recollect the many favours he received from his Grace, and several other noblemen and gentlemen, who showed a singular generosity towards him; only, I may say in general, that the goods which were given him, and which he carried over with him,

56. Sir Hans Sloane (1660–1753), physician and botanist; conducted research in the West Indies; president of the Royal Society (1727–41); president of the Royal College of Physicians (1719–35); First Physician to King George II.

57. John Montagu, second Duke of Montagu (d. 1749); courtier and one-time grantee of the West Indian islands of St. Vincent and St. Lucia; a noted Afrophile and patron of visiting Africans and Negro Americans.

were worth upwards of 500 pounds; besides which, he was well furnished with money, in case any accident should oblige him to go on shore, or occasion particular charges at sea. About the latter end of July last [1734] he embarked on board one of the African Company's ships, bound for Gambia; where we hope he is safely arrived, to the great joy of his friends, and the honour of the English nation.

SECTION III

I don't pretend here, as I hinted before, to trouble the reader or my self with a full and regular history of Job's country. Those who have the curiosity to inform themselves more particularly in the history of those parts of the world, may consult the voyages that are already published on that subject. I shall only take notice of some occasional remarks upon the customs of the country, as I had them in conversation from Job himself.

It is pretty commonly known that the Africans in general, especially those in the inland countries, are inured from their infancy to a hard and low life, being great strangers to the luxury and delicacy of most of the countries of Europe. They have the necessaries of life, 'tis true, and might have many of the conveniences of it too; but such is the simplicity of their manners, occasioned chiefly by their ignorance, and want of correspondence with the politer part of the world, that they seem contented enough with their plain necessaries, and don't much hanker after greater manners, tho' their country in many places is capable of great improvements.

In Job's country the slaves, and poorer sort of people, are employed in preparing the bread, corn, etc. And here they labour under a great many difficulties, having no proper instruments either for tilling the ground, or reaping the corn when it is ripe; insomuch that they used, in harvest-time, to pull it up, roots and all.[58] To reduce their corn to flower, they rub it between two stones with their hands, which must be very tedious. Nor is their fatigue in building and carriage less, for they perform the whole by mere dint of strength, and

58. This is another instance of Ayuba's failure to make himself fully understood. The "corn" which the Bondunkobe pulled up roots and all was, of course, peanuts, which was already a common food crop and has since become the principal cash crop of the country.

downright labour. The better sort of people, who apply themselves to study and reading, are obliged to read whole nights together by the light of the fire (having no candles or lamps, as we have) which must be very troublesome in that hot, sultry country. These, and several other difficulties which these people labour under, we hope will be removed by Job's return; his friends here having suited their presents very judiciously to the necessities of his countrymen; and there is scarce any tool or machine, that can be of real use to them, which Job has not had from some friend or other, and their several uses have been shown to him with a great deal of care.

Some of those people spend a great part of their time in hunting; particularly after the elephants, with whose teeth they drive a great trade. One of those hunters affirmed to Job, that he had seen an elephant surprize a lion (to which beast, it seems, the elephant bears a very great hatred) and carry him to a tree, which he split down, and putting the lion's head thro', let the tree close again on the lion's neck, and there left him to perish. Job did not say that he knew this fact to be true; but it seems to be the more probable, upon account of what he assured me he had been a witness to himself, viz. that an elephant having catched a lion, carried him directly to a great slough, and thrusting the lion's head under the mud, held him there till he was smothered.

One day Job finding a cow of his father's, that had been killed, and partly devoured, resolved, if possible, to surprize the devourer. Accordingly he placed himself in a tree, near the remains of the cow; and, in the close of the evening, he saw two lions making up to it with great caution, moving slow, and looking carefully about them. At last one came up, which Job shot with a poisoned arrow, and wounded so deadly, that he fell immediately upon the spot; the other coming up soon after, Job shot another arrow, and wounded him; upon which he roared out and fled, but the next morning was found dead about 300 yards from the place.

The poison they dip their arrows in, is the juice of a certain tree; and is of such a nature, that it infects the blood in a short time, and makes the creature quite stupid and senseless. Altho' it is so deadly a poison, it does not hinder their eating the flesh of the animal that is shot; for as soon as it is stupified enough to drop down, they catch it, cut its throat, etc. as their law directs, and then eat it. If a man is wounded with one of these arrows, they have an herb, which, if immediately applyed, is a sure remedy, and extracts the poison.[59]

And here I would observe two things, as well from my own observations abroad, as from what I have just mentioned. First, that in all countries, where these wild beasts are, at least where I have been, providence has so ordered it, that they will all fly at the sight of a man, and will never attack him, if they have any room to escape by flight. Secondly, that all poisons, of what nature soever, have their antidotes generally near them. One instance of which I shall mention, as being somewhat extraordinary.

The milk, or liquor that is squeezed from the cassavi,[60] or cassader roots (of which roots is made the bread of that name, used in Barbadoes, Jamaica, and all the Leward [sic], Caribbe Islands) is so deadly a poison, that one pint of it will soon kill any creature that drinks it. Yet I knew a cow, which drank a hearty draught of it, and immediately (as if sensible of the danger she was in) went and fed on a shrub, which grows common there, called the sensitive plant,[61] from the shrivelling up of its leaves upon the least touch; and altho' we expected every minute to see her fall down dead, it so expelled the poison, that she received not the least hurt by it.

The manner of their marriages and baptisms is something remarkable. When a man has a mind to marry his son (which they generally do much sooner than in England) and has found out a suitable match for him, he goes to the girl's father, proposes the matter to him, and agrees for the price that he is to pay for her; which the father of the woman always gives to her as a dowry. All things being concluded on, the two fathers and the young man go to the priest,

59. The poison is probably *Strophanthus hispidus*, widely cultivated in West Africa for the seeds, which form the base of the fluid extract into which arrows were dipped. Antidotes were usually kept secret, but several have been reported, including *Garcinia kola*, or bitter kola, a forest plant which was nevertheless marketed in precolonial times in the savanna country as far north as Bondu (J. M. Dalziel, *The Useful Plants of West Tropical Africa* [London, 1948], pp. 91, 379–80; A. Chevalier, "Nos connaissances actuelles sur la géographie botanique et la flore économique du Sénégal et du Soudan," in Lasnet, Chevalier, Cligny, and Rambaud, *Une mission au Sénégal* [Paris, 1900]).

60. Bitter cassava, *Manihot esculenta*, native to America but widely used in West Africa as a staple food. The poisonous hydrocyanic acid of the sap is removed by squeezing or soaking in water before cooking.

61. Sensitive plant, *Mimosa pudica*, used as forage for cattle in certain parts of West Africa (Dalziel, *Useful Plants*, p. 217). I have seen no evidence that it neutralizes the hydrocyanic acid in uncooked cassava.

and declare their agreement; which finishes the marriage. But now comes the great difficulty, viz. how the young man shall get his wife home; for the women, cousins, and relations, take on mightily, and guard the door of the house to prevent her being carried away; but at last the young man's presents and generosity to them, makes them abate their grief. He then provides a friend, well mounted, to carry her off; but as soon as she is up on horseback, the women renew their lamentations, and rush in to dismount her. However, the man is generally successful, and rides off with his prize to the house provided for her. After this they make a treat for their friends, but the woman never appears at it; and tho' the ladies here in England are generally more free after marriage than before, with the women in Job's country it is quite contrary; for they are so very bashful, that they will never permit their husbands to see them without a veil on for three years after they are married; insomuch, that altho' Job has a daughter by his last wife, yet he never saw her unveiled since marriage, having been married to her but about two years before he came from home. To prevent quarrels, and keep peace among their wives, the husbands divide their time equally betwixt them; and are so exact in this affair, that if one wife lies in, the husband lies alone in her apartment those nights, that are her turn, and not with the other wife. If a wife proves very bad, they put her away, and she keeps her dowry, and any one may marry her after her divorce; but they don't use to put them away upon slight occasions. If a woman puts away her husband, she must return him her dowry; and she is looked upon always after as a scandalous person, no man caring to have any thing to do with her.[62]

All their male children are circumcised; but, besides, they have a kind of baptism for all children, of both sexes. When the child is seven days old, the people that are invited meet together at the father's house; the father names the child, and the priest writes the name of the child on a piece of smooth board. Then the father kills a cow or sheep, according to his ability; part of which is dressed for the company, and the rest distributed amongst the poor: after which the child is washed all over with fair water, and then the priest

---

62. For Fulbe marriage customs, see Monteil, *Les Khassonké*, pp. 170–214; Derrick J. Stenning, *Savannah Nomads* (London, 1959), pp. 111–16; and Marguerite Dupire, *Peuls nomades* (Paris, 1962), pp. 232–47.

writes the child's name on paper, which is rolled up, and tied about the child's neck; where it remains, till it is wore or rubbed off.

The ceremony at their burials has nothing remarkable in it. They put the dead body in the earth, and cover it up as we do in England, saying some prayers over it, which Job told me were intended only for the benefit of the bystanders, and not of the dead person; for they are not of opinion that the dead can reap any advantage by their devotion at that time.

Their opinions and traditions, in matters of religion, are much the same with those of the generality of the Mahometans;[63] tho' the learned sort of them give a more plausible and refined turn to the gross and sensual doctrines of the Koran, than those in Turkey, and some other places They have a strong aversion to the least appearance of idolatry, insomuch that they will not keep a picture of any kind whatsoever in their houses; and the popish worship, at the French factory in their neighbourhood, has much confirmed them in an opinion that all Christians are idolaters. But I shall not say any more here upon this head, since their religion, and the ceremonies relating to it, are pretty well known.

I might add several other particulars, concerning their dress, their houses, oeconomy, and the like; but these too being described at large in several books already published, I shall make an end of this section, and so pass on.

SECTION IV

Job was about five feet ten inches high, strait limbed, and naturally of a good constitution; altho' the religious abstinence which he observed, and the fatigues he lately underwent, made him appear something lean and weakly. His countenance was exceeding pleasant, yet grave and composed; his hair long, black, and curled, being very different from that of the Negroes commonly brought from Africa.

63. Bluett was misinformed. European travellers to Bondu in the later eighteenth century reported that a significant part of the population was still polytheist, and that the religion of the clerical class as well as popular Islam had important polytheistic elements at that time as it does today; see Park, *Travels*, 1:78, 89; and D. Houghton in *Proceedings of the Association for Promoting the Discovery of the Interior Parts of Africa* (2d ed., 2 vols., London, 1810), 1:247.

His natural parts were remarkably good; and I believe most of the gentlemen that conversed with him frequently, will remember many instances of his ingenuity. On all occasions he discovered a solid judgment, a ready memory, and a clear head. And, notwithstanding the prejudices which it was natural for him to have in favour of his own religious principles, it was very observable with how much temper and impartiality he would reason in conversation upon any question of that kind, while at the same time he would frame such replies, as were calculated at once to support his own opinion, and to oblige or please his opponent. In his reasonings there appeared nothing trifling, nothing hypocritical or over-strained; but, on the contrary, strong sense, joined with an innocent simplicity, a strict regard to truth and a hearty desire to find it. Tho' it was a considerable disadvantage to him in company, that he was not sufficient master of our language; yet those who were used to his way, by making proper allowances, always found themselves agreeably entertained by him.

The acuteness of his genius appeared upon many occasions. He very readily conceived the mechanism and use of most of the ordinary instruments which were showed to him here; and particularly, upon seeing a plow, a grist mill, and a clock taken to pieces, he was able to put them together again himself, without any further direction.

His memory was extraordinary; for when he was fifteen years old he could say the whole Alcoran by heart, and while he was here in England he wrote three copies of it without the assistance of any other copy, and without so much as looking to one of those three when he wrote the others. He would often laugh at me when he heard me say I had forgot any thing, and told me he hardly ever forgot any thing in his life, and wondered that any other body should.

In his natural temper there appeared a happy mixture of the grave and the chearful, a gentle mildness, guarded by a proper warmth, and a kind and compassionate disposition towards all that were in distress. In conversation he was commonly very pleasant; and would every now and then divert the company with some witty turn, or pretty story, but never to the prejudice of religion, or good manners. I could perceive, by several slight occurrences, that, notwithstanding his usual mildness he had courage enough, when there was occasion for it: and I remember a story which he told me of himself, that is some proof of it. As he was passing one day thro' the country of the

Ayuba Suleiman Diallo. From *Gentleman's Magazine*, 20:272 (1750).

Arabic manuscript letter from Ayuba Suleiman to Sir Hans Sloane, James Fort, Gambia, 8 December 1734. From Sloane Papers, Ad. MSS 4053, British Museum. Reproduced by courtesy of the British Museum.

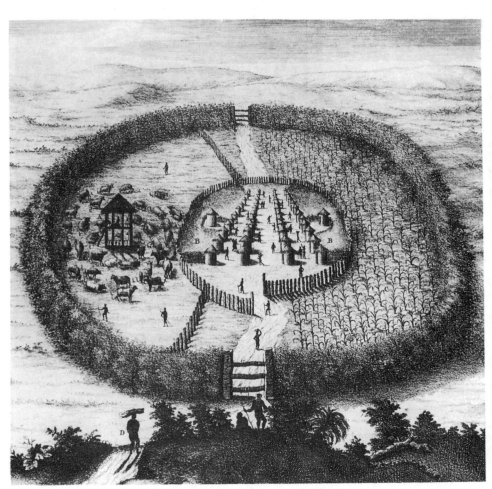

Settlement of pastoral Fulbe near the Gambia, *ca.* 1730. From Francis Moore, *Travels into the Inland Parts of Africa.*

Arabs,[64] on his way home, with four servants, and several Negroes which he had bought, he was attacked by fifteen of the wild Arabs, who are known to be common bandetti or robbers in those parts. Job, upon the first sight of this gang, prepared for a defence; and setting one of his servants to watch the Negroes, he, with the other three, stood on his guard. In the fight one of Job's men was killed, and Job himself was run thro' the leg with a spear. However, having killed two of the Arabs, together with their captain and two horses, the rest fled, and Job brought off his Negroes safe.

Job's aversion to pictures of all sorts, was exceeding great; insomuch, that it was with great difficulty that he could be brought to sit for his own. We assured him that we never worshipped any picture, and that we wanted his for no other end but to keep us in mind of him. He at last consented to have it drawn; which was done by Mr. Hoare. When the face was finished, Mr. Hoare asked what dress would be most proper to draw him in; and, upon Job's desiring to be drawn in his own country dress, told him he could not draw it, unless he had seen it, or had it described to him by one who had: upon which Job answered, if you can't draw a dress you never saw, why do some of you painters presume to draw God, whom no one ever saw? I might mention several more of his smart repartees in company, which showed him to be a man of wit and humour, as well as good sense: but that I may not be tedious, what I have said shall suffice for this head.

As to his religion, 'tis known he was a Mahometan, but more moderate in his sentiments than most of that religion are. He did not believe a sensual paradise, nor many other ridiculous and vain traditions, which pass current among the generality of the Turks. He was very constant in his devotion to God; but said, he never prayed to Mahommed, nor did he think it lawful to address any but God himself in prayer. He was so fixed in the belief of one God, that it was not possible, at least during the time he was here, to give him any notion of the Trinity; so that having had a New Testament given him in his own language, when he had read it, he told me he had perused it with a great deal of care, but could not find one word in it of three Gods, as some people talk: I did not care to puzzle him, and therefore answered in general, that the English believed only in one

64. This could refer to any of the Arabic-speaking region north of the Senegal in present-day Mauritania.

God. He showed upon all occasions a singular veneration for the name of God, and never pronounced the word Allah without a peculiar accent, and a remarkable pause: and indeed his notions of God, Providence, and a future state, were in the main very just and reasonable.

His learning, considering the disadvantages of the place he came from, was far from being contemptible. The books in his country are all in manuscript, all upon religion; and are not, as I remember, more than thirty in number. They are all in Arabick; but the Alcoran, he says, was originally wrote by God himself, not in Arabick, and God sent it by the Angel Gabriel to Ababuker, some time before Mahommed was born; the Angel taught Ababuker to read it, and no one can read it but those who are instructed after a different manner from that in which the Arabick is commonly taught. However, I am apt to think that the difference depends only upon the pointing of the Arabick, which is of later date. Job was well acquainted with the historical part of our Bible, and spoke very respectfully of the good men mentioned in Scripture; particularly of Jesus Christ, who, he said, was a very great prophet, and would have done much more good in the world, if he had not been cut off so soon by the wicked Jews; which made it necessary for God to send Mahomet to confirm and improve his doctrine.

AYUBA'S RETURN TO AFRICA

Ayuba Suleiman's return to Africa was reported by Francis Moore at James Fort on the Gambia. The following four extracts are from Moore's journal, originally published in his *Travels into the Inland Parts of Africa* (London, 1738), pp. 202–3, 205–9, 223–24, and 230–31. They are reprinted without change other than the modernization of the typography.

The next day [8 August 1734] about noon came up the *Dolphin* snow, which saluted the fort with nine guns, and had the same number returned; after which came on shore the captain, four writers, one apprentice to the Company, and one black man, by name Job Ben Solomon, a Pholey [Pulo] of Bundo in Foota, who in the year

1731, as he was travelling in Jagra [Jarra], and driving his herds of cattle across the countries, was robbed and carried to Joar, where he was sold to Captain Pyke, commander of the ship *Arabella,* who was then trading there. By him he was carried to Maryland, and sold to a planter, with whom Job lived about a twelve month without being once beat by his master; at the end of which time he had the good fortune to have a letter of his own writing in the Arabic tongue conveyed to England. This letter coming to the hand of Mr. Oglethorpe, he sent the same to Oxford to be translated; which, when done, gave him so much satisfaction, and so good an opinion of the man, that he directly ordered him to be bought from his master, he soon after setting out for Georgia. Before he returned from thence, Job came to England; where being brought to the acquaintance of the learned Sir Hans Sloane, he was by him found a perfect master of the Arabic tongue, by translating several manuscripts and inscriptions upon medals: he was by him recommended to his Grace the Duke of Montague, who being pleased with the sweetness of humour, and mildness of temper, as well as genius and capacity of the man, introduced him to court, where he was graciously received by the Royal Family, and most of the nobility, from whom he received distinguishing marks of favour. After he had continued in England about fourteen months, he wanted much to return to his native country, which is Bundo (a place about a week's travel over land from the Royal African Company's factory at Joar, on the River Gambia) of which place his father was High-Priest, and to whom he sent letters from England. Upon his setting out from England he received a good many noble presents from her most Gracious Majesty Queen Caroline, his Highness the Duke of Cumberland,[65] his Grace the Duke of Montague, the Earl of Pembroke,[66] several ladies of quality, Mr. [Samuel] Holden, and the Royal African Company, who have ordered their agents to show him the greatest respect.

· · · · · · · · · · · ·

Job Ben Solomon having a mind to go up to Cower [Kau-Ur][67] to talk with some of his countrymen, went along with me. In the

65. William Augustus (1721–65), third son of George II and Queen Caroline.
66. Henry Herbert (1693–1751), ninth Earl of Pembroke.
67. Then one of the most important markets on the river, located in the state of Salum.

evening we weighed anchor, saluting the fort with five guns, which returned the same number.

On the 26th [of August, 1734] we arrived at the Creek of Damasensa,[68] and having some old aquaintances at the town of Damasensa, Job and I went up in the yawl; in the way, going up a very narrow place for about half a mile, we saw several monkeys of a beautiful blue and red, which the natives tell me never set their feet on the ground, but live entirely amongst the trees, leaping from one to another at so great distances, as any one, were they not to see it, would think improbable.

In the evening, as my friend Job and I were sitting under a great tree at Damasensa, there came by us six or seven of the very people who robbed and made a slave of Job, about thirty miles from hence, about three years ago; Job, tho' a very even-tempered man at other times, could not contain himself when he saw them, but fell into a most terrible passion, and was for killing them with his broad sword and pistols, which he always took care to have about him. I had much ado to dissuade him from falling upon the six men; but at last, by representing to him the ill consequences that would infallibly attend such a rash action, and the impossibility of mine or his own escaping alive, if he should attempt it, I made him lay aside the thoughts of it, and persuaded him to sit down and pretend not to know them, but ask them questions about himself; which he accordingly did, and they anwered nothing but the truth. At last he asked them how the king their master did; they told him he was dead, and by further enquiry we found, that amongst the goods for which he sold Job to Captain Pyke there was a pistol, which the king used commonly to wear slung about his neck with a string; and as they never carry arms without being loaded, one day this accidentally went off, and the ball's lodging in his throat, he died presently. At the closing of this story Job was so very much transported, that he immediately fell on his knees, and returned thanks to Mahomet for making this man die by the very goods for which he sold him into slavery; and then turning to me, he said, "Mr. Moore, you see now God Almighty was displeased at this man's making me a slave, and therefore made him die by the very pistol for which he sold me; yet I ought to forgive him, says he, because had I not been sold, I should

68. In Jarra, the south-bank state in which Ayuba was captured.

neither have known any thing of the English tongue, nor have had any of the fine, useful and valuable things I now carry over, nor have known that in the world there is such a place as England, nor such noble, good and generous people as Queen Caroline, Prince William, the Duke of Montague, the Earl of Pembroke, Mr. Holden, Mr. Oglethorpe, and the Royal African Company."

On the 1st of September we arrived at Joar, the freshes being very strong against us. I immediately took an inventory of the company's effects, and gave receipts to Mr. Gill for the same. After which we unloaded the sloop, and then I sent her to Yanimarew [Niani-Maro][69] for a load of corn for James Fort, where she stayed till the 25th, and then came back to Joar, during which time I made some trade with the merchants, though at a pretty high price.

On Job's first arrival here, he desired I would send a messenger up to his own country to acquaint his friends of his arrival. I spoke to one of the blacks which we usually employ upon those occasions, to procure me a messenger, who brought to me a Pholey, who knew the High Priest his father, and Job himself, and expressed great joy at seeing him in safety returned from slavery, he being the only man (except one) that was ever known to come back to this country, after having been once carried a slave out of it by white men. Job gave him the message himself, and desired his father should not come down to him, for it was too far for him to travel; and that it was fit for the young to go to the old, and not for the old to come to the young. He also sent some presents by him to his wives, and desired him to bring his little one, which was his best beloved, down to him. After the messenger was gone, Job went frequently along with me to Cower, and several other places about the country; he spoke always very handsome of the English, and what he said, took away a great deal of the horror of the Pholeys for the state of slavery amongst the English; for they before generally imagined, that all who were sold for slaves, were generally either eaten or murdered, since none ever returned. His description of the English gave them also a great notion of the power of England, and a veneration for those who traded amongst them. He sold some of the presents he brought with him from England for trading-goods, with which he bought a woman-slave and two horses, which were very useful to him there, and

69. About twenty-five miles upstream from Joar and Kau-Ur.

which he designed to carry with him to Bundo, whenever he should set out thither. He used to give his country people a good deal of writing-paper, which is a very useful commodity amongst them, and of which the Company had presented him with several reams. He used to pray frequently, and behaved himself with great mildness and affability to all, so that he was very popular and well-beloved. The messenger not being thought to return soon, Job desired to go down to James Fort to take care of his goods, I promising to send him word when the messenger came back, and also to send some other messengers, for fear the first should miscarry.

On the 26th [of September] I sent down the *Fame* sloop to James Fort, and Job going along with her, I gave the master orders to show him all the respect he could.

. . . .

On the 29th [of January, 1734/35] came up from Damasensa in a canoa Job Ben Solomon, who, I forgot to say, came up in the *Fame* sloop along with me from James Fort on the 26th of December last, and going on shore with me at Elephants Island, and hearing that the people of Joar were run away,[70] it made him unwilling to proceed up hither, and therefore he desired Conner to put him and his things ashore at a place called India, about six miles above Damasensa, where he has continued ever since; but now hearing that there is no farther danger, he thought he might venture his body and goods along with mine and the Company's, and so came up.

On the 14th [of February] a messenger, whom I had sent to Job's country, returned hither with letters, and advice that Job's father died before he got up thither, but that he had lived to receive the letters sent by Job from England, which brought him the welcome news of his son's being redeemed out of slavery, and the figure he made in England. That one of Job's wives was married to another man; but that as soon as the husband heard of Job's arrival here, he thought it advisable to abscond: that since Job's absence from this country, there has been such a dreadful war, that there is not so much as one cow left in it, tho' when Job was there, it was a very noted country for numerous herds of large cattle. With this messenger came a good many of Job's old acquaintance, whom he was ex-

70. On account of a dynastic war in Salum during the latter part of 1734.

ceeding glad to see; but notwithstanding the joy he had to see his friends, he wept grievously for his father's death, and the misfortunes of his country. He forgave his wife, and the man that had taken her; for, says he, Mr. Moore, she could not help thinking I was dead, for I was gone to a land from whence no Pholey ever yet returned; therefore she is not to be blamed, nor the man neither. For three or four days he held a conversation with his friends without any interruption, unless to sleep or eat.

.   .   .   .

On the 8th [of April, 1735], having delivered up the company's effects to Mr. James Conner, and taken proper discharges for the same, I embarked on board the Company's sloop *James,* to which Mr. Hull accompanied me, and parted with me in a very friendly manner. Job likewise came down with me to the sloop, and parted with me with tears in his eyes, at the same time giving me letters for his Grace the Duke of Montague, the Royal African Company, Mr. Oglethorpe, and several other gentlemen in England, telling me to give his love and duty to them, and to acquaint them, that as he designs to learn to write the English tongue, he will, when he is master of it, send them longer epistles, and full accounts of what shall happen to him hereafter; desiring me, that as I had lived with him almost ever since he came here, I would let his Grace and the other gentlemen know what he had done, and that he was the next day going with Mr. Hull[71] up to Yanimarew, from whence he would accompany him to the gum forest, and make so good an understanding between the Company and his country people, that the English nation should reap the benefit of the gum trade; saying at last, that he would spend his days in endeavouring to do good for the English, by whom he had been redeemed from slavery, and from whom he had received such innumerable favours.

71. Thomas Hull, nephew of Richard Hull who was then governor at James Fort.

CHAPTER 2

OLAUDAH EQUIANO
OF THE NIGER IBO

G. I. Jones

Olaudah Equiano was kidnapped as a boy from his home in what is now the Benin province of Nigeria. After several changes of ownership he was sold to British slavers in 1756 and brought by them to Barbados. From here he was taken to Virginia, where a British naval officer bought him and took him to England as a servant, giving him the name of Gustavus Vasa. He served with his master in the British navy during the Seven Years' War, being present at the siege of Louisburg and at the capture of Belle Isle. At the end of the war in 1763 he had hopes of acquiring his freedom, but his master returned him instead to the West Indies for resale. This time he was bought by a Quaker merchant from Philadelphia trading in the Leeward Islands, and became assistant to the captain of one of his schooners. Through this captain's support and help he was able to engage in petty trade on his own account and in this way to acquire the £40 needed to buy his freedom in 1766. In 1767 he returned to England, where he qualified in London as a barber, and thereafter he varied periods of employment ashore as a personal servant with service afloat, in the course of which he travelled to places as widely separated as the Levant, New England, Nicaragua, and Greenland. In 1786 he was involved in the preparations for the expedition of the "Black Poor" which resulted in the foundation of Freetown, Sierra Leone; and in 1788, when he brings his memoirs to a close, he was actively associated with the British antislavery movement and was petitioning the Queen to support the abolition of this trade.

The memoirs which Olaudah published in 1789 represent a uniquely detailed account of an African's movement out of slavery. The descriptions of Olaudah's home and of his travels in Nigeria, however, are disappointingly brief and confused. He was only eleven years old when he was kidnapped, and the little he can remember of his travels is naturally muddled and incoherent, nor can we fill out many of the gaps by referring to present-day ethnography, for no detailed studies have yet been made of this part of Nigeria.[1] It is clear from his name (Equiano, or Ekwuno, is a common Ika and riverain Ibo name) and from the few vernacular words he uses that Olaudah was an Ibo, and we can locate his home with some certainty in the northern Ika Ibo region, which is in the eastern part of the present Benin province. This is a tropical forest country, a light-soiled flat peneplain which declines gradually from north to south till it becomes submerged in the Niger Delta. Apart from the Niger River which bounds it on the east, there are no large rivers or waterways until one reaches its southern margin. Trade routes led across it in Olaudah's day linking Benin with various places on the Niger— Idah in the northeast, Asaba and Onitsha in the center, and Aboh in the southeast at the apex of the Niger Delta. Another route, possibly the one referred to by Olaudah, led into it from the south by way of the Ase River as far as it was navigable and then northward on foot.

The region has no traditions of wars or other disturbances leading to large-scale movements of population. People seem to have drifted into the area in small groups and from different directions. Some, speaking various dialects of the Edo language, came from the west; others, speaking Ibo, came from the east and probably from the Nri-Awka area on the other side of the Niger. Recently, these Ibo communities formed the Asaba and Aboh administrative divisions of the Midwest Region and have been classified ethnographically as the

1. For past and present Ibo ethnography in general, however, see John Barbot, *A Description of the Coasts of North and South Guinea and of Ethiopia Inferior, Vulgarly Angola* (London, 1746 [first published 1732]); G. T. Basden, *Among the Ibos of Nigeria* (London, 1921), and *Niger Ibos* (London, 1938); R. E. Bradbury, *The Benin Kingdom and the Edo-Speaking Peoples of South-Western Nigeria* (London, 1957); D. Forde and G. I. Jones, *The Ibo and Ibibio-Speaking Peoples of South-Eastern Nigeria* (London, 1950); Northcote W. Thomas, *Anthropological Report on the Edo-Speaking Peoples of Nigeria*, Part I (London, 1910), and *Anthropological Report on the Ibo-Speaking Peoples of Nigeria*, Parts I and IV (London, 1914).

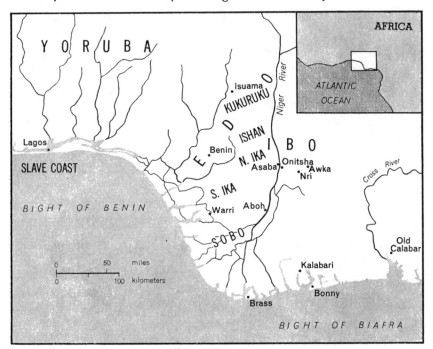

Map 5. The homeland of Olaudah Equiano.

Northern and Southern Ika, and as the Riverain Ibo, mainly as the former. North of them were the Edo-speaking divisions of Ishan and Kukuruku; south and southwest were the Urhobo and Sobo Edo of the Warri province.

These Ibo and adjacent Edo communities came under the political influence of Benin city, and most of their oral histories record alternating peaceful and hostile relations with it, a situation summed up very accurately by Olaudah: "Our subjection to the king of Benin was little more than nominal; for every transaction of the government . . . was conducted by the chiefs or elders of the place." The region also felt the ritual influence of the Ibo town of Nri, whose itinerant "priests" and "medicine men" travelled widely in the area removing "abominations" and nullifying breaches of taboos through the power of their sacred king, the Eze Nri. Other Ibo craftsmen and traders from east of the Niger also operated in the area—the *Oye Eboe* referred to by Olaudah.

The customs and social organizations of these Ibo- and Edo-speaking communities are very similar. In many respects, also, they more closely resemble those of the Ibo groups on the eastern side of the Niger than those of Benin and Yoruba peoples in the west. They are organized into small independent tribal states whose populations number between 2,000 and 10,000 people today, and were probably proportionately smaller in the past. Each consists of one or more villages held together by sentiments of sharing a common way of life and by common religious beliefs, more especially ancestor cults. All this was reinforced by a myth of patrilineal descent from a common founder or founders who came into the area from somewhere else—from Benin or from Nri, names which in most cases probably indicated direction rather than actual derivation. Residence was patrilocal, and each village of any size was subdivided into wards or quarters (*ogbe, idumu*). These comprised extended families whose members belonged to a minimal lineage—the lowest unit in a segmentary lineage structure which embraced the whole ward and in many cases extended to the whole village, or even more broadly.

Authority was based primarily on age, the oldest man in each segment or ward being its ritual head as representative of its founding ancestor. Where wards were ranked in order of seniority, the head of the senior ranking ward was regarded as the ritual head of the community. Male and female adults of the community were organized into age grades and usually into age sets. In its simpler form this consisted of a division into the grades of elder men (*edion* or *ndichie*) and elder women, of men and women, and of young men and young women, each with specific public duties and privileges.

This age organization was modified, however, by the institutions usually referred to as "title associations," whereby wealthy men, by payment of fees to existing title-holders, could secure accelerated promotion to the senior grades or to specific associations of title-holders. Power and authority in these communities was vested in these titled men and in the ritual heads of lineages and wards, referred to by Olaudah as "chiefs or elders." These titles were not hereditary; they had to be gained afresh by each aspirant. Title associations were of two main types: the Ozo system, diffused from Nri, in which the titled members bore on their foreheads the distinguishing *itchi* scarification and held the common title of *onye nze* or *onye itchi;* and the Benin system, which in a modified and attenuated form has now diffused to most of the northern Ika and riverain Ibo communities. Many of the title associations have also obtained from Benin the hereditary titled office of king (*obi*). Today almost every traditional state in the Asaba division has its *obi* and its own particular combination of age-title organization. Some of these kingly offices are of long standing; others are more recent innovations in response to political needs and aspirations which made themselves felt in the period of local-government reorganization carried out by the colonial government in the years 1929 to 1940.

Olaudah's home town had no *obi,* and the fact that its chiefs were *Ndi-itchi* (*embrenche*), titled men of the *ozo* title system, is interesting inasmuch as this system today is only found east of the Niger. He calls this town Essaka. There is no such name in government or ethnographical records, and we can either assume that the community has disappeared in the course of the last 150 years or that it is now known under another name. There is an Ashaka village group in the Aboh division, but this is on the Ase River and anyone brought up there must have been familiar with water and water transport—and Olaudah was not ("I had never before seen any water larger than a pond or rivulet"). The fact that the palm wine drunk in his town came from the sap of oil palms also suggests a more northern location. In the southern Ika it is obtained from raffia palms.

Villages and houses in the northern Ika area are transitional between what can be called a western or Yoruba style and an eastern style typified by Nri-Awka Ibo villages. In the materials of which these houses are built the area is again transitional, this time between the rectangular houses with wattle-and-daub walls and with roofs of mats made from raffia palm leaves, typical of the southern Edo and Ibo peoples, and the square to rectangular houses with solid earth walls, which are roofed with grass by the northern Ibo peoples and with broad-leafed reeds (*Thaumatococci* sp.) by the Yoruba and northern Edo. Yoruba houses are many-roomed and may accommodate a single or an extended family. They are built foursquare around a central courtyard with the rooms facing inward and entered from the outside by a single door which gives access to the veranda surrounding the courtyard. A number of these houses built close together and aligned into one or more streets form the village, which (where needed) is surrounded by an earth wall, beyond which is a narrow belt of forest. Beyond this again lie the farms and gardens of the village, bounded either by high forest or by the farming territory of another village. In the Nri-Awka Ibo each family lives apart in a walled compound which contains the separate houses of the household head and of his wives, unmarried children, and other dependents, plus his *obu,* a low walled or unwalled meetinghouse where he can entertain his visitors and where other members of the household can shelter from the sun or rain while they carry out their various domestic occupations. Nearby will be similar compounds of his brothers, married sons, and other patrilineal relatives. These compounds are dispersed in a maze of forest and cultivated trees, of shade gardens, of secondary forest growth, and of paths that connect the compounds and lead to open spaces which are kept clear and are used as village and ward meeting places. Beyond this inner area of forest and compounds lie the farm lands of the community.

Today most northern Ika villages and houses conform to the Benin pattern, which is similar to the Yoruba. In Olaudah's day they resembled the Nri-Awka Ibo, but their houses combined features not found today in any region, namely wattle-and-daub walls and reed thatch.

Their method of farming, a combination of male and female labor, seems to have been the same in the eighteenth century as it is today. So do their food crops, with the exception of cassava, or manioc. Its introduction into the area seems to have been comparatively recent, and Olaudah's statements provide negative corroboration of this. Yet we know from Barbot's description, which refers to the period 1680–1700, that cassava was the staple food of Warri, a town less than seventy miles distant. Tobacco is no longer grown locally. Olaudah's statement that cotton grows wild is an exaggeration—it has to be cultivated—and locusts do not destroy their harvests. Swarms of adult locusts still occasionally come as far south as the forest region but, apart from maize, they do not eat any cultivated food crops, and they are themselves collected and eaten by the farmers, who consider them a welcome addition to their diet.

Cotton, except in a few areas where it has been introduced from Igala, is not grown by Ibo east of the Niger, and raffia replaces cotton as fiber for weaving into clothes and bags. Similarly indigo dyeing is confined to the western side of the Niger and to Igala; and red, derived from powdered camwood, was the characteristic color east of the Niger, being rubbed on the body and into cloaks and other garments—hence, no doubt, Olaudah's reference to Ibo traders as "red men." Today blue is no longer a fashionable color for the cloaks and shawls still worn in the northern Ika area; they are either locally woven white cotton, or imported cotton prints.

The political situation in this area at the end of the nineteenth century seems to have been much the same as in Olaudah's day. Each little group lived with its neighbors in a state of armed neutrality which periodically gave way to open hostility. Warfare consisted of raids, ambushes, and engagements in more open country—typically, areas of farmland. Wars were seldom decisive, the combatants being too evenly matched in numbers and equipment. In the nineteenth century the combatants normally contented themselves with firing muskets and throwing spears at each other but avoided coming to close quarters. The reference to women taking an active part in fighting is surprising. The traditional role of Ibo women was that of opposition to fighting; and indeed, owing to rules of exogamy and patrilocal residence, many women would be unable to take an active part in local fighting, as their husbands' enemies might well be their own fathers and brothers. There are recorded cases, however, of Isuama Ibo villages which were smaller than their neighbors and which made up for their deficient manpower by encouraging their womenfolk to fight alongside their husbands in defense of their farmlands. This may possibly have been more general in the eighteenth century and in Olaudah's area. The weapons used in these engagements seem to have been much the same as at the end of the nineteenth century, except that by then bows and arrows had disappeared. While most of the later swords and cutlasses had a single edge, many of them were curved and some were of European manufacture. Barbot, however, has a drawing of a pointed dagger or short sword "made by the Hackbous [Ibo] blacks" which could well be a two-edged weapon.[2] In contrast to the slow spread of cassava, muskets seem to have diffused very rapidly into the hinterland. We know from Barbot that in his time (the end of the seventeenth century) muskets were not a normal article of trade in the bights of Benin and Biafra, though a few were being distributed as presents to kings and chiefs. The army of Benin, he says, were armed only with "pikes, javelins, bows and poisoned arrows, cutlaces and bucklers or shields; but so slight, and made of small bamboos, that they cannot ward off anything that is forcible."[3] The large shields described by Olaudah seem to have been

2. Barbot, *North and South Guinea*, p. 462.
3. Barbot, *North and South Guinea*, p. 369.

more robust. Later shields from this area were smaller, covering only a man's body, and were made from slatted pieces of wood or palm branches.

Olaudah's description of the domestic occupations of cooking, eating, or making libations to deceased relatives and ancestors, shows that they have changed but little. His description of marriage ceremonies could apply equally to Ibo or Edo communities, though the emphasis today is more on the bride wealth (gifts which the parents of the bridegroom present to those of the bride). Both Ibo and Edo require the bride to be supplied with all the property and gear needed by a married woman, and wealthy fathers liked in addition to present their daughters with slaves and other property to take with them to their new home.

The native currency of the Nri-Awka and northern Ika Ibo in the nineteenth century was the cowrie, which was also the currency of the Yoruba and Benin people. Barbot records that merchants were already flooding the Slave Coast with cowries in the latter part of the seventeenth century. The currency of the eastern Nigerian trading ports at this time and later consisted of brass rings (manillas) and copper or brass rods, while that of the eastern Nigerian hinterland seems to have been based on iron in various pointed forms. Very small pieces of this iron currency, variously described as conventionalized fishhooks or arrowheads, have survived down to the twentieth century in a few remote areas. It would seem, from Olaudah's description, that this sort also existed west of the Niger and that the diffusion of the cowrie currency into this area must have occurred later than 1756.

The method of Olaudah's kidnapping can be paralleled in innumerable police records and criminal depositions of this century. The dispersion of compounds made such crimes easier to commit, and once such children had been smuggled out of the territory of their own state, relatives could not easily follow them, as they were then in strange and hostile country and liable themselves to fall into ambushes.

It is clear that Olaudah did not travel very far in Nigeria. He tells us that the country remained the same in its vegetation and food crops and methods of agriculture. Had he been taken west to the Yoruba he would have passed through larger towns and encountered different methods of farming; had he moved north he would have been out of the forest belt and would have met with guinea corn and other grain crops and with different methods of cultivating yams. To begin with, he remained in his own language area; that is, within the present Asaba and Aboh divisions. His first master was probably a worker in brass, not gold; there is no gold in this part of Nigeria, and people are too poor to be able to import it. Most of their jewelry is made of brass with some silver and other white alloys.

Timnah, the next place he mentions, cannot be identified with any present-day community. Its water supply and coconut trees suggest a place nearer the coast, and the use of cowries there suggests some contact with the western trading area of the Slave Coast—though not a very close contact, for cowries were being imported on this coast by the barrel and valued by the hundredweight,[4] while the price paid for Olaudah was only 172 cowries. His treatment there in close association with the only son of a wealthy woman suggests a widespread African practice, that of the ritual association of two persons for the purpose, in this case, of diverting or transferring evil influences intended to harm the son to his associate who was then removed from the community.

The strange uncircumcised people who made no sacrifices or offering and to whom he was next taken provide another enigma. Ethnographers now maintain that all southern Nigerian peoples are circumcised, but it may well be that some groups in the past may have sought to differentiate themselves from their neighbors by remaining uncircumcised. Facial marks and teeth filing do not help much in identification. They are fashions which are widely distributed and which are also very unstable. There are two ethnic groups in the northeast of the Benin province—the Ivbiosakan and the Etsako—whose names signify "those who file their teeth"; but the use of iron cooking pots (a costly European import) and of European cutlasses and crossbows suggests a trading area nearer the coast, possibly Warri. Barbot tells us that they were "not all fond of idol-worship or pagan priests" having been formerly under the influence of Portuguese missionaries,[5] and modern ethnographers report that these people (the Jekri) do not "circumcise" their women and that they were formerly distinguished by facial marks consisting of three small vertical cuts below each eye, often supplemented by small lines

4. Barbot, *North and South Guinea,* p. 339.
5. Barbot, *North and South Guinea,* p. 378.

known as "fowl's toes" radiating from the corners of the eye towards the ears. It was on reaching this place that Olaudah saw his first large river and travelled by water for the first time. From Warri he could have been taken by water either to Lagos and the Slave Coast ports or to those of the eastern delta—Brass, New Calabar (Kalabari), or Bonny. It was probably one of the latter, as he found some slaves "of his own nation" already on board the slave ship which took him to the West Indies.

THE EARLY TRAVELS
OF OLAUDAH EQUIANO

The Interesting Narrative of Olaudah Equiano, or Gustavus Vasa, the African (2 vols., London, 1789) was published as Olaudah's autobiography, though the style is far too close to the literary standards of the period to have been entirely his own work. The selections below are the first two chapters (pp. 1–57) of the first volume, dealing with Olaudah's African home and his travels up to his first arrival in the West Indies. They are printed without omissions or changes, other than modernization of typography. The notes of the original author are indicated by an asterisk; additional annotation is by G. I. Jones.

CHAPTER I

I believe it is difficult for those who publish their own memoirs to escape the imputation of vanity; nor is this the only disadvantage under which they labour; it is also their misfortune, that whatever is uncommon is rarely, if ever, believed; and what is obvious we are apt to turn from with disgust, and to charge the writer with impertinenc. People generally think those memoirs only worthy to be read or remembered which abound in great or striking events; those, in short, which in a high degree excite either admiration or pity: all others they consign to contempt and oblivion. It is, therefore, I confess, not a little hazardous, in a private and obscure individual, and a stranger too, thus to solicit the indulgent attention of the public; especially when I own I offer here the history of neither a saint, a hero, nor a tyrant. I believe there are a few events in my life which have not happened to many; it is true the incidents of it are numerous; and, did I consider myself an European, I might say my sufferings were great; but, when I compare my lot with that of most of my countrymen, I regard myself as a particular favourite of Heaven, and acknowledge the mercies of Providence in every occurrence of my life. If, then, the following narrative does not appear sufficiently interesting to engage general attention, let my motive be some excuse for its publication. I am not so foolishly vain as to expect from it either immortality or literary reputation. If it affords any satisfaction to my numerous friends, at whose request it has been written or in the smallest degree promotes the interests of humanity, the ends for which it was undertaken will be fully attained, and every wish of my heart gratified. Let it therefore be remembered that, in wishing to avoid censure, I do not aspire to praise.

That part of Africa, known by the name of Guinea, to which the trade for slaves is carried on, extends along the coast above 3,400 miles, from Senegal to Angola, and includes a variety of kingdoms. Of these the most considerable is the kingdom of Benin, both as to extent and wealth, the richness and cultivation of the soil, the power of its king, and the number and warlike disposition of the inhabitants. It is situated nearly under the line, and extends along the coast about 170 miles, but runs back into the interior part of Africa, to a distance hitherto I believe unexplored by any traveller; and seems only terminated at length by the empire of Abyssinia, near 1,500 miles from its beginning. This kingdom is divided into many provinces or districts: in one of the most remote and fertile of which I was born, in the year 1745, situated in a charming fruitful vale, named Essaka. The distance of this province from the capital of Benin and the sea coast must be very considerable; for I had never heard of white men or Europeans, nor of the sea; and our subjection to the king of Benin was little more than nominal; for every transaction of the government, as far as my slender observation extended, was conducted by the chiefs or elders of the place. The manners and government of a people who have little commerce with other countries are generally very simple; and the history of what passes in one family or village, may serve as a specimen of the whole nation. My father was one of those elders or chiefs I have spoken of, and was styled Embrenché [*Mbreechi*];[6] a term, as I remember, importing

6. A person bearing the *itchi* facial marks of the *ozo* title society.

the highest distinction, and signifying in our language a mark of grandeur. This mark is conferred on the person entitled to it, by cutting the skin across at the top of the forehead, and drawing it down to the eye-brows; and, while it is in this situation, applying a warm hand, and rubbing it until it shrinks up into a thick weal across the lower part of the forehead. Most of the judges and senators were thus marked; my father had long borne it: I had seen it conferred on one of my brothers, and I also was destined to receive it by my parents. Those Embrenché, or chief men, decided disputes, and punished crimes; for which purpose they always assembled together. The proceedings were generally short; and in most cases the law of retaliation prevailed. I remember a man was brought before my father, and the other judges, for kidnapping a boy; and, although he was the son of a chief, or senator, he was condemned to make recompense by a man or woman slave. Adultery, however, was sometimes punished with slavery or death; a punishment, which I believe is inflicted on it throughout most of the nations of Africa: so sacred among them is the honour of the marriage-bed, and so jealous are they of the fidelity of their wives. Of this I recollect an instance: a woman was convicted before the judges of adultery, and delivered over, as the custom was, to her husband to be punished. Accordingly, he determined to put her to death; but, it being found, just before her execution, that she had an infant at her breast, and no woman being prevailed on to perform the part of a nurse, she was spared on account of the child. The men, however, do not preserve the same constancy to their wives which they expect from them; for they indulge in a plurality, though seldom in more than two. Their mode of marriage is thus: Both parties are usually betrothed when young by their parents (though I have known the males to betroth themselves). On this occasion a feast is prepared, and the bride and bridegroom stand up in the midst of all their friends, who are assembled for the purpose, while he declares she is thenceforth to be looked upon as his wife, and that no person is to pay any address to her. This is also immediately proclaimed in the vicinity, on which the bride retires from the assembly. Some time after she is brought home to her husband, and then another feast is made, to which the relations of both parties are invited: her parents then deliver her to the bridegroom, accompanied with a number of blessings; and at the same time they tie round her waist a cotton string, of the thickness of a goose-quill, which none but married women are permitted to wear; she is now considered as completely his wife; and at this time the dowry is given to the new married pair, which generally consists of portions of land, slaves, and cattle, household goods, and implements of husbandry. These are offered by the friends of both parties; besides which the parents of the bridegroom present gifts to those of the bride, whose property she is looked upon before marriage; but, after it, she is esteemed the sole property of the husband. The ceremony being now ended, the festival begins, which is celebrated with bonfires, and loud acclamations of joy, accompanied with music and dancing.

We are almost a nation of dancers, musicians, and poets. Thus every great event, such as a triumphant return from battle, or other cause of public rejoicing, is celebrated in public dances, which are accompanied with songs and music suited to the occasion. The assembly is separated into four divisions [or age grades], which dance either apart or in succession, and each with a character peculiar to itself. The first division contains the married men, who, in their dances, frequently exhibit feats of arms, and the representation of a battle. To these succeed the married women, who dance in the second division. The young men occupy the third; and the maidens the fourth. Each represents some interesting scene of real life, such as a great achievement, domestic employment, a pathetic story, or some rural sport; and, as the subject is generally founded on some recent event, it is therefore ever new. This gives our dances a spirit and variety which I have scarcely seen elsewhere.[7*] We have many musical instruments, particularly drums of different kinds, a piece of music which resembles a guitar, and another much like a stickado.[8] These last are chiefly used by betrothed virgins, who play on them on all grand festivals.

As our manners are simple, our luxuries are few. The dress of both sexes are nearly the same. It generally consists of a long piece of callico,[9] or muslin, wrapped loosely round the body, somewhat in the form of a highland plaid. This is usually dyed blue,[10] which is

7*. When I was in Smyrna I have frequently seen the Greeks dance after this manner.
8. The *sticcado pastorale,* an Italian musical instrument resembling a xylophone.
9. Indian calico cloths began to be imported into Nigeria at about this time, but not in large quantities. The cloths referred to here were probably locally woven cotton cloths.
10. With local indigo dye.

our favourite colour. It is extracted from a berry, and is brighter and richer than any I have seen in Europe. Besides this, our women of distinction wear golden ornaments, which they dispose with some profusion on their arms and legs. When our women are not employed with the men in tillage, their usual occupation is spinning and weaving cotton, which they afterwards dye, and make into garments. They also manufacture earthen vessels, of which we have many kinds. Among the rest tobacco pipes, made after the same fashion, and used in the same manner, as those in Turkey.[11*]

Our manner of living is entirely plain; for as yet the natives are unacquainted with those refinements in cookery which debauch the taste: bullocks, goats, and poultry, supply the greatest part of their food. These constitute likewise the principal wealth of the country, and the chief articles of its commerce. The flesh is usually stewed in a pan. To make it savoury we sometimes use also pepper and other spices; and we have salt made of wood ashes. Our vegetables are mostly plantains, eadas,[12] yams, beans, and Indian corn. The head of the family usually eats alone; his wives and slaves have also their separate tables. Before we taste food, we always wash our hands; indeed our cleanliness on all occasions is extreme; but on this it is an indispensible ceremony. After washing, libation is made, by pouring out a small portion of the drink on the floor, and tossing a small quantity of the food in a certain place, for the spirits of departed relations, which the natives suppose to preside over their conduct, and guard them from evil. They are totally unacquainted with strong or spirituous liquors; and their principal beverage is palm wine. This is got from a tree of that name, by tapping it at the top, and fastening a large gourd to it; and sometimes one tree will yield three or four gallons in a night.[13] When just drawn, it is of a most delicious sweetness; but in a few days it acquires a tartish and more spirituous flavour: though I never saw any one intoxicated by it. The same tree

11*. The bowl is earthen, curiously figured, to which a long reed is fixed as a tube. This tube is sometimes so long as to be borne by one, and frequently, out of grandeur, by two boys. [Olaudah is probably referring to the pipes he later saw in the Levant. There is no record of pipes of such length in southern Nigeria.]

12. Taro (*Colocasia esculenta*), also called coco yams.

13. No oil palm tree will yield as much as this unless it is felled and the entire sap withdrawn through the crown. This is the Yoruba method. The present-day Ibo method is to climb the living tree and to tap it through a draining tube inserted just below the inflorescence. Palm wine, if allowed to ferment, can become very intoxicating.

also produces nuts and oil. Our principal luxury is in perfumes; one sort of these is an odoriferous wood of delicious fragrance: the other a kind of earth; a small portion of which thrown into the fire diffuses a most powerful odour.[14*] We beat this wood into powder, and mix it with palm-oil; with which both men and women perfume themselves.

In our buildings we study convenience rather than ornament. Each master of a family has a large square piece of ground, surrounded with a moat or fence, or inclosed with a wall made of red earth tempered, which, when dry, is as hard as brick. Within this are his houses to accommodate his family and slaves; which, if numerous, frequently present the appearance of a village. In the middle stands the principal building, appropriated to the sole use of the master, and consisting of two apartments; in one of which he sits in the day with his family, the other is left apart for the reception of his friends. He has besides these a distinct apartment, in which he sleeps, together with his male children. On each side are the apartments of his wives, who have also their separate day and night houses. The habitations of the slaves and their families are distributed throughout the rest of the inclosure. These houses never exceed one story in height; they are always built of wood, or stakes driven into the ground, crossed with wattles, and neatly plastered within and without. The roof is thatched with reeds.[15] Our day houses are left open at the sides;[16] but those in which we sleep are always covered, and plastered in the inside with a composition mixed with cow dung,[17] to keep off the different insects which annoy us during the night. The walls and floors also of these are generally covered with mats. Our beds consist of a platform, raised three or four feet from the ground, on which are laid skins, and different parts of a spungy tree called plantain.[18] Our covering is calico or muslin, the same as our dress.

14*. When I was in Smyrna I saw the same kind of earth, and brought some of it with me to England; it resembles musk in strength, but is more delicious in scent, and is not unlike the smell of a rose.

15. A species of *Thaumatococci,* a plant with a long reedlike stem which expands into a broad leaf at the tip.

16. This suggests the Ibo type of meetinghouse, called *obu.*

17. Floors and walls of southern Nigerian houses are rubbed with a preparation of cow dung to repel jiggers, a type of burrowing tick.

18. This may refer to the pliable sleeping mats made locally from the screwpine (*Pandanus*). There is no ethnographic reference to using plantain stems for sleeping on.

The usual seats are a few logs of wood; but we have benches, which are generally perfumed, to accommodate strangers: these compose the greater part of our household furniture. Houses so constructed and furnished require but little skill to erect them. Every man is a sufficient architect for the purpose. The whole neighborhood afford their unanimous assistance in building them, and in return receive and expect no other recompense than a feast.

As we live in a country where nature is prodigal of her favours, our wants are few, and easily supplied; of course we have few manufactures. They consist for the most part of calicoes, earthen ware, ornaments, and instruments of war and husbandry. But these make no part of our commerce, the principal articles of which, as I have observed, are provisions. In such a state money is of little use; however we have some small pieces of coin, if I may call them such. They are made something like an anchor; but I do not remember either their value or denomination. We have also markets, at which I have been frequently with my mother. These are sometimes visited by stout mahogany-coloured men from the south-west of us: we call them Oye-Eboe, which term signifies red men living at a distance. They generally bring us firearms, gunpowder, hats, beads, and dried fish. The last we esteemed a great rarity, as our waters were only brooks and springs. These articles they barter with us for odoriferous woods and earth, and our salt of wood-ashes. They always carry slaves through our land; but the strictest account is exacted of their manner of procuring them before they are suffered to pass. Sometimes indeed we sold slaves to them, but they were only prisoners of war, or such among us as had been convicted of kidnapping, or adultery, and some other crimes, which we esteemed heinous. This practice of kidnapping induces me to think, that, notwithstanding all our strictness, their principal business among us was to trepan our people. I remember too they carried great sacks along with them, which not long after I had an opportunity of fatally seeing applied to that infamous purpose.

Our land is uncommonly rich and fruitful, and produces all kinds of vegetables in great abundance. We have plenty of Indian corn, and vast quantities of cotton and tobacco. Our pine apples grow without culture; they are about the size of the largest sugar-loaf, and finely flavoured. We have also spices of different kinds, particularly pepper; and a variety of delicious fruits which I have never seen in

Europe; together with gums[19] of various kinds, and honey in abundance. All our industry is exerted to improve those blessings of nature. Agriculture is our chief employment; and every one, even the children and women, are engaged in it. Thus we are all habituated to labour from our earliest years. Every one contributes something to the common stock; and, as we are unacquainted with idleness, we have no beggars. The benefits of such a mode of living are obvious. The West India planters prefer the slaves of Benin or Eboe to those of any other part of Guinea, for their hardiness, intelligence, integrity, and zeal. Those benefits are felt by us in the general healthiness of the people, and in their vigour and activity; I might have added too in their comeliness. Deformity is indeed unknown amongst us, I mean that of shape. Numbers of the natives of Eboe, now in London, might be brought in support of this assertion; for, in regard to complexion, ideas of beauty are wholly relative. I remember while in Africa to have seen three negro children, who were tawny, and another quite white, who were universally regarded by myself and the natives in general, as far as related to their complexions, as deformed. Our women too were, in my eyes at least, uncommonly graceful, alert, and modest to a degree of bashfulness; nor do I remember to have ever heard of an instance of incontinence amongst them before marriage. They are also remarkably cheerful. Indeed cheerfulness and affability are two of the leading characteristics of our nation.

Our tillage is exercised in a large plain or common, some hours walk from our dwellings, and all the neighbours resort thither in a body. They use no beasts of husbandry; and their only instruments are hoes, axes, shovels, and beaks, or pointed iron to dig with. Sometimes we are visited by locusts, which come in large clouds, so as to darken the air, and destroy our harvest. This however happens rarely, but when it does a famine is produced by it. I remember an instance or two wherein this happened. This common is often the theatre of war; and therefore when our people go out to till their land, they not only go in a body, but generally take their arms with

19. There is no record of any trade in gums from the West African rain-forest areas. Indeed, the commercially exploited gum tree (*Acacia senegal*), which figures in the European rivalries over Senegambian trade, would not produce in such a humid area. Olaudah may refer to forest rubber, which figured in the trade of this region in the early twentieth century.

them, for fear of a surprise; and, when they apprehend an invasion, they guard the avenues to their dwellings, by driving sticks into the ground, which are so sharp at one end as to pierce the foot,[20] and are generally dipt in poison. From what I can recollect of these battles, they appear to have been irruptions of one little state or district on the other, to obtain prisoners or booty. Perhaps they were incited to this by those traders who brought the European goods I mentioned amongst us. Such a mode of obtaining slaves in Africa is common; and I believe more are procured this way, and by kidnapping, than any other. When a trader wants slaves, he applies to a chief for them, and tempts him with his wares. It is not extraordinary, if on this occasion he yields to the temptation with as little firmness, and accepts the price of his fellow creature's liberty with as little reluctance, as the enlightened merchant. Accordingly, he falls on his neighbours, and a desperate battle ensues. If he prevails, and takes prisoners, he gratifies his avarice by selling them; but, if his party be vanquished, and he falls into the hands of the enemy, he is put to death: for, as he has been known to foment their quarrels, it is thought dangerous to let him survive; and no ransom can save him, though all other prisoners may be redeemed. We have fire-arms, bows and arrows, broad two-edged swords and javelins; we have shields also, which cover a man from head to foot. All are taught the use of these weapons. Even our women are warriors, and march boldly out to fight along with the men. Our whole district is a kind of militia: On a certain signal given, such as the firing of a gun at night, they all rise in arms, and rush upon their enemy. It is perhaps something remarkable, that, when our people march to the field, a red flag or banner is borne before them. I was once a witness to a battle in our common. We had been all at work in it one day as usual, when our people were suddenly attacked. I climbed a tree at some distance, from which I beheld the fight. There were many women as well as men on both sides; among others my mother was there, and armed with a broad sword. After fighting for a considerable time with great fury, and many had been killed, our people obtained the victory, and took their enemy's chief prisoner. He was carried off in great triumph; and, though he offered a large ransom for his life, he was put to death. A virgin of note among our enemies

20. These approaches were also guarded by pitfalls lined with such stakes.

had been slain in the battle, and her arm was exposed in our market-place, where our trophies were always exhibited. The spoils were divided according to the merit of the warriors. Those prisoners which were not sold or redeemed we kept as slaves: but, how different was their condition from that of the slaves in the West-Indies! With us they do no more work than other members of the community, even their master. Their food, clothing, and lodging, were nearly the same as theirs, except that they were not permitted to eat with those who were free born; and there were scarce any other difference between them than a superior degree of importance which the head of a family possesses in our state, and that authority which, as such, he exercises over every part of his household. Some of these slaves have even slaves under them, as their own property, and for their own use.

As to religion, the natives believe that there is one Creator of all things, and that he lives in the sun, and is girded round with a belt, that he may never eat or drink; but according to some, he smokes a pipe, which is our own favorite luxury. They believe he governs events, especially our deaths or captivity; but, as for the doctrine of eternity, I do not remember to have ever heard of it: some however believe in the transmigration of souls in a certain degree. Those spirits, which are not transmigrated, such as their dear friends or relations, they believe always attend them, and guard them from the bad spirits of their foes. For this reason, they always, before eating, as I have observed, put some small portion of the meat, and pour some of their drink, on the ground for them; and they often make oblations of the blood of beasts or fowls at their graves. I was very fond of my mother, and almost constantly with her. When she went to make these oblations at her mother's tomb, which was a kind of small solitary thatched house, I sometimes attended her. There she made her libations, and spent most of the night in cries and lamentation. I have been often extremely terrified on these occasions. The loneliness of the place, the darkness of the night, and the ceremony of libation, naturally awful and gloomy, were heightened by my mother's lamentations; and these concurring with the doleful cries of birds, by which these places were frequented, gave an inexpressible terror to the scene.

We compute the year from the day on which the sun crosses the line; and, on its setting that evening, there is a general shout throughout the land; at least, I can speak from my own knowledge, throughout our vicinity. The people at the same time made a great noise with rattles not unlike the basket rattles used by children here, though much larger, and hold up their hands to heaven for a blessing. It is then the greatest offerings are made; and those children whom our wise men foretel will be fortunate are then presented to different people. I remember many used to come to see me, and I was carried about to others for that purpose. They have many offerings, particularly at full moons, generally two at harvest, before the fruits are taken out of the ground; and, when any young animals are killed, sometimes they offer up part of them as a sacrifice. These offerings, when made by one of the heads of a family, serve for the whole. I remember we often had them at my father's and my uncle's, and their families have been present. Some of our offerings are eaten with bitter herbs. We had a saying among us to any one of a cross temper, "That if they were to be eaten, they should be eaten with bitter herbs."

We practised circumcision like the Jews, and made offerings and feasts on that occasion in the same manner as they did. Like them also our children were named from some event, some circumstance, or fancied foreboding, at the time of their birth. I was named Olaudah, which, in our language, signifies vicissitude, or fortune also; one favoured, and having a loud voice, and well spoken. I remember we never polluted the name of the object of our adoration; on the contrary, it was always mentioned with the greatest reverence; and we were totally unacquainted with swearing, and all those terms of abuse and reproach which find their way so readily and copiously into the language of more civilized people. The only expressions of that kind I remember were "May you rot, or may you swell, or may a beast take you."

I have before remarked, that the natives of this part of Africa are extremely cleanly.[21] This necessary habit of decency was with us a part of religion, and therefore we had many purifications and washings; indeed almost as many, and used on the same occasions, if my recollection does not fail me, as the Jews. Those that touched the dead at any time were obliged to wash and purify themselves before they could enter a dwelling-house. Every woman too, at certain times, was forbidden to come into a dwelling-house, or touch any

21. By comparison with eighteenth-century Europeans, Edo and Ibo people were remarkably cleanly and attached great importance to washing.

person, or anything we eat. I was so fond of my mother I could not keep from her, or avoid touching her at some of those periods, in consequence of which I was obliged to be kept out with her in a little house made for that purpose, till offering was made, and then we were purified.[22]

Though we had no places of public worship, we had priests and magicians, or wise men. I do not remember whether they had different offices, or whether they were united in the same persons, but they were held in great reverence by the people. They calculated our time, and foretold events, as their name imported, for we called them Ah-affoe-way-cah, which signifies calculators or yearly men, our year being called Ah-affoe. They wore their beards; and, when they died, they were succeeded by their sons. Most of their implements and things of value were interred along with them. Pipes and tobacco were also put into the grave with the corpse, which was always perfumed and ornamented; and animals were offered in sacrifice to them. None accompanied their funerals, but those of the same profession or tribe. These buried them after sunset, and always returned from the grave by a different way from that which they went.

These magicians were also our doctors or physicians. They practised bleeding by cupping; and were very successful in healing wounds, and expelling poisons. They had likewise some extraordinary method of discovering jealousy, theft, and poisoning; the success of which no doubt they derived from the unbounded influence over the credulity and superstition of the people. I do not remember what those methods were, except that as to poisoning. I recollect an instance or two, which I hope it will not be deemed impertinent here to insert, as it may serve as a kind of specimen of the rest, and is still used by the negroes in the West Indies. A young woman had been poisoned, but it was not known by whom: the doctors ordered the corpse to be taken up by some persons, and carried to the grave. As soon as the bearers had raised it on their shoulders, they seemed seized with some sudden impulse, and ran to and fro, unable to stop themselves. At last, after having passed through a number of thorns and prickly bushes unhurt, the corpse fell from them close to a

---

22. It is still customary for Ibo women to avoid normal dwelling houses during their menstrual periods and to sleep in small houses specially built for their use during these occasions.

house, and defaced it in the fall; and the owner being taken up, he immediately confessed the poisoning.[23]*

The natives are extremely cautious about poison. When they buy any eatable, the seller kisses it all round before the buyer, to show him it is not poisoned; and the same is done when any meat or drink is presented, particularly to a stranger. We have serpents of different kinds, some of which are esteemed ominous when they appear in our houses, and these we never molest.[24] I remember two of those ominous snakes, each of which was as thick as the calf of a man's leg, and in colour resembling a dolphin in the water, crept at different times into my mother's night-house, where I always lay with her, and coiled themselves into folds, and each time they crowed like a cock. I was desired by some of our wise men to touch these, that I might be interested in the good omens, which I did, for they are quite harmless, and would tamely suffer themselves to be handled; and then they were put into a large open earthen pan, and set on one side of the high-way. Some of our snakes, however, were poisonous. One of them crossed the road one day as I was standing on it, and passed between my feet, without offering to touch me, to the great surprise of many who saw it; and these incidents were accounted, by the wise

23*. An instance of this kind happened at Montserrat in the West Indies in the year 1763. I then belonged to the *Charming Sally,* Capt. Doran. The chief mate, Mr. Mansfield, and some of the crew one day on shore, were present at the burying of a poisoned negro girl. Though they had often heard of the circumstance of the running in such cases, and had even seen it, they imagined it to be a trick of the corpse bearers. The mate therefore desired two of the sailors to take up the coffin, and carry it to the grave. The sailors, who were all of the same opinion, readily obeyed; but they had scarcely raised it to their shoulders before they began to run furiously about, quite unable to direct themselves, till at last, without intention, they came to the hut of him who had poisoned the girl. The coffin then immediately fell from their shoulders against the hut, and damaged part of the wall. The owner of the hut was taken into custody on this and confessed the poisoning—I give this story as it was related by the mate and crew on their return to the ship. The credit which is due to it I leave with the reader.

24. In the Niger Delta and its hinterland, pythons were very frequently considered under the protection of (or mystically associated with) the tutelary deities of particular communities. For example, Article XII of the Treaty with the Kings and Chiefs of Brass, November 1856, stated that "long detentions having heretofore occurred in trade and much angry feeling having been excited in the natives from the destructions by white men, in their ignorance of the superstitions and customs of the country, of certain species of boa-constrictor that visits the cask-houses, and which is a 'jew-jew' or sacred to the Brass men, it is hereby forbidden to all British subjects to harm or destroy any such snake: but they are required upon finding the reptile on their premises, to give notice to the Chief's man in Twaw, who is to come and remove it away."

men, and likewise by my mother and the rest of the people, as re-markable omens in my favour.

Such is the imperfect sketch my memory has furnished me with of the manners and customs of a people among whom I first drew my breath. And here I cannot forbear suggesting what has long struck me very forcibly, namely, the strong analogy which even by this sketch, imperfect as it is, appears to prevail in the manners and customs of my countrymen, and those of the Jews, before they reached the Land of Promise, and particularly the patriarchs, while they were yet in that pastoral state which is described in Genesis—an analogy which alone would induce me to think that the one people had sprung from the other.[25]* Indeed this is the opinion of Dr. Gill, who, in his *Commentary on Genesis,* very ably deduces the pedigree of the Africans from Afer and Afra, the descendants of Abraham by Keturah his wife and concubine (for both these titles are applied to her). It is also conformable to the sentiments of Dr. John Clarke, formerly Dean of Sarum, in his *Truth of the Christian Religion:* Both these authors concur in ascribing to us this original. The reasonings of those gentlemen are still further confirmed by the *Scripture Chronology* of the Rev. Arthur Bedford; and, if any further corroboration were required, this resemblance in so many respects, is a strong evidence in support of the opinion. Like the Israelites in their primitive state, our government was conducted by our chiefs, our judges, our wise men, and elders; and the head of a family with us enjoyed a similar authority over his household with that which is ascribed to Abraham and the other patriarchs. The law of retaliation obtained almost universally with us as with them: and even their religion appeared to have shed upon us a ray of its glory, though broken and spent in its passage, or eclipsed by the cloud with which time, tradition, and ignorance, might have enveloped it: for we had our circumcision (a rule I believe peculiar to that people): we had also our sacrifices and burnt-offerings,[26] our washings and purifications, on the same occasions as they had.

As to the difference of colour between the Eboan Africans and the modern Jews, I shall not presume to account for it. It is a subject

---

25*. See 1 Chron. i.33. Also John Brown's *Dictionary of the Bible* on the same verse.
26. There are no "burnt offerings" in Ibo rituals, nor are any reported for the Edo or Ibo peoples. Olaudah is no doubt speaking symbolically of non-Christian practices in general.

which has engaged the pens of men of both genius and learning, and is far above my strength.[27] The most able and Reverend Mr. T. Clarkson, however, in his much admired *Essay on the Slavery and Commerce of the Human Species,* has ascertained the cause in a manner that at once solves every objection on that account, and, on my mind at least, has produced the fullest conviction. I shall therefore refer to that performance for the theory,[28*] contenting myself with extracting a fact as related by Dr. Mitchel.[29*] "The Spaniards who have inhabited America, under the torrid zone, for any time, are become as dark coloured as our native Indians of Virginia, of which I myself have been a witness." There is also another instance[30*] of a Portuguese settlement at Mitomba, a river in Sierra Leona, where the inhabitants are bred from a mixture of the first Portuguese discoverers with the natives, and are now become, in their complexion, and in the wooly quality of their hair, perfect negroes, retaining, however, a smattering of the Portuguese language.

These instances, and a great many more which might be adduced, while they show how the complexions of the same persons vary in different climates, it is hoped may tend also to remove the prejudice that some conceive against the natives of Africa on account of their colour. Surely the minds of the Spaniards did not change with their complexions! Are there not causes enough to which the apparent inferiority of an African may be ascribed, without limiting the goodness of God, and supposing he forebore to stamp understanding on certainly his own image, because "carved in ebony"? Might it not naturally be ascribed to their situation? When they come among Europeans, they are ignorant of their language, religion, manners, and customs. Are any pains taken to teach them these? Are they treated as men? Does not slavery itself depress the mind, and extinguish all its fire, and every noble sentiment? But, above all, what advantages do not a refined people possess over those who are rude and uncultivated? Let the polished and haughty European recollect, that his ancestors were once, like the Africans, uncivilized, and even barbarous. Did Nature make them inferior to their sons, and should they too

27. The nature and origins of racial difference were much discussed in eighteenth-century England. For a summary of English racial thought regarding Africans at this period, see P. D. Curtin, *The Image of Africa* (Madison, Wis., 1964), pp. 28–57.

28*. pp. 178–216.

29*. *Philos. Trans.* No. 476. Sect. 4, cited by the Rev. Mr. Clarkson, p. 205.

30*. Same page

have been made slaves? Every rational mind answers, No. Let such reflections as these melt the pride of their superiority into sympathy for the wants and miseries of their sable brethren, and compel them to acknowledge, that understanding is not confined to feature or colour. If, when they look round the world, they feel exultation, let it be tempered with benevolence to others, and gratitude to God, "who hath made of one blood all nations of men for to dwell on all the face of the earth;[31]* and whose wisdom is not our wisdom, neither are our ways his ways."

CHAPTER II

I hope the reader will not think I have trespassed on his patience in introducing myself to him with some account of the manners and customs of my country. They had been implanted in me with great care, and made an impression on my mind, which time could not erase, and which all the adversity and variety of fortune I have since experienced served only to rivet and record; for, whether the love of one's country be real or imaginary, or a lesson of reason, or an instinct of nature, I still look back with pleasure on the first scenes my life, though that pleasure has been for the most part mingled with sorrow.

I have already acquainted the reader with the time and place of my birth. My father, besides many slaves, had a numerous family, of which seven lived to grow up, including myself and a sister, who was the only daughter. As I was the youngest of the sons, I became, of course, the greatest favourite with my mother, and was always with her; and she used to take particular pains to form my mind. I was trained up from my earliest years in the arts of agriculture and war: my daily exercise was shooting and throwing javelins; and my mother adorned me with emblems, after the manner of our greatest warriors. In this way I grew up till I was turned the age of eleven, when an end was put to my happiness in the following manner:—Generally, when the grown people in the neighbourhood were gone far in the fields to labour, the childen assembled together in some of the neighbour's premises to play; and commonly some of us used to get

31*. Acts xvii. 26.

up a tree to look out for any assailant, or kidnapper, that might come upon us; for they sometimes took those opportunities of our parents' absence, to attack and carry off as many as they could seize. One day, as I was watching at the top of a tree in our yard, I saw one of those people come into the yard of our next neighbour but one, to kidnap, there being many stout young people in it. Immediately, on this, I gave the alarm of the rogue, and he was surrounded by the stoutest of them, who entangled him with cords, so that he could not escape till some of the grown people came and secured him. But alas! ere long, it was my fate to be thus attacked, and to be carried off, when none of the grown people were nigh. One day, when all our people were gone out to their works as usual, and only I and my dear sister were left to mind the house, two men and a woman got over our walls, and in a moment seized us both; and, without giving us time to cry out, or make resistance, they stopped our mouths, and ran off with us into the nearest wood. Here they tied our hands, and continued to carry us as far as they could, till night came on, when we reached a small house, where the robbers halted for refreshment, and spent the night. We were then unbound; but were unable to take any food; and, being quite overpowered by fatigue and grief, our only relief was some sleep, which allayed our misfortune for a short time. The next morning we left the house, and continued travelling all the day. For a long time we had kept the woods, but at last we came into a road which I believed I knew. I had now some hopes of being delivered; for we had advanced but a little way before I discovered some people at a distance, on which I began to cry out for their assistance; but my cries had no other effect than to make them tie me faster and stop my mouth, and then they put me into a large sack. They also stoped my sister's mouth, and tied her hands; and in this manner we proceeded till we were out of the sight of these people. When we went to rest the following night they offered us some victuals; but we refused them; and the only comfort we had was in being in one another's arms all that night, and bathing each other with our tears. But alas! we were soon deprived of even the smallest comfort of weeping together. The next day proved a day of greater sorrow than I had yet experienced; for my sister and I were then separated, while we lay clasped in each other's arms: it was in vain that we besought them not to part us: she was torn from me, and immediately carried away, while I was left in a state of distraction not to be described. I cried and grieved continually; and for several days did not eat any thing but what they forced into my mouth. At length, after many days travelling, during which I had often changed masters, I got into the hands of a chieftain, in a very pleasant country. This man had two wives and some children, and they all used me extremely well, and did all they could to comfort me; particularly the first wife, who was something like my mother. Although I was a great many days journey from my father's house, yet these people spoke exactly the same language with us. This first master of mine, as I may call him, was a smith; and my principal employment was working his bellows, which were the same kind as I had seen in my vicinity. They were in some respects not unlike the stoves here in gentlemen's kitchens; and were covered over with leather; and in the middle of that leather a stick was fixed, and a person stood up, and worked it, in the same manner as is done to pump water out of a cask with a hand pump. I believe it was gold he worked, for it was of a lovely bright yellow colour, and was worn by the women on their wrists and ancles. I was there I suppose about a month, and they at least used to trust me some little distance from the house. This liberty I used in embracing every opportunity to inquire the way to my own home: and I also sometimes, for the same purpose, went with the maidens, in the cool of the evenings, to bring pitchers of water from the springs for the use of the house. I had also remarked where the sun rose in the morning, and set in the evening, as I had travelled along; and I had observed that my father's house was towards the rising of the sun. I therefore determined to seize the first opportunity of making my escape, and to shape my course for that quarter; for I was quite oppressed and weighed down by grief after my mother and friends; and my love of liberty, ever great, was strengthened by the mortifying circumstance of not daring to eat with the free-born children, although I was mostly their companion. While I was projecting my escape one day, an unluckey event happened, which quite disconcerted my plan, and put an end to my hopes. I used to be sometimes employed in assisting an elderly woman slave to cook and take care of the poultry; and one morning, while I was feeding some chickens, I happened to toss a small pebble at one of them, which hit it on the middle, and directly killed it. The old slave, having soon after missed the chicken, inquired after it; and on my relating the accident (for I told her the truth, because my mother would never suffer me to tell a lie), she flew into a violent passion, threatening that I should suffer for it; and, my master being out, she immediately went and told her mistress what I had done. This alarmed me very much, and I expected an instant flogging, which to me was uncommonly dreadful; for I had seldom been beaten at home. I therefore resolved to fly; and accordingly I ran into a thicket that was hard by, and hid myself in the bushes. Soon afterwards my mistress and the slave returned, and not seeing me, they searched all the house, but not finding me, and I not making answer when they called to me, they thought I had run away, and the whole neighbourhood was raised in the pursuit of me. In that part of the country (as well as ours) the houses and villages were skirted with woods or shrubberies, and the bushes were so thick, that a man could readily conceal himself in them, so as to elude the strictest search. The neighbours continued the whole day looking for me, and several times many of them came within a few yards of the place where I lay hid. I expected every moment, when I heard a rustling among the trees, to be found out, and punished by my master; but they never discovered me, though they were often so near that I even heard their conjectures as they were looking about for me; and I now learned from them that any attempt to return home would be hopeless. Most of them supposed I had fled towards home, but the distance was so great, and the way so intricate, that they thought I could never reach it, and that I should be left in the woods. When I heard this I was seized with a violent panic, and abandoned myself to despair. Night too began to approach, and aggravated all my fears. I had before entertained hopes of getting home, and had determined when it should be dark to make the attempt; but I was now convinced it was fruitless, and began to consider that, if possibly I could escape all other animals, I could not those of the human kind; and that, not knowing the way, I must perish in the woods. Thus was I like the hunted deer:

"Ev'ry leaf, and ev'ry whisp'ring breath
Convey'd a foe, and ev'ry foe a death."

I heard frequent rustlings among the leaves; and being pretty sure they were snakes, I expected every instant to be stung by them. This increased my anguish; and the horror of my situation became now quite insupportable. I at length quitted the thicket, very faint and hungry, for I had not eaten or drank any thing all the day, and crept to my master's kitchen, from whence I set out at first, and which was an open shed, and laid myself down in the ashes with an anxious wish for death to relieve me from all my pains. I was scarcely awake in the morning, when the old woman slave who was the first up, came to light the fire, and saw me in the fire place. She was very much surprised to see me, and could scarcely believe her own eyes. She now promised to intercede for me, and went for her master, who soon after came, and, having slightly reprimanded me, ordered me to be taken care of, and not ill-treated.

Soon after this my master's only daughter and child by his first wife sickened and died, which affected him so much that for some time he was almost frantic, and really would have killed himself, had he not been watched and prevented. However, in a small time afterwards he recovered; and I was again sold. I was now carried to the left of the sun's rising, through many dreary wastes and dismal woods, amidst the hideous roarings of wild beasts. The people I was sold to used to carry me very often, when I was tired, either on their shoulders or on their backs. I saw many convenient well-built sheds along the roads, at proper distances, to accomodate the merchants and travellers, who lay in those buildings along with their wives, who often accompany them; and they always go well armed.

From the time I left my own nation I always found somebody that understood me till I came to the sea coast. The languages of different nations did not totally differ, nor were they so copious as those of the Europeans, particularly the English. They were therefore easily learned; and, while I was journeying thus through Africa, I acquired two or three different tongues. In this manner I had been travelling for a considerable time, when one evening, to my great surprise, whom should I see brought to the house where I was but my dear sister? As soon as she saw me she gave a loud shriek, and ran into my arms—I was quite overpowered: neither of us could speak, but, for a considerable time, clung to each other in mutual embraces, unable to do any thing but weep. Our meeting affected all who saw us; and indeed I must acknowledge, in honour of those sable destroyers of human rights, that I never met with any ill treatment, or saw any offered to their slaves, except tying them, when necessary, to keep them from running away. When these people knew we were brother and sister, they indulged us to be together; and the man, to whom I supposed we belonged, lay with us, he in the middle, while she and I held one another by the hands across his breast all night; and thus for a while we forgot our misfortunes in the joy of being together; but even this small comfort was soon to have an end; for scarcely had the fatal morning appeared, when she was again torn from me forever! I was now more miserable, if possible, than before. The small relief which her presence gave me from pain was gone, and the wretchedness of my situation was redoubled by my anxiety after her fate, and my apprehensions lest her sufferings should be greater than mine, when I could not be with her to alleviate them. Yes, thou dear partner of all my childish sports! thou sharer of my joys and sorrows! happy should I have ever esteemed myself to encounter every misery for you, and to procure your freedom by the sacrifice of my own! Though you were early forced from my arms, your image has been always riveted in my heart, from which neither time nor fortune have been able to remove it: so that, while the thoughts of your sufferings have damped my prosperity, they have mingled with adversity, and increased its bitterness. To that Heaven which protects the weak from the strong, I commit the care of your innocence and virtues, if they have not already received their full reward; and if your youth and delicacy have not long since fallen victims to the violence of the African trader, the pestilential stench of a Guinea ship, the seasoning in the European colonies, or the lash and lust of a brutal and unrelenting overseer.

I did not long remain after my sister. I was again sold, and carried through a number of places, till, after travelling a considerable time, I came to a town called Timnah, in the most beautiful country I had yet seen in Africa. It was extremely rich, and there were many rivulets which flowed through it, and supplied a large pond in the centre of the town, where the people washed. Here I first saw and tasted cocoa nuts, which I thought superior to any nuts I had ever tasted before; and the trees, which were loaded, were also interspersed amongst the houses, which had commodious shades adjoining, and were in the same manner as ours, the insides being neatly plastered and whitewashed. Here I also saw and tasted for the first time sugar-cane. Their money consisted of little white shells, the size of the fingernail: they were known in this country by the name of core.[32] I was sold here for one hundred and seventy-two of them by a merchant who lived and brought me there. I had been about two or three days at his house, when a wealthy widow, a neighbour of his, came there one evening, and brought with her an only son, a young gentleman about my own age and size. Here they saw me; and, having taken a fancy to me, I was bought of the merchant, and went home with them. Her house and premises were situated close to one of those rivulets I have mentioned, and were the finest I ever saw in Africa: they were very extensive, and she had a number of slaves to attend her. The next day I was washed and perfumed, and when mealtime came, I was led into the presence of my mistress, and eat and drank before her with her son. This filled me with astonishment; and I could scarce help expressing my surprise that the young gentleman should suffer me, who was bound, to eat with him who was free; and not only so, but that he would not at any time either eat or drink till I had taken first, because I was the eldest, which was agreeable to our custom. Indeed every thing here, and all their treatment of me, made me forget that I was a slave. The language of these people resembled ours so nearly, that we understood each other perfectly. They had also the very same customs as we. There were likewise slaves daily to attend us, while my young master and I, with other boys, sported with our darts and bows and arrows, as I had been used to do at home. In this resemblance to my former happy state, I passed about two months, and I now began to think I was to be adopted into the family, and was beginning to be reconciled to my situation, and to forget by degrees my misfortunes, when all at once the delusion vanished; for, without the least previous knowledge, one morning early, while my dear master and companion was still asleep, I was awakened out of my reverie to fresh sorrow, and hurried away even amongst the uncircumcised.

Thus, at the very moment I dreamed of the greatest happiness, I found myself most miserable; and it seemed as if fortune wished to give me this taste of joy only to render the reverse more poignant. The change I now experienced was as painful as it was sudden and

32. Cowrie, a sea shell obtained from the Maldive Islands and used as currency in many parts of West Africa.

unexpected. It was a change indeed from a state of bliss to a scene which is inexpressible by me, as it discovered to me an element I had never before beheld, and till then had no idea of, and wherein such instances of hardship and fatigue continually occurred as I can never reflect on but with horror.

All the nations and people I had hitherto passed through resembled our own in their manners, customs, and language; but I came at length to a country, the inhabitants of which differed from us in all those particulars. I was very much struck with this difference, especially when I came among a people who did not circumcise, and eat without washing their hands. They cooked also in iron pots, and had European cutlasses and cross bows, which were unknown to us, and fought with their fists among themselves. Their women were not so modest as ours, for they eat, and drank, and slept with their men. But, above all, I was amazed to see no sacrifices or offerings among them. In some of those places the people ornamented themselves with scars, and likewise filed their teeth very sharp. They wanted sometimes to ornament me in the same manner, but I would not suffer them; hoping that I might some time be among a people who did not thus disfigure themselves, as I thought they did. At last, I came to the banks of a large river, which was covered with canoes, in which the people appeared to live with their household utensils and provisions of all kinds. I was beyond measure astonished at this, as I had never before seen any water larger than a pond or a rivulet; and my surprise was mingled with no small fear, when I was put into one of these canoes, and we began to paddle and move along the river. We continued going on thus till night; and, when we came to land, and made fires on the banks, each family by themselves, some dragged their canoes on shore, others stayed and cooked in theirs, and lay in them all night. Those on the land had mats, of which they made tents, some in the shape of little houses: In these we slept; and, after the morning meal, we embarked again, and proceeded as before. I was often very much astonished to see some of the women, as well as the men, jump into the water, dive to the bottom, come up again, and swim about. Thus I continued to travel, sometimes by land, sometimes by water, through different countries, and various nations, till, at the end of six or seven months after I had been kidnapped I arrived at the sea-coast. It would be tedious and uninteresting to relate all the incidents which befel me during this journey, and which I have not yet forgotten; of the various lands I passed through, and the manners and customs of all the different people among whom I lived: I shall therefore only observe, that, in all the places where I was, the soil was exceedingly rich; the pomkins, eadas, plantains, yams, etc., were in great abundance and of incredible size. There were also large quantities of different gums though not used for any purpose; and every where a great deal of tobacco. The cotton even grew quite wild; and there was plenty of red wood.[33] I saw no mechanics whatever in all the way, except such as I have mentioned. The chief employment in all these countries was agriculture, and both the males and females, as with us, were brought up to it, and trained in the arts of war.

The first object which saluted my eyes when I arrived on the coast was the sea, and a slaveship, which was then riding at anchor, and waiting for its cargo. These filled me with astonishment, which was soon converted into terror, which I am yet at a loss to describe, nor the then feelings of my mind. When I was carried on board I was immediately handled, and tossed up, to see if I were sound, by some of the crew; and I was now persuaded that I had got into a world of bad spirits, and that they were going to kill me. Their complexions too differing so much from ours, their long hair, and the language they spoke, which was very different from any I had ever heard, united to confirm me in this belief. Indeed, such were the horrors of my views and fears at the moment, that, if ten thousand worlds had been my own, I would have freely parted with them all to have exchanged my condition with that of the meanest slave in my own country. When I looked round the ship too, and saw a large furnace or copper boiling, and a multitude of black people of every description chained together, every one of their countenances expressing dejection and sorrow, I no longer doubted of my fate; and, quite overpowered with horror and anguish, I fell motionless on the deck and fainted. When I recovered a little, I found some black people about me, who I believed were some of those who brought me on board, and had been receiving their pay; they talked to me in order to cheer me, but all in vain. I asked them if we were not to be eaten by those white men with horrible looks, red faces, and long hair. They told

33. This could refer to camwood, but more probably to mahogany.

me I was not; and one of the crew brought me a small portion of spirituous liquor in a wine-glass; but, being afraid of him, I would not take it out of his hand. One of the blacks therefore took it from him, and gave it to me, and I took a little down my palate, which, instead of reviving me, as they thought it would, threw me into the greatest consternation at the strange feeling it produced having never tasted any such liquor before. Soon after this, the blacks who brought me on board went off, and left me abandoned to despair. I now saw myself deprived of all chance of returning to my native country, or even the least glimpse of hope of gaining the shore, which I now considered as friendly; and I even wished for my former slavery, in preference to my present situation, which was filled with horrors of every kind, still heightened by my ignorance of what I was to undergo. I was not long suffered to indulge my grief; I was soon put down under the decks, and there I received such a salutation in my nostrils as I had never experienced in my life; so that, with the loathsomeness of the stench, and crying together, I became so sick and low that I was not able to eat, nor had I the least desire to taste any thing. I now wished for the last friend, death, to relieve me; but soon, to my grief, two of the white men offered me eatables; and, on my refusing to eat, one of them held me fast by the hands, and laid me across, I think, the windlass, and tied my feet while the other flogged me severely. I had never experienced any thing of this kind before; and, although not being used to the water, I naturally feared that element the first time I saw it; yet, nevertheless, could I have got over the nettings, I would have jumped over the side; but I could not; and, besides, the crew used to watch us very closely who were not chained down to the decks, lest we should leap into the water: and I have seen some of these poor African prisoners most severely cut for attempting to do so, and hourly whipped for not eating. This indeed was often the case with myself. In a little time after, amongst the poor chained men, I found some of my own nation, which in a small degree gave ease to my mind. I inquired of them what was to be done with us? they gave me to understand we were to be carried to these white people's country to work for them. I then was a little revived, and thought, if it were no worse than working, my situation was not so desperate: but still I feared I should be put to death, the white people looked and acted, as I thought, in so savage a manner; for I had never seen among any people such instances of brutal cruelty; and this not only shown towards us blacks, but also to some of the whites themselves. One white man in particular I saw, when we were permitted to be on deck, flogged[34] so unmercifully with a large rope near the foremast, that he died in consequence of it; and they tossed him over the side as they would have done a brute. This made me fear these people the more; and I expected nothing less than to be treated in the same manner. I could not help expressing my fears and apprehensions to some of my countrymen: I asked them if these people had no country, but lived in this hollow place the ship? they told me they did not, but came from a distant one. "Then," said I, "how comes it in all our country we never heard of them?" They told me, because they lived so very far off. I then asked, where were their women? had they any like themselves? I was told they had. "And why," said I, "do we not see them?" they answered, because they were left behind. I asked how the vessel could go? they told me they could not tell; but that there were cloth put upon the masts by the help of the ropes I saw, and then the vessel went on; and the white men had some spell or magic they put in the water when they liked in order to stop the vessel. I was exceedingly amazed at this account, and really thought they were spirits. I therefore wished much to be from amongst them, for I expected they would sacrifice me: but my wishes were vain; for we were so quartered that it was impossible for any of us to make our escape. While we staid on the coast I was mostly on deck; and one day, to my great astonishment, I saw one of these vessels coming in with the sails up. As soon as the whites saw it, they gave a great shout, at which we were amazed: and the more so as the vessel appeared larger by approaching nearer. At last she came to an anchor in my sight, and when the anchor was let go, I and my countrymen who saw it were lost in astonishment to observe the vessel stop; and were now convinced it was done by magic. Soon after this the other ship got her boats out, and they came on board of us, and the people of both ships seemed very glad to see each other. Several of the strangers also shook hands with us black people, and made motions with their

34. Such brutal floggings were at this time considered essential to the maintenance of discipline in the British navy and on ships engaged in the slave trade. Flogging is not an Ibo and Edo form of punishment, as it is, for example, farther north in the Hausa country.

hands, signifying, I suppose, we were to go to their country; but we did not understand them. At last, when the ship we were in had got in all her cargo, they made ready with many fearful noises, and we were all put under deck, so that we could not see how they managed the vessel. But this disappointment was the least of my sorrow. The stench of the hold while we were on the coast was so intolerably loathsome, that it was dangerous to remain there for any time, and some of us had been permitted to stay on the deck for the fresh air; but now that the whole ship's cargo were confined together, it became absolutely pestilential. The closeness of the place, and the heat of the climate, added to the number in the ship, which was so crowded that each had scarcely room to turn himself, almost suffocated us. This produced copious perspirations, so that the air soon became unfit for respiration, from a variety of loathsome smells, and brought on a sickness amongst the slaves, of which many died, thus falling victims to the improvident avarice, as I may call it, of their purchasers. This wretched situation was again aggravated by the galling of the chains, now become insupportable; and the filth of the necessary tubs, into which the children often fell, and were almost suffocated. The shreiks of the women, and the groans of the dying, rendered the whole a scene of horror almost inconceivable. Happily perhaps for myself I was soon reduced so low here that it was thought necessary to keep me almost always on deck; and from my extreme youth I was not put in fetters. In this situation I expected every hour to share the fate of my companions, some of whom were almost daily brought upon deck at the point of death, which I began to hope would soon put an end to my miseries. Often did I think many of the inhabitants of the deep much more happy than myself; I envied them the freedom they enjoyed, and as often wished I could change my condition for theirs. Every circumstance I met with served only to render my state more painful, and heighten my apprehensions and my opinion of the cruelty of the whites. One day they had taken a number of fishes; and when they had killed and satisfied themselves with as many as they thought fit, to our astonishment who were on the deck, rather than give any of them to us to eat, as we expected, they tossed the remaining fish into the sea again, although we begged and prayed for some as well as we could, but in vain; and some of my countrymen, being pressed by hunger, took an opportunity, when they thought no one saw them, of trying to get a little privately; but they were discovered, and the attempt procured them some very severe floggings.

One day, when we had a smooth sea, and moderate wind, two of my wearied countrymen, who were chained together (I was near them at the time), preferring death to such a life of misery, somehow made through the nettings, and jumped into the sea; immediately another quite dejected fellow, who, on account of his illness, was suffered to be out of irons, also followed their example; and I believe many more would very soon have done the same, if they had not been prevented by the ship's crew, who were instantly alarmed. Those of us that were the most active were in a moment put down under the deck; and there was such a noise and confusion amongst the people of the ship as I never heard before, to stop her, and get the boat out to go after the slaves. However, two of the wretches were drowned, but they got the other, and afterwards flogged him unmercifully, for thus attempting to prefer death to slavery. In this manner we continued to undergo more hardships than I can now relate; hardships which are inseparable from this accursed trade. Many a time we were near suffocation, from the want of fresh air, which we were often without for whole days together. This, and the stench of the necessary tubs, carried off many. During our passage I first saw flying fishes, which surprised me very much: they used frequently to fly across the ship, and many of them fell on the deck. I also now first saw the use of the quadrant. I had often with astonishment seen the mariners make observations with it, and I could not think what it meant. They at last took notice of my surprise; and one of them, willing to increase it, as well as to gratify my curiosity, made me one day look through it. The clouds appeared to me to be land, which disappeared as they passed along. This heightened my wonder: and I was now more persuaded than ever that I was in another world, and that every thing about me was magic. At last, we came in sight of the island of Barbadoes, at which the whites on board gave a great shout, and made many signs of joy to us. We did not know what to think of this; but, as the vessel drew nearer, we plainly saw the harbour, and other ships of different kinds and sizes: and we soon anchored amongst them off Bridge Town. Many merchants and planters now come on board, though it was in the evening. They put us in separate parcels, and examined us attentively. They also made us jump, and pointed to the land, signifying we were to go there. We thought by this we should be eaten by these ugly men, as they appeared to us; and when, soon after we were all put down under the deck again, there was much dread and trembling among us, and nothing but bitter cries to be heard all the night from these apprehensions, insomuch that at last the white people got some old slaves from the land to pacify us. They told us we were not to be eaten, but to work, and were soon to go on land where we should see many of our country people. This report eased us much; and sure enough, soon after we landed, there came to us Africans of all languages. We were conducted immediately to the merchant's yard, where we were all pent up together like so many sheep in a fold, without regard to sex or age. As every object was new to me, everything I saw filled me with surprise. What struck me first was, that the houses were built with bricks, in stories, and in every other respect different from those I have seen in Africa: but I was still more astonished on seeing people on horseback. I did not know what this could mean; and indeed I thought these people were full of nothing but magical arts. While I was in this astonishment, one of my fellow prisoners spoke to a countryman of his about the horses, who said they were the same kind they had in their country. I understood them, though they were from a distant part of Africa, and I thought it odd I had not seen any horses there; but afterwards, when I came to converse with different Africans, I found they had many horses amongst them, and much larger than those I then saw. We were not many days in the merchant's custody, before we were sold after their usual manner, which is this: on a signal given (as the beat of a drum), the buyers rush at once into the yard where the slaves are confined, and make choice of that parcel they like best. The noise and clamour with which this is attended, and the eagerness visible in the countenances of the buyers, serve not a little to increase the apprehension of the terrified Africans, who may well be supposed to consider them as the ministers of that destruction to which they think themselves devoted. In this manner, without scruple, are relations and friends separated, most of them never to see each other again. I remember in the vessel in which I was brought over, in the men's apartment, there were several brothers who, in the sale, were sold in different lots; and it was very moving on this occasion to see and hear their cries at parting. O, ye nominal Christians! might not an African ask you, learned you this from your God? who says unto you, Do unto all men as you would men should do unto you. Is it not enough that we are torn from our country and friends to toil for your luxury and lust of gain? Must every tender feeling be likewise sacrificed to your avarice? Are the dearest friends and relations, now rendered more dear by their separation from their kindred, still to be parted from each other, and thus preventing from cheering the gloom of slavery with the small comfort of being together, and mingling their sufferings and sorrows? Why are parents to love their children, brothers their sisters, or husbands their wives? Surely this is a new refinement in cruelty, which, while it has no advantage to atone for it, thus aggravates distress, and adds fresh horrors even to the wretchedness of slavery.

CHAPTER 3

PHILIP QUAQUE OF CAPE COAST

Margaret Priestley

Unlike most other narrators in this volume, Philip Quaque[1] was connected with the slave trade through the merchants who carried it on—not as one of the human cargo. Born on the Gold Coast in 1741, his community was Cape Coast, the town outside the walls of Cape Coast Castle, the principal British trade castle on the West African coast. In 1754, at the age of thirteen, he was sent to England for education, sponsored by the Society for the Propagation of the Gospel in Foreign Parts (S.P.G.), and he was ordained as a priest of the Church of England, the first African to attain this distinction. In 1766, the Reverend Philip Quaque returned to the Gold Coast as a missionary to his own people. Over the next half-century, he wrote a series of letters to S.P.G. headquarters in London. The text that follows is a selection of this correspondence.

Quaque's appointment was sponsored by the S.P.G. in conjunction with the Company of Merchants Trading to Africa, the association of British merchants engaged in the slave trade, charged with the management of the fortified trading posts along the African coast. His position was defined by the Society as "Missionary, School Master, and Catechist to the Negroes on the Gold Coast," and by the Company as "Chaplain" at Cape Coast Castle. He continued to play this

1. Quaque is an eighteenth-century English version of Kweku, a common Fanti name, given to a boy born on Wednesday. Philip was Quaque's Christian name, received on baptism at St. Mary's Church, Islington, in 1759.

dual role until his death on 17 October 1816, and his grave can still be seen in the courtyard of the Castle.[2]

Quaque's life and circumstances are of interest from a number of points of view—religious, educational, and social. In modern Ghana he is remembered, not only as an early Protestant missionary of indigenous birth, but as one of the pioneers of educational development.[3] He exemplifies, furthermore, the interaction of cultures—European and African—and some of the problems of adjustment to the process of Westernization, which was already beginning in the second half of the eighteenth century. While much correspondence by Europeans on the Gold Coast has survived from this period, Quaque's record is most unusual, giving as it does the personal account of his work and of his reactions to his own society from the point of view of a Western-educated African.

The society in which Quaque was born and lived his adult life was a special creation of Afro-European relations in the era of the slave trade. Along the turbulent shore of the Gulf of Guinea, Europeans had begun to erect trading forts in the late fifteenth century, mainly for the gold trade which rivaled the importance of the slave trade on this section of the African coast. In time, these solid and imposing edifices were scattered along the Gold Coast more densely than in any other part of Africa. Built with the consent of the local population, they possessed no territorial sovereignty. Their continued existence depended on a working partnership between an African society and the British, Dutch, or Danish merchants in the forts—a partner-

2. See Committee of the Company of Merchants Trading to Africa to Governor and Council, Cape Coast Castle, 29 October 1765 (African Companies' Records) Treasury Papers, Public Record Office, London (hereafter abbreviated T.) 70/69, ff. 59–60; C. F. Pascoe, *Two Hundred Years of the S.P.G., 1701–1900* (London, 1901), pp. 256–58; C. P. Groves, *The Planting of Christianity in Africa* (4 vols., London, 1948–58), 1:175–77; F. L. Bartels, "Philip Quaque, 1741–1816," *Transactions of the Gold Coast and Togoland Historical Society*, 1:153–77 (1955).

3. He was not, however, the first Protestant missionary of African origin. In 1737, Rev. Christian Protten, born in Accra of a Danish father and an African mother and educated in Denmark and Saxony, returned to the Gold Coast with a European colleague "as the first Protestant missionary." Protten worked intermittently in Accra, but he seems to have achieved little, spending much of his time in Europe. In 1742, Jacobus Eliza Capitein, an African educated in the Netherlands and ordained in the Dutch Reformed Church, was appointed preacher and schoolmaster at Elmina Castle, the Dutch headquarters on the Gold Coast. See R. M. Wiltgen, *Gold Coast Mission History, 1471–1880* (Techny, Ill., 1956); and F. L. Bartels, "Jacobus Eliza Capitein, 1717–1747," *Transactions of the Historical Society of Ghana*, 4:3–13 (1959).

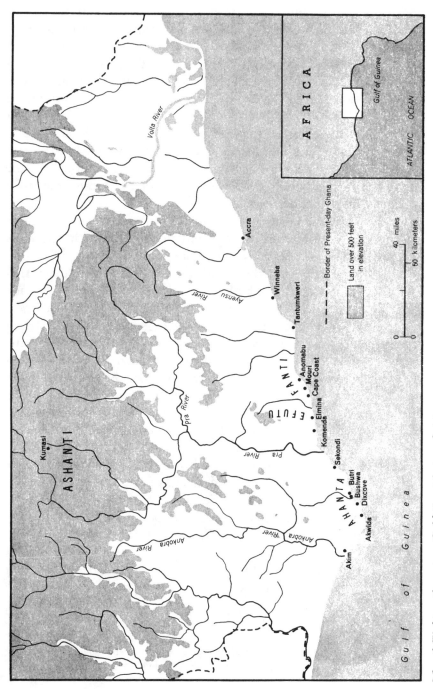

Map 6. Eighteenth-century Gold Coast forts and states.

ship based on a mutual assessment of advantages. In spite of their limited commercial objectives, the forts served over the long run as crucial points for the diffusion of European culture during the four centuries of maritime contact that preceded the colonial era. "Nowhere else," it has been said, "have small and transitory communities of traders so changed the life of the alien peoples who surrounded them, and indirectly of a vast region beyond."[4] The Westernizing agencies at work—trade, education, and Christianity—are clearly brought to light by Philip Quaque's career. As one of a small group of Africans selected for education overseas, he returned to the "mixed" world of the coast town and the fort and became himself a harbinger of further change.

Quaque's life span of seventy-five years (1741–1816) coincided with notable occurrences in Europe and West Africa, reflected in his correspondence and partially conditioning his own activities. One factor of importance was the British mode of organizing their African trade. The Company of Merchants, which governed that trade from the 1750's to 1821, was not a joint-stock company dealing in slaves on its own account, like its predecessor, the Royal African Company. It was limited instead to the function of maintaining the forts out of an annual parliamentary grant. British merchants trading to Africa were obliged to join the company, but the membership fee was nominal, and membership gave them a voice in the selection of the African Committee, the executive organ for the Company as a whole.[5] It was this Committee that appointed Quaque to its staff in 1765, though the appointment was made at the request of the S.P.G. and the two bodies joined in meeting his salary.[6]

Cape Coast, the African headquarters of the Company of Merchants, might seem remote from Europe, but it was not cut off from the repercussions of European war and peace. When Quaque returned in 1766, the Seven Years' War was a recent memory, which included an enemy bombardment of Cape Coast Castle in 1757 and the general disturbance of the sea lanes to Europe and America. But Britain had emerged as the world's foremost commercial and mari-

4. A. W. Lawrence, *Trade Castles and Forts of West Africa* (London, 1963), p. 29.
5. E. C. Martin, *The British West African Settlements, 1750–1821* (London, 1927), *passim.*
6. Committee of the Company of Merchants to Governor and Council, Cape Coast Castle, 29 October 1765, T. 70/69, ff. 59–60; Bartels, "Philip Quaque," p. 161.

time power; and until the abolition of the British slave trade in 1808 she was to be the dominant supplier of African slaves to the American plantations. The maritime war that accompanied the war of the American Revolution (1776–83) again brought a disruption of the sea lanes and Anglo-Dutch conflict on the Gold Coast itself, but the British position was already assured.

At the beginning of Quaque's ministry, few voices were raised against the slave trade, either in Britain or in Africa. By the end of the century, however, new currents were flowing in this as in other matters. Ideas of liberty and the natural rights of man appeared as a political force during the American and French revolutions. A humanitarian concern in Britain, directed principally against the slave trade from the 1780's onward, was finally crowned by Wilberforce's successful parliamentary campaign to end the trade, only a few years before Quaque's death. As his chaplaincy, contemporaneous with so much of moment in the world, drew to a close, West Africa stood on the threshold of a new phase in its history. The former *raison d'être* of the trade forts was removed, and a commercial revolution began as West Africa gradually moved from the export of slaves to the export of different products.

Other forces, much closer at hand, were emerging, and they too would help shape the future of the Gold Coast. Prominent among these was the rise and expansion of Ashanti. From origins in the late seventeenth century, it was pressing southward toward the European settlements with the aim of direct trade that would cut out native middlemen. To the Fanti, profitably engaged in this business, the development carried the menace of economic ruin and political subjugation. In 1765, the year before Quaque returned to West Africa, an Ashanti army had penetrated almost to the seaboard, encamping a few miles behind the forts at Cape Coast and Anomabu. During the rest of the century Europeans on the coast feared a major clash between Ashanti and Fanti, and Quaque's horizon was overshadowed by this uncertainty, expressed in his letters.[7] When the invasion finally came in 1807, the year the British Parliament acted against the slave trade, it brought a new era of political and military, as well as economic, unsettlement to the Gold Coast.

7. M. Priestley, "The Ashanti Question and the British: Eighteenth Century Origins," *Journal of African History*, 2:35–59 (1961).

The growth of Ashanti's inland power was paralleled on the coast by a strengthening and consolidation of Fanti in ways that were particularly relevant to Quaque's career. Fanti was at first confined to a narrow stretch of land to the east of Cape Coast, but during the eighteenth century it extended its influence, associating with nearby territories in a loose confederation of independent states. The inclusion of Cape Coast was especially significant. Originally part of the separate and culturally distinct kingdom of Efutu, the town gradually entered into the Fanti orbit, absorbing many Akan customs.[8] From the mid-century, this process gained momentum under the threat of danger from the interior and through the integrating tendencies of European commerce. Fanti had long been an established center of British trade. It contained several important forts, notably the fort at Anomabu, built by the new Company in the 1750's and linked with the headquarters at Cape Coast through the network of indigenous society, as well as by the formal relations between the neighboring European garrisons.[9] Trade and politics alike conspired to bring Cape Coast and Fanti closer together.

A figure of note, Cudjo Caboceer of Cape Coast, was very much involved in these developments.[10] Employed at the Castle by the Royal African Company during the 1720's, he still served the successor Company at the time of his death in 1776. Cudjo's career admirably illustrates the intermingling of two worlds and the dependence of the European trading community on African good will. His position at the fort was that of linguist, the governor's intermediary and spokesman in dealing with neighboring peoples. It carried responsibilities of a semidiplomatic nature, since the linguist was supposed to ensure smooth and amicable relations between the trade partners.

8. H. Meredith, *An Account of the Gold Coast of Africa* (London, 1812), pp. 95–96, 111–12; W. E. F. Ward, *A History of the Gold Coast* (London, 1952), pp. 136–37; J. B. Christensen, *Double Descent among the Fanti* (New Haven, 1954), pp. 8–10. The Fanti, like the Ashanti, are Akan people. According to tradition, they migrated from the interior to the coast.

9. M. Priestley, "Richard Brew: an Eighteenth Century Trader at Anomabu," *Transactions of the Historical Society of Ghana*, 4:33–34 (1959).

10. Known in African circles as Birempon Cudjo. Cudjo (Kudwo) is the day name for a male child born on a Monday. "Caboceer" is from the Portuguese *caboceiro* (captain), a term used in the past by Europeans to denote a man of rank; and "birempon" (*brempon*) is a Fanti word indicating a person wealthy through trade or inheritance; see J. M. Sarbah, *Fanti Customary Laws* (London, 1904), pp. 11–12, 55; Bartels, "Philip Quaque," p. 153.

Hence it called for considerable local standing.[11] Cudjo's high status in the town and its surrounding area is clearly depicted in Quaque's letters, especially in the account of Cudjo's funeral.

A Fanti by birth, Cudjo was brought to Efutu in infancy. He rose to prominence through his mother's remarriage to the local ruler, through his consequent line with the royal household, and through his wealth from trade, acquired with the aid of his personal connection at the fort.[12] He held the rank of Chief of Cape Coast, but it was he (not his half-brother, now king) who wielded real power in the middle of the century, and he was still the effective ruler of Efutu twenty years later. Cudjo also exercised wide authority in Fanti, so that he was able to forge links between Fanti and Efutu, as well as establishing a notable dynasty in his adopted town.

The British also held him in high esteem: a visiting missionary referred to his considerable knowledge of the English language and government, and official dispatches show him as an invaluable ally—guardian of British commercial interests against the encroachments of European rivals or interruptions of trade brought about by African political changes. It was only natural, therefore, that Cudjo should have been consulted in the 1750's about the choice of candidates for the rare privilege of education in England. Three boys were selected. One of them, Philip Quaque, was related to Cudjo; and he followed in the footsteps of Cudjo's own son, Frederick Adoy, who had been educated in London a few years earlier by an Anglican clergyman.[13]

11. Cudjo's name appears on the establishment list of Cape Coast Castle in 1729 among "Linguists and Messengers." He was then in a junior capacity receiving £24 a year. By 1750, his pay as linguist had risen to £72 a year. The many diplomatic missions on which he was engaged for the British included negotiations with Fanti in 1752 to exclude the French from settling on the stretch of coast under Fanti control. His death in 1776 was regarded as a great loss by the British (Castle Charge Book, 1729, T. 70/1450, f. 3; List of Persons in the Company's Service, 1750, T. 70/1516; Governor and Council, Cape Coast Castle, to Committee of the Company of Merchants, 23 September 1752, C.O. 388/45 [Board of Trade and Plantations, Original Correspondence, Public Record Office, London]; the same to the same, 7 May 1776, T. 70/32, f. 33).

12. E. J. P. Brown, *Gold Coast and Asianti Reader* (2 vols., London, 1929), 1:122–25. Cudjo's parents came from Ekumfi-Adansi in Fanti. After divorcing her husband, his mother married Egyir Panyin, King of Efutu and Cape Coast.

13. Governor and Council, Cape Coast Castle, to Committee of the Company of Merchants, 23 July 1751, C.O. 388/45; the same to the same, 25 September 1778, T. 70/32, f. 82; T. Thompson, *An Account of Two Missionary Voyages* (facsimile reprint, London, 1937), pp. 34–35, 67; Brown, *Gold Coast Reader*, 1:130 ff.

Quaque, indeed, is sometimes referred to as Cudjo's son, though it seems improbable that this was so in a strict European sense.[14] More likely, Quaque was a "son" only in the classificatory sense of the Fanti kinship system. He refers to Cudjo as "grandfather," a highly respected title, and also the normal title of address for chiefs (*nana*). A junior member of the family, or even a non-related dependent, might equally well be addressed as "son."[15] Quaque's letters convey the impression of a bond that involved social obligations, but was otherwise not particularly close. His comments about the Caboceer are detached and impersonal, and, while he indicates that Frederick Adoy was an actual son of Cudjo, there is little to suggest that he himself fell into the same category. The Reverend Thomas Thompson, who made the arrangements for the visit to England, also expressly mentions Frederick as Cudjo's son, while he refers to the other three boys as "a Relation to Cudjo and the other two sons of Cabosheers."[16]

Thomas Thompson played a major part in Quaque's advancement. As the first missionary sent to West Africa by the S.P.G., it was he who set in motion the plan to train young Africans for Christian

14. Pascoe, *S.P.G.*, p. 256; Brown, *Gold Coast Reader*, 1:125, 129; Bartels, "Philip Quaque," p. 153. The first contemporary reference in the S.P.G. manuscripts to Cudjo Caboceer as Quaque's father occurs, not at the time Quaque was sent over to England by Rev. Thomas Thompson, but after he had returned to the coast in 1766. Quaque's first letter to the Society after arrival at Cape Coast is reported in the Society's *Journals* (17: 134, S.P.G. Archives, London), where it is noted that "his Father Cabosheer Cudjo" had promised to assist his work and thanked the Society "for the care they have taken in the education of his son." Unfortunately, this letter has not survived, but it seems very probable that in it Quaque may have quoted Cudjo Caboceer using the word "son," as he did in the letter of 28 September 1766 (see n. 15, below), although to denote a relationship of a different kind. Thompson's letter of 2 April 1754, in which he announced that he was sending over three boys from Cape Coast, was minuted in the Society's *Journals* (12:391). One of them was described in the minutes as "related to Cudjo, the principal Caboceer, and the other two sons to men of figure in this town."

15. See Quaque's letters to the S.P.G., 28 September 1766 and 5 September 1769, "C" MSS, West Africa, S.P.G. Archives, London (for portions not included in the present selection). He refers to Cudjo as "the old man" and quotes him as saying, "Pray son, don't you think that I am too old to enter into covenant with God?" In the Fanti extended family, all persons of the same generation are customarily addressed by the same title—a daughter, for example, referring to her maternal aunt as "mother." The names of Quaque's parents were not entered in his baptismal record (Christensen, *Double Descent among the Fanti*, p. 20; Bartels, "Philip Quaque," p. 154).

16. Thompson, *Two Missionary Voyages*, p. 67. The introduction to this work (p. xii) describes Quaque as Cudjo's son, though this is not what Thompson says in the text.

work among their own people. Throughout his residence in Cape Coast, from 1752 to 1756, he had numerous dealings with Cudjo, whom he described as the person with greatest influence in the town. Cudjo was interested in "some kind of learning" for its children, and Thompson, by starting a school in response to this interest, paved the way for his African successor. Further consultation led to the dispatch, in 1754, of three youths to be educated by the Society—not for the usual employment as writers in a fort, but for the more elevated vocation of Anglican missionary. Only Quaque, however, stayed the course. The other two died in England, Thomas Coboro of tuberculosis, and William Cudjo after a mental breakdown.[17]

The Society's young protégé was to be profoundly influenced by the eleven years spent in a new environment, and by the education he received there. Information is somewhat scanty as to the curriculum he followed; but religious instruction was well to the fore, and it seems likely that in later stages there was also an element of classics. Until 1759, when Quaque was baptized in Islington Parish Church, his tutor was the local schoolmaster, Mr. Hickman. Afterwards, he came under the guidance of the Reverend John Moore, Curate and Lecturer of St. Sepulchre's Church, in the Holborn area. For the space of seven years, he lived at Moore's house in Charterhouse Square. Good progress was made during this time: Moore later reported that his pupil had improved "in every branch of knowledge necessary to the station for which he was designed, and it is hoped will prove a worthy missionary." On 25 March 1765, Quaque was ordained deacon by the Bishop of Exeter, and on 1 May of the same year, he was ordained priest by the Bishop of London. In each case, the setting was a distinctive one—the Chapel Royal, St. James' Palace.

He began now to look ahead to the work of conversion awaiting him in West Africa. Appointed by the Society as missionary, and then by the African Committee as chaplain of Cape Coast Castle, Quaque arrived there in February 1766. He was accompanied by an English wife, Catherine Blunt, whom he had married in London on 2 May 1765. Quaque's salary was sixty pounds a year, plus an allowance of thirteen pounds a year for Mrs. Quaque, as the "usual

17. Thompson, *Two Missionary Voyages*, esp. pp. 34–35, 41–42, and 67; Bartels, "Philip Quaque," pp. 153–54.

encouragement" given to white women residing on the coast.[18]

Unlike Thomas Thompson, who was appointed solely by a missionary society, the Reverend Philip Quaque came into the official establishment of a British trading fort. There he joined a small European staff and was allotted accommodation by the governor-in-chief. In this commercial environment, Quaque lived and carried out his duties for the best part of fifty years—a fact that must be borne in mind in any critical assessment of his work. Trade conditions necessitated close contact between African and European, and racial barriers were less pronounced than they were to be in the ensuing colonial period. While Quaque experienced occasional pinpricks, the general attitude toward him was one of acceptance, along with indifference to his special calling. He was accorded the status of a European officer, for example, and temporarily commanded outforts at Dixcove, Sekondi, and Komenda during the absence of their governors. Apart from such visits, and a brief spell in England in 1784–85 in connection with his children's education, it was at Cape Coast that he spent the greatest part of his time, and it is there that his life's work must be examined.

For a British company to appoint a chaplain on the west coast was a new departure. It has been said that the British paid "notably less" attention to the "spiritual health of their servants" than other powers did; the Danes, for example, had provided for the spiritual welfare of their servants in West Africa since the seventeenth century.[19] European personnel at Cape Coast now came under Quaque's religious

18. Committee of the Company of Merchants to Governor and Council, Cape Coast Castle, 29 October 1765, T. 70/69, ff. 59–60; Diocese of London, Ordinations, MSS 9535, Bk. III, f. 341 (Guildhall Library, London); Bartels, "Philip Quaque," pp. 153–57. Some writers, such as J. Beecham, *Ashantee and the Gold Coast* (London, 1841), p. 258, and Sarbah, *Fanti Laws,* have associated Quaque with Oxford University, but Mr. Bartels, in his study of the S.P.G. records, finds no reference to this connection.

19. Lawrence, *Trade Castles,* p. 63; Wiltgen, *Mission History,* pp. 106–8: H. Debrunner, "Notable Danish Chaplains on the Gold Coast," in *Transactions of the Gold Coast and Togoland Historical Society,* 2:13–29 (1956). During the early period of European contact, the Catholic Portuguese had been considerably more active in spiritual matters than their immediate successors were to be. The Royal African Company, it should be noted, had asked the S.P.G. in 1720 to recommend suitable people as chaplains at the forts; following this, Rev. Thomas Thompson was the first British clergyman to be sent to West Africa, although in the capacity of S.P.G. missionary. It seems that he voluntarily performed the additional duties of chaplain at Cape Coast Castle (Pascoe, *S.P.G.,* pp. 254–55; Groves, *Christianity,* 1:174–75).

charge, though there is little doubt that he himself gave first priority to the conversion of the indigenous population. Running through his letters is a note of pessimism about his achievements on either score. Soon after arrival, he told the Society on 28 September 1766: "All my hopes, I am afraid are in vain." Forty-five years later, on 13 October 1811, he reported that "this unsuccessful mission . . . at present on the face of things bears but an indifferent aspect." The African Committee might decree compulsory attendance at divine service every Sunday for all officers at the Castle, defaulters to pay a fine of seven shillings and sixpence, but the African Committee was far away in London. In practice, much depended on the attitude of individual governors, whose concentration on their private trade, in addition to the Company's affairs, often led them to neglect less worldly matters.[20]

Quaque found uphill work, too, leading his own people "to the truth of the glorious light of the Gospel of our Lord and Saviour."[21] He extended the range of his activities from fort to town, preaching and conducting services before Cudjo Caboceer, as Thomas Thompson had done, impressing them with the necessity of baptism and urging the universal truth of Christianity. But he encountered a deeply entrenched traditional religion, integral to Akan social and political structure. This religion included belief in a Supreme Being, widespread ancestor worship, and investing natural objects—sun, moon, sea, and rocks—with deistic qualities. But ancestor worship prevailed.[22] These forces would long be resistant to missionary persuasion, and Quaque's efforts represent only an early and isolated stage of the missionary effort. While he experienced moments of satisfaction from the baptism and Christian instruction of mulatto children, his main religious contribution was in preparing the ground for another and more far-reaching stream of missionary enterprise in the 1830's—that of the Wesleyan Methodists.[23]

His educational work is often considered to have been more impor-

20. Lawrence, *Trade Castles*, pp. 63–64.
21. Bartels, "Philip Quaque," p. 156.
22. J. W. de Graft Johnson, *Historical Geography of the Gold Coast* (London, 1929), p. 122; Brown, *Gold Coast Reader*, 1:166; Ward, *History of the Gold Coast*, pp. 95–96.
23. The S.P.G. connection with the Gold Coast lapsed in 1824 and was not resumed until the early twentieth century. Meanwhile, the Wesleyan Methodist Church made such gains that it was described in the 1920's as the "National Church of the Gold Coast" (De Graft Johnson, *Historical Geography*, p. 121; Wiltgen, *Mission History*, p. 109).

tant for modern Ghana than his missionary efforts.[24] Resuming the endeavors of Thomas Thompson, he set up a school in 1766 and began to teach mulatto boys and girls in his room at the Castle. Religious knowledge, reading, writing, and arithmetic made up the course of study. The number of students, however, never exceeded sixteen, and on occasion fell to one or even none. Quaque always hoped for a separate school building, which was never provided; and the school struggled along in a precarious and rudimentary fashion.

Its most organized phase came after Quaque had been on the coast for some twenty years. In 1787, the Torridzonian Society was founded under the presidency of the governor-in-chief, the other members being gentlemen of the trading establishment. The Society's original purpose was "mutual harmony and social conviviality," but it was later decided that funds should be used instead to start a form of charity school in the fort with twelve needy mulatto children as boarders. Quaque was placed in charge, assisted by his son Samuel, lately returned from his education in England. Both the S.P.G. and the African Committee gave their blessing and sent out funds and textbooks—primers, spelling books, testaments, and Bibles. Quaque was delighted with this new and promising departure, and it seems that for a few years the school lived up to expectations. By 1791, general progress could be reported. This optimism, however, came too soon. Friction arose within the Torridzonian Society, and the school declined as the Society's members withdrew their attention from the philanthropic experiment.[25]

What was the outcome of Philip Quaque's labors as a teacher sporadically encouraged by a missionary society and a company of merchants engaged in the slave trade? As with his evangelization, he met with difficulties in the prevailing culture. Though men like Cudjo Caboceer were progressive and enlightened in many respects, and though the practical value of education was recognized in the maritime towns, attachment to the traditional way of life remained

24. Bartels describes Quaque's school as one of the foundation stones of the modern Ghanaian educational system ("Philip Quaque," p. 174), but it was not the first step toward Western-style education on the Gold Coast. In the sixteenth century, the Portuguese had carried out some educational work at São Jorge da Mina, the first European fort on the coast. Later on, Danish chaplains at Christianborg Castle, Accra, taught mulatto children there in a castle school (Wiltgen, *Mission History*, pp. 15–17; Debrunner, "Danish Chaplains," pp. 22–23).

25. Bartels, "Philip Quaque," pp. 153, 157–66.

strong. Limited support from his own people, the fluctuating interest at the Castle, and generally unsettled political conditions all hindered the progress of the school. Yet, on however small a scale, Quaque assisted in the evolution of primary education on the Gold Coast. Some of his pupils themselves became teachers, and a schoolmaster was appointed to succeed him. The Government School in nineteenth-century Cape Coast stood in a direct line of descent from his modest establishment.[26]

Quaque was also influential in shaping the course of future social change. His pupils were mainly mulatto children, the offspring of Afro-European unions, and these mulattoes and their descendants, particularly in Fanti, were to be prominent nineteenth-century innovators, forming the nucleus of an educated class of clerks, teachers, and lawyers.[27] Even in the field of conversion to Christianity he had some long-range success: former pupils of the Castle School helped to bring the Wesleyan Methodists to Cape Coast in 1835.[28]

From the time of his first visit to England in 1754, Quaque himself moved in the two worlds of change and tradition, with the expected conflicts. After eleven impressionable years in England, "that blessed Christian country,"[29] and then as a member of the European establishment on the coast, his outlook and mode of behavior were shaped by this experience. He lived in European style, with books and mahogany furniture, and his first wife was an Englishwoman.[30] Like his colleagues at the fort, he engaged in trade—made necessary by the fact that the African Committee paid his salary in goods. At times he was expected to carry out the duties of any other officer of the administration. A gulf thus grew between Quaque and his traditional origins: he ceased to be fluent in any African language, depending on the services of an interpreter, and he continuously attacked traditional polytheism as false and idolatrous.

26. Bartels, "Philip Quaque," p. 174; also De Graft Johnson, *Historical Geography*, pp. 119, 126.

27. A Ghanaian scholar has recently summed up Quaque's success in the "dynamic activities" of these few students (address by Dr. J. W. de Graft Johnson at an Annual Service of Remembrance, Christ Church, Cape Coast, 16–17 October 1960).

28. De Graft Johnson, *Historical Geography*, pp. 119–21, 126–27; Groves, *Christianity*, 1:301–3; Bartels, "Philip Quaque," p. 174. Rev. Joseph Dunwell, the first Wesleyan missionary, arrived at Cape Coast on 1 January 1835.

29. Quaque to S.P.G., 11 April 1777.

30. Entries of 28 January and 21 March 1780, Rough Journal, Cape Coast Castle, T. 70/1480, f. 66; Bartels, "Philip Quaque," pp. 170–73.

He also encountered problems of culture-conflict at a personal level, resenting the claims made on him from within the African community. At the root of the trouble was a fundamental difference of attitude toward society—Western individualism as against his duties to the extended family.[31] After his period in England, Quaque regarded these duties as an infringement of private spheres of action. But he was also criticized from the European side for his involvement in Cape Coast town. By the 1790's, he had built a family house there, and his second and third wives were both African women.[32] The opinions he expressed to the missionary Society, therefore, must not be interpreted to mean a total dissociation with his own culture, and he may have drawn closer to it in the later years of his life.[33]

In any event, Quaque's achievements and failings cannot be fairly measured against the more rapid changes of the nineteenth century. He belongs to the eighteenth-century era of the slave trade, when no one accomplished more than he in his chosen field of endeavor. Not only was the partnership of the S.P.G. and the Company of Merchants a difficult master; the Society's correspondence with its agent left much to be desired. It was seven years before Quaque received his first letter from its London headquarters, in February 1773, and during the next twenty years, he received only two others. Under the circumstances, it is remarkable that he kept in touch with the Society for nearly fifty years.[34] Yet, at the age of seventy, and writing "much in pain," he could still send a report of baptisms and services at Cape Coast. This alone is some evidence of character and sense of purpose, however slight the immediate returns might appear to be. Considered as literature, Quaque's letters undoubtedly have shortcomings. But they still convey a realistic and informative picture of life on the West African coast in the eighteenth century, from the point of view of an African who was caught up in the problem of bridging two worlds.

31. Sarbah, *Fanti Laws;* De Graft Johnson, *Historical Geography*, p. 150; Christensen, *Double Descent among the Fanti*, pp. 19 ff.

32. Governor and Council to African Committee, Cape Coast Castle, 20 June 1791, T. 70/33, f. 274. Quaque reported the death of his first wife to the Society in his letter of 7 March 1767. Subsequent marriages were reported in 1769 and 1772.

33. According to an account published in the nineteenth century, Quaque had traditional rites performed when he felt his own death approaching (R. Lee, *Stories of Strange Lands* [London, 1835]). The author of these *Stories* had lived at Cape Coast Castle when her husband, T. E. Bowdich, was in the service of the Company of Merchants.

34. Bartels, "Philip Quaque," p. 172.

THE LETTERS OF PHILIP QUAQUE

These letters are contained in the Archives of the Society for the Propagation of the Gospel, London, designated as: "C" Manuscripts. West Africa. Letters of Philip Quaque, or Kweku, from Cape Coast Castle, 1765–1811.

Ten letters of a representative nature have been selected for publication here in shortened form. Omitted passages within a paragraph are indicated by three ellipsis points; where a complete paragraph or more of the original is left out, the omission is shown a full line of ellipsis points. In editing the letters, spelling has been modernized with respect to abbreviations, contractions, and capitalization, and has occasionally been otherwise modified for the sake of clarity; punctuation is adjusted in view of Quaque's lengthy sentences. Very occasionally, wording has been amended in order to facilitate the reading of a letter, but with the object of departing as little as possible from the original style. Two examples only are given of the formal closing, since this followed the same general pattern.

References to Quaque's letters in the notes are to sections of the correspondence not printed in this volume.

Cape Coast Castle
Africa
September 28th, 1766

Reverend Sir,

Since my late letter to the venerable body dated in February 1766,[35] I am induced to acquaint them that all my hopes, I am afraid, are in vain. Governor Hippisley, Esq., whom Mr. Thompson was so kind as to recommend us to, is very lately dead, after having been stationed here only five months and eleven days, with a very short illness. He indeed proved to us in all points a worthy friend, as was described by Mr. Thompson to the Society. He showed himself a man of feeling for the distresses of others, very humane and hospita-

---

35. Quaque had arrived back on the Goal Coast from his English education at the beginning of February 1766. His letters to the S.P.G. were addressed to its Secretary, a post then held by Rev. Dr. Daniel Burton. Communication with Europe was a slow process; a letter sent via the West Indies, following the route of the triangular trade, might take up to six months to reach its destination. Outward letters from Europe to West Africa came more quickly and directly, sometimes in two months or even less.

ble, a sincere lover he was of his profession and a great observant of the public worship of Almighty God.[36] . . . But since he is dead, all my expectations are foiled and are also buried with him. We have no other whom we can call a friend, that wishes us health and prosperity. And as for those fair promises of the Caboceer's mentioned in my last, I am greatly afraid that all that will now dwindle into nothing, as my chief agent is now no more. The only reason and inducement of his then fair promises, I since find to have been nothing else but a sinister view of getting from me, if possible, the little income I have from the African Committee into his own custody, notwithstanding he being a person of great repute and substance and I being then only as a newcomer, not knowing the manners and customs of my native place, made him proceed to such unreasonable steps. But seeing himself with all my numerous family greatly disappointed in their aim, are therefore become very careless and thoughtless about us.[37]

36. Although John Hippisley's tenure as governor-in-chief at Cape Coast Castle was so brief, he had spent a number of years on the coast. He was governor of the fort at Sekondi in 1755 and at Winneba in 1759, his career in the service then being interrupted by a period of suspension, the not uncommon result of coastal factions. Hippisley was the author of three essays dealing with the African trade, which were published in London in 1764. A point of special interest about them, in view of Quaque's high opinion of the governor, was his awareness, unusual for the time, of the inhuman aspects of the slave trade. But it could never be dropped, he wrote, because of the impossibility of doing without slaves in the West Indies. "The absolute necessity, then, of carrying it on, must, since there is no other, be its excuse" (*Essay on the Populousness of Africa* [London, 1764]). Rev. Thomas Thompson, Quaque's predecessor and the S.P.G.'s first missionary in West Africa, reached Cape Coast Castle on 13 May 1752, after calling at the Gambia and Sierra Leone. He conducted a service at the Castle on the following Sunday, the congregation including Cudjo Caboceer of Cape Coast. Ill health caused Thompson to return to England in 1756, and he died in 1773. The previous year he had published a defense of the slave trade.

37. This passage illustrates a recurrent theme in Quaque's letters—his criticism of African society after the experience of a European environment. The particular subject at issue here was the claim of the extended family, through a senior representative, on the wealth acquired by one of its members (property, under the traditional structure, being corporately owned by the family as a social group). In coastal towns, however, the impact of European trade was slowly giving rise to new ideas of individual ownership of property and a conflict of attitudes was therefore bound to occur, heightened in Quaque's case by the long period he had spent overseas. Cudjo Caboceer, although acting here in accordance with customary practice, was among those whose wealth and influence were to a considerable extent the result of new forces. As linguist for many years to the governor of Cape Coast Castle, he was at the center of the British trading network in Fanti. For an analysis of family, property, and inheritance on the coast, see Sarbah, *Fanti Laws*.

. . . The factory at present is in very poor condition, all falling down over our heads. It's a very ancient building, upwards of a hundred and eleven years standing in these parts, so that at the time of our severe rainy season every individual are almost drowned in their apartments by leaking, during which I was forced to strip and quit my two rooms of all my furniture, encumbering others who were in a better condition than I with them, and I and my spouse partaking with whomsoever we could. This accident and trouble of moving we shall be liable to every season if no remedy is found out in time to prevent it.[38] My poor spouse and bosom companion has been but very indifferent since we came upon the coast, who now lies at the point of death and every moment expecting it to be her last.[39]

. . . .

At the Feast of Easter there was no duty, owing to a very great indisposition of body I was in by a severe fit of the flux and fever,[40] but

38. Cape Coast Castle dated from the mid-seventeenth century; it was built on the headland which the Portuguese called Cabo Corso (Short Cape). In 1649, the English had a trading post there from which they were ousted by the Swedes, who then began to erect the more substantial structure of a fort. After several changes of ownership among Swedes, Danes, and Dutch, the fort was captured by the English in 1664 during the second Anglo-Dutch war and considerably enlarged in the later seventeenth century to become the headquarters of the Royal African Company. On the latter's replacement in 1750 by the Company of Merchants Trading to Africa, the Castle continued as British headquarters on the Gold Coast. Not until 1877 did it lose this position to Accra. In describing Cape Coast Castle as a "factory," Quaque is using the term in a generalized sense. Strictly speaking, a factory, as distinct from a fort, was a trading post housed in a less solid and permanent building. Europeans in West Africa were faced with the perennial problem of keeping their forts in a good state of repair, and the rainy season, extending from about May to October, caused frequent damage. A further difficulty was labor and materials and the need to import so much from Europe (Lawrence, *Trade Castles*, pp. 90–95, 183–98; "A New Check List of the Forts and Castles of Ghana," *Transactions of the Historical Society of Ghana*, 4:57–67 [1959]).

39. This is a reference to Catherine Blunt, the Englishwoman whom Quaque had married in London on 2 May 1765, in a ceremony performed by his tutor, Rev. John Moore. Writing to the governor of Cape Coast Castle on 29 October 1765 about Quaque's appointment, the African Committee announced that his wife was coming with him to West Africa, accompanied by a woman companion. It was rare to find a white woman on the coast in the eighteenth century. A mixed marriage of the kind contracted by Quaque was unusual, although liaisons between European traders and local women were not. Mrs. Quaque died at Cape Coast Castle in November 1766.

40. Flux (dysentery) ranked among the most common tropical ailments of the time, along with malaria, yellow fever, and smallpox; all took their toll of Europeans. Inoculation was introduced against smallpox, a number of Africans being treated thus at Cape

all the other festivals following were duly performed to the best of my power with universal satisfaction. But still found none of what sect or denomination soever that was willing or disposed to commence communicants, and the only plea they offer is that while they are here acting against light and conscience, they dare not come to that holy table, so that while I remain in these remote soils that branch of duty will never be exercised in public, unless it be to myself and spouse.

.   .   .   .

. . . On Sunday the 22nd of June 1766 I baptised two little infants . . . and on the 29th baptised also the son of the deceased John Hippisley, Esq., aged 12 years, who was called after the name of his father.[41] He was by the desire of his father under my inspection long before and after his baptism, but since the death of his father he has quite deserted me. Now with regard to the baptism of infants here, I shall be glad to know from the respectable Society whether it will be deemed lawful for me to baptise them without sponsors, or whether the standard of heathen parents will be altogether sufficient on that head? . . .

Coast Castle in 1796. The forts had surgeons on their staff; sometimes they rose to command of an establishment, even of Cape Coast Castle itself. William Mutter, for example, governor there in 1763, had been a surgeon's mate ten years earlier; and Archibald Dalzel, governor in 1792, had been a surgeon at Anomabu in the 1760's.

41. One of the important features of European settlement on the Gold Coast was the form of local marriage that developed between traders and their "wenches," as the women were called. Such unions might last for a number of years, and they led to a mulatto element in coastal society. In many cases, the trader assumed responsibility for his family. Sons might be sent to Europe for education, and, on final departure from the coast, some provision was made for the wench. The Danes drew up definite regulations on this matter, stipulating, for instance, that the woman must be given the chance to join her husband in Europe if she so wished. There are numerous references in the British African Companies' records (T. 70 classification, Public Record Office, London) to the mulatto offspring of governors of forts. In 1779, for example, Governor Richard Miles of Cape Coast Castle told a correspondent that he had had seven children by his wench, of whom only two were still alive, and Governor Gilbert Petrie, after leaving the coast for good, received news of his African family, including the information that he now had a grandchild. Mulattoes were to form a substantial part of an educated élite in Gold Coast society during the nineteenth century. They must not be thought of, however, as detached from the African setting: the situation was very much the reverse. For a nineteenth-century account of local marriage, see G. E. Brooks, Jr., "The Letter Book of Captain Edward Harrington," *Transactions of the Historical Society of Ghana,* 6:73–77 (1963).

Salutation and signature of the Reverend Philip Quaque's letter to the Society for the Propagation of the Gospel, 28 September 1766.

Cape Coast Castle.
Photograph by
P. D. Curtin.

Canoes under the walls
of the trade castle,
Anomabu. Photograph
by P. D. Curtin.

This country is very destructive to the health of men of British constitutions and though myself being a native by birth, yet am not exempted from undergoing the common fate equally with those who are not. And as a proof to this assertion, we have had for the little time we have been here the third part out of five and twenty soldiers dead; a factor, the nephew of the present Bishop of Waterford, and a surveyor. Several others very sick and infirm besides many others of an older standing, together with six or seven captains of ships suddenly cut off by a very short illness.[42]

Number of communicants—none. Visitants since are ten, buried fourteen; Papists, Quakers and Anabaptists—none here. Now the consideration of the things that has been alleged will, I hope, be duly looked upon and noticed by my great benefactors, the venerable Society.

.   .   .   .

And believe me to be with the utmost respect and esteem,
  Reverend Sir,
   Your most dutiful brother and obedient servant,
            Philip Quaque

          Cape Coast Castle
          Africa
          March 7th, 1767

Reverend Sir,

On the last account given to the venerable Society of my arduous mission in September 28th last, I therein took the freedom in stating before them, as well as able, the confinement I was then under with respect to my spouse's ill state of health, and withal the impossibility of her recovery if nothing in time was found out for her immediate relief. I do now, with great regret, inform them by this favourable

42. While health risks for Europeans in West Africa were high and an epidemic might bring a sudden wave of mortality, instances of lengthy residence can also be found. Richard Brew, whom Quaque mentions in his letter of 7 March 1767, spent thirty years on the coast, going back only once to Britain; and Governor Richard Miles, preparing to leave Cape Coast Castle in 1780, told his father that he thought fifteen years quite sufficient for Africa—though he returned for a brief period, 1782–84. Despite Quaque's doubts about his own health, he survived the rigors of the coast for fifty years. See P. D. Curtin, *The Image of Africa* (Madison, Wis., 1964), pp. 71–78.

conveyance of the heaviness which surrounds me at this time for the loss of so dear and worthy a spouse, whom Providence in pity and for wiser ends (I hope) has thought proper to deprive me of and the sweet consolations I received from her tender breast on November last.[43] . . .

. . . But sometime before her death, I was requested by the earnest importunity of Gilbert Petrie, our present Governor,[44] whether I should choose to take the trouble of an arduous task upon me in the education of children. I made an answer that that was one of my chief employment and had already begun in private, but not publicly, as yet, and about ten or eleven days after the decency of my confinement began by a slow gradation to dissipate a little, I established a seminary, by his order, in my own bedchamber for the instruction of mulatto children only of both sexes, the number of which at present is but ten, who seem to take their learning surprisingly well and some have made a very good progress, considering the very short space of time they have been with me. And do intend shortly, God willing, to take a few of the rougher kind to see what can be really made out of them.[45] . . .

. . . The morning after New Year's Day, I took my first visit to Anomabu where I lodged in the house of one Richard Brew, Esq., an English merchant, by the kind recommendation of Samuel Smith, Esq. (his bosom friend) who was then a member of the Committee,

43. Quaque made two further marriages on the coast. The next one, in 1769, was to his late wife's "waiting maid"; she died the following year, giving birth to a daughter. His third marriage, to an "adult black girl" whom he had first baptized, was reported in a letter dated 8 March 1772.

44. Gilbert Petrie was governor-in-chief at Cape Coast Castle between 1766 and 1769, an extremely disturbed period politically, owing to friction between the Ashanti and Fanti, and fear of invasion from the interior. Petrie was involved in European attempts to mediate, the prospect of a war being viewed with apprehension in the forts, as likely to have detrimental effects on trade. Quaque said in a letter of 15 April 1769 that Petrie had been fourteen or fifteen years on the coast and had made an "immense fortune."

45. Here can be seen the modest beginnings of Quaque's school for mulatto children, whom he obviously regarded as the more promising material. In the early 1750's, Rev. Thomas Thompson had started a school at Cape Coast in a private room, but the local population, according to his report, quickly lost interest in it.

and aboded with him for the space of a week, during which time he behaved in the most polite manner imaginable. And on the Sunday read prayers and preached in his most noble hall to a very good audience. The divine service being ended, I immediately reported to the table where I had already fixed my element for christening and did then and there lawfully baptise his two mulatto daughters, by his own earnest desire, and three others besides, to the universal satisfaction of the whole congregation both white and black then assembled, and gave certificates before I took my farewell of him.[46] . . .

. . . .

From hence I returned back to the place of my situation and on the Sunday, the 28th of January, performed the office of matrimony for the first time between Alias Andrew, a Corporal of this fort and Hannah Neirah, an English woman. They both came here lately from England. I made no scruple of conscience but examined them well first before I performed the solemn office, and asked them when and where they were married and by whom, which they answered that they had been at Senegal for four years and were married there by the Reverend Mr. Smith, Chaplain to the regiment that is stationed there,[47] and showed me some kind of a certificate, but could

46. Richard Brew, a merchant of Irish origin, was a prominent figure in the European coastal community during the second half of the eighteenth century. Serving as governor of the forts at Tantumkweri and Anomabu in the 1750's and 1760's, he eventually settled at Anomabu as a private trader in an impressive establishment built after the style of the fort there and called Castle Brew. It was equipped with mahogany furniture, silverware, pictures, and books. The "most noble hall," for example, contained a glass chandelier and an organ, doubtless played on the occasions of religious services. The mulatto daughters whom Quaque baptized were called Eleanor and Amba; Brew made a bequest to them and to their mother in his will. He died on 5 August 1776. Samuel Smith was Brew's London partner and was concerned in coastal administration for some years as a member of the African Committee. The Smith-Brew trading partnership ran into serious financial difficulties, and, in 1774, two years before Brew died, Smith was declared a bankrupt.

47. Britain had captured the Senegalese trading posts from the French during the Seven Years' War (1756–63), uniting them with her trading posts on the Gambia to form the first British Crown Colony in West Africa—the province of Senegambia (1765). During the war of the American Revolution, further Anglo-French hostilities took place in this region and at the Treaty of Versailles in 1783, Senegal was restored to France. Britain retained the Gambia settlements but the Crown Colony experiment ended and the African Company resumed control.

not make a word out of it. But desired that I would perform the office for them again as they have now come into a strange place, that they might live free from molestation, whereby also they might be able to silence the cavils of unreasonable and gainsaying people, especially here where they are so very censorious.[48] This I did accordingly and sometime after I gave them a certificate. . . .

By the goodness of Mr. John Hippisley, deceased, I have had a letter from Vincent Biscoe, Esq., who informed me that in consideration of his kind letter in recommendation of me and my wife and laying before them the scantiness of my salary as a clergyman in a proper light, have increased it to £100 *p.a.* coast currency, which is a further help to me in these parts where there is no manner of perquisites whatsoever and provision excessively dear.[49] . . .

. . . .

And now remain with the utmost esteem and sincerity,
    Reverend Sir,
      Your most obedient and very humble brother,
                         Philip Quaque

48. Gossip and scandal were rife in the small European settlements, restricted in outlet, lacking variety of companionship, and living under the strain of a tropical climate. When Quaque remarried in 1769, he told the Society that he had done so in order to silence the "scandalous tongues" from which he had suffered since the death of his first wife.

49. Quaque is referring here to the proposed increase of his salary from its initial £60 a year, although according to his next letter dated 1767, the governor of Cape Coast Castle was recommending otherwise to the Committee. As there was no regular minted or paper currency on the coast, salaries were paid partly in food and clothing and partly in goods for barter. Hence, all fort personnel traded, and Quaque was no exception. Price was reckoned in different ways, gold forming a standard of value. The coast price of stores sent out to maintain the forts and pay salaries, however, was arrived at by adding 50 per cent to the price paid in England (Martin, *West African Settlements*, pp. 44–49). The records of the African Companies show Quaque's salary as £150 a year in 1797. This compared favorably with the salaries of Europeans. Writers, for example, got between £60 and £80, while at Anomabu fort, in 1764, the governor received £400, including his table allowance; the surgeon, £100; and the gardener (a European), £36. Quaque's remark about the high cost of provisions is interesting. Supplies of meat, bread, butter, cheese, and flour were shipped out to the forts from Europe, but they had to be supplemented by local foodstuffs. Forts were popular with African traders because they created a local demand for eggs, fowls, and plantains; and the Fanti proved particularly adept at taking advantage of this. When the British were building a new fort at Anomabu in the early 1750's, the high prices charged by the Fanti evoked their unfavorable comment.

Cape Coast Castle
1767

Reverend Sir,

With these I make bold to address the Society that since my last Notitia Scholastica and other Accompti in March the 7th 1767 . . . I was in hopes of being favoured with a few lines long before this from the Society, but as that long wished for period has failed me, do herewith trouble them with my half yearly transaction to their judicious perusal. That with respect to the school the number still remains, out of which three of them reads their primers surprisingly well and with regard to their Catechism, most of them say as far as to the first Commandment incomparable well. They behave very orderly and mostly appear extremely decent. The continuance of their growth in grace and progress in further knowledge, I trust in the divine disposal of all events for future success, if they are not overcorrupted through the infamous practices of their relations. . . .

I sincerely wish, in God's name, it was in my power to give a much better pleasing account to the Society of the inhabitants of the garrison than what I shall anon relate concerning these illiterate people, but find it an impossibility of attempting it, as they now grow more degenerate than before.[50] For at first, I must really say, in the reign of John Hippisley, Esq., deceased, that they resorted or met together almost every Sunday for that purpose or the public services of Almighty God. But now deviates much from it as they formerly frequented it. . . . And moreover have heard that Mr. Brew, the person whom I spoke so kindly of in my last, and his civilities and friendship shown as well as private councils when with him, should now say to the Chief of Anomabu through an injurious pique lately had, occasioned by trifling words passed between us, that he would never come to Cape Coast to be subservient to and to sit under the nose of a black boy to hear him pointing or laying out their faults before them.[51] . . . At the hearing of this and a few others ensuing, I can't say but I was somewhat discouraged. . . .

50. In this letter, a lengthy one much abridged for present purposes, Quaque enlarges on the difficulties facing him as chaplain to the European community in the fort and describes his missionary endeavors among the indigenous population, of whose traditional polytheism he strongly disapproved.

51. Richard Brew was distinguished by irascibility. There was nothing unusual about his quarrel with Philip Quaque: he had many similar episodes with British and Dutch residents on the coast. Good relations were eventually restored, and, in 1775, Brew was

... On Saturday the 26th June had a conference with Caboceer Cudjo concerning the utility and legality of the ordinance of baptism, at which time I stated also before him the excellency of our religion above that of any other in the world.[52] . . . From hence I continued silent till the 2nd day of August, kept in suspense by the Governor for upwards of eight weeks in expectation of his desiring prayers, but all to no purpose. Took the opportunity, as on this day, of performing divine service for the first time before Caboceer Cudjo and many of the Cape Coast people, seemingly to their satisfaction. At which time the Caboceer expressed again his earnest desire of having the school house built to contain two long rooms, one side for the worship of God and the other as a school house, for the instruction of the younger branch.[53]

·　·　·　·　·　·　·　·　·　·　·

The following Sabbath day, perceiving no sign of prayers in the fort, went as usual to town and read the service for the day to the Caboceer and about eleven of the Cape Coast penins, the first time of any of their attendance, and many of the principal people belonging to this town.[54] The number of the whole congregation then present were between forty and fifty, both mulattos and black. Prayers being ended, they expressed a great thankfulness by obeisance and immediately returned to what they term the liquor of life. This sudden motion being started, I made a very great objection against it and told them that what they have now heard teaches them no such thing, but on the contrary far from it. . . . I went to them again in the evening about four o'clock, where I gave a specimen of what was intended

present at Cape Coast Castle when Quaque conducted prayers there. "Chief of Anomabu" in this context means, of course, governor of the fort.

52. Soon after arrival on the coast, Quaque had tried to persuade Cudjo Caboceer to be baptized, arguing that Cudjo's subjects would then follow his example. The Caboceer's reply was that he was "too old to enter into covenant with God" (see n. 15, above).

53. Thomas Thompson had testified to the progressive outlook of Cudjo Caboceer in the matter of education, and to his interest in a school at Cape Coast. Cudjo's interest, however, was not shared by all the elders of Cape Coast.

54. A penin, or elder, was the head of the extended family in Fanti. Knowledgeable in customary law and generally of advanced years, he controlled the family's affairs, including its property, and settled disputes. Chiefs were assisted in their government of a town or state by a council of elders.

more fully when Mr. Frederic Adoy comes from his kroom [village], the person who assisted Mr. Thompson in his employment. I imitated [*sic*] to explain the necessity and reasonableness of the sacrament of baptism in my own lingo, as well as I was able, to about 25 of them in number and told them that what they have now imperfectly heard from me will be, I hope, more perfectly or clearly laid open to them at his return.[55] And on the morrow . . . told them that now they must not neglect of coming whenever I officiate in town, to which they made an answer that they would not.

. . . .

Miracles, I believe, never will cease, as Gilbert Petrie, Esq., condescended at last to write me a note relative to prayers, to my great wonder and amazement. It runs to this effect. Mr. Quaque, our duty put from necessity being long omitted, therefore let us have one of Mr. Yorick's *Discourses,* that is but adapted for explication. This unaccountable action I never dreamed of ever having it more wrought upon me. By the manner of his writing, it appears to me also not to spring out of any real good intention or earnest desire in the request, but on the contrary, rather out of shame for long neglect of duty. . . .

. . . .

I had the pleasure on this day of dining with him, at which time he seemed to express a great delight, and passing some encomiums upon my deliverance and pronunciation, I took then the liberty of hinting to him about conferring the ordinance of baptism on his four children, three girls and one boy,[56] being his own promise from the beginning as they have not yet been admitted into covenant with their unknown Creator through that sacrament, the only means made by Christ for our acceptance with God. He paused and reflected much, but gave me no answer. Many agreeable subjects having passed away, I retired about the hour of three and made my way for town in hopes of meeting with the Cape Coast penins at the Caboceer's house in readiness, according to the agreement made by them-

55. One of Quaque's problems after returning from England, accentuating his differences with African society, was that he had ceased to be fluent in the vernacular which he now despised, describing it as a "vile jargon" in the letter of 20 October 1781.

56. In 1779, arrangements were being made for Petrie's mulatto son, Bob, to come to England. His father had left West Africa some years earlier.

selves. When I went, I was greatly disappointed by not seeing a soul
there. I immediately went to the chief of them to know the reason of
their proving so very deceitful to their words, to which he sent me
word back that they were tired and had but just departed from
Cudjo's house upon settling a long and tedious palaver[57] and begged
to be excused coming, as they were going to get something to corroborate themselves with, not having as yet broke their fast. However,
not to be disappointed in my view, I read the service to my scholars
who were in great decorum before me, the Caboceer, a gentleman in
the fort and to Mr. Aqua[58] and a few others, and then departed
without offering the discourse intended for the penins of Cape Coast.

. . . On this day, the 20th instant . . . in the afternoon I went to
town . . . where also I both read and preached to about 35. . . .

.   .   .   .

Here I introduced for the first time the singing of Psalms and was
assisted by Mr. Aqua, the reason of which was they being fond of
music, that by its pleasing sound it might attract them the more, as
nothing can be more stealing upon the minds of the ignorant than
the harmonious strains of the Prophet. They hearkened to it with
due attention and expressed a great veneration towards it.

.   .   .   .

Mr. Frederic Adoy and Mr. John Aqua would esteem it as honour
whenever the house for education is erected for the good of the
young children, to be listed in the Society's service as a kind of a
small assistance in the school, if approved of, provided the number
of scholars increase. And are of opinion, as well as myself, that the

57. "Palaver," a word still in common usage on the west coast, was a corruption of
the Portuguese *palabra*. It denoted the discussion of an issue with the object of arriving
at a settlement, and, in a more general sense, it also came to mean the issue itself. Palavers between Europeans and Africans over trade and associated matters were frequent
and were usually accompanied by appropriate European gifts. Many examples can be
found of Portuguese influence on the vernacular languages of the west coast as well as
on pidgin English.

58. John Aqua, like Frederic Adoy, acted as Quaque's interpreter. He, too, had been
educated in England in the early 1750's, along with another local youth. The African
Committee paid the expenses of Aqua and his companion, amounting to over £600,
causing the Committee to have doubts about a repetition of the policy unless it was
judged essential on the coast in the interests of trade (Bartels, "Philip Quaque," p. 155).

promise of the old men in building a small seminary will be the very same as it was with the Reverend Mr. Thompson. . . .

July 30th, 1775

Reverend Sir,

. . . Being weary of confining my time to one spot to no secret satisfaction was obliged, one day, to accept of an invitation from a friend, one of our Chiefs belonging to Dixcove Castle, with whom I resided happily upwards of eight months.[59] The intention of my staying here so long was chiefly owing to the information I had from this gentleman, who gave me to understand that his neighbours, the Dutch Chiefs,[60] receiving intelligence by him of my travelling up so far, expressed their earnest desire of embracing the opportunity of initiating their children into the sacred order of baptism, and faithfully promised at my arrival to put their God-like design into execution, which were the means of my taking so long a season. But when it came to a matter of consideration, their hearts failed them and no doubt dispositions changed from their original proposal. Before I advance any further in my narration, I can't help observing that in all my travels from Cape Coast up to windward, the remarkable difference there is between the Fantis and Ahanta people (for so the windward blacks from Sekondi up as far as Axim are called). By what little I could discern of the natives of these places, find that they are of a quiet temper, a ready mind and easy to be governed, their disposition and manner of behaviour entirely foreign from those of the Fanti nations, who are of a turbulent spirit, strangers to civil discipline and inveterate enemies of public tranquillity.[61] . . .

59. Dixcove fort, on the western Gold Coast (Quaque's "windward"), was built by the English in the 1690's and enlarged in the middle of the eighteenth century. It was transferred to the Dutch during the Anglo-Dutch exchange of forts in 1868, the occasion of considerable local disturbance. In 1872, Dixcove reverted to its original ownership, by British agreement with the Dutch on the latter's final withdrawal from the Gold Coast. "Dixcove" is an abbreviated form of Dick's or Dickie's Cove, the name given to the adjoining bay where Europeans had traded before a fort was built.

60. There were a number of Dutch forts on the western part of the Gold Coast. Those nearest to Dixcove were Fort Dorothea at Akwida and Fort Batensteyn at Butri, both dating from the seventeenth century.

61. Quaque is repeating here the usual European opinion of his time. Fanti political structure—a form of confederation—allowed great independence to the component

The different excursions of the Chief down to Cape Coast, where his presence was immediately required on affairs of importance, afforded me an opportunity of acting in my ministerial function, then mixed with the charge and care of the public fort and business, almost every Sabbath day, sickness only excepted. . . . Whilst I resided at this place there happened, in the absence of the Chief, a very lamentable circumstance between the Dutch subjects and our townspeople at Dixcove, which commotion terminated in a devastation of blood, the consequence thereof would have been much slaughter and confusion had not the interposition of Providence ordered me as a patron and a mediator between them. It perhaps may seem incredible when I take upon me to declare that had not my zealous efforts, with indefatigable diligence, been used in this affair (thinking it to be a part of my profession), with the kind assistance of a worthy gentleman, a Dutch Chief at Butri, destruction upon destruction most assuredly would have followed. For from the 21st of February 1775, the day on which this wicked stratagem was conspired against the lives of many, I ceased not in giving my attendance daily to Bushwa Town, distant from the fort about three computed miles, under a very spacious tree instituted in the days of old, as I am informed, for hearing causes. From the hour of eight in the morning successively for eight days have I deserted the fort, and not been able to enter its gates till ten or eleven o'clock at night on foot, notwithstanding the strenuous arguments and reasonings made use of both by the Dutch Chief and myself as a sure prevention against the impending danger.[62] . . .

---

states. Disputes between them were common, impeding the development of centralized government, although in the late eighteenth and early nineteenth centuries there was a trend towards closer cooperation. Some British traders of the period believed that political disunity was desirable, so as to give them a better bargaining position in commercial dealings. For the same reason, they believed that control of the coast by Ashanti would not be to their advantage. But Fanti disunity was not always to the British advantage—far from it. The Fanti attitude of independence and hard bargaining took commercial as well as political forms.

62. It has been said that "no other European station resisted as many sieges as the English fort at Dixcove," and the troubles in that area illustrate very well the entanglement of European commercial rivalry with African politics. The town of Dixcove, independent of the surrounding Ahanta people and ruled by its own chiefs, had found an English alliance useful against the Ahanta since the foundation of the fort in the late seventeenth century. The Ahanta, on the other hand, received the backing of the Dutch, who had a fort at Butri in their territory—hence Quaque's description of them as "Dutch subjects." The result was that differences between the two peoples often led to Ahanta attacks on Dixcove town and fort, each of the rival European powers tending to encourage its local ally. In the 1775 episode, it appears that the Ahantas restricted themselves

Leaving this for my nomination (the distance of which is judged to be upwards of thirty or forty leagues), in my way down, I stopped both at Sekondi and Komenda forts and luckily the charge and care of these also fell under my custody for the space of a month or two.[63] At last, being released from my faithful services to community, I arrived at my district on Monday, the 19th day of June 1775, where I believe curiosity instead of the true spirit of devotion led on the Governor to have prayers on the 9th of July before an auspicious audience, at which time were present Richard Brew, Esq., and Horatio Smith, Esq., from Anomabu.[64] And the Sunday ensuing baptised a mulatto infant of two months old, which makes, in the whole, two this year. My school, which consisted some years ago of sixteen scholars, are now no more than two in number, one a black boy and the other a mulatto. The former pupils of both sexes, by whom I promised myself great comfort and satisfaction in their education, the parents, judging them to advance on with swift succession to years of maturity, have thought it expedient to initiate the male kind as soldiers and fifers in the service of the African Committee[65] and the female, who are also become marriageable, into the busy cares of life. Hence the Society may judge of the independency of these people, a state on which there is no reliance. . . .

January 17th, 1778

Reverend Doctor,

Since my last Notitia of the 11th April last to the venerable Society . . . I have with anxious eyes and confident hope expected to have

to the town, and, on this occasion, the Dutch governor at Butri joined forces with Quaque in a policy of mediation conducted at Bushwa, in Ahanta country—a good example, in fact, of a palaver (Lawrence, *Trade Castles,* pp. 292–311).

63. The British forts at Sekondi and Komenda dated from the late seventeenth century; the Dutch also had forts at these places. Like Dixcove, Sekondi was plundered by the Ahanta on more than one occasion.

64. Brew had obviously departed from his earlier view "that he would never come to Cape Coast to be subservient to and to sit under the nose of a black boy." Horatio Smith, cousin of Samuel Smith, Brew's London partner, was assistant to Brew in his trading concern at Anomabu.

65. Each fort had a garrison for defense, varying in size according to the fort; mulattoes were often taken into the establishment as soldiers. In Cape Coast town itself, there were a number of military companies or *asafu*—a typical Fanti institution persisting into the twentieth century. One company, made up of mulattoes and their descendants, acquired a drum and fife band as a distinguishing mark of its European origin. See J. C. de Graft Johnson, "The Fanti Asafu," *Africa,* 5:310–11, 321 (1932).

been honoured with their most gracious indulgence ere now. But fallen short of my expectation, due obedience of orders and love of duty therefore inspires me to send in this narrative, which I confess ought to have pursued its travels two months sooner. But considering the lamentableness of the times, the uncertainty of a safe voyage, together with the melancholy news of the African merchant ships being apprehended and properties confiscated, as well as letters of private persons seized and destroyed by the Africans [*sic*] was the sole reason of my not expediting this sooner, and even the safety of this I have my doubts about me.[66] However, since the appointment of Richard Miles, Esq., to the command of the African Committee's affairs here (as a successor to David Mill, Esq., late Governor of this Castle, who is since dead and whose untimely end, we here learn, was occasioned by the accident of his falling into the hands of the rebels after his departure from the coast and conveyed to the Island of Antigua, where he died with immense property totally lost), I have no small satisfaction of acquainting them that the true spirit of devotion and due observance of a Sabbath holy to God, much neglected in the former Governor's time, begins under the present one (though not yet confirmed) to illumine the mind as the morning sun enlightens the fertile earth.[67] . . . There are yet several children belonging to different gentlemen of this Castle unbaptised, notwithstanding the many remonstrances made touching the utility of their admission into that sacred function, both in public and private, but it has not as yet had any impression. Trusting therefore to that powerful agency, voluntary choice, I hope it will hereafter have the desired

66. This is an allusion to the war of the American Revolution (1776–83) and its effect on the African trade through privateering in the Atlantic; "destroyed by the Africans" is obviously a misnomer for "destroyed by the Americans." One instance was the seizure of the proceeds of Richard Brew's estate, which were being shipped to Europe after his death on the coast in 1776.

67. Richard Miles, who has been described as "the most energetic and enterprising of the Governors in the eighteenth century," had a long career in West Africa. He was appointed a writer in 1765 at £60 a year, and progressed upwards to become governor of Cape Coast Castle on 1 January 1777. In 1779, he was suspended, and he returned to London in the following year to defend himself before the African Committee. Restored to favor, Miles was again governor-in-chief between 1782 and 1784 (Martin, *West African Settlements*, p. 43). David Mill, predecessor to Miles, became governor at Cape Coast in 1770. He was a member of a family much concerned in the African trade. In a letter of 11 April 1777, Quaque praised Mill for his personal qualities, but admitted that he had been neglectful of religious observance.

influence upon their hearts and minds and that process of time will discover. The funeral ceremony of the late Cudjo Caboceer, whose death I mentioned in my last account, was pompously exhibited on the 20th day of October last after the blacks' usual custom or manner of burying their deceased. This performance or funeral grandeur was accompanied with incessant firing of muskets from that time successfully for eight days, together with little or no intermission. But the Society will please to observe that this mighty exhibition could not well be acted without songs of shouting, drinking and that to a very great excess, with dancing and all kinds of juvenile festivity, which scene appeared to me more like their harvest feasts than that of mourning or sorrow. This, however, was continued on by a vast concourse of different neighbouring caboceers along the sea coast, their attendances and townspeople, besides many other caboceers from the inland countries and villages adjacent. The computation of the number of souls that came to perpetuate the memory of their deceased monarch might be upwards of a million. But the manner in which they make their public entrance on these occasions deserves a place in this cursory description, as it is not only laughable but curious withal, in which drama you will find the generality of them equipped with their warlike apparel. Some are covered with a cap of a tiger's skin, others again with deer's, a third the skins of monkeys, the fourth and fifth have on porcupine's skins and also wild boar's and the sixth, straw bonnets and cockle shells strung and ornamented about their necks and legs, together with their numerous charms. . . . They likewise paint themselves, both men and women, some with white chalk, others yellow earth and a number of others, in order to make their hue appear more odious, daub themselves with powdered charcoal. But the most detestable scene in all their actions is the barbarous and inhuman practice of sacrificing innocent lives as attendances to the great folks only in the other world, which diabolical custom and a mistaken vile notion seems to prevail much with them when any of their reputed head[s] dies.[68] . . . On the 15th day of last December, the supposed heir to the stool so called (or in other words, the crown of the late Cudjo Caboceer) was publicly installed by a grand proces-

68. In this extremely interesting passage, Quaque gives an eyewitness account of the funeral of a Gold Coast chief in the eighteenth century and reveals his attitude, akin to that of the later European missionaries, towards traditional religious practice. Funerals were occasions of great importance in Fanti, their significance turning on the part played

sion, in their own way, by the consent both of the townspeople, the principals of Anomabu and Elmina, people and properties of the stool, with songs of shouting, dancing and drinking as before described, decorated with all their usual apparatus. He then passes through a kind of an oath of supremacy before the concourse of both strangers and his own alliances publicly assembled, after which he and his attendant train comes into the Castle to pay his respects, where he takes upon him the oath of allegiance before the Governor, clothed in his war robe and having in his right hand a three edged sword, with which he swears himself faithfully the subject of Great Britain, binding the same with a sacred oath to defend the rights and privileges belonging thereto by night or day. On his leaving the fort, he and his numerous retinue receives a customary gratuity granted on these occasions from the Governor, with the honour of nine saluting guns as a compliment from the Castle, denoting, I imagine, the public consent as well as the British attachment and protection of them.[69] The Society may also remember of my hinting to them in my last favour the unavoidable expense I was likely to be involved in by the

---

by ancestor worship and the belief that both living and dead were linked together in permanent association. Since the spirits of departed ancestors were thought to guide and influence the fortunes of their clan on earth, it followed that the living must pay constant attention to the dead in order to ensure a favorable ordering of events. These beliefs explain much of the ritual marking entry into the spirit world, including human sacrifice to provide appropriate retinue for a man of distinction. The magnitude of the ceremony was determined by the worldly position of the deceased, and it was believed that the failure to stage an appropriate celebration would bring down the displeasure of the spirit world. This accounts for the grandeur of the ceremony held for Cudjo. Quaque's imagination nevertheless ran riot in assessing the numbers in attendance at perhaps "upwards of a million."

69. Quaque's report of the enstoolment, or installation, of Cudjo Caboceer's successor raises an important question, namely, the relationship between fort and town at Cape Coast. His reference to the chief as "the subject of Great Britain" must be interpreted to mean, rather than political sovereignty, the special type of connection based on trade, not territorial rights, that grew up around a European fort. Despite occasional disputes, there were a number of interests that bound a fort and town together—commercial privileges on the one hand and protection against hostile African neighbors on the other. The role of Dixcove fort against the Ahanta ("Dutch subjects") is a case in point. Trade, therefore, can be said to have had political implications. At Cape Coast, a close tie developed in the eighteenth century, much assisted by Cudjo Caboceer. Promoting British trade in every possible way, Cudjo and his successors became "the subjects of Great Britain"—the recipients of material favors and some protection in return for good will. But it was the British object to limit active protection to the minimum and to steer clear, as far as they could, of direct involvement in African politics. In nineteenth-century Fanti, however, this proved impossible because of recurrent attacks by Ashanti.

death of this great man, which so poor as I am amounts to £127 7s. 6d. I mention this merely to show them the difficulties I frequently labour under through numerous family connections, whose sole dependence rest entirely upon me, exclusive of domestic care, a wife and two children and another shortly expected, by God's blessing.

By the paper on which I write, you may easily perceive how short I am of stationery and if I recollect aright, I think you promised to indulge me with the anniversary sermons preached at St. Martin's le Bow yearly. . . . Pray may I also presume so far as to ascertain from you of what is become of the Reverend Mr. John Moore, son of my worthy tutor, the late Reverend Mr. John Moore, Lecturer of St. Sepulchre's Parish, Snowhill. . . . Likewise shall be infinitely indebted to you to be informed whether the Reverend Thomas Thompson, my predecessor, is still in being or translated into the bliss above, there to receive the recompense of his labour reserved for him in the Kingdom of our Father.[70] The knowledge of these and the above requests will for ever confer an additional duty and brotherly love on him who ardently wishes you all desirable health, and every valuable blessing this sublunary paradise of ours is capable of affording, and remain with love unfeigned always in due submission to your commands.

Cape Coast Castle
October 20th, 1781

Reverend Doctor,

. . . I have now, blessed be God, three children, a son and two daughters. The eldest girl and lad I purpose, God willing and with their permission, soon to send to England to receive a very liberal education as far as my poor finances in life will possibly afford. . . . There is no parent existing but what has a natural feeling or affection for his children, for which reason, therefore, I could wish that these two children may become useful to the community. In consequence, therefore, I have pitched upon this method to secure their tender minds from receiving the bad impressions of the country, the vile customs and practices and above all, the losing their mother's vile jargon, the only obstacles of learning in these parts. Besides, I may yet hope that this will be an everlasting provision for them after

70. He had died in 1773.

I am annihilated and interred in the sepulchre of my ancestors. For it is reasonable to suppose that by their thus gaining a superior knowledge of things over their countrymen, should it please the Almighty Director of all events to spare their lives and to return back here again to endeavour the prosecution of their errand, must certainly be a very great antidote against the frequent troubles and palavers or lawsuits which I foresee would unavoidably harass and distress them, through the inconsiderate behaviour of mercenary relations, and for ought I know, reduce them to penury and the extremest of wants.[71]

Cape Coast Castle
February 8th, 1786

Reverend Doctor,

Since my last narrative of my safe arrival to the place of my destination,[72] I am exceedingly happy to inform the venerable Society that although I meet with no visible appearance as yet of performing divine service in the public hall, for want of the chapel being erected as specifically ordered by the African Committee[73] (the prosecution of which being suppressed by the Governor and Council till further orders of a more forcible nature is obtained by them), I have been so fortunate as to perform divine service regularly every Sunday in my own room, where more or less of the gentlemen frequently give their attendance at morning and evening service. . . . It may be uncharitable in me to observe, and indeed it is hard to say what will really be

71. In this further criticism of African culture, including its language, Quaque shows the importance he attached to education for his children as a means of social mobility. The suggestion that a daughter as well as a son should be educated overseas was unusual. After returning from London, Samuel Quaque was appointed assistant to his father at the Charity School set up in Cape Coast Castle in the late 1780's. In 1797, Quaque applied unsuccessfully to the governor for the admission of his son as writer in the African Committee's service. Whether this was Samuel is not known, although the Charity School had run into difficulties by then and Samuel Quaque may no longer have been employed there.

72. Quaque had visited England for a short while in 1784–85 in connection with his children's education.

73. At the end of December 1784, the African Committee informed the governor of Cape Coast Castle that, at Quaque's request, they had sent out vestments and other necessities for the chapel which was to be allotted to him in the new building. During his visit to England he would certainly have seen both the Committee and the S.P.G.

the ultimacy of this part of the country in the course of a few years, for it is grown to such a pitch of daring insolence, the foundation of which arises chiefly from the ill management of the European settlers here, that I fear there will be no such thing as living in Africa. Nothing reigns nowadays but confusion and anarchy, dissipation and discontent throughout the country, for since the short period of my residence, I have experienced nothing else but perpetual disquietude, with threats of danger, by those for whom Providence originally ordained this spot as their portion. The calamities and distresses they themselves feel is pitiable, and yet no argument can move their obdurate hearts to a better mode of thinking; it therefore seems to me that the justice of God's proceedings with impenitent sinners still pursues this race of men, if I may be allowed the expression, for their unjust dealings and practices.

On Tuesday the 18th of last October, happened a most melancholy and unhappy circumstance in the Road of Mouri belonging to the Dutch settlement,[74] where was riding at anchor a Dutch ship full of slaves almost ready to take her departure from the coast. But the ill treatment of the unfeeling Captain incensed the poor captives so highly that they rose upon the ship's crew in his absence and took possession of the vessel. They consisted in number about 150. But the most dreadful circumstance of all is that after having laid their scheme with subtlety and art, and decoying as many of their countrymen who came far and near to plunder on board and near the ship, and also some white sailors from an English ship in hopes of relieving them, were all indiscriminately blown up to upwards of three or four hundred souls. This revengeful but very rash proceeding we are here made to understand to be entirely owing to the Captain's brutish behaviour, who did not allow even his own sailors, much more the slaves, a sufficient maintenance to support nature. If this is really the case, can we but help figuring to ourselves the true picture of inhumanity those unhappy creatures suffer in their miserable state of bondage, under the different degrees of austere masters they unfortunately fall in with, in the West Indies?[75] The next observation that

74. Mouri was in Fanti, between Cape Coast and Anomabu, and was the site of an early Dutch fort, built in 1612 and known as Fort Nassau. British and Dutch settlements along the Gold Coast were thus closely interspersed.

75. This is one of Quaque's rare direct references to the slave trade, the mainspring of Afro-European commerce and the reason for Quaque's own presence on the staff of a

occurs is that on the 14th of November last, the whole body of the slaves belonging to this garrison, of different occupation, deserted and did not return back till the 14th December, but the real cause of their desertion is not yet ascertained. Still, it is easy to conceive that the evils which they seem to complain of, to bear an affinity to the excess of burden the Children of Israel suffered in the reign of Pharaoh, King of Egypt, under their task masters.[76] Not long after this follows another lamentable but very bitter portion indeed, a scene that has not been seen or heard of in the memory of man for ages before. The town of Cape Coast, by some unforeseen accident or other, suffered a most dreadful conflagration on the 27th November which consumed every dwelling house excepting very few, and in endeavouring to secure the different effects belonging to the gentlemen and myself that were exposed to irreparable danger in the said town, we unfortunately had the greatest part burnt and lost, among which I had a large chest of books burnt into ashes. But of such things of the poor natives as they could possibly save were permitted also to be lodged in the fort, and many of them were obliged to take shelter there as the only secure place of refuge. Several, however, lost their lives and vast properties destroyed. . . . Thus is the present state of this country and I leave you to judge of the bitter consequences that may attend it hereafter.

On Sunday the 29th January, I have the satisfaction of informing the Society that I had the honour of baptising a male white infant, born here of European parents. And am in great hopes soon of initiating two more infants of the Governor into that sacred ordinance, which leaves me to conclude, by fervent prayer, that God may in His

---

British fort. At this period, both European merchants and African middlemen viewed the trade simply as an economic transaction that was mutually advantageous. In 1772, even Rev. Thomas Thompson had written in defense of the trade (*Two Missionary Voyages,* p. xiv). Governor John Hippisley, on the other hand, had shown some awareness of its grim side. See Curtin, *Image of Africa,* for the changing British attitudes from the 1780's onward.

76. Each fort had its complement of "castle slaves," male and female. They performed domestic duties and rough work for the garrison, though some of the men were skilled artisans. Like all fort personnel, they were paid in the form of goods for barter, and a system of pensions existed. Strict rules governed their treatment, and they could not be sold off the coast except for the most serious offenses. Desertion seems, in general, to have been rare. Though Quaque gives the impression of considerable hardship, there is no doubt that the castle slaves were much better off than those shipped across the Atlantic (Lawrence, *Trade Castles,* pp. 49–56).

appointed time be gracious unto this land, enlighten their dark minds and to open their eyes to see the wonderful things of His laws.

Cape Coast Castle
January 28th, 1789

Reverend Sir,

I have the honour to address myself to you on a subject, the first of any consequence since my last arrival in Africa worthy the Society's knowledge, which I have no doubt will afford pleasure to my patrons and benefactors as it promises the appearance of conversion and light to the ignorant and infidel. Before I proceed, you will permit me to premise that it is the first real and important circumstance that has happened by the information of which I could justify the trouble I am about to give you. A Society of gentlemen (of which the Governor in Chief is a patron), have entered into an association for the purpose of clothing, feeding and educating twelve coloured children of this country, principally the offspring of distressed and deceased parents, who have no regular mode of support and who are consequently led into the commission of crimes for their support, which oftentimes involves them in trouble and disgrace. These gentlemen, who style themselves Torridzonians (a name analogous to the climate), have appointed me the care of them and my little boy Samuel, lately under the tuition of the Reverend Mr. Fountaine at Marylebone, my assistant. . . . For my part, nothing shall be wanting that can promote so desirable an end and should it continue to exist, I have no doubt of its having due weight and efficacy with other of the natives who appear to admire the institution.

On Sunday the 28th September, I held a general baptism, at which time were received within the pale of Christ's Church ten of the above-mentioned children, who I trust will fight manfully in defence of His doctrine. The sight was truly awful but pleasing; all the gentlemen were present and some one or other of them stood their sponsors. Since this, another essential benefit has been produced, I mean the regular and due performance of divine service at which the children attend, dressed in plain blue cloth and always clean and neat. In addition to the above twelve, there are four more considered in the light of day scholars. These are the children of gentlemen and others and are more independent than the former. For the little time I have had the tuition of them, they have made a tolerable progress in the English language and Catechism, and I have very little doubt but that they will, in the due course of time, prove useful to the community and grateful to their God who has enlightened them. I have to request from the Society a few useful books for their instruction, such as spelling books, copying and cyphering books, together with such tracts in divinity as the Society in their profound wisdom shall deem necessary.[77] . . .

Cape Coast Castle
July 21st, 1792

Reverend Sir,

Since my last letter to the venerable Society, having nothing material occurring to engage your attention has been the cause of my remaining silent so long as I have done. But now having happily overcome, blessed be God, some disagreeable matter that transpired here, of which I did not think it prudent at the time it happened to trouble the Society with till I had vindicated my conduct to the satisfaction of the public, and having gained my point without the least difficulty, I am the more induced to acquaint them with the circumstance thereof. On the 11th day of May 1791, I received a peremptory order from the Governor, William Fielde, Esq., by the Secretary about the hour of six o'clock in the evening, to attend him and others to Anomabu to take up arms in the defence of that fort, the Chief

77. Quaque's educational efforts, conducted in his own room at Cape Coast Castle from 1766, had not been encouraging. The new departure of a Charity School, initiated by the Torridzonian Society, therefore gave him special satisfaction. The society, of which Quaque was a member, had been founded at Cape Coast on 28 July 1787, first as a social club (a Freemasons' lodge of the same name in 1810 may have been a development from it). Its president was the governor-in-chief, and the society's motto—"Friendship ardent as the clime"—was inscribed on a gold medal worn by members. One of the features of the boarding school which it set up for twelve mulatto children lacking proper means of support, was the introduction of school uniforms, distinguished by "a blue jacket with red cuffs and cape, to which was affixed on the left side a badge marked TZS," hence Quaque's reference to his pupils "dressed in plain blue cloth." The four day-scholars, whom he mentions as more independent than the boarders, included the offspring of gentlemen of the trading establishment. Although short-lived, the Torridzonian educational venture was an interesting reflection of philanthropic trends in Europe. The Danes, it should be noted, embarked during the same period on a similar scheme at Christiansborg Castle, their fort in Accra (see Bartels, "Philip Quaque," pp. 161–66).

thereof having created great disturbance with the natives of the town which afterwards terminated with great slaughter and devastation. And because I strongly argued and opposed the order, which I conceived highly inconsistent and injurious to my profession and the station I hold in the African Committee's service, I was in consequence of my refusal most spitefully and maliciously suspended by him and Council, and was obliged to quit the fort to go to reside in Cape Coast town.[78] But during my emigration there, I wrote to the Committee stating fully the cause of my suspension, and in that situation waited upwards of eleven months till their will and pleasure was known which, God be praised, had the desired effect and on the 8th day of April last, I had the satisfaction to receive the abstracts and orders of the Committee's minutes, my reappointment to my office and station as Chaplain only in their service with an addition of £10 *p.a.* annexed to my former salary, to the great mortification and shame of those that had ill will against me and rejoiced at my trouble. . . .

. . . .

P.S. I forgot to acquaint you by way of information, and a most striking circumstance I ever met with, that our periodical rains being almost ended, commenced on the 27th instant the celebration of the jubilee or the first fruits offering with the natives of Africa, which they generally term blacks' Christmas. This custom, I learn, is a traditional institution handed down to them time immemorial by the ancients, the performance of which is held sacred by them annually.[79]

78. The incident of Quaque's suspension brings to light the difficulties of his position as a priest appointed in the service of an administration designed to promote the interests of trade. Writing critically to the African Committee about his behavior, the governor said that Quaque had pleaded the illness of his children as an excuse for not helping to keep watch at Anomabu when staff was short there. Disturbances between fort and town were periodic occurrences on the coast, sometimes resulting in physical attack on a governor. At Anomabu, the Fanti adopted a particularly independent attitude. Although governors used force from time to time, it was generally as a last resort, since this course of action upset the normal processes of trade.

79. The annual yam custom, celebrating the new harvest of a staple foodstuff, was one of the great traditional festivals on the Gold Coast and the occasion, also, of commemorating ancestral spirits. The European forts made gifts at this time to the chiefs and elders of a town, as their contribution towards the festival. "Blacks' Christmas," as described by a nineteenth-century writer, followed immediately after the yam custom and was a period marked by social activity and visiting (Beecham, *Ashantee and the Gold Coast*, pp. 238–41).

But the most remarkable circumstance is that the day never varies, except the day of the month.

Cape Coast Castle
October 13th, 1811

Reverend Doctor,

During the course of nature within these four years past, I have been wretchedly reduced and debilitated in such a dreadful manner, through a complication of various disorders that has rendered me incapable of doing anything whatever, nay not even scarce to go about my room, being weak and feeble.[80] . . . The state of the country is grown worse and worse than ever, nothing but confusion and rumours of wars on every side;[81] but as for my own part, the disagreeable disadvantage I am at present involved in is too shocking to relate. My own family, whom I have brought up, one would naturally imagine would be the most near and dear a tie to me, but instead of which they are plotting my ruin, more particularly by raising up a malicious dispute with Mrs. Quaque merely through jealousy and hatred and envy, and opposing every measure I take for the future benefit of my wife, as if a man has not power and authority to do and dispose of his own property as he pleaseth, without the controlling or interferring of anyone. This they have done without any dread or fear of conscience, and have grossly assaulted and maltreated her so shamefully as to cast a disgrace and infamy upon my character. Thus you see the avaricious disposition of the blacks, who are all for themselves and wish not that the inferior people should ever rise in equality with themselves.[82] It is no wonder and too true a say-

80. The last of Quaque's letters in the S.P.G. Archives, written in haste when its author was old and in ill health, is more difficult to decipher than the earlier ones; and there is an element of pathos running through it. Two themes of the letter of 28 September 1766 are echoed here, almost half a century later—Quaque's conflict with traditional society and his despondency about the success of his mission.

81. The Ashanti invasion of Fanti in 1807 and attack on Anomabu town and fort were followed by almost seventy years of uncertainty and disturbance along the seaboard, one consequence of which was a series of Anglo-Ashanti wars. In 1811, Ashanti armies had again come down to the coast.

82. As in 1766, Quaque was still at odds with the communalism of the African family, the dispute in this instance arising over inheritance. Since the Akan kinship structure was based on the matrilineage, it followed that a man's wife and children were excluded from the bulk of the husband's inheritance. Changing circumstances, however,

ing of our blessed Lord, that a man's foes shall be they of his household and that a prophet has no honour in his own country. Thus is the case now with me and I am fully convinced that the more a man do to these kind of people, the more ungrateful and unthankful they seem to be; it is like casting so many pearls before swine.

.   .   .   .

The state of this unsuccessful mission, I formerly had some hopes of its growth, but at present on the face of things bears but an indifferent aspect. I have my doubt of its increase unless a new change should take place for the better. I could wish to say more on this topic, but I write much in pain and time fails me as His Majesty's ship the *Thaïs,* Captain Scobell, goes away from hence tomorrow morning without fail, and therefore hope your goodness will excuse this scrawl as I have no time to lose. But beg leave to inform the Society that within these few years, I have buried two and fifty persons and baptised eleven children. Prayers regularly every day in my room and on Sundays some of the gentlemen do attend. I hope to be more explicit in my next, should God permit me my health. Accept of my sincere and hearty wishes and prayers for your health and continuance.

---

were even then bringing the modified view that "self-acquired" property was distinct from family property and was at the disposal of the person who had acquired it. His reference to "the inferior people" is not easy to interpret as it stands, but it may relate to the status of his third wife.

PART II

*Travellers
in the
Gold Coast
Hinterland*

Although Europeans in the eighteenth-century Gold Coast rarely penetrated into Ashanti, and those of the early nineteenth century went no farther than Kumasi, they were extremely interested in the geography of the farther hinterland—especially in the mysterious city of Timbuktu and in the course and termination of the Niger River.[1] These interests led to the preservation and publication of three narratives by non-Europeans who had travelled down to the Gold Coast and could report on Ashanti and the lands beyond.

Ṣāliḥ Bilāli was born about 1770 in Massina, a Pulo like Ayuba Suleiman. He was captured, enslaved, and shipped from the Gold Coast in about 1790, passing within twenty miles of Philip Quaque's headquarters at Cape Coast. Abū Bakr al-Ṣiddīq followed a similar route into slavery some fifteen years later. He was born in Timbuktu itself, but spent most of his life in Africa farther south, in Jenne and in Bouna, just beyond the Ashanti frontier. He was from much the same social class as Ayuba; but he was better edu-

1. The Niger was an unsolved puzzle to Europeans until the early decades of the nineteenth century. European traders, anchoring their ships in the mouths of the Niger, had supposed the delta to be a series of individual rivers, and had not been tempted to explore upstream through the pestilential swamp, which extends inland for a hundred miles to the apex of the delta. Final evidence linking the Niger Delta with the upper reaches of the river came in 1830, when the Landers emerged at the mouth after having approached the river by an overland route, from Badagry to Bussa in Nupe, and explored the lower course by canoe.

cated, and his original account in Arabic is the only one of the present collection written down by the narrator himself in an African language. The third traveller, Wargee of Astrakhan, was not so intimately connected with the slave trade. He was not a slave himself, nor is there evidence that his commercial dealings were connected with the slave trade. His information on the routes of commerce in the Gold Coast hinterland, however, is extremely valuable. His is the first published account of a north-south crossing of western Africa, from the Mediterranean to the Gulf of Guinea—seven years before René Caillié, who is usually credited with this achievement. He also gives one of the rare pre-European accounts of Timbuktu, and in 1821–22 he followed the same route from the north as Ṣāliḥ and Abū Bakr.

The three narratives can therefore be read together, even though they describe events at fifteen year intervals. Taken together, they add greatly to the otherwise partial and scattered sources for the history of this region. European explorers came in the 1820's and later, but they came in the wake of the great religious revolutions that swept the Western Sudan in the earlier decades of the century. Abū Bakr and Ṣāliḥ Bilāli, in particular, show their societies on the eve of these revolutions, and Wargee's passage from Timbuktu to the Gold Coast came at a period before the Muslim Fulbe reformers of Massina were fully established in power under *Shehu* Ahmadu.

CHAPTER 4

ṢĀLIḤ BILĀLI OF MASSINA

Ivor Wilks

Ṣāliḥ Bilāli, known more prosaically as Tom, became head driver of Hopeton Plantation, Georgia, in 1816, having worked there since his purchase from the Bahama Islands sixteen years earlier.[1] At the time the following account was written he had been in America some forty years, but still read (though did not write) Arabic, and was described as "a strict Mahometan [who] abstains from spirituous liquors, and keeps the various fasts, particularly that of the Rhamadan."[2]

Ṣāliḥ was a Massina Pulo (or Fulani), having been born about 1770 at Kianah on the Niger River near the present town of Mopti. Seized by slave raiders—presumably Bambara—when only about twelve years old, he was taken to the Bambara capital, Segu, and, being passed from hand to hand, was finally sold into slavery in the Bahama Islands from Anomabu on the Gold Coast.[3]

In the late eighteenth century Massina was an area of complex ethnic, religious, and economic diversity, where in close interrelationship lived sedentary Fulbe, Bambara, and Songhai farmers, nomadic Fulbe cattle herders, Bozo fisherman, and, in the towns, So-

1. The sole source for Ṣāliḥ Bilāli is a letter written by his American master, probably in the late 1830's. His name is given there as Sali-bul-Ali, which presumably represents Ṣāliḥ Bilāli—the name *Bilāli*, being that of the Prophet's African muezzin, having had a certain vogue in West Africa.

2. The fast of Ramadan is one of the five pillars of Islam, obligatory upon all Muslims.

3. Ṣāliḥ Bilāli was thus transported from the same part of the Gold Coast as his younger contemporary Abū Bakr al-Ṣiddīq (see Chap. 5) though a few years earlier.

ninke and Dyula[4] traders, and the cosmopolitan '*ulamā*', men for whom learning was a way of life. Many Massina communities were completely polytheistic; others Muslim, with centuries of adherence to the faith behind them; many existed in an intermediate state, still devoted to the ancient gods but progressively adopting Islamic practices. While Massina was ruled by its non-Muslim Fulbe *ardos,* who recognized intermittently the overlordship of the non-Muslim Bambara kings of Segu, the Muslim communities, responsive to the teachings of the Qādiriyya *shaykh* Sidi al-Mukhtar al-Kunti,[5] and aware of the consolidation of Fulbe Muslim power in Futa Jallon to the west,[6] awaited the reformer, the *mujaddid,* who would free them from polytheistic domination.

Ṣāliḥ Bilāli was born into a Muslim Fulbe community, in which, as he tells us, "all the children are taught to read and write Arabic by the priests." It was from this same stratum of Massina society that Ahmadu bi Hammadi came, who, born in 1775/6, was an almost exact contemporary of Ṣāliḥ Bilāli. In the early years of the nineteenth century, when Ṣāliḥ Bilāli was aspiring to the position of head driver on Hopeton Plantation, Ahmadu bi Hammadi, or *Shehu* Ahmadu as he became better known, came under the influence of 'Uthmān dan Fodio (d. 1817) and his brother Abdullahi (d. 1829), whose jihad of 1804 led to the creation of the Fulbe emirates of the caliphate of Sokoto, in what is now northern Nigeria (see below, pp. 195–98). *Shehu* Ahmadu, in consultation with Sokoto, in turn called for jihad in Massina, probably in 1818. Rallying the Muslim Fulbe to his support, he established his capital at Hamdullahi, overthrew the *ardos*, and cast off Bambara overlordship to establish the imamate of Massina with himself as *amīr al-mu'minīn,* commander of the faithful.[7] Ruled with the strictest adherence to Islamic practice,

4. *Diula* or *Dyula* is a term with slightly different meanings in different parts of West Africa. It was originally simply the word for merchant in several of the Mande languages, and it is still used in this sense in the literature concerning the Senegambia and its hinterland. In the region between Ashanti and the upper Niger around Jenne and Segu, however, the Malinke-speaking merchants were sufficiently different from the rest of the population to be considered a separate ethnic group, usually called Dioula or Dyula in the literature.

5. Al-Mukhtar al-Kunti (1729–1811) was head of the Qādiriyya in the Western Sudan, and greatly influenced the leaders of the jihads of the early nineteenth century.

6. The Pulo Karamoko Alfa called for jihad in about 1725, and his nephew Ibrāhīm Sōri carried it through to a successful conclusion some half a century later to establish the imamate of Futa Jallon.

7. For an account of the imamate, from traditional sources, see H. Ba and J. Daget, *L'Empire Peul du Macina* (Paris, 1955).

to which even the '*ulamā*' of Jenne had difficulty in conforming, the imamate survived the death of *Shehu* Ahmadu in 1843/44 by some twenty years, and collapsed before the power of a new reformer, *al-Ḥājj* 'Umar al-Fūtī, also known as Sheiku Umar Tall in his native Futa Toro.

The narrative of Ṣāliḥ Bilāli is of interest mainly for the glimpses it gives us of Massina Muslim Fulbe society some forty years before the creation of the imamate. For it was in this society—rather than in that of the Jenne '*ulamā*' to which Abū Bakr al-Ṣiddīq belonged—that the jihad had its roots.

ṢĀLIḤ BILĀLI'S RECOLLECTIONS OF MASSINA

The text that follows contains the reminiscences of Ṣāliḥ Bilāli as reported in a letter of James Hamilton Couper, of Hopeton Plantation, published by William Brown Hodgson in *Notes on Northern Africa, the Sahara, and the Soudan* (New York, 1844), pp. 68–75. It is reprinted here in full and without changes other than modernization of the spelling of place names where the identification is certain.

His native town is Kianah, in the district of Temourah, and in the Kingdom of Massina.[8] Kianah is a considerable town, within half a mile of a great river, nearly a mile wide, which is called Mayo;[9] and which runs from the setting to the rising sun, and this, to the north of the town. To the east of Kianah, this river unites with another large river which flows into it from the south. On this southern river, the large towns of Kuna and Jenne are situated; and he believes that the two unite beyond the latter town.[10]

Kuna is situated on the north side of the southern river, immediately on its banks; and is two days' journey, in a south-west direction, from Kianah. It is a very large town, and an extensive market is

8. I cannot identify Kianah. It must, however, have been near the confluence of the Niger and the Bani, and a little west of the present town of Mopti.

9. The Niger, still known to the Fulbe as the Mayo.

10. Kuna and Jenne are both on the Bani, which joins one of the branches of the Niger at Mopti. Kuna was visited by René Caillié in 1828; see *Travels through Central Africa to Timbuctoo* (2 vols., London, 1830), 2:4–7. It was then a small but flourishing river port and market, occupied by Fulbe. H. Barth described it half a century later as "a small town, but an important market place"—*Travels and Discoveries in North and Central Africa* (3 vols., New York, 1859), 3:708.

held, on stated days, on the opposite bank of the river. Beyond Ki-anah, up the same river, but on the south side of it, is Jenne. It lies south-west from Kianah, and is also about two days' walk from it. It is a very large town, being a day's ride in circuit, for a man on horse-back. The head priest resides at Jenne, and is called *Al-mami*.[11] He has been frequently at Kuna and Jenne; and has heard of a large town on the great river, higher up than Jenne, which is west south-west from Kianah, and which is called Segu, and is the principal town of the Kingdom of Bambara.[12] Another great town, the largest in the country, also lies on the great river, on the north side of it. It lies north-east from Kianah, and is called Timbuktu. It is a great dis-tance from Kianah, more than two hundred miles.[13]

Arab traders, who are nearly white, Mahometans in religion, and who speak the languages both of the Koran and the country, trade between Timbuktu, Kuna, Jenne and Segu. They travel in large boats, covered with awnings, and propelled by poles. They are armed, wear turbans, and travel in large parties, having frequently thirty or forty boats together. They bring for sale, salt in large thick slabs, blankets, guns, pistols, cotton cloth, beads, shell money,[14] and sometimes horses. These traders differ from the natives in color, hair and dress, and come from a distant country beyond Timbuktu.

He has never been at Timbuktu. The natives he has seen, from that town and Jenne, speak a different language from his own, which

11. That is, the imam of the Jenne mosque. Jenne had long been an important religious center, with a large and cosmopolitan ʻulamāʼ class. Al-Saʻdi, the seventeenth-century author of the *Taʼrīkh al-Sūdān,* remarked how "God has brought to this fortunate city a number of learned and holy men, strangers to the country, who have come to live here. They are from different peoples and countries."

12. Mungo Park, visiting Segu in the late eighteenth century, remarked: "The view of this extensive city; the numerous canoes upon the river; the crowded population; and the cultivated state of the surrounding country, formed altogether a prospect of civiliza-tion and magnificence, which I had little expected to find in the bosom of Africa"—*Travels in Africa* (new ed., 2 vols., London, 1817), 1:297. Although the Bambara kings of Segu at this period were not Muslim, it is clear that Segu already had a large and politically influential Muslim population. It was, of course, the rise of this kingdom in the early eighteenth century that influenced the flow of slaves toward the Senegambia and the position of Ayuba Suleiman there.

13. Timbuktu is in fact a little under two hundred miles northeast of the region of Kianah.

14. Cowries, current over a large part of West Africa at this time. They were im-ported from the Maldive Islands by way of North Africa. The other products came from North Africa or the Sahara.

is that of the Kingdom of Massina; but the traders understand both.[15] Mahometanism is the religion of all. He knows of but one race of negroes, occupying the country of Timbuktu, Kuna, Jenne and Massina. They vary somewhat in color. That most prevalent is a yellowish brown, lighter than his own, which is brownish black. He recollects no difference in the hair, which is woolly in himself.

I infer from his conversation, that the town of Kianah, or perhaps the Kingdom of Massina, is a Foulah [Fulbe] or Fellatah colony, established among the older nations of the Soudan, and differing from them in language.[16] I can draw no inference as regards any difference of physical appearance. He is not aware of any difference of origin.

The houses consist of two kinds. Those occupied by the richer classes are built of *cylindrical* bricks, made of clay mixed with rice chaff, and dried in the sun. They contain two rooms only; one of which is used as a store-room, and the other as an eating and sleeping apartment, for the whole family. They are of one story high, with flat roofs, made of joists, overlaid with strips of wood, and plastered with a very white clay. The inhabitants sleep on raised platforms, covered with mats; and during the cold weather, which occurs about the season of the rice harvest, blankets of wool made from their own sheep, are used. The fires are made on the floors, and the smoke escapes by a hole left in the roof. The poorer classes live in small conical huts, made of poles, connected at the tops, and covered with straw.[17]

The churches (mosques) are built of dried bricks, like the best class of houses. They contain a recess,[18] towards the east or rising sun, towards which the *Al-Mami* turns his face, when he prays—towards Mecca. The houses of the head men do not differ in size from those of the better classes.

15. Ṣāliḥ Bilāli's language, of which Couper gives a specimen, was of course that of the Fulbe (called Pular in the west and Fulfulde in the east). In both Timbuktu and Jenne, Songhai would be widely spoken.

16. Fulbe groups had been moving into Massina from the west from probably the fourteenth century onwards, and by the late eighteenth century were numerically dominant in many areas. Ṣāliḥ's ancestry, like that of Ayuba Suleiman, thus goes back to the Senegal Valley.

17. Ṣāliḥ Bilāli's description of the two types of dwellings, the mud-brick rectangular, and the grass circular, would still apply today.

18. The *mihrāb,* always orientated to Mecca.

The natives cultivate the soil, and keep large droves of horses, cows, sheep, goats, and some asses. The great grain crop is rice. As a preparation for it, the soil is turned with a sharp pointed hoe. The seed is then sown broad cast, and is covered with the same hoe. The ground continues dry, until the rice is nearly two feet high; when the river rises, and inundates the country. The water continues up, until the rice is ripe; and it is harvested in canoes, and carried to the high ground, to which the inhabitants retire during the freshets.[19] Besides rice, they cultivate a species of red maize, millet and Guinea corn. They also grow beans, pumpkins, okra, tomatoes, cucumbers and cotton. They have cocoa-nuts, pine-apples and small yellow figs, which grow on very large trees.

The usual food is rice, milk, butter, fish, beef and mutton. The domesticated animals are horses, used for riding, asses and camels for carrying loads; cattle, the bulls of which have lumps on their shoulders,[20] for milk and meat—sheep, with very long wool, for food and wool—goats and poultry, and dogs for guards. They have no hogs.

The wild animals are lions, hyenas, elephants and hippopotami, called *gabou.*

The usual dress of the men, is a large pair of cotton trowsers, and a shirt with a conical straw hat, without a rim. They manufacture their own cotton cloth; and dye it of a very fine blue better than any he has seen here. They also wear blankets, made from the long wool of their sheep.

The hair of the natives is curled and woolly; and both men and women wear it in long plaits, extending down the sides of their heads. In war, they use shields and spears, but not bows and arrows. All the children are taught to read and write Arabic, by the priests (Maalims).[21] They repeat from the Koran, and write on a board, which when filled, is washed off. There are no slaves. Crimes are punished by fines. The men work in the fields, fish, herd cattle, and weave. The women spin, and attend to household duties, but never work in the field.

His father and mother, were persons of considerable property.

19. An accurate description of cultivation in the middle Niger delta, which is in flood for about half the year from around July.

20. The humped zebu cattle.

21. Arabic *mu'ālim,* Hausa *malam,* etc., a man of learning.

When about twelve years old, as he was returning from Jenne to Ki-anah, alone, on horseback, he was seized by a predatory party and carried to Segu, and was transferred from master to master, until he reached the coast, at Anomabu. During his journey, he passed a high range of mountains, on the slopes of which, he met with a nation of cannibals.[22] After leaving Bambara, to use his own expression, the people had no religion, until he came to this country.

22. Ṣāliḥ Bilāli's route from Segu on the Niger to Anomabu on the Gold Coast is unfortunately not recorded. The "high range of mountains," however, is presumably a reference to the cliffs of Banfora, south of the headwaters of the Black Volta. The inhabitants were probably not cannibals: Muslim Africans of the Western Sudan tended to attribute cannibalism to many of the polytheistic peoples living nearby, just as many West Africans believed the Europeans practiced cannibalism.

CHAPTER 5

ABŪ BAKR AL-ṢIDDĪQ
OF TIMBUKTU

Ivor Wilks

Abū Bakr al-Ṣiddīq was born in Timbuktu about 1790, but he was brought up in Jenne from the age of two.[1] He belonged to one of the *Shurfa* groups of the Western Sudan, claiming descent from the Prophet; and the founder of his line was one *Shaykh* 'Abd al-Qādir, who has so far not been identified.[2] The family was clearly one of some standing, its members for generation after generation belonging to the class of the *'ulamā'*, or men of learning, in whose hands the conduct of public affairs largely rested. Abū Bakr's father, Kara Mūsā,[3] is described as *tafsīr*, a grammatically corrupt form (though common in the Western Sudan) of *mufassir* (one learned in Koranic exegesis). His paternal great-grandfather, 'Umar, is described as a *qa'īd*, and his maternal great-grandfather, as *shāhid 'l-malik* (the king's witness, presumably a jurisconsult). Unfortunately a gap of a century prevents our linking the family with any of the prominent figures of Timbuktu

1. The principal sources for his life are the autobiographical fragments incorporated in the text that follows. Additional material is found in R. R. Madden, *Twelve Months Residence in the West Indies* (2 vols., London, 1837), 2:183–89; G. C. Renouard, "Routes in North Africa, by Abú Bekr eṣ ṣiddík," *Journal of the Royal Geographical Society*, 6:100–113 (1836); *The Friend of Africa*, 1, No. 4 (25 February 1841); 1, No. 10 (August 1841); 2, No. 18 (April 1842).

2. For the *Shurfa* families of Timbuktu, see P. Marty, *Études sur l'Islam et les tribus du Soudan* (4 vols., Paris, 1920–21), 2:10–14.

3. Probably a shortened form of Karamo or Karamoko, a widespread Malinke title meaning a man of learning.

and Jenne known through the sixteenth- and seventeenth-century chronicles, the *Ta'rikh al-Fattash* and the *Ta'rikh al-Sudan*.[4]

Abū Bakr al-Ṣiddīq tells us that he received his early education at Jenne, where he was "fully instructed in reading and construing the Koran." At the age of nine, in charge of his tutor, he commenced an extended tour of the south. One year was spent in the important Dyula trading center of Kong, fifteen to twenty days' journey from Jenne, where one of his paternal uncles, 'Abd ar-Rahmān, lived. They next moved to Bouna, another ancient trading center eight days to the east, where a second uncle, Mahmūd, lived, and where Abū Bakr's father was buried, having died there about 1794 while trading in gold.

In Bouna, Abū Bakr continued with his education—more advanced work on the Koran, since, he tells us, he was still too young to proceed to the studies of logic, rhetoric, and *tafsīr*. Abū Bakr's information upon the organization of learning in Bouna, where 'Abdallāh ibn al-Ḥājj Muḥammad al-Watarāwi presided over a community of scholars drawn from many parts of the Western Sudan, is of great interest. The existence of this center of learning so far south, on the frontiers of the Ashanti Empire, is otherwise known only from Barth's short reference to it, as "a place of great celebrity for its learning and its schools, in the countries of the Mohammedan Mandingoes to the south,"[5] though extant works in Arabic of eighteenth-century date and western Gonja provenance also clearly presuppose a flourishing tradition of scholarship in the region of which Bouna was part.[6]

At the beginning of the nineteenth century Ashanti was torn by revolution. Although there were many aspects to this struggle, it was partly a clash between Islam and polytheism, perhaps not entirely unrelated to the tide of Muslim reform that was rising throughout the Western Sudan. The *asantehene* Osei Kwame was deposed about 1801, because of "his attachment to the Moslems

4. The most recent editions of these works, in French translation, are published under authors' names transliterated as Abderrahman al-Sa'di and Mahmoud Kati, respectively (Paris, 1964).

5. H. Barth, *Travels and Discoveries in North and Central Africa* (5 vols., London, 1857–58), 5:239–40.

6. See for example the mid-eighteenth-century *Kitab Ghunja* (*The Book of Gonja*), an edition of which is being prepared by I. Wilks and N. Levtzion.

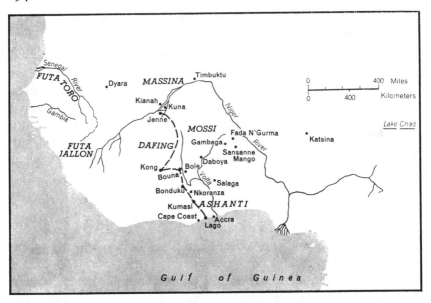

Map 7. Abū Bakr's route to the coast.

and, as it is said, his inclination to establish the Korannic law for the civil code of the empire.'"[7] His deposition provoked a violent reaction in the Muslim-dominated northwestern parts of the empire. Western Gonja and Bonduku, with the support of Kong and probably of Bouna, led a revolt intended to restore Osei Kwame to the throne. It was not until 1804, after a series of expeditions had been dispatched against the rebels, that the Ashanti government succeeded in reasserting its authority in the northwest.

One of the last of these campaigns seems to have been that of the *gyamanhene* Adinkra—an Ashanti nominee then in power in Bonduku—against Bouna.[8] This is the campaign that ended in the defeat of Bouna, and it is described in some detail by Abū Bakr al-Ṣiddīq. Abū Bakr himself was taken prisoner and carried off first to Adinkra's capital at Bonduku, then to Kumasi, seat of the *asantehene,* and so by the old slave route to the port of Lago where the English intermittently occupied a small fortified lodge some thirty-five miles east of Cape Coast. There, in about 1805, he was sold to an English ship and transported to the West Indies.

He first became the slave of a stonemason, Donellan, then of an

7. J. Dupuis, *Journal of a Residence in Ashantee* (London, 1824), p. 245.
8. See Ivor Wilks, *The Northern Factor in Ashanti History* (Legon, 1961), pp. 22–24.

absentee landowner named Haynes, who had him baptized as Edward Donellan (variously spelled as Donlan or Doulan); and finally in 1823 he was sold to Alexander Anderson, who employed him as a storeman. Abū Bakr kept the accounts in Arabic, since he had learned only to speak English, not to read or write it. In 1834, Anderson was persuaded to free Abū Bakr, through the exertions of Dr. R. R. Madden, a Special Magistrate in Jamaica concerned with the supervision of the Emancipation Act of 1833. The inhabitants of Kingston donated £20 to Abū Bakr by public subscription.

On Madden's return to England in 1835, he approached the Royal Geographical Society with the suggestion that Abū Bakr be employed as guide for some future expedition into the Western Sudan. The idea was rejected by the Society, on the grounds that having spent almost thirty years in Jamaica, he would be a stranger in his own country. Notwithstanding this discouraging response, Abū Bakr was brought to England by Captain Oldrey, another Special Magistrate from Jamaica, and Madden commended him to John Davidson, who was then sponsoring, and planning to lead, a private expedition to Timbuktu.

In September 1835, Davidson embarked for Gibraltar, taking Abū Bakr with him. In Morocco Davidson, who had read medicine at Edinburgh, placed his knowledge at the disposal of the sultan and treated, so he claimed, 1,200 patients. Abū Bakr's situation was probably less arduous, since Davidson reported that "he was fully acknowledged, and my dragoman had orders from the palace to treat him with respect, as he was a Mulay (prince)."[9] The travellers also learned in Morocco that one of Abū Bakr's relatives had become "sheik of Tomboktu." The combination of Davidson's medical knowledge and Abū Bakr's noble ancestry was sufficient to induce the sultan reluctantly to give them permission to proceed into the desert—though not, as originally hoped, by way of Fez and Tafilelt, but by the more westerly route from Wadi Nun across Wadi Dra.

The expedition left Wadi Nun late in November 1836. Some three weeks later, on 18 December, it was attacked, and Davidson was killed. Reports reached London, however, that Abū Bakr al-

---

9. For the Davidson expedition, see T. Davidson (ed.), *Notes Taken during Travels in Africa by John Davidson* (London, 1839). The chief source of information about Abū Bakr after his departure from the West Indies is *The Friend of Africa*, 1, No. 4, and 2, No. 18.

Ṣiddīq had been spared, a possibility not incompatible with other accounts that the merchants of Tafilelt had hired the Al Harīb to prevent the Christian Davidson from prying into their commercial activities. Be that as it may, the likelihood of Abū Bakr's survival brought Madden back into the picture. In 1841, as newly appointed Commissioner of Inquiry on the state of the British forts on the Gold Coast, he distributed leaflets for circulation into the interior, offering one hundred dollars reward for information about Abū Bakr's whereabouts. The information could be turned in to any British settlement on the Guinea Coast or to the commanding officer of the Niger Expedition then about to set out. Of various reports received, the most satisfactory reached Morocco. In June 1841, the British vice-consul at Mogadore received word from a man recently returned by caravan from Timbuktu and described as "a friend of the Sheikh," that Abu Bakr al-Ṣiddiq had returned to Jenne.

THE AFRICAN TRAVELS
OF ABŪ BAKR AL-ṢIDDĪQ

Abū Bakr al-Ṣiddīq left two autobiographical fragments dealing with his life in Africa. The first of these was given to R. R. Madden in Jamaica in 1834. It was written in Arabic, though Abū Bakr himself translated it orally for Madden, and presumably Madden had further assistance in preparing the English version for publication. The second version was also written originally in Arabic, this time in England, "in the neighbourhood of London" and dated 29 August 1835. This version was translated and published by G. C. Renouard, who also saw a third version, now lost, which was written on board ship between the West Indies and England. Renouard, however, notes that this version resembled the one he published "almost word for word." Neither of the Arabic originals is know to be extant. The two versions are so much alike that both were probably based on still another that Abū Bakr kept for himself. The Renouard text, however, is fuller, though sections are identical with the Madden text. There is little doubt that Renouard's translation, obviously made by a competent Arabist, is preferable to that of Madden in collaboration with Abū Bakr himself.[10] The text that follows is therefore based mainly on the Renouard version, though in places Madden's is preferred. Variant readings

10. Both versions have been reprinted or paraphrased, Madden's in Wilson Armistead, *A Tribute to the Negro* (London, 1848), pp. 245–47; Renouard's in *The Friend of Africa*, 1(10):151–53.

are identified by letter, *A* for Renouard, and *B* for Madden. Orthography has been modernized, including the spelling of place names, except where there is doubt about the intended form. Notes marked with an asterisk are by Renouard.

A: "This is an account of the beginning of my life," in G. C. Renouard, "Routes in North Africa, by Abú Bekr es ṣiddīk," *Journal of the Royal Geographical Society,* 6:102-7 (1836).

B: "The History of Abon Becr Sadiki, known in Jamaica by the name of Edward Donlan," in R. R. Madden, *Twelve Months Residence in the West Indies* (2 vols., London, 1837), 2:183–89.

My name is Abū Bakr al-Ṣiddīq, my birthplace Timbuktu. I was educated in the town of Jenne, and fully instructed in reading and construing the Koran—but in the interpretation of it with the help of commentaries. This was done in the city of Bouna,[11] where there are many learned men [*'ulamā'*], who are not natives of one place, but each of them having quitted his own country, has come and settled there. The names of these *sayyids* [masters] who dwelt in the city of Bouna were as follows: 'Abdallāh ibn al-Ḥājj; Muḥammad Watarāwī;[12] Muḥammad al-Muṣṭafā; Fatik al-Abyaḍ [the white man]; *Shaykh* 'Abd al-Qādir Sankari, from the land of Futa Jallon;[13] Ibrāhīm ibn Yūsuf, from the land of Futa Toro;[14] Ibrāhīm ibn Abī 'l-Hasan from Silla by descent, but born at Dyara.[15] These men used to meet together to hear the instructions of 'Abdallāh ibn al-Ḥājj Muḥammad Tafsīr.[16]

My father's name was Kara Mūsā the Sharīf ("of a noble tribe"), Watarāwī,[17] *Tafsīr.* His brothers were named Idrīs, 'Abd

11. For Bouna, Abū Bakr used the usual Arabic literary form of *Ghūnah.* Text B clarifies the point that most of his education was in Bouna, and Renouard noted that even after thirty years in Jamaica, he still knew the Koran "almost by heart."

12. Both versions include the semicolon between these two names, but they might equally well be one. Watarāwī means "of the Watara," a Dyula lineage in such southern trading centers as Kong, Bonduku, and Bouna.

13. Sankari would be the Fulbe *yettodé,* Sangare.

14. The presence of Fulbe scholars from Futa Jallon and Futa Toro, both of which had by this time passed through their religious revolutions and were under the rule of *almamis,* indicates one of the routes by which the Muslim reform movement spread to other parts of the Western Sudan.

15. An ancient Diawara Soninke center near Nioro, on the present-day frontier of Mali, north of Bamako. Silla probably refers to the prominent Diawara clerical lineage of that name, rather than to the town of Silla, a little to the west of Jenne.

16. Presumably the 'Abdallāh already mentioned. *Tafsīr* means a Koranic commentator.

17. The *Shurfa* of Timbuktu bore Mande lineage names (Marty, *L'Islam et les tribus du Soudan,* 2:10).

ar-Rahmān, Mahmūd, and Abū Bakr. Their father, my grandfather, was Mār,[18*] al-qāʾid,[19] ʿUmar ibn Shahīd al-Malik [son of the King's witness or chief law officer]; he lived in the cities of Timbuktu and Jenne. He was also called ibn Abū Ibrāhīm, because Ibrāhīm (may his grave be visited!) was of this country. [*B:* Some say he was the son of Ibrāhīm, the founder of my race in the country of Jenne.][20] He [Kara Mūsā] was their father's first-born, and for that reason I was called by the name of his brother, Abū Bakr.

After their father's death, my grandfather's, there was dissension between them and their families, and they separated and went into different countries of the Sudan. Idrīs went to the country of Massina, where he dwelt in Diawara, and married a daughter of Mār, al-qāʾid Abū Bakr:[21] her name was Ummuyu. ʿAbd ar-Rahmān travelled as far as the land of Kong. He married the daughter of Abū Thaūmā Alī [*B:* Samer Ali],[22] lord of that country, and dwelt there. The name of his wife was Sārah. Mahmūd travelled to the city of Bouna, and settled there [*B:* . . . and married the daughter of the king of Bouna]. His wife's name was Zuhrā. Abū Bakr remained at Timbuktu with the rest of the family. He was not married at the time I left our country.

Before all these things happened, my father used to travel about. He went into the land of Katsina and Bornu.[23] There he married my mother, and then returned to Timbuktu, to which place my mother followed him. After two years had elapsed, my father thought about his brothers, whom he repented having parted with,

18*. The same as Emír.

19. A title that appears to have enjoyed a particular vogue in the Western Sudan, usually equivalent to *amīr*.

20. The sense of either text is obscure, but they may intend to say that Abū Bakr's grandfather was known as ʿUmar ibn Abū Ibrāhīm, and that Ibrāhīm (or Abū Ibrāhīm?) was the first to settle in Jenne as opposed to Timbuktu.

21. It is impossible to know exactly what office is meant. The only Diawara ruler of this name, Boukari, is traditionally placed later, in 1826–31 (G. Boyer, *Un peuple de l'ouest soudanais: Les Diawara* [Dakar, 1953], annexe I).

22. There was no ruler of Kong by that name, but a Soma Ali was subordinate ruler of the northeastern provinces at the relevant period. He was grandson of Zambakari, who was in turn third son of Seku Watara, founder of the ruling Dyula dynasty of Kong. A less likely identification is with Soma Oule, grandson of Seku Watara. See E. Bernus, "Kong et sa région," *Études éburnéennes*, 8 (1960).

23. In present-day northern Nigeria. Katsina was of great importance in the eighteenth century as a southern terminus of the central Saharan caravan and pilgrim route to the Fezzan and beyond—the route later used by Wargee to reach the Western Sudan.

which grieved him exceedingly. He then ordered his slaves to make ready for their departure with him to visit his brothers, and see whether they were in health or not. They therefore obeyed their master's orders, and did so; and went to the town of Jenne, and from there to Kong, and from there to Bouna, where they stopped.[24] There they abode, and continued to serve their master, collecting much gold from him there. In that country much gold is found in the plains, banks of rivers, rocks and stones.[25] They have to break the stones, and grind them, and reduce them to dust. This is then put into vessels and washed with water till the gold is all collected under the water in the vessels and the dust lies above it. They then pour out this mud upon the ground, and the gold remains in the vessels. They spread it out to dry. After that they assay it, and make such things of it as they are able. For money or exchange they use a shell, al-wada'[cowries], gold, and silver. They also barter goods for goods, according to the measure of their value.

My father collected much gold in that country, and sent much to his father-in-law. My father also sent horses, asses, mules, and very valuable silks brought from Egypt, with much wealth, as presents to him. He was my mother's father, al-Ḥājj Muḥammad Tafsīr, of the countries of Bornu and Katsina, both inhabited by his family.[26]

After this my father fell ill of a fever, and died in the city of Bouna. He was buried there, and his brothers went and made a great lamentation for him. At that time I was a child; I knew nothing of this, but some of my old relations told me all about the life of my departed father. My uncles, after the death of my father, returned to their different countries, and Mahmūd alone was left in the city of Bouna.

My mother's name was Nāghōdī, that is, in the Hausa tongue; but her real name was Ḥafṣah. Her brothers were named 'Abdallāh Tafsīr aṣ-Ṣifā [the purified], Ya'qūb, Yaḥyā, Sa'ad, Ḥāmid Bābā,

24. See Appendix 1, at end of chapter, for route information printed in Renouard's version.

25. There are important gold fields both to the north and to the south of Bouna, and commercial mining has been carried on in this century.

26. There was a flourishing gold trade between such southern centers as Bouna and the regions to the northeast, as is borne out by Dupuis, *Journal of a Residence in Ashantee*, pp. lvii–lviii. These routes, however, were of even greater importance for the kola trade, which Abū Bakr does not mention. Although Abū Bakr clearly never travelled the road from Bouna to the northeast, he gave a report of the route (see Appendix 2).

Mū'min, 'Uthmān, and 'Abd al-Karīm. Her sisters were Ḥabībah, Fāṭimah, Maryam, and Maimūnah. Their father was named *al-Ḥājj* Muḥammad Tafsīr, of the cities of Katsina and Bornu.[27] Her father, when he went to perform the pilgrimage, left her mother suckling her, on which account her name was called Nāghōdī [Hausa: "I am thankful"]. My brothers were named 'Umar, Ṣāliḥ, Sa'īd, Mūsā Bābā, Mū'min, 'Abdallāh, Sulaymān, Muṣṭafā, Yūsuf, and 'Abd ar-Rahmān, but by my mother's side, Ṣāliḥ only. My sisters were 'Ayishah, Āminah, Ṣalīmah, Ḥawā', and Keltūm; but Āminah only on my mother's side. These men and these women issued, all of them, from the stock of the *Shaykh* 'Abd al-Qādir the Sharīf, and their family name is Mōr.

About five years after the death of my father I asked my instructor, who taught me the Koran to go with me to the city of Bouna to visit my father's grave. He answered, "Yes, Abū Bakr al-Ṣiddīq, if it pleases God, I will do that thou dost desire." He then prepared himself, and sought for provision for the road; and he was followed by a large company of disciples, who bewailed him [28]* [B: . . . and took along with us many of his oldest scholars to bear us company]. We departed, and, after long fatigue, we arrived at the city of Kong. From there we went on to the city of Bouna, and stopped there for a long time, reckoning that country as our own. We found protection[29]* in that country [B: having much property therein]. Two years after our arrival in Bouna, it entered into my teacher's heart to set out on the pilgrimage; and while he was making diligent inquiries from people who performed the pilgrimage, some men told him of the business of Muḥammad Keshīn [of Katsina?] and his brother 'Umar, and Adama, of the land of Bonduku.[30] He then began to make inquiries of the people of Bonduku, and they told him that 'Umar and Muḥammad Keshīn had already gone, and had left Adama behind; that he was not now going but wished to go. My master made haste to seek for him in some of the towns, and left me in the city of Bouna with my uncle Mahmūd.

At this time we heard the news of the business of Adinkra, Sultan

27. The capital of Bornu, at this time Birnin Gazargamo.

28*. *Ghilmān* means "young men," but it also means "slave"; however, Abū Bakr seems to have used it in the sense here given.

29*. *Sultānān* may mean "a Sultan"; but the power of living securely is probably what is here meant.

30. Capital of Gyaman, about 80 miles south of Bouna. Like Kong and Bouna, Bonduku was largely a Dyula town.

of Bonduku,[31] after the Sultan of Banda or Nkoranza, who was named Fua,[32] had been killed. [B: In the meantime we heard that Adinkra, king of Bonduku, having slain Fua, the king of Banda, in battle, also wanted to kill Kwadwo, the captain of an adjoining district.] They say Adinkra wished to kill Kwadwo, governor of Kolongzhwi, a town belonging to the Sultan of Bouna.[33] He wished to kill him because of what happened between him and Dikki, his deputy. Adinkra therefore wished to put the latter to death by way of retaliation. Adinkra, Sultan of Bonduku, sent to Kwadwo, requiring him to pay a great deal of gold as a ransom for his life, and Kwadwo sent what he required. But he refused to accept it, and said to Kwadwo's messenger: Return to your master, and say to him, "Unless you increase it by 200 times as much, I will not accept it [B: if he does not send two hundred pieces of gold, I will not be satisfied]; but my sword shall take his head from off his neck. You shall die a swift death." When the messenger returned to his master, and told him these words, Kwadwo stretched out his hand, took back the gold, and kept it; and likewise sent a messenger to the Sultan of Bouna to tell him what had happened.

When Adinkra came to hear of Kwadwo sending to inform the king of Bouna of his doings, he became very wroth, and he ordered all his captains to gather all their soldiers together, and follow him to make war against Kwadwo and to kill him, that they might avenge the death of his servant Dikki. When the Sultan of Bouna heard that Adinkra, Sultan of Bonduku, and his army had come against them to kill them, he and all his host, together with Kwadwo, rose up to meet them, and marched against them as far as the town of Bole,[34] choosing to attack them there. They fought from the middle of the day until night. Then they went to their different

31. Adinkra, the non-Muslim *gyamanhene,* came to the throne about 1800, at which time he was considered to be a tool of the Ashanti government (G. A. Robertson, *Notes on Africa* [London, 1819], p. 177). He assisted Ashanti in suppressing the revolts in the northwestern, Muslim-dominated provinces following the destoolment of -the *asantehene,* Osei Kwame, whose proclivity for Islam was well known. The campaign against Bouna, which Abū Bakr describes here, occurred in the context of these anti-Muslim moves by Ashanti (see Wilks, *Northern Factor in Ashanti History,* pp. 22–24).

32. The *nkoranzahene* Guakro Fua II. Banda and Nkoranza were neighboring provinces of Ashanti.

33. Kwadwo is a common Akan name often spelled Cudjoe in eighteenth-century English, but Kolongzhwi has not been identified.

34. In western Gonja, about 30 miles southeast of Bouna and 70 miles north-northeast of Bonduku.

camps. Seven days afterwards they again gathered themselves together, and engaged in battle at the town of Anwiego.[35] It was a hard-fought battle, and many lives were lost on both sides on that day. But Adinkra's army, being stronger than the king of Bouna's took possession of the town. The people of Bouna fled, and some of them passed on to the city of Kong.

On that very day they made me a captive. They tore off my clothes, bound me with ropes, gave me a heavy load to carry, and led me to the town of Bonduku, and from there to the town of Kumasi, where the king of Ashanti reigned, whose name is Osei.[36] From there through Akisuma and Ajumako, in the land of the Fanti, to the town of Lago, near the salt sea (all the way on foot, and well loaded).[37]

There they sold me to the Christians, and I was bought by a certain captain of a ship at that time. He sent me to a boat, and delivered me over to one of his sailors. The boat immediately pushed off, and I was carried on board of the ship. We continued on board ship, at sea, for three months, and then came on shore in the land of Jamaica. This was the beginning of my slavery until this day. I tasted the bitterness of slavery from them, and its oppressiveness. But praise be to God, under whose power are all things. He does whatsoever He wills! No one can turn aside that which He has ordained, nor can anyone withhold that which He has given. As God Almighty himself has said: Nothing can befall us unless it be written for us (in his book)! He is our master: in God, therefore, let all the faithful put their trust!

The faith of our families is the faith of Islam. They circumcise the foreskin;[38] say the five prayers; fast every year in the month of Ramadan; give alms as ordained in the law; marry four free women—a fifth is forbidden to them except she be their slave; they fight for the faith of God; perform the pilgrimage to Mecca, i.e. such as are able to do;[39] eat the flesh of no beast but what they have slain for them-

35. About six miles south of Bouna.

36. Osei Tutu Kwame, later known as Osei Bonsu, reigned *ca.* 1801–24. Abū Bakr gave Renouard the additional route information shown in Appendix 3.

37. Abū Bakr's supplementary route information is shown in Appendix 4.

38. The emphasis placed by Abū Bakr on circumcision—which is not enjoined by the Koran—presumably reflects the popularity in West Africa of the *Risāla* of Ibn Abī Zayd, in which it is regarded as commanded (*wājib*).

39. Prayer, fasting for Ramadan, giving of alms, and the pilgrimage to Mecca are, to-

selves; drink no wine, for whatever intoxicates is forbidden to them; they do not keep company with those whose faith is contrary to theirs, such as worshippers of idols, men who swear falsely by the name of the Lord, who dishonour their parents, commit murder or robbery, bear false witness, are covetous, proud, insolent, hypocrites, unclean in their discourse, or do any other thing that is forbidden: they teach their children to read, and instruct them in the different parts of knowledge; their minds are perfect and blameless according to the measure of their faith. Verily I have erred and done wickedly, but I entreat God to guide my heart in the right path, for He knoweth what is in my heart, and whatever can be pleaded in my behalf.

Abū Bakr al-Ṣiddīq

ABŪ BAKR IN JAMAICA

Very little is known about the African Muslim communities created in the New World as a result of the slave trade. Two fragments of Arabic correspondence, translated and published by R. R. Madden, are therefore of particular interest. One wonders, for example, to what extent the Jamaica Muslims were able to keep informed of events in West Africa—presumably not a simple matter after the abolition of the slave trade by Britain in 1807. Had Abū Bakr al-Siddīq any knowledge of the great changes that were occurring in the Western Sudan during the period of his exile from about 1804 to about 1840?—of 'Uthmān dan Fodio's call for jihad in 1804, of *Shehu* Ahmadu's call in 1818, and of the extension of his power to Timbuktu in 1826–27, or of *al-Hajj* 'Umar al-Futi's claims to be a *khalifa* of the Tijaniyya upon his return from Mecca in the 1830's?

Certainly some communication between the Muslims in Jamaica and their homeland existed: B. Angell gave Madden an interesting account of a *wathīqa* —a "pastoral" letter—which circulated in Jamaica and came into the hand of Muḥammad Kaba, a slave in Manchester Parish: "About three years ago [1831], he received from Kingston, by the hands of a boy, a paper written in Africa forty-five years previously. He knew it to be of this date, as the paper purported to have been written in the forty-third year of the age of the King, Allaman Talco,[40] who was thirty-five years old when he (Robert Peart) left the

gether with the profession of faith, the five pillars of Islam. The other injunctions, however, are also Koranic, and the communal obligation of holy war (jihad) was greatly stressed in the Western Sudan in the late eighteenth and early nineteenth centuries.

40. Dating by reference to the ruler's age would be most unlikely. There may be a

country. The paper exhorted all the followers of Mahomet to be true and faith-ful, if they wished to go to Heaven, etc."[41] The *wathīqa* was destroyed by Muḥammad Kaba's wife at the time of the slave rebellion of January 1832, because of its dangerous nature.

Muḥammad Kaba was enabled to correspond with Abū Bakr in 1834 by the passage of the Emancipation Act, in 1833, giving all the slaves in Jamaica the status of "apprentices" and bringing a corps of Special Magistrates from Britain to supervise their transition to freedom. These Special Magistrates, like William Oldrey and R. R. Madden, opened communication between men who had left Africa many decades before—some fifty-six years in the case of Muḥammad Kaba, and almost thirty years for Abū Bakr himself. Muḥammad Kaba (alias Robert Peart, alias Robert Tuffit) was born, of Mandingo parentage, in Bouka, a short distance east of Timbo in Futa Jallon, about 1758. His father, 'Abd al-Qādir, is described as "a substantial yeoman, possessing 140 slaves, several cows and horses, and grounds producing quantities of cotton, rice, and provisions, which he exchanged for European and other commodities brought from the coast by the Higglers."[42] The family was Muslim, and Muḥammad Kaba was educated by his father and by his uncle, Muḥammad Batūl, "a great lawyer." About 1778, shortly after Ibrāhīm Sōri had become head of the new imamate of Futa Jallon centered on Timbo, Muḥammad Kaba fell into the hands of robbers and was carried off to the coast and sold.

The two letters that follow are reprinted from R. R. Madden, *Twelve Months Residence in the West Indies* (2 vols., London, 1837), 2:199–201, without alteration other than corrected spelling of place names.

Muḥammad Kaba to Abū Bakr al-Ṣiddīq

In the name of God, Merciful omnificent, the blessing of God, the peace of his prophet Mahomet.

This is from the hand of Mahomed Caba, unto Bekir Sadiki Scheriffe. If this comes into your hands sooner or later, send me a satisfactory answer for yourself this time by your real name, don't you see I give you my name, Robert Tuffit, and the property is named Spice Grove. I am glad to hear you are master of yourself, it is a heartfelt joy to me, for Many told me about your character. I thank you to give me a good answer, "Salaam aleikoum." Edward Doulan,

---

misunderstanding of a phrase such as "in the 43rd year [after the year 1200 of the hegira]," which would be A.D. 1827/28. *Almami* Talko has not been identified, though he was apparently a figure in Muḥammad Kaba's home country of Futa Jallon.

41. B. Angell to R. R. Madden, 7 October 1834, in Madden, *West Indies*, 2:198.
42. Madden, *West Indies*, 2:196–98.

A Kong Muslim of the early nineteenth century. From J. Dupuis, *Journal of a Residence in Ashantee.*

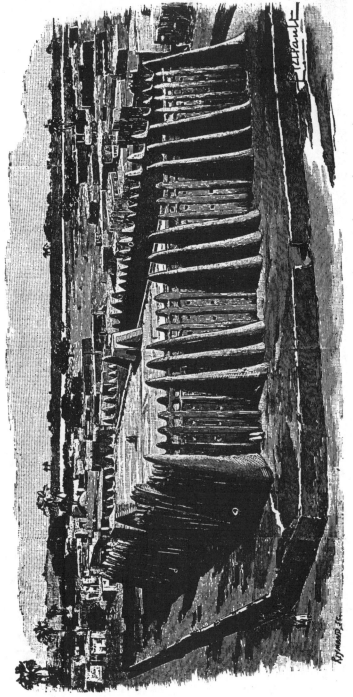

Jenne Mosque before its destruction by *Shaykh* Ḥamad, *ca.* 1830. From F. Dubois, *Timbuctoo the Mysterious.*

I hear of your name in the paper: the reader told me how so much you write.

Robert Tuffit

Manchester parish
(God bless you, give me an answer by Dr. Madden, King's Magistrate, Kingston.)

Abū Bakr al-Ṣiddīq to Muḥammad Kaba

Kingston, Jamaica, October 18, 1834

Dear Countryman,

I now answer your last letter, my name, in Arabic, is Abon Becr Sadiki, and in Christian language, Edward Doulan, I born in Timbuktu, and brought up in Jenne; I finished read the Coran in the country of Bouna, which place I was taken captive in war. My master's name in this country is Alexander Anderson. Now my countryman, God hath given me a faithful man, a just and a good master, he made me free; and I know truly that he has shown mercy to every poor soul under him. I know he has done that justice which our King William the Fourth commanded him to do (God save the king) and may he be a conqueror over all his enemies, from east to west, from north to south, and the blessing of God extend over all his kingdom, and all his ministers and subjects. I beseech you, Mahomed Caba, and all my friends, continue in praying for my friend, my life, and my breadfruit, which friend is my worthy Dr. Madden, and I hope that God may give him honour, greatness, and gladness, and likewise his generation to come, as long as Heaven and Earth stands. Now my countryman, these prayers that I request of you is greater to me than any thing else I can wish of you; and also you must pray that God may give him strength and power to overcome all his enemies, and that the King's orders to him be held in his right hand firmly. The honour I have in my heart for him is great; but God knows the secrets of all hearts. Dear countryman, I also beseech you to remember in your prayers my master Alexander Anderson, who gave me my liberty free and willingly; and may the Almighty prosper him, and protect him from all dangers.

Whenever you wish to send me a letter, write it in Arabic language; then I will understand it properly.

I am, dear Sir,

Your obedient servant,

Edward Doulan

APPENDIX I:
ROUTE FROM JENNE TO KONG TO BOUNA

[The spelling is modernized except for unidentified towns, which are marked with asterisks.]

Jenne

The country of the Soninke [to the south of Jenne]: Muslims and Kafirs

Simfuya, also called Bā Kwē*: Muslims

Kewei, a city belonging to Korongō: Muslims and Kafirs

Mossi [an ethnic group]: Muslims and Kafirs

Dafing or *Marka* [an ethnic subgroup of Soninke]: Muslims and Kafirs in equal numbers

*Ba lōk**: the same

Kong

The exact route is not clear, but it would be an easterly one, along the edge of the Mossi country and through the Dafing-Marka around Safane. It took Abu Bakr two months for this journey, but he thought it could be done in fifteen days. His route then continued eastward to Bouna, an eight-day journey:

Kong

Kongolu [about 10 miles east of Kong. Abū Bakr reported that the king's name was Makka, a common personal name among the Mande-speaking Watara, who provided the rulers of Kong. For modern Kongolu, see Bernus, "Kong et sa région."]

Kaware [near Kolon, about 20 miles southeast of Kongolu]

Koniéné [about four miles east of Kolon]

Sambata [Abū Bakr reported that "as far as Sambata the ground is level and clear with occasional patches of wood. Near that place, after crossing a hill (the Gorohoui Kongoli range), the road leads down to the river (the Komoe), which divides Balobolo from Donsadugu."]

Balobolo [The village has disappeared, but the name is remembered as that of a place near the crossing of the Komoe.]

Donsadugu, the first place in the kingdom of Bouna.

*Kungzhīyah**

Yalo [about 14 miles west of Bouna]

*Purrā**

Bouna

Abū Bakr noted that the people of the towns were Muslim, but subject to polytheists. The numerically dominant elements in the region would be Senufo west of the Komoe River and Kulango to the east of it.

APPENDIX II:
ROUTE FROM BOUNA TO DABOYA TO HAUSA

Bouna

Cross the *Black Volta* at *Vonkoro* [the border between Bouna and western Gonja]

Bole, a country or province [most westerly of the nine divisional chiefdoms of Gonja]

Yagbum or *Nyanga* [about 25 miles north-northeast of Bole, and until this century the seat of the ruler of Gonja]

Daboya [on the White Volta about 70 miles east-northeast of Nyanga. It is one of the nine divisional chiefdoms of Gonja and is important, as Abū Bakr reported, for its salt industry. The Bouna-Daboya journey was eight days, according to Abū Bakr.]

On Gonja generally, Abū Bakr reported that the people were half Muslim and half polytheists, that they called themselves *Ngbanya* [sing., *ka-gbanya*], and that others called them *Inta*. In fact, they are called *Nta* by the Akan to the south, and the more familiar term, *Gonja,* is the Hausa rendering of *Ngbanya*.

Gambaga [about 90 miles northeast of Daboya]: inhabitants called Dagomba [which is incorrect, since Gambaga was actually the capital of the sister state of Mamprussi]

Salaga: inhabitants Gonja [about 90 miles southeast of Daboya, an extremely important center for the kola trade, and the market for Kpembe, one of the nine divisions of Gonja]

Cross a river

Boghyori, Boghayiri, Poghoyiri, or *Boghodi* [not identified, though the name is either Dagamba or Mamprussi in form]

Sansanné-Mango [an important trading center about 60 miles east of Gambaga]

Fada-N'Gurma [about 140 miles northeast of Gambaga]

This route actually represents two alternative routes from Daboya to Hausa—one through Salaga and one through Gambaga. Numerous route-books in Arabic circulated in Gonja and neighboring areas at this time, and Abū Bakr's routes may be compared with those published, for example, by Dupuis, *Residence in Ashantee*, pp. cxxiv–cxxxv.

APPENDIX III:
ROUTE FROM BOUNA TO KUMASI (11–12 DAYS)

Bouna
Anwiego [in Bouna], one-half day
Bonduku, four days
Kyekyewere [in Bonduku, not located], one day
Nyami [a small village in Ashanti, west of the road from Bonduku via Sampa to Berekum, about 30 miles south of Bonduku], one day
Ansiri, near a lake [There is actually no lake on this route; possibly the River Offin is meant.], two days
Kumasi, capital of Ashanti, one day

Since the total journey from Bouna to Kumasi is more than 200 miles, the captives must have travelled about 20 miles each day. The section Bonduku-to-Kumasi is the same as that given by T. E. Bowdich, in *A Mission from Cape Coast to Ashantee* (London, 1819), pp. 169, 482; but Bowdich thought this section alone would take eleven days.

APPENDIX IV:
ROUTE FROM KUMASI TO THE SEA (2–3 DAYS)

Kumasi
Lake of Bosum Pra [actually a river, whose crossing at Praso lay some 55 miles south of Kumasi]
Wassaw [actually an ethnic group much farther west], one and one-half days
Asikuma [a Fanti town, about 35 miles southeast of Praso]
Ajamako [12 miles farther south]
Lago, a little below Accra [actually some 45 miles west of Accra], one night

Abū Bakr's recollection of this part of the journey is obviously defective. The total distance is almost 120 miles as the crow flies, and because of the dense forest it was generally considered impossible to average even 10 miles a day.

CHAPTER 6

WARGEE OF ASTRAKHAN

Ivor Wilks

In May 1822, there were persistent rumors in Cape Coast, where the English had their headquarters on the Gold Coast, of the presence of Europeans in Kumasi, capital of Ashanti. On 1 June 1822, an elderly white man arrived in Cape Coast, with an escort provided by the king of Ashanti, Osei Bonsu. Finding that the stranger spoke no European language known to them, the English authorities in the Castle finally established a measure of communication through the medium of a Hausa-speaking boy there: the stranger speaking in Hausa, the boy translating into Fanti, and one of the Castle interpreters, into English. Since the stranger's Hausa, the boy's Fanti, and the interpreter's English were all somewhat inadequate, it is remarkable that considerable information was elicited from the traveller.[1]

The name of the stranger was transliterated as Wargee. He was born at Kisliar, then in the province of Astrakhan, on the west shore of the Caspian Sea. He was a Tatar, and therefore probably Muslim.[2]

---

1. *The Royal Gold Coast Gazette,* which first printed this account, described the text as "by favour of Capt. J. Thursfield Pierce of the Cape Coast Militia." Somewhat later, however, A. Gordon Laing, the first nineteenth-century European to reach Timbuktu, identified the English amanuensis as a Mr. Williams. (See E. W. Bovill [ed.], *Missions to the Niger* [Cambridge, 1964], 1:371.) Did Williams report an interview that Pierce conducted?

2. Williams observed that Wargee was "no Mussulman himself." This seems unlikely for many reasons—Wargee's Tatar origins, his visit to Mecca (made, moreover, at the time of the pilgrimage), his release from slavery in Istanbul, and his subsequent residence there.

He appears to have been about fifteen years of age at the time of the Turko-Russian war of 1787–92 when, accompanying his brother to the front, he fell into the hands of the Turks and became a slave of Saladar, "a person of high authority," before procuring his freedom. He then set himself up as a trader in Istanbul. In 1822, he described some of his early voyages: one notable journey took him by camel caravan from Istanbul to Smyrna, Damascus, Mosul, and Baghdad; by boat down the Tigris and Euphrates rivers to Basra at the head of the Persian Gulf; by Muscat ship to Muscat itself, in the Oman, and across the Indian Ocean to Surat, Bombay, Malabar, Madras, and Calcutta, and thence to Java. In India he traded his merchandise, sheet copper, against silks and muslins. On his return, he resided for some time at Mocha in the Yemen, and from there visited Mecca, finally arriving back in Istanbul after an absence of two years. On a second and more modest expedition he sailed to Malta, Tripoli, Tunis, and Gibraltar, and it was perhaps at this time that the idea of crossing the Sahara began to take shape in his mind. His African journey, commenced apparently in 1817, led him across the continent from the Mediterranean to the Gulf of Guinea, through towns then the object of absorbing interest in Europe—Kano, Jenne, Kong, and Timbuktu. As Williams, his first editor, mildly remarked, "the circumstance could not fail to excite a considerable degree of curiosity."

Wargee began this journey by sailing to Tripoli, where he remained for some time before joining a camel caravan for the south. His account of crossing the Sahara, through Murzuk in the Fezzan and Agades in Asben to the Hausa town of Katsina, is brief. He followed a well-known route, much the same as that taken by Barth thirty years later and fully described by him.[3] Wargee is similarly uninformative about his stay in Katsina and subsequently in Kano, then two of the leading emirates in the Fulbe caliphate of Sokoto. Nor, unfortunately, does he report in any detail his journey from Kano south to more outlying parts of the caliphate—to Raba, the capital of Nupe, and to the Yoruba town of Ilorin, then probably already dominated by Mallam Alimi. Ali Eisami and Samuel Crowther (see Chaps. 7 and 9) were able to report on events in Oyo in greater detail. Ali Eisami had, indeed, crossed Hausa as a slave within a dec-

3. H. Barth, *Travels and Discoveries in North and Central Africa* (3 vols., New York, 1859); see 1:150–488 for the route from Murzuk to Katsina, traversed in 1850, and 3:626–30 for the route from Murzuk to Tripoli via Sokna in 1855.

Map 8. Wargee's route across Africa.

ade before Wargee's journey, but he was sold from Old Oyo to the coast about the time Wargee set out from Tripoli. Wargee probably made his journey as far as Ilorin with authorization from Sokoto, and was thus unable to proceed across the military frontier into Yoruba-held territory and on to the coast in the vicinity of Lagos. As Clapperton found four years later, the Fulbe authorities exercised strict control over the movement of visitors into the southern domains.[4]

Returning from Ilorin to Kano, Wargee left again on the western route to Timbuktu. This was probably towards the end of 1820. The main line of his journey seems reasonably clear: from Kano he travelled through Zamfara territory to the Gaya crossing of the Niger, and from there through Fada N'Gurma and Hombori to Kabara and Timbuktu, where he arrived in March or April, 1821. In the Gaya area he appears to have made several shorter journeys. In particular, he visited Yawuri or Yauri, about a hundred miles down the Niger. In Birnin Yawuri he met two white men who have not been identified—though, as shown by the case of Wargee himself, there may have been numbers of strangers in the Western Sudan at this time who, unsponsored by governmental or other institutions, have remained unknown.

He then moved on to Timbuktu, which in 1821 was experiencing a period of brief and uneasy independence. The Bambara kings of Segu, who had intermittently asserted their suzerainty over Timbuktu in the eighteenth century, were preoccupied with the revolt of the Fulbe of Massina under *Shehu* Ahmadu, whose power was to be extended over Timbuktu itself only five years later. The Tuareg, who also were accustomed to taking control of the town from time to time, appear to have been quiescent. Timbuktu was governed by *Sultan* Muḥammad[5] and his *wazīr*—both, we may assume, members of the *arma,* the Songhai nobility who claimed descent from the Moroccans who had settled there after al-Mansur's invasion of 1591. Wargee's description of Timbuktu is perhaps the most valuable part of his narrative: it is detailed and, insofar as this can be independently checked, accurate. Earlier accounts of Timbuktu exist, by such

4. D. Denham and H. Clapperton, *Narrative of Travels and Discoveries in Northern Central Africa* (London, 1826), esp. Clapperton's narrative, pp. 88–89.

5. I know of no independent source for dating *Sultan* Muḥammad, who Wargee suggests succeeded *Sultan* Abū Bakr in about 1814. For a modern study of Timbuktu, see H. Miner, *The Primitive City of Timbuctoo* (Princeton, 1953).

North African travellers as Leo Africanus and *al-Ḥājj* 'Abd al-Salam Shabīnī, and by such Western Sudanese writers as Mahmūd Kati and al-Sa'di, but Wargee's account is the earliest we have by a non-African: he preceded Laing to Timbuktu by five years, and Caillié by seven.

From Timbuktu, Wargee travelled by boat through the middle Niger delta to Jenne: the vessel was carrying a cargo of salt from the Taodeni mines in the central Sahara. Of Jenne, unfortunately, Wargee says little, though he stayed there long enough to take a wife. From Jenne he followed one of the major routes to the south, through the Dyula trading towns of Bobo-Dioulasso, Kong, and Bouna. At Kong he remained for some seven weeks, and he gives a short description of that center, the earliest we have. From Bouna he entered Ashanti territory through Banda, where he was detained by officials of the Ashanti king, members of the *nkwansrafo,* or road-wardens, described more fully by Bonnat later in the century:

> The great roads which lead there [to Kumasi] are guarded by the *Nquam-Sarafa* or guardians, who question the stranger when he presents himself, and send one of their number to inform the king of the stranger's arrival and of the purpose of his journey. Meanwhile another guardian leads the traveller to the nearest village, where he awaits the royal authorization to continue his journey to the capital.[6]

Wargee was in fact taken a considerable way from Banda, through Daboya to the great Ashanti-dominated kola market of Salaga in eastern Gonja, where he remained for over three months before obtaining permission to proceed to Kumasi. He spent almost a month in the Ashanti capital, where the king, Osei Bonsu, well known for his courtesy towards strangers, treated him hospitably and finally provided him with an official escort to Cape Coast.

Since his departure from Tripoli some five years earlier, Wargee had travelled five thousand miles or more on his circuitous route to Cape Coast. While it was not unknown for North African merchants to find their way to the Guinea Coast or into its immediate hinterland at this time and even earlier (such as the Fezzan trader Sharīf

6. J. Gros, *Voyages, aventures et captivité de J. Bonnat chez les Achantis* (Paris, 1884), p. 178.

Imhammad in the late eighteenth century),[7] the English in Cape Coast were understandably surprised at the arrival from the interior of a Tatar—and especially one "clothed in an old uniform of the African Company," though presumably this had been given him by the Ashanti king.

Interest in the exploration of the Niger was great in Britain at this period: 1821 was, for example, the year of the government's decision to sponsor the Denham, Clapperton, and Oudney expedition. It seems most unlikely that the English authorities in Cape Coast would have failed to arrange for Wargee's passage to England, where his knowledge of the interior of West Africa would have been at a premium. Nevertheless, no report of Wargee's career after leaving Cape Coast—if indeed he did—has yet come to light.

THE AFRICAN TRAVELS OF WARGEE

The text that follows was taken down through double translation from Hausa (which Wargee had only begun to learn in his old age), to Fanti, to English. It is therefore necessarily corrupt in certain respects, but the parts that can be checked are remarkably accurate, and Mr. Williams, the English reporter of the narrative, was careful of detail—largely because of the contemporary fascination with the problem of the Niger and the nature of the African interior. The report was first printed in the *Royal Gold Coast Gazette* for 31 December 1822 and 7 January 1823.[8] The present version is a complete reprinting of the African portions of the original, without omissions from the text itself, though some footnotes have been left out. Interpolations within parentheses are in the original. Original footnotes are marked with an asterisk. Spellings of identifiable place names and other proper nouns have been modernized; unidentified names are placed within quotation marks.[9]

He describes the commencement of his last or present journey to have taken place about five years ago. He sailed from Istanbul in a

7. J. Dupuis, *Journal of a Residence in Ashantee* (London, 1824), pp. xiv–xv; *Proceedings of the Association for Promoting the Discovery of the Interior Parts of Africa* (London, 1791), pp. 263–64.

8. It was reprinted in the *Royal Gazette and Sierra Leone Advertiser* (Freetown), 8 and 15 March 1823, and in *The Asiatic Journal*, 16:16–23 (London, 1823), and later in Charles Hulbert, *African Fragments* (London, 1826), pp. 33–49. A French translation appeared in *Journal des voyages*, 20:121–44 (November 1823).

9. The editor wishes to acknowledge the assistance of Mr. Gerald Hartwig of the University of Indiana in the preparation of this edition.

Turkish vessel, commanded by an Armenian named Abdu, and navigated by twelve men, to Alexandria, and thence to Tripoli; he paid the master of the vessel the value of forty-four dollars[10] for his passage. His merchandize consisted of iron, jewellery, silks, and some spirits, to the value of 1,500 dollars. At Tripoli he remained a considerable time: he then proceeded towards Murzuk, in company with a caravan of forty-five camels. He had three camels and two servants, his slaves; one of the camels carried water, another provisions, and the third merchandize. In thirty-five days they arrived at Sokna; eight days from Sokna to Murzuk.[11] At Murzuk he sojourned two months, and again advanced by Ghat, to Assode,[12] and thence to Agades, one day's journey from which they crossed a river of great breadth.[13]* It being then the dry season, it was shallow; still it was as much as the camels could do to cross it, the water being up to their shoulders: in the rains it is impassable, except by boats. Agades is in Tuareg,[14] through which country this river winds. One day's journey from Agades is Katsina.[15] The caravan was sixty days in travelling from Murzuk to Katsina. At "Galibaba,"[16] in Katsina, he was robbed of much of his property.

From Katsina he advanced to Kano [95 miles], in five days. Close to Kano is a large water, whether a river or lake could not be clearly understood, called the river "Goorbie Mak Hadgee,"[17] which he described as being about a hundred and fifty yards broad, but narrow during the dry season; because in the rains there is communication

10. Probably the Austrian "Maria Theresa" dollars, still in circulation in some parts of the Western Sudan, though they have been minted in many other places since their eighteenth-century origin. Their early nineteenth-century value was about five English shillings.

11. Sokna is about 300 miles south-southeast of Tripoli; and Murzuk, one of the principal towns of the Fezzan, is 230 miles farther.

12. Ghat (Chanab or Ganat in the text) is an important trade center, some 230 miles from Murzuk. About 450 miles farther on is Assode in the Asben massif, another trade center visited by Barth (*Travels*, 1:303).

13*. As broad as from the castle-gate [of Cape Coast] to the female school, being about four hundred yards.

14. Agades, another 100 miles beyond Assode, is itself a Songhai town, though the surrounding region was dominated by the Tuareg.

15. Actually, about 280 miles south of Agades—more than one day's march.

16. Probably Garun Babba, a common place-name in the region.

17. Possibly the Gulbin Magaga, one of the upper tributaries of the Chalawa River, but very much smaller than the stream Wargee describes.

between the Niger, which will be again spoken of, and the "Goorbie Mak Hadgee." On it are numerous boats (canoes); in one of which, paddled by four men, he was conveyed over. His camels were tied by the neck to the canoe, and swam over.

The houses of Kano are circular, and built of mud. It is subject to the Sultan of Hausa, who is a Muslim: his name is Bello, that of his capital Sokoto.[18] In the neighbourhood of Kano, territory of Nupe,[19] he remained a considerable time, and appears to have travelled from that point in several directions; for instance, from Kano to Zaria in five days, "Malica" three, Farin Dutse two, "Rollah" two, Domah three, "Hanafa" six, Galadima five; from Galadima to Tudun, "Abazee" and "Koorkoonon" two, Bokani and Raba one, Jebba one, Ilorin five—total, thirty-five days.[20]

Several of the principal towns on this part appear to have ditches around them for their defence; and the approach to them, from what could be understood of his description of Raba, must be extremely rude. He drew circles and lines to represent the ditch and entrance across it by a board. This his camels could not pass, he was therefore obliged to leave them behind, and the weather being wet and bad, they soon died.[21]

Having again returned to Kano, he undertook another journey from Kano to Terna three days, "Galata" two, Zamfara two, Banaga five, "Doweassim" seven, Yawuri six—twenty-five days.[22]

At Yawuri he sojourned for some time, and travelled thence to Zugu, and again from Yawuri to Gaya in three days, Foga one, Kir-

18. Muḥammad Bello (d. 1837), who succeeded his father 'Uthmān (Hausa: Usuman) dan Fodio (d. 1817) as amīr al-muʾminīn, with his capital at Sokoto.

19. A confusion of the text, since Nupe lies some 230 miles to the southwest.

20. Some of these place-names cannot now be identified. Others, like Farin Dutse (Falandoosa in the original), are too common to be located with certainty; but this Farin Dutse may be the one in eastern Kano near Argungu. The Domah mentioned here may also be the one in eastern Kano. Galadima is another common name, this one probably being Anguwan Galadima, just to the south of Kaduna and about eight miles from Tudun (Tootoo in the original).

21. Camels are rarely used today south of Kano, on account of the disease problems of the relatively humid savanna, including tse-tse. To take camels as far south as Raba, as the text seems to imply, would have been foolhardy.

22. A swing through western Hausa. There is a Terna to the northwest, near Maradi. Zamfara was capital of a Fulbe emirate, and Banaga was in south Zamfara. Yawuri (Laooree in the original) must remain a tentative identification, but it is suggested both by the direction of travel and its importance at this period.

mam one, Kamba one: at Kamba he crossed the Niger, a large river, much larger than the "Goorbie Mak Hadgee."[23] He was about one hour in crossing it in a boat (canoe), paddled by sixteen men. When questioned as to the course of this river, he asserted that the current ran from the direction of the rising sun towards its setting.[24] Having crossed the Niger, he arrived, after a ten days' journey, at Fada N'Gurma and in ten days more at Mossi.[25] Proceeding onwards, he arrived in ten days more at Hombori.[26]* Between Hombori and Mossi, he crossed no water. From Hombori he travelled onwards five days, and then reached another larger river, called the Niger,[27] over which he was ferried in a boat (canoe), managed by ten men. The passage occupied half an hour. After a walk of about three hours, he arrived at Kabara, a town on the banks of a small river called "Mazzr," and in three hours more, from Kabara he reached Timbuktu.[28]*

23. Gaya is actually on the Niger, while Kamba (Cumba in the original) is ten miles away. Zugu (Zoogoh in the original) might possibly be Zougou, some hundred miles to the southwest in present-day Dahomey, but it is more likely another Zugu, in Nigeria, a hundred miles east of Kamba in the direction of Kano. Foga (Fogan in the text) is also a puzzle. The Dallol Foga joins the Niger eighteen miles below Gaya, after having passed Kamba on its left bank. Still another and less likely Foga is an island in the Niger just above Bussa.

24. In fact, the Niger at this point flows toward the southeast, but there was a persistent North African belief over centuries that the Niger flowed to the west (see Chap. 1, n. 31). To the extent that Wargee is correctly reported, he was probably echoing this theory.

25. Fada N'Gurma was then capital of one of the Mossi states. The Mossi (Moosh in the original text) to which Wargee refers may well have been Wagadugu, the capital of another Mossi state, since it would lie on a possible route to Hombori, his next stop.

26*. In endeavouring to trace the course he took in the several excursions from Kano and to this place; his invariable reply was, that the rising sun was at his back, varying a little to the right or left.

27. In this instance he calls the Niger the "Barneel" (Baḥr al-Nīl being the usual Arabic name for the Niger), while earlier he referred to it as the "Quolla."

28*. Wargee says, it is three hours' walk from Timbuktu to Kabara (on the "Mazzr," a branch of the "Bar-Neel" or Niger, but not navigable), and three hours more from Kabara to the junction of the "Mazzr" with the main stream of the Niger. That Wargee's information on this point is correct there can be no doubt, for he illustrated it by a rude sketch. [Timbuktu is, in fact, about five miles north of its port, Kabara, which lies on a partly artificial branch of the Niger, running north from the main channel. The river must have been exceptionally low when Wargee was there, at the end of the dry season of 1821, since traffic is seldom unable to reach Kabara even at this least favorable time.]

The island formed by the "Mazzr" (the "Jinbelah" of the maps), Wargee calls Kabara. He states its breadth to be about three hours' walk, and its length about two days' journey; he saw numbers of asses and cattle grazing on it.

[The following paragraph appeared as an endnote to the original text.]

He neither heard of any white man having been at Timbuktu, nor of any having been seen on the Niger: but he asserts that about three years ago, when he was upon one of his excursions from the vicinity of Kano, he arrived at a place called Birnin Yawuri, on the banks of the Niger; he saw a crowd collected, and inquired what was the cause; he was told that two white men had been brought there who had been cast away. The river being very rapid as well as rocky in this place, the boats struck on one of the rocks; some of the natives seeing this, swam off to plunder, but the head man of the place sent some people to their assistance, and got their things restored. The whole of the people were kind to them, particularly the head man, in whose house they lodged, and who gave them fowls, etc. and a girl to wait on them. He was in the room in which they were, but could not talk to them; saw no books or papers. Whilst he was there a large hair trunk was brought in; it was carried on a pole on the shoulders of two men; saw also a large bundle, which he thinks contained bedding. The two men were quite white; one appeared about thirty years of age, the other a few years older; they wore green coats and woollen caps striped blue and white; they also wore gaiters, which he described by wrapping the skirt of his coat round his leg, and pointing to buttons; and had dirks or daggers (several were shown to him, but the one he fixed upon as being similar is a short dirk about fourteen inches, with no guard; what they were, he said, were like that, but with guards about four inches, which he showed by placing his fingers across the dirk) with body belts. He only remained at Birnin Yawuri two days, then crossed the river and proceeded to Yawuri, which is only half a day's walk from its banks: never heard anything of them after that time, neither did he learn from whence they came. He did not again visit Birnin Yawuri, which is in the territory of "Ganaganah."[29]

29. The Gangawa, the people of riverain Yawuri. Wargee apparently distinguished between Yawuri (Laooree) and Birnin Yawuri (Lahoorpoor) by using the Persian suffix *pūr* in place of the Hausa *birnin* for city or capital. Wargee's Birnin Yawuri is probably Yelwa, the present capital on the banks of the Niger. His Yawuri may well be the old capital, some seven miles back from the river; this distance being reasonably close to the half day's walk of Wargee's estimate.

The few following particulars respecting Timbuktu are the substance of replies to numerous questions, reiterated on several occasions, and thereby corrected, as far as the very limited and defective method of communication would admit.

Timbuktu he represents as a large town, much larger than Cape Coast, and much larger than Kumasi; the houses far better and more regular. It has one long street intersected by others, but not very regular. The houses are built of mud. The house in which he lodged belonged to the Sultan Muḥammad, who has seven houses, superior to those of his subjects; it was two stories high, and had several apartments on the ground floor, occupied by attendants; on the first floor were the apartments in which the Sultan entertained his friends, and in the upper story he and his wives lived. The house had a flat roof, surrounded, except in the front, by a wall enclosing a large yard, in which the camels and other cattle were kept, and situated in the center of the town. It was tolerably well plastered; had doors and windows of boards, and was whitewashed with lime brought from Jenne. Much trouble was taken to ascertain the truth of this fact. He clearly described a kind of oven (drawing a rude plan on paper) in which stones were heated, and imitated the hissing noise it made when water was thrown over it to slake it. To prove this the more strongly, he was shewn the lime kiln at Cape Coast Castle, and said it was something like that, but very small, and stones burnt in it, not shells. A basket was shewn to him which might contain about a bushel and a half, and he was asked what the price of the quantity of lime it would hold might be. The answer was, about the value of a dollar at Jenne, at Timbuktu perhaps four. He heard it used to be brought to Timbuktu as presents to the chief men, who made presents of cloth in return: it is only used by the superior people. He believes the roofs of the houses to be only covered with clay, but is ignorant whether anything is mixed with it to make a cement. The houses of the rich people are all built in the same style as that of the Sultan; and he mentioned that of *Kahia,* whom he called Muḥammad's *wazir,*[30] as almost equal to the Sultan's. The dwellings of the common people are small round huts, covered with thatch. The Sultan is fat, stout, and good looking, having a few grey hairs in his

30. *Kahia* is strictly speaking a military rank and the title of the administrative chief. It is still used by one of the most important *arma* families of Timbuktu (P. Marty, *Études sur l'Islam et les tribus du Soudan* [4 vols., Paris, 1920–21], 2:8).

The landing place at Kabara, the port of Timbuktu. From F. Dubois, *Timbuctoo the Mysterious.*

A street in Timbuktu, *ca.* 1895. From F. Dubois, *Timbuctoo the Mysterious.*

Agades, *ca.* 1850. From H. Barth, *Travels and Discoveries in North and Central Africa.*

Kano, *ca.* 1850. From H. Barth, *Travels and Discoveries in North and Central Africa.*

beard, and is a peaceable good man: he is a Muslim, and dresses handsomely in the Muslim style; [he] has seen him occasionally wear silks, but principally white cloth and muslins.

The king's wives wear a lower cloth fastened round them, and another thrown over their bodies; these are generally white, but the lower one sometimes blue; indeed, he says, coloured cloths are rarely to be seen; white and blue are the prevailing colours, varying in their quality according to the station in life of the wearer. On the head they (the king's wives) wore a kind of red cap, just covering the crown, which has some gold ornament, or gold lace on the top of it. They wear silver ornaments on the arms and ankles, and ear-rings of gold or silver. They also wear silver chains on their forehead, round the neck and round the waist; these chains are made at Sansanding, and silver is so much prized at Timbuktu that they balance them for gold. The Sultan had in his possession many muskets and blunderbusses, inlaid and ornamented with silver. He had also several soldiers. Muskets are also to be seen in the possession of many persons of note, but they are not common. The value of a very common musket is ten dollars,[31*] of a long gun sixteen dollars: the latter guns are used for killing elephants. He says that the hunters go on foot to search for the herds; watch for a fair aim, and if the shot does not take immediate effect, the hunter climbs a tree for safety, and watches the animal. They have often been tracked for days after they have been shot, before they die. Elephants are also killed with arrows, the length of which he described by stretching out his arms, then pointing from the shoulder to within about three inches of the wrist, and saying it was wood; and again to the end of his fingers, which part he said was iron. These arrows are rubbed over with a liquid poison. This, he says, he saw; but knows not of what it is composed: it is of a yellow colour, and of the consistency of palm-oil.

In the "Mazzr" small fish are taken, but there are no canoes on it. They are far more abundant in the Niger: many kinds are caught by the natives (who go on the river in small canoes) with lines and nets; some of them are very large. He said he had seen some as large as a boy about eight years old, whom he pointed out, but those were

31*. Dollars are mentioned, not as being current in Timbuktu, but because their value was understood by him. [This appears to be incorrect; the silver dollar was known in Timbuktu even earlier. See the trading account of al-Ḥājj Ḥamad al-Wangārī, in J. G. Jackson, *An Account of Timbuktu and Houssa* (London, 1820), pp. 347–48.]

not eaten. In the Niger are also some large animals, with heads as big as those of elephants, and having teeth, which were sold to the traders from Fez. These were killed with a kind of spear or harpoon, ten or twelve feet long. Some of the common people eat the flesh.[32]* They, as well as alligators, are numerous, both in the Quolla and Bar-Neel [i.e., in both cases, the Niger; see n..27].

About Timbùktu and Jenne, wild owls [guinea fowl?] are very plentiful, as are also poultry, particularly ducks; there are also great numbers of cattle, goats, sheep (very large), a few small horses, no camels, except what are brought by the traders; asses without number, and dogs. Of wild animals he mentioned the elephant, antelope, lynx, and fox; tame rabbits of different colours are kept in the house. The difficulty of acquiring this information, through an interpreter ignorant of the names, was obviated by a reference to the plates of a work on natural history.[33]

The food of the principal people consists of poultry, the flesh of cattle, goats and sheep, and of fish, which they have various modes of dressing, boiling, frying, etc.; he has seen some fish brought into the market for sale, fried. Much butter is made at Timbuktu and Jenne, from goat and cows' milk; this they use to dress their fish, etc. with, and eat it with their bread, but never use it to rub over their bodies.

They grind their corn on stones, and make a kind of bread of it; this the common people eat with goats' milk. There are some pits at Timbuktu from which the common people procure their water; but that which is used by the superior class is brought from the "Mazzr": this water, which he says is excellent, is carried in skins on asses, and it takes them about three hours to go there. Milk is also drunk, and, by those who can afford it, a kind of fermented beer called *giya*,[34] made of Indian corn; he is ignorant of the process of making it: being shewn some of the beer which is common on some parts of the Gold Coast, called Pitto, he said that it was like that, but not so good.

The rich people use spoons and forks; he has seen there some spoons made of gold, some of silver, and some of iron; they also use

32*. Hippopotami: he was much pleased at recognizing the tooth of one, which the writer happened to show him at the moment.

33. The difficulties were clearly not fully overcome!

34. The Hausa word for alcohol or beer.

plates. When questioned how they procure them, his reply was, that they were brought by the traders, and they got them from Gibraltar.[35] The common people use their fingers, and eat out of wooden bowls.

No cocoa-nuts at Timbuktu; neither did he see them in any part until he came to Cape Coast. No yams, no plantains; water melons in great plenty, and other fruit which could not be recognized by his description. No pineapples at Timbuktu, but saw some at Jenne; honey plentiful; and at Timbuktu they have a particular kind of bread, in which honey is mixed when they are making it. He describes the climate of Timbuktu as extremely hot. The rainy season he understood to be approaching at the time he was at Timbuktu, which he thinks was about thirteen months ago. The rains, he heard, continued about four months: during the first two they are very heavy, and after that, for the next two months, light. After the first two months the caravans come from the Desert, to the number of many hundred camels. About midway between Taodeni and Timbuktu, at a place called Arawan, they often separate, some going to Sandsanding and Segu, some to Timbuktu.[36]

The Timbuktu traders have a particular room or shop in their houses, in which their goods are packed up in boxes; they have also many pieces of cloth hung on a line exposed to view opposite the door, but those inside of the houses are for show. He understood it took the caravans of the Arab traders from Fez and Meknes three months to perform their journey to Timbuktu. The articles of trade which they bring are cotton cloths, clothing, silks, iron, beads, silver, tobacco in rolls, paper, earthenware, and tar; in exchange for which they get gold-dust, ivory, the teeth of the hippopotami, gum, and ostrich feathers;[37]* slaves also form a considerable portion of their re-

35. Barth later observed that "all cutlery in Timbuktu is of English workmanship" (*Travels,* 3:367)

36. The salt-mining center of Taodeni was 400 miles north of Timbuktu on the track through Taghaza to Akka in southern Morocco, where the Timbukti merchants had their agents (see Jackson, *An Account of Timbuktu and Houssa,* pp. 347–48). Arawan was about 150 miles north of Timbuktu on the same track, and it was, as Wargee notes, the junction point for the secondary route to the Bambara kingdom of Segu. Jackson notes that a complete caravan perished on the Taodeni track in 1805, with the loss of 2,000 persons and 1,800 camels.

37*. Very few ostriches are to be seen within a considerable distance from Timbuktu; the feathers are brought there by the traders from Bornu.

turns. He states the price of a man slave, if handsome, to be about the value of thirty dollars, if otherwise sixteen dollars; of a young female, about twenty-five dollars. The price of gunpowder is high at Timbuktu; when he was questioned on this point, he looked about him, and seeing a small crystal basin on the sideboard, he took it up, and said that as much as such as that would hold (about one pound and a half) would cost the value of three dollars at Timbuktu, two dollars at Salaga, how much at Kumasi he did not know. Gunpowder is not brought to Timbuktu by the Arabs, but by the merchants from Kong, and other places immediately connected with the Ashanti trade.[38] Never heard of any copper mines in the interior; neither did he see any iron manufactured in any part he had visited. They get their iron at Timbuktu from Fez, and it is conveyed in short bars on each side of the camels. When inquiry was made as to its price, he measured twice the length of his arm from the elbow, to which he added one span, and said it was worth five dollars.

There is much gold at Timbuktu, but not so much as at Sansanding, where he had heard there are valuable gold mines;[39] and a great number of Arabs resort there to trade. Cowries are current at Timbuktu for the purchase of provisions, but they are not taken in trade by the Arabs; about 3,000 of them are the value of a dollar.[40]

Their musical instruments are of a kind of rude fiddle, flutes, and drums. All offences are punished by order of the Sultan. Great offences, particularly meddling with any of the Sultan's wives, are punished by hanging. He did not see any one hanged, but saw a gallows there; he described the process by making two men stand at a short distance from each other, and placing a stool between them, put his stick on their heads, with his handkerchief on it touching the stool, which he then kicked away. The punishment for theft is confinement, flogging, and restitution of the value, and servitude until paid. He says there is a house appropriated to the purpose of confinement, and which is guarded by four men with muskets. Cir-

---

38. Commercial relations between Ashanti and Kong would thus seem to have become normal by 1821. The earlier part of the century had been marked by the decline of trade along this route, following the Ashanti-Kong hostilities in which Abū Bakr al-Ṣiddīq was involved.

39. Sansanding, on the Niger above Timbuktu, was an important center of the distributive trade—not of gold extraction.

40. The value of the cowrie fluctuated. In 1821 it would appear to have been low.

cumcision is general among the people at Timbuktu, who are all Muslim. He does not know the exact number of mosques, but recollects three large ones, two of which were built by the king, and one by the Arab traders.[41]

He heard that Timbuktu was formerly subject to Bambara, but ceased to be so since the latter had a war with the Fulbe, in which they were defeated;[42] Sultan Muḥammad is therefore independent, although not powerful; for he says, that his control does not extend much beyond Timbuktu itself. Muḥammad succeeded Sultan Abū Bakr, who, he heard, died about eight years ago; is ignorant who was his predecessor. Abū Bakr was extremely rich. Wargee remained at Timbuktu five weeks, during which time he lived in Sultan Muḥammad's house, and was treated by him with the greatest kindness. He never heard of any white man having been at Timbuktu.

Leaving Timbuktu, Wargee embarked on the Niger (to which goods are transported on camels and asses) in a large boat, which was sometimes paddled by ten men, and sometimes pushed forward with long poles. The river near Timbuktu is deep, and flows in a direction contrary to that in which they were going; its breadth is about 200 yards. The boat had a considerable quantity of salt in it, which had been brought from Taodeni to Timbuktu, and they stopped at several places to dispose of it. Eleven days after they left Timbuktu, and at a place called "Koonah," the river, which had been hitherto of nearly an equal width, spread out into a large lake, which was very shallow near to the shore: here small canoes came to receive the salt. It continued thus spread out for four days, until they arrived at "Koonannah," where it narrowed to its former breadth. When asked if the lake had different names, he replied it was called "Baharee," or "Bar Hareh"; its breadth he observed was about the length of the Salt Pond at Cape Coast, say about half a mile.[43] At the expiration of twenty-two days from their departure from Timbuktu they arrived at Jenne, which is built in a similar manner to Timbuktu, but not nearly

41. He probably refers to the three large and ancient mosques—Jingereber (the great mosque), Sankore, and Sidi Yahya. There are various accounts of the origins of these; see, for example, Barth, Travels, 3:325; Miner, Timbuctoo, passim.

42. This probably refers to Shehu Ahmadu's call for jihad in 1818, when the Fulbe of Massina finally threw off Bambara overlordship.

43. "Koonah" is not the Kuna reported by Ṣāliḥ Bilāli, since that town was much farther south, on the Bani above its junction with the Niger. The lake was Lake Débo. Bar Hareh is simply baḥra, Arabic for pond.

so large; he remained at Jenne a long time. He says the country about Timbuktu and Jenne is flat and fertile, and well adapted for pasturage, and that the number of cattle is considerable.[44] From Jenne he went forward by land to Souroutouna, in twenty-five days, remaining at several places; the distance is ten days' journey. From Souroutouna he advanced to Kouri, to "Samaco," to Bobo-Dioulasso, to Kong, in thirty-three days.[45] In travelling from Jenne to Souroutouna, to Kouri, to "Samaco," to Bobo-Dioulasso, and to Kong, the rising of the sun was to his left. From Kouri he diverged to the westward, and after a journey of ten days he arrived at Folona, a large town, the capital of a country of the same name, which he says is next to Bambara; from thence again he returned to Kouri.[46]

Between Kong and Bobo-Dioulasso is a considerable river, which he was obliged to cross by a canoe; its name he had forgotten; he describes its breadth by saying it was as far as from the castle to the house in which he lived (about 100 yards), and its direction from the rising towards the setting of the sun.[47] Kong is a town of considerable size, but not so large as Timbuktu; the inhabitants are Muslim; they employ themselves much in trading with the Ashanti in one direction, also with Fulbe Sansanding in the other; the houses are of mud, flat-roofed, two stories high, some of them are good, but not equal to those at Timbuktu.[48]

Wargee remained at Kong fifty days. Having taken a wife at

44. The commercial prosperity of Jenne was closely linked with that of Timbuktu. "It is because of this holy town," wrote al-Sa'di of Jenne, "that caravans come to Timbuktu from all points of the horizon" (*Ta'rīkh al-Sūdān*).

45. The route is Jenne to Souroutouna (65 miles), to Kouri (70 miles), to Bobo-Dioulasso (75 miles), to Kong (140 miles). This is one of the most important of the historic north-south routes in the Western Sudan, and the Bobo-Dioulasso-to–Jenne section is that followed by the modern north-south road. South of Bobo-Dioulasso, however, the modern route is deflected to the west to follow that of the Ivory Coast railway. See I. Wilks, "A Medieval Trade Route from the Niger to the Gulf of Guinea," *Journal of African History*, 3:337–41 (1962).

46. Folona is the region of the Senufo Pamporo, south of Sikasso. The Muslim Dyula had established settlements among the Pamporo over a period of time, and the town of Folona was probably dominated by them in 1821. The area was shortly to be incorporated into the kingdom of Kenedugu, under the Taraure rulers of Sikasso.

47. The Komoé River, though the direction of its flow is wrongly noted.

48. Kong was an important Dyula trading center lying on the main northwestern route from Ashanti to the Niger in the region of Jenne. The Sansanding mentioned lay on the main Niger, a little downstream from Segu. It was then under the control of the Fulbe followers of *Shehu* Ahmadu. See E. Bernus, "Kong et sa région," *Études éburnéennes*, 8 (1960).

Jenne, she fell sick at Kong, which caused his remaining so long. It would seem by this time his means had dwindled very materially, and on his being questioned, he acknowledged that, in addition to his loss at "Galibaba," he had expended much of his property, and much had been extorted from him. We find him at Kong retailing in the market some material in small bottles, which was much prized by them to darken their eyelids and eyebrows and making a profit by selling it; this he said was called by the Arabs "Hainar," and by the Kongs "Incassah."[49] It was understood, in the first instance, that this was purchased from the Arabs; but at a subsequent interview, he declared it was procured from a country called "Namnam," about fifteen days' journey from Kano, the inhabitants of which are cannibals. Observing that this was much doubted, he again seriously repeated his assertion, and declared, that when he was at Kano, the Sultan was at war with Mallam Jago, King of "Namnam," and he saw several of these people who were made prisoners sold in the market; that one day a slave having died, the Sultan, who doubted the fact of their being cannibals, paid the master for the body and gave it to them, and they ate it; to this he said he was an eyewitness.[50]

Being asked if he had seen any mountains near to Kong, his reply was that he had seen several large mountains, but he had either not noticed or did not recollect their direction, neither could it be understood that there was a continued chain.[51] From Kong he travelled to Bouna in fifteen days,[52] but rested at different places some days; his

49. There appears to be a confusion here between the vegetable dye, henna (Arabic: *hinnā'*), which is used on the body, and the mineral dye kohl (Arabic: *kuḥl*), particularly used around the eyes.

50. *Nam-nam, nyam-nyam, yam-yam,* and the like, are generic Western Sudanese terms for cannibals, probably meaning the Yakoba of the Bauchi plateau in this case. "Sultan" here simply stands for ruler; that is, *Emir* Dabo Cigari of Kano, who was installed in 1819 and who put down much violent opposition during the early years of his reign. *Mallam* Jago may have been a Hausa ruler of Ningi, southeast of Kano. The chiefs of Ningi have traditionally borne the title of *mallam* (though it normally means simply a learned man, roughly equivalent to the *alfa* of the Senegambia). Hausa control, however, may date only from the middle of the nineteenth century, when a band from Kano under *Mallam* Hamzatu occupied the area. For the region in general, see H. Gunn, *Pagan Peoples of the Central Area of Northern Nigeria* (London, 1956).

51. This questioning about mountains reflects the common European belief of the period that the "mountains of Kong" formed a continuous chain from east to west, cutting off easy access from the coastal region to the northern savannas.

52. The Dyula town and center of Muslim learning where Abū Bakr al-Ṣiddīq obtained his education.

course was now to the eastward, that is, his face was towards the rising sun. From Bouna to "Foula" in eight days, "Foula" to Banda[53] in twelve days, travelling in a different direction, that is, with the sun to his left. Banda is under the frontier of Ashanti, and a dependency of that kingdom; here he was stopped by an Ashanti chief, who told him he would not allow him to advance until he had sent to consult the king. From Banda he was ordered to go to Daboya, twelve days' journey eastward;[54] and from Daboya to Salaga[55] in a southerly direction, eight days. Inquiry being made if he had heard of Dagomba, he said it was thirty-three days' journey from Kong. He further said, that Dagomba and Yendi were the same place, being called by the former name by the Hausa and Marawa people, and by the latter by that of Mossi.[56] Salaga is five days' journey in a southerly direction from Dagomba; Salaga, as well as all the Marawa people, including Hausa, pay tribute annually to Bornu.[57]

At Salaga he sojourned three months and ten days; and, at the expiration of that time, people came from the King of Ashanti, to tell him he might advance. Went by another route, and passed many towns, but could not learn their names, there being no people who could speak to him. In fourteen days arrived at a village near Kumasi, where he was ordered to remain, and received a present of a sheep, a flask of rum, and some yams, from the king; four days after this he was allowed to go to Kumasi, and saw the king [Osei Bonsu], from whom he again received a present of a sheep, a pig, some rum, yam, plantains, and gold. When asked where he was going, he told the king that he had travelled very far, and hearing the English had a place not very far off, he was desirous of getting

53. It is possible that Williams, who used "Foula" for Fulbe, was searching for a familiar rendering of "Fughula," the name by which Banda was known to Muslims. Banda, which also figures in Abū Bakr's account, had been a dependency of Ashanti since the mid-eighteenth century.

54. It is difficult to see why this indirect route should have been taken from Banda. Daboya, a divisional chiefdom of Gonja, lies on the White Volta some 110 miles northeast of Banda.

55. An important Muslim-dominated kola entrepôt in eastern Gonja and the center of Ashanti administration in the northeast. Many Kumasi officials were stationed there.

56. In fact, Yendi was the capital of the Dagomba kingdom, which had become an Ashanti protectorate in the middle of the eighteenth century.

57. A clear case of misunderstanding. Not only was Dagomba under Ashanti hegemony at this period, but Bornu itself was having difficulties maintaining its independence in the face of attacks from the Sokoto caliphate. See the account of Ali Eisami, below.

there, because he knew they would help him to find his way back to his own country. The king replied that was well, and that he should be sent to Cape Coast Castle soon. He was kept at Kumasi twenty-five days, when the king appointed messengers to escort him to Cape Coast Castle, where he arrived in twenty-one days, as they travelled by very easy journeys, and rested about every other day.[58] During his whole stay at Kumasi, the king behaved towards him with much kindness and attention.

[*The concluding two paragraphs appeared as endnotes to the original text.*]

Being questioned what route he would take if he were obliged to return to Timbuktu, he stated the following as the most direct: from Cape Coast to Kumasi nine days, to Salaga fourteen days, Dagomba five, Sansanné-Mango five, Koupéla [Koomfiela, in text] fifteen, Boussouma seven, Mané three, Hombori ten, Timbuktu five—in all seventy-three days.[59]

Sept. 30. Wargee's account relative to the setting in of the rains at Timbuktu was given some time since; when again questioned on the subject, he said, that from his leaving Timbuktu to his arrival at Salaga was seven moons, his stay at Salaga three moons and ten days, journeying thence to Kumasi fourteen days, at Kumasi twenty-five days, journey from Kumasi to Cape Coast twenty-two days. Since his arrival, in which he was correct to a day, four moons and ten days, making seventeen moons. This will make his departure from Timbuktu to have been about the 10th of June.

58. Compare with Abū Bakr's overoptimistic memory that a similar trip from Kumasi to the coast could be made in two and a half days. The situation in Cape Coast had not changed in its essentials since Philip Quaque's death in 1816. The Company of Merchants Trading to Africa was replaced by a royal government in June 1821, but the extent of British control beyond the forts themselves was much as it had been.

59. This route would, in short, follow the traditional northwesterly route from Ashanti toward Hausa as far as Sansanné-Mango in the north of present-day Togo—from there north and slightly west through Upper Volta, passing midway between Wagadugu and Fada N'Gurma.

PART III

Four Nineteenth-Century Nigerians

F̲o̲u̲r̲ of the narratives in this collection come from the territory of present-day Nigeria, and the men who provided them shared elements of a common background. They were contemporaries, and each observed a different aspect of the many-sided war and revolution that swept through Yoruba and the savanna country to the north and northeast during the early decades of the nineteenth century. Ali Eisami was born in the later 1780's in Bornu, enslaved in about 1810, and sold from one master to another until he was finally shipped from Porto Novo (now in Dahomey) in 1818. The other three were all Yoruba, though each came from a distinct part of the broad Yoruba-speaking region. Osifekunde was born in Ijebu about 1798, enslaved and shipped from the coast at Warri in 1820. Samuel Crowther was born in the Ibarapa district of the declining kingdom of Oyo in about 1806. He was enslaved in 1821 and sailed from Lagos in 1822. Joseph Wright belonged to the Egba subgroup of the Yoruba. He was born about 1815, and he was enslaved and shipped from Lagos in 1826 or 1827. Thus, though the four differed considerably in age, all were embarked for tropical America within in single decade. All four narratives deal with the experience of enslavement, and those by Ali Eisami, Crowther, and Wright also include the similar experience of capture at sea by British cruisers and landing in Sierra Leone to begin a new life of freedom in a Western cultural setting. It was, indeed, this stroke of luck that led to the recording and ultimate publication of their accounts. But any one of the four combines his own particular view of his place and time with an account of personal disaster they shared with thousands of others of their generation.

All four report some view of major events in Nigerian history, particularly the break-up of the formerly powerful state of Oyo and the beginning of the Yoruba Wars that were to occupy most of the remainder of the nineteenth century.[1] At the eighteenth-century peak of its power, Oyo controlled most of the savanna-forest borderland in present-day western Nigeria, though its center of power was well north, in the savanna near the border between the former northern and western regions. It was therefore not really a forest state, and forest people like the Ijebu and the Egba were only on the fringes of its influence. Oyo had once held hegemony over the Egba towns, but its control lapsed well before the date of the final collapse. Ijebu was never under Oyo domination, though it was to play a key role in the nineteenth-century disorders of southern Yoruba. Even Ali Eisami from distant Bornu travelled to the coast by way of Yoruba and was an eyewitness to a crucial phase in the destruction of Oyo.

The precise causes for the collapse of Oyo are not well understood, but I. A. Akinjogbin has suggested recently that the disintegration began in about 1793 when the *Alafin* (or ruler), Aole, ordered an attack on the town of Apomu.[2] This action was not merely a routine military operation. Apomu belonged to the independent state of Ife, and Ife was both a major religious center and the traditional home of the Yoruba people. An attack on Ife was contrary to the Oyo coronation oath. In response to the attack, leading Oyo officials and military officers repudiated the *Alafin's* authority; and the constitutional practice of Oyo required the *Alafin* to commit suicide, which he did in about 1796.

Two short and ineffective reigns followed, but neither of these *Alafins* enjoyed real power, and they were followed by some twenty years of interregnum (*ca.* 1797–1817). It was during this interregnum that a number of leading generals and provincial governors began to carve out little kingdoms for themselves and to behave as

1. For a general account of the Yoruba Wars, see J. F. Ade Ajayi and R. S. Smith, *Yoruba Warfare in the Nineteenth Century* (Cambridge, 1964).

2. I. A. Akinjogbin, "The Prelude to the Yoruba Civil Wars of the Nineteenth Century," *Odu*, 1 (new ser.):24–46 (1965). See also R. S. Smith, "List of Alafin of Oyo," *The African Historian: Journal of the Historical Society, University of Ife*, 3 (March 1965).

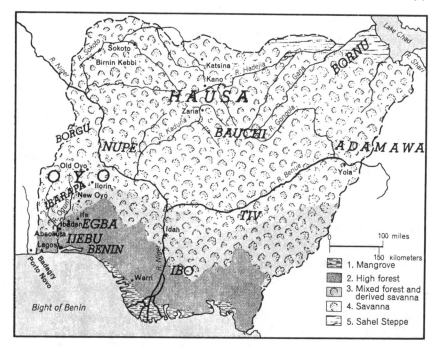

Map 9. Vegetation zones in Nigeria.

independent rulers. Political instability and economic dislocation in central Oyo became so widespread that many people began to desert the metropolitan provinces and move southward. A little later, Oyo began to feel the impact of a major religious revolution taking place still farther north in the Hausa city-states.

Islam had been present in Hausa since the fourteenth century, but it was only one religion among a variety of polytheistic cults, enjoying no special status. Some Hausa rulers called themselves Muslim and favored Islam. Others called themselves Muslim, but did nothing to further their religion. And religious diversity was combined with ethnic diversity. The Hausa cities contained several minority groups, including a class of Fulbe or Fulani scholars and teachers who had wandered eastward from their homeland in Futa Toro. They were, in short, much the same kind of people as Ayuba Suleiman of Bondu, though the principal leaders were far better educated. In the countryside there were also larger groups of Fulbe herdsmen who practiced transhumant pastoralism, wandering north with their cattle during the rains and southward in the dry season. Over several centuries they too had been gradually drifting eastward, and they shared certain ties of kinship and language with the urban Fulbe, as well as recurrent friction with the sedentary Hausa.

By the beginning of the nineteenth century, the religious discontents of the urban Fulbe Muslims were combining with those of the Fulbe herdsmen, and they were joined by others that were neither serious Muslims nor Fulbe. The way was open for a general series of revolts in the name of Islam and under the leadership of a rising class of Fulbe warrior-scholars. These revolts in Hausa began in 1804 in the state of Gobir with a revolt of the Muslim Fulbe under the leadership of the reformer, *Shehu* Usuman (or 'Uthmān) dan Fodio.[3] At first it was simply an attack on this single Hausa government, but it rapidly spread, through a series of sympathetic risings against other Hausa states. Muslim leaders, again mainly Fulbe, also began to seize power among the non-Hausa peoples of the Bauchi plateau, the Gongola and upper Benue valleys, and eventually in Nupe and northern Yoruba. These events occupied the first three decades of the nineteenth century, and they ultimately involved the whole region between the Niger and Lake Chad.

The long-run consequences were truly revolutionary. After the jihad, Islam became the permanent state religion in Hausa, and under this regime the old cults lost their influence (though they remain here and there, even today). To the south and southeast of Hausa proper, Islam came in as virtually a new religion carried by military invasion. Here too, Islamic forms of government were set up, and their establishment led to a gradual conversion, which has continued up to the present. Everywhere, old rulers were overthrown and replaced by the new class of Fulbe aristocrats, whose descendants still enjoy a dominant social position in much of northern Nigeria. For the first time in history, the majority of the people were brought under a degree of centralized political control. Not only the Hausa states, but also the many smaller governments outside of Hausa were divided into emirates, all dependent on a central government in the newly developed city of Sokoto (with a subsidiary capital for the western emirates located at Gwandu).

It was the eastward spread of the Fulbe wars that made Ali Eisami

3. There is, as yet, no comprehensive history of this movement, nor has the rich and voluminous source material in Arabic been fully exploited by scholars. See H. F. C. Smith, "A Neglected Theme in West African History," *Journal of the Historical Society of Nigeria*, 2:169–95 (December 1961), and the works there cited.

a slave and resulted in his travels across Hausa and southward through Yoruba to the sea. And he passed through Oyo at precisely the period when the general Islamic revolution began to be most serious for the Oyo empire. Samuel Crowther was also present as a teenage boy, so that he too saw something of the impact of this revolution on the Yoruba. Until this time, the troubles in Oyo had been mainly internal revolt under Yoruba leadership. Gradually, Afonja, the *are-one-kakanfo* (or senior military officer) built a combined force of Oyo Muslims, foreign Muslim slaves, and Fulbe emissaries from the revolts farther north. This combination soon grew into the most effective fighting force amid the prevalent anarchy. But a little later (after Ali Eisami and Crowther had left the scene), its character changed. The leadership passed to the immigrant Fulbe and Hausa, and the revolt became more nearly a foreign invasion, directed from Sokoto. A new Islamic political unit, the emirate of Ilorin, came into existence and spread its control over the region that had once been central Oyo. Yoruba migration to the relative safety of the forest fringe increased to a flood. By 1837, the old capital was abandoned and a new city of Oyo was founded to the south. There, the old name and the title of *Alafin* lived on, but it never regained its former influence among the Yoruba.

These events in Oyo necessarily had an impact on interstate relations in southern Yoruba. The earliest phases of Oyo weakness had forced the *Alafin* to withdraw his claims to hegemony over the congeries of virtually independent walled towns in the Egba forest, but the first two decades of the nineteenth century—the early youth of Osifekunde in Ijebu and Joseph Wright in Egba—were a period of relative peace. But already the Ijebu were beginning to come into closer contact with the European slave dealers at coastal points such as Lagos, and they began to carry on an active commerce in the prisoners of war taken in the northern fighting. Osifekunde says nothing about this new, Ijebu-managed slave trade (and he himself was kidnapped during a coastal trading expedition), nor was it at first a threat to the Egba towns. Their fortifications allowed each to go its own way in minor warfare based on petty quarrels among themselves, while the forests protected them from the full force of Oyo or Fulbe cavalry from the savanna. There is, indeed, no evidence that southern Yoruba was a large supplier of slaves to the Atlantic trade at any period before the 1820's.

But then the crisis came to southern Yoruba, and it came from two sources. The Ijebu began to arm themselves with firearms bought from the European slave dealers on the coast—and bought, apparently, with the proceeds of the earlier southward flow of prisoners. Thus the anarchy in Oyo indirectly bred more violence. The weakening of Oyo also removed a strong state, which had previously been a source of stability. The balance of power had shifted abruptly. Much as in European international relations, major wars in southern Yoruba were the result, as each state struggled to preserve or improve its position in the new political and military setting. Owu, which had rather indefinite friendly connections with the Egba cities, was one of the strongest states in the south. It was attacked and finally overwhelmed by a coalition of enemies including Ife, Ijebu, and groups of refugee fighting men from Oyo. This war—the Owu War—broke out in 1818 or 1820 and lasted to 1825, and it brought an end to stability for many decades. As the wars continued after the fall of Owu, spreading desolation among the Egba towns, Joseph Wright's town of Oba was captured and he was made a slave. By 1830 most of the Egba towns had been destroyed. The people were pushed westward toward the Ogun River, where they established a new united Egba city at Abeokuta, drawing in refugees from Owu as well. A second new city and center of power grew up around the ruins of Ibadan, a small Egba town which first became the war camp for the victorious coalition and then grew larger as it attracted many of the continuing stream of refugees from Oyo and the north. Within a few decades the new cities, Abeokuta and Ibadan and new Oyo among others, had replaced the old centers of power like Owu. The political map of southern Yoruba was remade as effectively as the creation of the emirate of Ilorin or the caliphate of Sokoto had remade the political map in the savanna country.

None of the four Nigerians represented here fully understood the broader pattern of events in which he moved. Each reported at a relatively early age, from the microcosmic web of family and personal relations, but each was caught up in the wider pattern of historical change in ways that will be explored by the editors of the four texts that follow.

CHAPTER 7

ALI EISAMI GAZIRMABE
OF BORNU

*H. F. C. Smith, D. M. Last
and Gambo Gubio*

Ali Eisami, or William Harding (as he was known in Sierra Leone), was born in Gazir, the metropolitan province of the empire of Bornu, in the later 1780's. His father was a Kanuri *mallam,* or teacher-scholar, and he in turn received a good education in the Islamic tradition of his country. He was about twenty years old when the Fulbe incursions brought the great religious revolution to his own section of Bornu in 1808.[1] From 1808 to 1818, Ali Eisami lived in a world of constant change. He was present at the first Fulbe sack of Birnin Gazargamo, the capital of Bornu. Later on, his family lost its home and he himself was enslaved, after which he passed through the great emirates of Kano and Katsina within a few years of the overthrow of the old Hausa dynasties. He witnessed the revolts in Oyo which finally overthrew the *Alafin* and established the the emirate of Ilorin. Finally, in 1818, he was transported to the coast and sold as a slave to European merchants in Porto Novo, shipped for the New World, captured at sea, and landed at Sierra Leone.

Ali Eisami's homeland was the ancient Kanuri empire of Bornu,

1. Errors of a chronological nature are to be expected in an oral account of this kind, remembered over several decades. Ali, however, appears to be substantially correct for most dates, except the ordering of events in the years 1808–9. Minor discrepancies, however, occur here and there in his account of time elapsed between events. His birth date, for example, can be calculated as 1794 from an eclipse of the sun he observed in 1807. On his own report of his father's words, however, he must have been born in 1786 or 1787. We have accepted the latter estimate as the more likely.

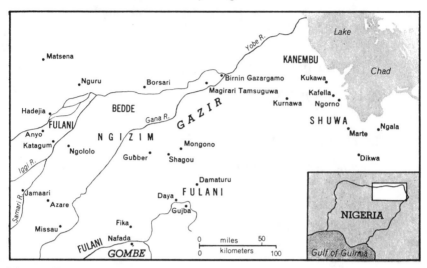

Map 10. Bornu, *ca.* 1810.

centered in the flood-plain of the Yo River.[2] This empire was ruled
by the ancient family of the Sefawa, which had already enjoyed nearly a millenium of political power in the lands east and west of the
Chad. Settling in the Bornu plain in the fifteenth century, the Sefawa
had built up a wide sphere of influence, extending, in the course of
the sixteenth and seventeenth centuries, far into Hausa. Certainly, by
the second half of the eighteenth century this once-great power was
showing signs of decay. But the final collapse of the Sefawa and the
destruction of Bornu influence in the west, which took place in the
first two decades of the nineteenth century, were the result of the
Fulbe incursions.

From 1806 or thereabouts, the Fulbe risings in Hausa were accompanied by revolt among the Fulbe populations living in western and
central Bornu. But here the religious setting was different from the
Hausa pattern. The Sefawa dynasty was the oldest Muslim dynasty in
the whole Sudan, and the Kanuri were well known for their Islamic
learning. The Fulbe of Bornu, however, were a discontented minority and claimed that polytheistic practices were widely tolerated in the
empire of Bornu. It was also said that the Sefawa were supporting
certain of the old Hausa states in opposition to the Fulbe jihad farther west.[3]

2. For the history of Bornu generally see Y. Urvoy, *Histoire de l'empire du Bornou*
(Paris, 1949), and works there cited.

3. The chief sources for the Fulbe risings in Bornu are Muḥammad Bello, *Infāq al-*

Whatever the facts of the matter, the outcome was momentous: the capital at Birnin Gazargamo was sacked, and the Sefawa government was put to flight. The Fulbe then annexed the old western marches of Bornu and organized them as the new emirates of Hadejia and Katagum, later creating two others, Missau and Jama'are. These new provinces owed allegiance to Sokoto, and the Bornuan governor of the western frontier, the *galadima*, was forced to withdraw his headquarters from Nguru to Borsari, far to the east.

These losses in the west were the beginning of the end for the Sefawa dynasty. They were forced to appeal for help from an influential scholar and merchant, Muḥammad al-Amin al-Kanemi,[4] who had built up a large and powerful following among certain minority and fringe elements found among the populations of eastern Bornu, particularly the Kanembu settlers and Shuwa Arabs near Lake Chad. Muḥammad al-Amin answered the appeal, temporarily restored the Sefawa government, and suppressed the Fulbe rising in the metropolitan province. The Sefawa, however, became mere puppet rulers, and real political power passed from the Kanuri of central Bornu to the Shuwa advisers of Muḥammad al-Amin, his slaves, and the Kanembu military leaders. The old capital at Birnin Gazargamo was abandoned, and Muḥammad al-Amin ordered another one built at Kukawa, in the part of the country where he enjoyed the greatest influence.

Some reflection of these events appears in Ali Eisami's text, but he was already gone from Bornu by 1820, when Muḥammad al-Amin had reached supreme power. He had been living in Sierra Leone for many years as William Harding, when, in 1846, 'Umar, the son of

---

Maysūr (ed. C. E. J. Whitting; London, 1951), partly paraphrased and summarized by F. J. Arnett, *The Rise of the Sokoto Fulani* (Kano, 1922); Usuman dan Fodio, *Ta'līm al-ikhwān* (Sokoto Arabic MSS, uncatalogued); Aḥmad b. al-Ḥājj, *Tārīkh Missau* (Ibadan Arabic MSS, uncatalogued); and the account given by Ali Eisami in S. W. Koelle, *African Native Literature* (London, 1854), pp. 212–48.

4. Material now available on Muḥammad al-Amin is comparatively scarce. D. Denham and H. Clapperton met him in the early 1820's and published their impressions in *Narrative of Travels and Discoveries in Northern Central Africa* (London, 1826). Copies of a few of his letters, a tract which he wrote (on the *shari'a* pertaining to marriage), and an elegy to him, by one of his friends, are among Ibadan Arabic MSS. His correspondence with the Sokoto reformers is copied in *Infāq al-Maysūr*. But there is, as yet, little else; and, though important, he therefore remains an obscure figure. His obscurity is increased by his misleading surname. His connections were not with Kanem, but with the Fezzan and the Arab world. To him Bornu was in many ways a foreign country, and this has to be taken into account in any appreciation of his work.

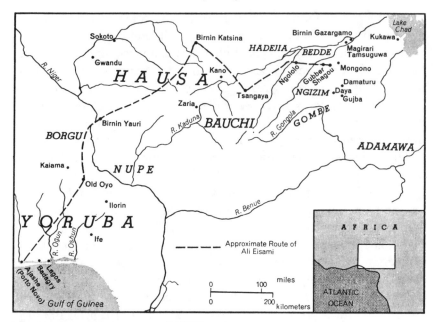

Map 11. Approximate route of Ali Eisami.

Muḥammad al-Amin, deposed and executed the last of the Sefawa. Thus he missed the end of this most ancient of Sudanese dynasties and the final political reordering which brought Muḥammad al-Amin's descendants, the *shehu* of Bornu, into the political eminence they still enjoy in northeastern Nigeria.

Ali Eisami's account of his westward travels through Hausa as a slave is disappointingly brief, but his sale to an important figure in Old Oyo again brought him into contact with the great events of his period. As a Muslim, though a slave, Ali Eisami became one of the potential fifth column in the heart of Oyo, which was used so effectively by Afonja to complete the destruction of that empire. At this point, Ali Eisami's narrative treats the same events described by Samuel Crowther. When Afonja, in 1817, offered freedom to slaves who enlisted in his forces, he was, in fact, recruiting the army that later sacked Crowther's town of Osogun. Ali, however, was sold to the coast by his Yoruba master to prevent his escape. Otherwise, he might well have participated in the enslavement of Crowther, rather than preceding him by four years on a similar path to the coast, capture at sea, and settlement in Sierra Leone.

From another point of view, however, Ali Eisami's arrival on the coast was fortunate—since he was ultimately captured at sea. The British had abolished their own slave trade in 1807, and, during the remainder of the Napoleonic wars, they made it a practice to capture slave ships at sea and to land the liberated recaptives at Sierra Leone, their only real territorial holding on the coast of West Africa. At the end of the war, they made a serious effort to obtain international support for the continuation of an anti-slave-trade blockade, but their effort to obtain a multilateral sanction for the capture of slave ships failed. The lack of a legal basis for the blockade brought a British court to hold in 1817 that the Navy could not seize or search foreign slavers on the high seas in peacetime. For a few months, therefore, the Navy had to give up strict enforcement of the antislavery blockade against foreign nations, though it maintained patrols against possible British slavers and against the pirates that infested the West African coast for a few years after the end of the wars.

Ali Eisami was therefore lucky to have been recaptured at all. He sailed from the coast at a peculiarly unpropitious time. Even though Britain rectified the legal problem later in 1817 by forcing Spain and Portugal to sign treaties giving bilateral sanction to the blockade, the slavers captured under these treaties had to be taken before an international Court of Mixed Commission, and the court at Freetown in Sierra Leone was not actually set up until 1819.[5] Meanwhile, the blockading force on the West African coast in the early part of 1818 consisted of only two vessels of the British Navy—the *Semiramis*, flagship of Commodore Sir James Lucas Yeo, and the *Cherub*. Though the *Cherub* cruised past Porto Novo near the time of Ali's departure, she apparently missed his ship, which was captured later and far at sea.

Once Ali had been landed in Sierra Leone, his narrative follows a pattern that was to be standard for many thousands of other recaptives, including Samuel Crowther and Joseph Wright. Under the governorship of Sir Charles MacCarthy (1814–24), the reception of recaptives was made more systematic than it had been in the past. They were first kept on board ship until the Court of Mixed Commission or Vice-Admiralty Court had completed the adjudication. If condemned, the ship was confiscated and the recaptives were landed and turned over to the Captured Negro Department (or Liberated

---

5. For the British suppression of the foreign slave trade see C. Lloyd, *The Navy and the Slave Trade* (London, 1949), esp. pp. 43–46, 67.

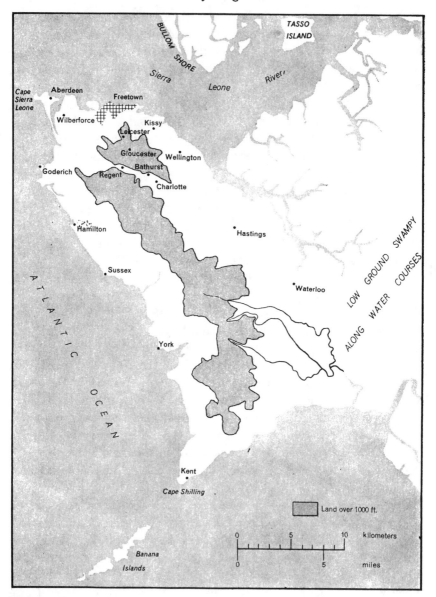

Map 12. Sierra Leone, *ca.* 1820.

African Department after 1822) of the Sierra Leone government, at its establishment called the King's Yard. Some were then apprenticed to the Negro settlers from America, or to recaptives who had arrived earlier and were already established. The rest were assigned to one of a series of villages established for the purpose. Each village, named after an English county or a prominent figure of the day, was under a European manager, who acted as magistrate, schoolmaster, and often as a missionary as well. Many, indeed, were agents of the Church Missionary Society, rather than simply government employees. The recaptives were subsidized at first at government charge, but they were supposed to fend for themselves as soon as they were able. Most took European names in addition to their own African names, often borrowing that of the family to which they were apprenticed or that of the superintendent of their original village.[6]

Ali Eisami was assigned to the village of Bathurst, then under the superintendency of the Reverend Mr. Decker of the Church Missionary Society—the same village to which Crowther was to be assigned four years later. Several recaptives who were later to achieve prominence took Decker's name, but Ali's choice of William Harding probably originated directly or indirectly from John Harding, a Maroon settler of Jamaican origin and clerk in the Captured Negro Department at the time of Ali's arrival.[7]

Little is known of Ali's life in Sierra Leone during the next two decades. Since he was already about thirty years old at the time of his arrival, he was apparently less able or less willing to accept Western culture than younger recaptives like Crowther and Wright. In any event, he became only a nominal Christian, and he remained illiterate in English to the end of his life. During his early years in Sierra Leone, some two hundred other Kanuri were also present, and Ali tended to live among his own countrymen.

The present narrative owes its existence to the arrival in 1847 of S. W. Koelle, the German linguist employed by the Church Missionary Society. Koelle's many-sided linguistic studies included Kanuri grammar and a selection of Kanuri readings with English translation and an extensive vocabulary. Koelle took Ali as a full-time informant during most of 1848 and again for a period of two years during 1849–52, by which time Ali was well into his sixties. Koelle's method of investigation was to write phonetically the examples of the

6. C. Fyfe, *A History of Sierra Leone* (London, 1962); J. E. Peterson, "Freetown: A Study of the Dynamics of Liberated African Society, 1807–1870" (unpublished Ph.D. thesis, Northwestern University, 1963), esp. pp. 98–109.

7. Fyfe, *Sierra Leone*, p. 167.

Kanuri language furnished by Ali and other informants. In this way, he accumulated a manuscript literature of some eight hundred pages, including stories, fables, and historical fragments, as well as the personal narrative that is reproduced here.[8]

The importance of this account is not that it contains much political history that cannot be read elsewhere, though the events described accord with what we know from other sources. Neither is it a work of historical interpretation: it is, indeed, doubtful that either Ali Eisami or Koelle appreciated the significance of the events they discussed. As a document of social history, however, it shows the impact of revolutionary changes on the life of an ordinary man. Such documents are rare for Ali's time and place, and it may serve to remind us that the study of the past is of little use unless it concerns itself with the fortunes of the *talaga* as well as the rise and fall of governments.

NARRATIVE OF THE TRAVELS OF ALI EISAMI

The narrative that follows was dictated by Ali Eisami to S. W. Koelle in Sierra Leone in about 1850. It was published in Koelle's *African Native Literature* (London, 1854), in Kanuri, pp. 115–21, and in English translation, pp. 248–56. The present version follows Koelle's translation, with some modernization of Koelle's English style and with a few corrections, including modern spellings for all the clearly identifiable place names. Minor obscurities in Koelle's translation have been disregarded, and some of Koelle's footnotes have been omitted; those that have been retained are marked with an asterisk.

In the town of Magriari Tapsoua, there was a man, named Mamade Atshi, son of Kodo,[9]* and he was my father.[10] He was already a *mal-*

---

8. S. W. Koelle, *Grammar of the Bornu or Kanuri Language* (London, 1854), pp. ii–x; *African Native Literature*, pp. v–viii; P. E. H. Hair, "Koelle at Freetown," in S. W. Koelle, *Polyglotta Africana* (2d ed., Graz, 1963), pp. 9*–12*.

9*. She was his mother.

10. "Magriari Tapsoua" is possibly Magirari Tamsuguwa. Both parts of this name are common as place-names in Bornu (*Magirari* means under the Queen Mother; *Tamsuguwa* means tamarind trees). There is a place of this name at a day's journey from Birnin Gazargamo. "Mamade Atshi" is Muḥammad al-Ḥājj. "Eisami" means "son of Aisha." The use of the matronymic is still a common feature of Kanuri society.

lam[11] when he went and sought to marry my mother: so when their elders had consulted together, and come to a mutual understanding, my father prepared himself, sought a house, and the time for the wedding was fixed, which having arrived, my mother was married, and brought into my father's house. After they had been living in their house one year, my elder sister, Sarah, was born, next my elder brother Mamade,[12]* and after him myself; next to me, my younger sister Pesam, and then my younger sister Kadei were born; on their being born, our mother did not bear any more. As to myself, I was put to school when I was seven years of age. Then my younger sister Kadei and my elder brother Mamade died, so that only three of us remained, of whom two were females and I alone a male. When I had been reading at school till I was nine years of age, they took me from school, and put me into the house of circumcision; and after passing through the rite of circumcision, I returned to school, and having remained there two years longer, I left off reading the Koran.[13] When I left off reading the Koran, I was eleven years old.

Two years later, there was an eclipse of the sun, on a Saturday, in the cold season.[14] One year after this, when, in the weeding time, in the rainy season, about two o'clock in the afternoon, we looked to the west, the Kaman-locusts[15] were coming from the west, forming a straight line across the sky, as if one of God's thunderstorms were coming, so that day was turned into night. When the time of the locusts was past, the famine Ngeseneski[16] took place, but did not last long, only three months. After it, the pestilence came, and made

11. A teacher-scholar. Ali later refers to his father also as *fugara,* or scholar-student, a less respected title.

12*. Muḥammad.

13. This could be translated: "completed reading the Koran"; that is, finished the standard primary education for Muslims.

14. An eclipse of the sun should have been visible in Bornu on Sunday, 29 November 1807, according to the path calculated in T. R. von Oppolzer, *Canon der Finsternisse* (Vienna, 1887; trans. Gingerich, New York, 1962), Chart 144. The confirmation of oral accounts by astronomical data is rare as yet for African history. The best known case is the eclipse recorded by E. Torday in the history of the Bushong (see B. Davidson, *Old Africa Rediscovered* [London, 1959], p. 26).

15. The species in question is likely to have been the desert locust, which is liable to do considerable damage during the months of September through November. In this case, the locusts appear to have come in July.

16. *Ngeseneski* means "I forgot."

much havoc in Bornu, completely destroying all the elderly.[17] Next, the wars of the Fulbe[18] came up. In the rainy season the Fulbe put to flight the king of Daya with his family,[19] and, as they were coming to our town, my father said to me, "My son, times will be hard for you: this year you are nineteen years of age, and though I said that, when you are twenty, I will seek a girl for you, and let you marry, yet now the Fulbe have unsettled the land, and we do not know what to do: but what God has ordained for us, that shall we experience." When the guinea-corn which we were weeding had become ripe, and the harvest was past, the Fulbe roused both us and the Dayans, so we went, and remained near the capital,[20] till the Fulbe arose and came to the capital, on a Sunday, about two o'clock in the afternoon. When they were coming, the *kaigamma*[21] went out to encounter them; but, after they had met and been engaged in a battle till four o'clock, the *kaigamma's* power was at an end. The *mai* arose, passed out through the east gate, and started for Kurnawa.[22] Then the *kai-*

17. The nature of this pestilence (*bamba*) is not known. The intensely hot, dusty months before the rains are the season for epidemics.

18. Ali Eisami used the Kanuri term, *Fulata*, but Koelle's translation used the form, *Phula*, more common in Sierra Leone. (The present text has been corrected to Fulbe, throughout.) The Fulbe had lived for a long time in western and southern Bornu. Here, as in Hausa, they preserved a tradition of Islamic learning, as is attested by the writings of the eighteenth-century scholar, Muḥammad al-Ṭāhir b. Ibrāhīm al-Fulāni, of which examples are to be found among the Ibadan Library Arabic MSS collection.

The Fulbe revolt in western Bornu actually began more than a year before these events, under the leadership of *Ardo* Lerlima and his associate Biyi Abdur. It had already brought about the death of *Galadima* Dunama, governor of the western frontier districts of Bornu. Eisami's account begins with a second revolt, that of the southern Fulbe under *Shaykh* al-Bukhari and Gwoni (the learned) Mukhtar, in 1808.

19. Daya, some twenty-six miles south of Damaturu and west of Gujba, is now deserted, but was then the main town of a district of that name. The "family" of the king of Daya probably means his people. Elsewhere (Koelle, *African Native Literature*, pp. 212 ff.) Ali Eisami says that Daya had been a center of disaffection for some time. Five years previously the *Mai* Daya, a supporter of the Fulbe, had apparently defied the government. He had been deposed for this, and replaced by his younger brother. The new governor of Daya subsequently fell into a dispute with the Fulbe, who are said to have migrated to Gujba whence they mounted the attack mentioned here.

20. Birnin Gazargamo, the deserted ruins of which lie some twenty-five miles east of modern Geidam in north-central Bornu. It had been the seat of government of the Sefawa since the late fifteenth century.

21. The slave commander-in-chief of the Bornu army. Ali Eisami claims (Koelle, *African Native Literature*, pp. 212 ff.) that three *kaigamma* had already been demoted for failing to deal with the trouble in Daya. "About two o'clock" is Koelle's translation of *zuhr*, the time of mid-day prayer; "four o'clock" is *'aṣr*, the afternoon prayer.

22. *Mai* is the traditional title of the Sefawa rulers of Bornu. The *mai* at this time

gamma left the Fulbe, and followed the king; on seeing which, all the Fulbe came and entered the capital.[23] After they had entered, the tidings reached us about seven o'clock in the evening. When the tidings came, none knew where to lay his head. On the following morning, a great Pulo *mallam*[24] said to us, "Let every one go and remain in his own village, the war[25] is over: let all the common people go, and each cultivate his land!" Then my father called his younger brother, and we arose and went to our town; but when we came, there was nothing at all to eat. So my father called my mother at night, when all the people were gone, and said to her, "Our town is ruined; if we remain, the Fulbe will make an end of us: arise, and load our things upon our children!" Now there was a town, Magerari[26] by name, which is subject to the Shuwa; and the Fulbe never meddle with any place that is subject to the Shuwa.[27] So we arose, and went to that town; but when we had lived there one year, the *mai* went, turned the Fulbe out of the capital, and went in himself and abode there.[28]

---

was Ahmad, son of Ali, who is said to have become blind. He abdicated after his arrival at Kurnawa in favor of his son, Dunama. It was also apparently at this time and from Kurnawa that the appeal for help was first made to Muḥammad al-Amin al-Kanemi. This particular Kurnawa, however, cannot be positively identified. It is a common place name, and at least two towns called Kurnawa are located to the east and southeast of Birnin Gazargamo. Ali Eisami deals with these events in greater detail in Koelle, *African Native Literature*, pp. 221 ff.

23. March-April 1808 (Muharram-Safar, A.H. 1223) is the most likely date for the first Fulbe occupation of Birnin Gazargamo (Ibadan Arabic MSS, Bornu 52; H. R. Palmer, *Gazetteer of Bornu Province* [Lagos, 1929], p. 18). Muḥammad al-Amin's first letter to the Fulbe leaders about the troubles in Bornu is dated May 1808 (Rab' I, A.H. 1223), though it does not actually mention the sack of the capital. Ali Eisami's account (reckoning from the eclipse in November 1807) would put the event after the rains in 1809. This is certainly too late.

24. Possibly Gwoni Mukhtar, the leader of the Daya Fulbe in this attack.

25. It is indicative that Ali Eisami used the ordinary Kanuri word for war, *krige*, and not the term *jihad*, which would have implied a recognition of the Fulbe religious goals.

26. Mongono Magirari (as this town is called below) is not precisely identified. There is a famous Mongono near the western shore of Lake Chad in what is now Shuwa country. Similarly, there is a Mongono in central Bornu, in the area allotted to the Shuwa by Moḥammad al-Amin after his reconquest.

27. The Shuwa Arabs were, like the Fulbe, a non-Kanuri minority, long domiciled in Bornu. The Fulbe did not, in truth, meddle with them, probably because of their respect for Arabic-speaking peoples and because the Shuwa way of life and their position in Kanuri society were similar in so many ways to their own.

28. This passage refers to the reoccupation of Birnin Gazargamo by the young *mai*, Dunama, with the help of Muḥammad al-Amin al-Kanemi, most probably before the rains

About one year after this event, when my father had died, as it were today, at two o'clock in the afternoon, and we had not yet buried him, intending to do so next day, then we slept, and on the following morning, my mother called me, and my elder and my younger sister, and said to us, "Live well together, you three; behold, your father lies here a corpse, and I am following your father." Now there was just then a *mallam* with us who said to my mother, "Why do you say such things to your children?" but my mother replied to the *mallam*, "I say these things to my children in truth." Then she called me, and I rose up, went, and sat down before her. When I had sat down, she said to me, "Stretch out your legs, that I may lay my head in your lap." So I stretched out my legs, and she took her head, and laid it on my lap; but when the *mallam* who was staying with us saw that my mother was laying her head on my lap he rose, came, sat down by me, stretched out his legs, and took my mother's head from my lap, and laid it upon his own. Then that moment our Lord took away my mother. After this tears came from my eyes, and when the *mallam* saw it, he said to me, "Let me not see tears in your eyes! will your father and your mother arise again, and sit down, that you may see them, if you weep?" I attended to what the *mallam* said, and did not weep any more. With the corpse of our father before us, and with the corpse of our mother before us, we did not know what to do, till the people of the town went and dug graves for both of them, side by side, in one place, and came back again, when we took the corpses, carried and buried them, and then returned.

After waiting two months at home, I took my younger sister, and gave her to a friend of my father's in marriage, my elder sister being already provided with a husband. On one occasion I got up after night had set in, without saying anything to my sister, took my father's spear, his charms, and one book which he had, set out on a journey, and walked in the night, so that it was not yet day when I reached the town of Shagou,[29] where there was a friend of my father's, a Shuwa; and, when I came to the dwelling place of this friend of my father's, they were just in the open space in front of the house. When I came to him, and he saw me, he knew me, and I

---

in early 1809. Gwoni Mukhtar, whose forces were largely dispersed with their cattle during the dry season, was killed (see Ali Eisami's more detailed account in Koelle, *African Native Literature*, pp. 222–23).

29. Probably the village of that name in south-central Bornu.

knew him. I having saluted him, he asked me, "Where is your father?" I replied to him, saying, "My father is no more, and my
mother is no more, so I left both my elder and my younger sister, and
came to you." Whereupon he said to me, "Come, my son, we will
stay together; your father did good to me, and now since he is no
more, and you did like me and come to me, I also like you: I will do
to you what I do to my own son."

After I had been there about three years, I called a companion,
saying, "Come and accompany me!" for I had a friend in the town
of the name of Gubber.[30] The youth arose, and we started together,
but as we were going towards the town of Gubber, seven Fulbe way-
laid us, seized us, tied our hands upon our backs, fettered us, put us
in the way, and then we went till it became day.[31] When it was day,
both they and we became hungry in a hostile place, the land being
the land of Ngizim.[32] In this place we sat down, and ate the fruit of
a certain tree called ganga, till it became dark, when they took us
again, and carried us to the town of Ngololo[33] to market. On that
day some Hausa bought us, took us into a house, and put iron fetters
on our feet; then, after five days, we set out, and were twenty-two
days, till we arrived in Hausa. When we arrived, we went to a town
called Tsangaya where there are a great many dates.[34] In this town
we remained during the months of Asham, Soual, and Kide,[35] but
when only three days of the [month of] Atshi were passed, they
roused me up, and in a week we came to Birnin Katsina, where they

30. A village some fifteen miles west of Shagou.
31. It is not surprising that Ali Eisami and his friend were captured, given the circumstances of the period. By this time, Birnin Gazargamo had again fallen to the Fulbe
under Ibrāhīm Zaki, the emir of Katagum. Mai Dunama was then deposed by his uncle,
Muḥammad Ngeleruma. Muḥammad succeeded in recapturing the capital, but he later
surrendered the office of mai to Ibrāhīm, Dunama's younger brother (Ali Eisami, in
Koelle, African Native Literature, pp. 224–26). Muḥammad al-Amin's role in this episode is not clear. Mai Muḥammad Ngeleruma probably tried to operate independently of
him. Mai Ibrāhīm, however, was certainly under his domination. The Fulbe, meanwhile,
mounted two further attacks on Birnin Gazargamo before it was finally abandoned by the
Kanuri in favor of the new capital at Kukawa.
32. The country lying to the north of modern Potiskum in western Bornu.
33. A village some fifty-five miles west of Shagou.
34. Tsangaya is southwest of Ngololo and southeast of Kano. Clapperton passed
through early in 1824 and described it as it then was, somewhat decayed as a result of
the wars, but still with the date trees Ali noticed (Denham and Clapperton, Travels in
Africa, p. 36).
35. That is, the Arabic months of Ramadan, Shawwal, and Dhu-l-qa'da, or September
to November, 1812.

slew the Easter-lamb,[36] and after five days they rose again, and we started for Yauri. After marching a fortnight, we arrived at Birnin Yauri. Here the Hausa sold us, and took their goods, whilst Borgawa[37] bought us. The Borgawa roused us up, and when we came to their town, the man who had bought me, did not leave me alone at all: I had iron fetters round my feet, both by night and by day. After I had stayed with him seven days, he took me, and brought me to the town of Sai,[38] where a Yoruba bought me.

The Yoruba who bought me was a son of the Katunga king;[39] he liked me, and called me to sit down before him, and, on seeing my tattoo-marks, he said to me, "Were you the son of a king in your country?" To this I replied, "My father, as for me, I will not tell lies, because times are evil, and our Lord has given me into slavery: my father was a scholar."[40] Then he said, "As for this youth and his father, his father must have been a fine man; I will not treat him ill," and so he kept me in his house. In this place I remained a long time, so that I understood their language. After I had been there four years, a war arose:[41] now, all the slaves who went to the war, became free; so when the slaves heard these good news, they all ran there, and the Yoruba saw it. The friend of the man who had bought me, said to him, "If you do not sell this slave of yours, he will run away, and go to the war, so that your cowries will be lost, for this fellow has sound eyes." Then the man took hold of me, and bound me, and

36. The "Easter" feast, *'Id al-kabir,* was celebrated in Katsina in December. It is curious that Ali Eisami went from Tsangaya to Katsina without passing through Kano, or, if he did, that he does not mention it.

37. The people of Borgu, the country lying west and southwest of Birnin Yauri. The Borgawa are not linguistically akin to the Hausa, and they were well known for their resistance to the Fulbe jihad.

38. Sai (or Saitu, as it appears in the Kanuri text) is not identified. It possibly lay in the now-deserted area between Old Oyo and Kaiami.

39. Katunga, meaning "the wall," is the Hausa name for Old Oyo. Hence, the Katungan king should be the *Alafin;* but it is probable that the office of *Alafin* was vacant until about 1817. However, the period was extremely confused in Old Oyo, and Ali's owner could equally well have been the son of a former *Alafin,* or else the son of a claimant to the title.

40. Here he uses the term *fugara,* a scholar-student.

41. There is little doubt that this war was Afonja's revolt. Specialists on Yoruba history incline to date this revolt in 1817, which is confirmed here by Ali Eisami and is congruent with the dates supplied by Crowther, who lived nearby (see below; Chap 9). Afonja's revolt is also associated with a flight of slaves from Old Oyo, such as is mentioned here (Samuel Johnson, *The History of the Yorubas* [Lagos, 1921], pp. 193 ff; see also H. Clapperton, *Journal of a Second Expedition into the Interior of Africa* [London, 1829], p. 39).

Ali Eisami Gazirmabe, alias William Harding, in Freetown about 1850. From
S. W. Koelle, *Grammar of the Bornu or Kanuri Language*.

A cavalryman of Bornu in the 1820's. From Denham and Clapperton, *Narrative of Travels and Discoveries in Northern Central Africa.*

his three sons took me to the town of Ajashe,[42] where white men had landed; then they took off the fetters from my feet, and carried me before them to the white people, who bought me, and put an iron round my neck. After having bought all the people, they took us, brought us to the seashore, brought a very small canoe, and transferred us one by one to the large vessel.

The people of the great vessel were wicked: when we had been shipped, they took away all the small pieces of cloth which were on our bodies, and threw them into the water, then they took chains, and fettered two together. We in the vessel, young and old, were seven hundred, whom the white men[43] had bought. We were all fettered round our feet, and all the oldest died of thirst, for there was no water. Every morning they had to take many, and throw them into the water: so we entreated God by day and by night, and, after three months, when it pleased God to send breezes, we arose in the morning, and the doors were opened. When we had all come on deck, one slave was standing by us, and we beheld the sky in the midst of the water.

When I looked at the horizon, my eye saw something far away, like trees. On seeing this, I called the slave, and said to him, "I see a forest yonder, far away." Whereupon he said to me, "Show it to me with your finger!" When I had shown it to him, and he had seen the place at which my finger pointed, he ran to one of the white men who liked me, and would give me his shirts to mend, and then gave me food, he being a benefactor; now, when the slave told it him, the white man who was holding a roasted fowl in his hand, came to me, together with the slave. This slave who understood their language, and also the Hausa,[44*] came and asked me, saying, "Show me with your finger what you see, that the white man also may see it!" I

42. The region of modern Porto Novo. The trade route between Old Oyo and Ajashe had long been a main artery of trade between the interior and the coastlands, passing as it did through the open country to the west of the Egba forest; and the *Alafin* had established his influence along this route as far back as the end of the seventeenth century (Johnson, *Yorubas,* pp. 74 ff., 183; A. Dalzel, *The History of Dahomey* [London, 1793], pp. 179 ff.; J. Adams, *Sketches Taken during Ten Voyages to Africa, 1786–1800* [London, 1822], p. 80). With the decline and abandonment of Old Oyo as a commercial center, this route was diverted—to the west through Borgu and to the east through Ilorin and eastern Yoruba.

43. The term used here for white men is *wasili,* the normal Kanuri word for the Tuareg and the North Africans. The white men in this case are said to have been Spaniards.

44*. Which Ali likewise speaks a little.

showed it, and when the white man brought his eye, and laid it upon my finger, he also saw what I pointed at. He left the roasted fowls which he held in his hand and wanted to eat, before me, and ran to their Captain. Then I took the fowl, and put it into my bag. All of them ran, and loaded the big big guns with powder and their very large iron. We, not knowing what it was, called the Hausa who understood it, and said to him, "Why do the white men prepare their guns?" and he said to us, "What you saw were not trees, but a vessel of war is coming towards us." We did not believe it, and said "We have never seen any one make war in the midst of water," and, after waiting a little, it came, and when it was near us, our own white men fired a gun at them; but it still went on. When the white men with us had fired a gun nine times, the white man-of-war was vexed and fired one gun at our vessel, the ball of which hit the middle mast with those very large sails, cut it off, and threw it into the water. Then the white men with us ran to the bottom of the vessel, and hid themselves. The war-chief, a short man, of the name of Captain Hick,[45]* brought his vessel side by side with ours, whereupon all the war-men came into our vessel, sword in hand, took all our own white men, and carried them to their vessel.[46] Then they called all of us, and when we formed a line, and stood up in one place, they counted us, and said, "Sit down!" So we sat down, and they took off all the fetters from our feet, and threw them into the water, and they gave us clothes that we might cover our nakedness, they opened the water-casks, that we might drink water to the full, and we also ate food, till we had enough. In the evening they brought drums, and gave them to us, so that we played till it was morning. We said, "Now

45*. I wrote this name from Ali's pronunciation, and so I am not quite sure whether it is correct: it might also be Heck, or Hicks, or Egg. [The commanders of the two ships then on West African Station for the Royal Navy were Yeo of the *Semiramis* and Willes of the *Cherub*. The individual in question, however, might possibly be Samuel Tuck, Master of the *Cherub*.]

46. The slave ship and its capture are hard to identify in British naval records of the period. Ali's description of his journey at sea, however, suggests that the ship dropped south of the equator in order to catch the southeast trades, and that it then was becalmed in the doldrums somewhere in mid-Atlantic. A foreign ship captured in this situation might well have been taken to Sierra Leone for condemnation. One captured in West Indian waters would more likely have been turned in to a vice-admiralty court there. Two pirates with slaves on board were captured late in 1817 or early in 1818 on the African coast itself (both by H.M.S. *Cherub*), but both were captured within sight of land, neither had a large number of slaves, and the descriptions of the engagements in the *Cherub's* log do not fit that given by Ali Eisami.

our Lord has taken us out of our slavery," and thanked him. Then
came a white man, stood before me, and after looking at me, slapped
both my cheeks, took me to the place where they cooked food, and
said to me, "You must cook, so that your people may eat." So I
cooked food, and distributed the water with my own hand, till they
brought us and landed us in this town [Freetown], where we were
a week in the king's house [King's Yard], and then they came and
distributed us among the different towns.

We went and settled in the forest[47]* at Bathurst.[48] We met a white
man in this town whose name was Mr. Decker, and who had a wife,
and was a reverend priest. On the following morning we all went,
and stood up in his house, and having seen all of us, he came, took
hold of my hand, and drew me into his house, and I did not fear
him; but I heard inside the house that my people without were talking, and saying, "The white man has taken Ali, and put him into the
house, in order to slaughter him."[49]* So I looked at the white people,
and they looked at me. When the white man arose and went to the
top of the house, I prepared myself, and thought, "If this white man
takes a knife, and I see it in his hand, I will hold it," but the white
man was gone up to fetch shirts, and trousers, and caps down. On
coming down, he said to me, "Stand up!" So when I stood up, he put
me into a shirt, put trousers over my legs, gave me a jacket, and put a
cap upon my head. Then he opened the door, and when we came
out, all our people were glad. He called a man who understood the
white man's language, and said to him, "Say that this one is the chief
of all his people."[50]* Then the man told me so. When they carried us
to the forest the day before, my wife followed after me; and on the
day after our arrival the white man married us, and gave me my
wife, so we went and remained in the house of our people.

The white man was a benefactor, and he liked me. But, after a
few days, his wife became ill, so we took her, and carried her to the
town of Hog-brook [later Regent]; and then the illness exceeded
her strength, and our Lord sought her. After this he arose in our

47*. As the neighborhood of Bathurst was in those days.

48. One of the villages for the reception of recaptives, Bathurst had only recently
been founded, in 1817, within a year of Ali's arrival there in April 1818.

49*. Many Negroes believed, on being shipped in slave vessels, that the white men
were cannibals who had almost eaten up their own countrymen, and now came to fetch
black men to gratify their appetite for human flesh.

50*. From that time Ali was for many years a constable.

town, and we took his things, and carried them to Freetown, where he said to us, "Go, and remain quiet; I go to our own country, not knowing whether I shall come back again, or not." Then he shook hands with us, bade us farewell, and went to their own country. We returned and settled down until the Lord brought the minister, Mr. Renner, to our town.[51]

Until now our Lord has preserved me, but "God knows what is to come," say the Bornuans. I also heard the great men say, "What is to come even a bird with a long neck cannot see, but our Lord only."— This is an account of what I experienced from my childhood till today, and what I have been telling you is now finished.

51. Rev. Melchior Renner, a German Lutheran who served the Church Missionary Society in Sierra Leone and Rio Pongas from 1804 until his death in 1821 (Fyfe, *Sierra Leone,* pp. 94–95, 130, 153).

CHAPTER 8

OSIFEKUNDE OF IJEBU

P. C. Lloyd

The story of Osifekunde is an appealing one. This Ijebu lad, seized by Ijo pirates in the lagoons of the Nigerian coast, was sold into slavery and spent almost twenty years in Brazil. Then he came to France, with his master, and subsequently lived in Paris, employed as a servant in several houses. Here he met Marie Armand Pascal d'Avezac-Macaya, vice-president of the Société Ethnologique of Paris and member of numerous geographical societies and associations with interests in Africa and the Orient. D'Avezac realized that Joaquim (as he was called in France) came from the kingdom of Ijebu on the Guinea Coast—a kingdom which had been named on the maps of the seventeenth and eighteenth centuries, but of which European travellers had less knowledge than of almost any other part of this coast. D'Avezac interrogated his informant for weeks on his homeland and its language. He also arranged for Osifekunde's return to Africa, but in the end Osifekunde preferred servitude under his former master in Brazil, where he could be with his own son, rather than passage to Sierra Leone—still far from his original home. He slipped away secretly from Le Havre and disappeared from history.

D'Avezac, in this account, not only tells the story of Osifekunde and of the family into which he was born; he also gives us a very full ethnographic account of the land and its people. This was published in 1845, having been written in about 1840 from Osifekunde's recollections of conditions in the 1810's. Yet even at this thirty-year remove, the information was a most significant addition to European knowledge of the Guinea Coast and the hinterland of Lagos. At the height of the slave trade a few decades earlier, Lagos had played only a minor role despite its strategic location at one of the few exits of the lagoon system into the sea. European slave ships entered the estuaries of the Niger Delta, but they left lagoon traffic to their African suppliers. Thus Adams' detailed report of trade conditions about 1800 gives only hearsay evidence of an Ijebu kingdom north of Lagos lagoon.[1]

The earliest Portuguese explorers had mentioned the city of Ijebu Ode in their reports,[2] and Ijebu legends relate that Portuguese people once lived in the Ijada quarter of the city. No contemporary records have come to light confirming this, however; almost everything that is known or surmised about pre-nineteenth-century Ijebu depends upon oral tradition. Ijebu myths relate that Obanta, founder of the present dynasty of rulers, came from the northeast by way of Ile Ife, the mythical cradle of all the Yoruba. A comparison with the myths of neighboring areas, however, suggests that Obanta may have been a rebel prince or warrior from Benin, who founded a kingdom at Ijebu Ode in the fourteenth or early fifteenth century. Obanta apparently entered an area that was already well settled, with several small kingdoms, each having its own ruler. Idoko seems to have been the largest of these political units, all of which were finally consolidated into a single kingdom. To the northeast of the Ijebu lay the powerful kingdom of Owu; to the north were the numerous small kingdoms of the Egba. Thick forests on the east separated Ijebu from the Ondo, and to the west were the small Egbado kingdoms and the Awori of the Lagos area.

With the rise of Lagos as the port of entry to the newly founded towns of Abeokuta and Ibadan in the nineteenth century and with the increasing importance of the arms trade in maintaining the Yoruba wars, Ijebu found itself in partial control of the major trade routes to the interior. The rise and expansion of Ibadan from the 1830's brought a new power into existence, replacing the strategic

1. J. Adams, *Remarks on the Country Extending from Cape Palmas to the River Congo* ... (London, 1823), esp. pp. 96–98.

2. One account describes it as being surrounded by a huge rampart (Duarte Pacheco Pereira, *Esmeraldo de Situ Orbis* [Portuguese text, with French trans., ed. Raymond Mauny, Bissau, 1956], pp. 130–31). The rampart may be the *eredo* of Sungbo described by P. C. Lloyd, "Sungbo's *Eredo*," *Odu*, 7:15–22 (1959).

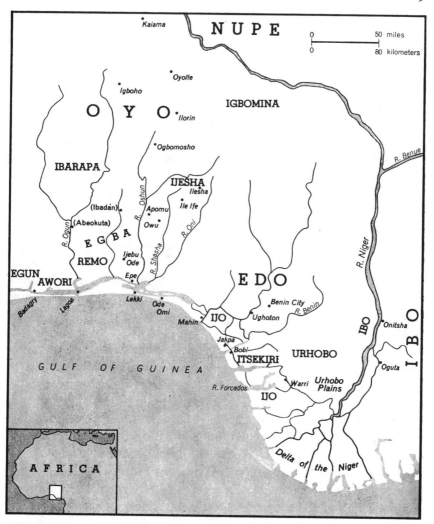

Map 13. Western and midwestern Nigeria, *ca.* 1820.

position once held by Owu. Ijebu, on the direct route to Ibadan, developed a chronic hostility toward the new Egba state of Abeokuta, which dominated the alternate route farther west, and toward Ibadan itself, which sought to control its own trade with Lagos. It is said that in order to maintain their hold over this trade the Ijebu forbade strangers to traverse their territory; and there have been further suggestions that, had strangers seen the small size of their capital, Ijebu Ode, the kingdom would have been quickly conquered.

This exclusiveness was ended in 1896 when a British expeditionary force landed at Epe and marched on Ijebu Ode, following an Ijebu closure of trade routes contrary to treaty agreements. Dating from this time, Ijebu swiftly became the vanguard of all Yoruba in acceptance of Western culture. By 1950, they had a higher proportion of children in school than any other Yoruba group and a smaller proportion of persons claiming, in census returns, to worship traditional Yoruba deities. With the *pax Britannica,* Ijebu travelled to all parts of Nigeria as traders and craftsmen, using their savings to build elaborate houses in their home towns and villages. Today the traditional ways of life are disappearing faster in Ijebu than in almost any other part of Yoruba.

Ijebu Ode lies on an escarpment of sedimentary rocks. The soil is porous: the valleys cut deeply into a predominantly flat landscape. Only in the north of the kingdom does one meet the crystalline rocks of the Basement Complex with its undulating scenery, heavier soils, and dense forests. Ijebu Ode remains to this day a relatively small town by Yoruba standards, having a population of only 26,000 (1952 census), while the present-day population of Ijebu as a whole is about a half million. The settlement pattern, however, is unlike that of most of Yoruba, in that the capital is immediately surrounded by more than a hundred small villages—units of permanent settlement and not hamlets to which the farming population commutes as they do from Ibadan or Abeokuta. This area around and including the capital has one of the highest population densities in Yoruba, and the antiquity of most of the villages suggests that a relatively high figure prevailed in the past. Today, the country has been largely stripped of its forest cover. Poor soils and insufficient land are probably one cause of the prevalent Ijebu emigration to work elsewhere as traders and craftsmen.

The most significant feature of D'Avezac's work with Osifekunde is the extent of its ethnographic detail, which is unique in the present collection. None of the other reporters in this volume had the scientific training of D'Avezac, nor the interest in pursuing a line of questioning that would reveal the whole pattern of an African way of life. D'Avezac-Macaya, moreover, was one of the important figures in the Société Ethnologique, the first professional society of the new science of anthropology. In 1841, the Society put together the first professionally oriented list of desiderata, in the form of a questionnaire for the guidance of field researchers—the direct forebear of similar guides still in use within the profession. D'Avezac was the first ethnographer to make systematic use of this document—not in the field, but in his questioning of Osifekunde in Paris.[3]

When, however, we attempt to estimate the reliability of his work, we are in immediate difficulty. There are no other precolonial accounts giving similar information which might be used to corroborate or refute the picture he gives us. In some fields, particularly religion and government, the traditional institutions have been so modified in the present century that we cannot tell whether the almost unrecognizable accounts given by D'Avezac represent inaccurate reporting or rapid change.

The source of these data certainly leaves something to be desired. Osifekunde was only twenty years old at the time of his enslavement —old enough to comprehend the details of domestic life, but surely immature as a politically conscious citizen. No modern anthropologist would use so young an informant for details of his society's political structure, particularly in the case of a centralized kingdom. A youth of this age, for example, would hardly be expected to understand the constitutional relationships between different grades of chiefs. Furthermore, we know nothing of the company in which Osifekunde spent his life in Brazil. Was he with other Ijebu, with whom he would presumably have discussed his homeland, or with other Yoruba? If the latter, he may have acquired a more generalized picture of Yoruba country, applicable only in part to Ijebu. If the former case, how far might these slaves have built up an overglamorized image of their homeland? A third caveat arises from the difficulty of communication between Osifekunde and D'Avezac. The informant knew little or no French, and their discussions were held in pidgin Portuguese. D'Avezac may well have reported Osifekunde's statements accurately, but, in the circumstances, ambiguities in elaboration of detail would have been difficult to resolve.

These caveats, however, vary in importance, depending on the area of knowledge Osifekunde was covering. One of D'Avezac's main tasks was to delineate the Ijebu kingdom: in Osifekunde he had a widely travelled informant. D'Avezac seems to have had quite a remarkable success in locating Ijebu Ode itself and the lagoonside

3. P. D. Curtin, *The Image of Africa* (Madison, Wis., 1964), pp. 329–32, 334–35.

towns. In fact, some of his estimates of distances, based on Osi-fekunde's units of "half day's journeys by canoe" seem uncannily close to reality. Yet at other times Osifekunde's data are markedly inconsistent. His descriptions of routes into the interior are difficult to comprehend. Some of the towns mentioned cannot now be iden-tified, though possibly they were relatively small places destroyed in the wars of the early nineteenth century. Others, which can be iden-tified, are obviously misplaced. Although Osifekunde claims to have travelled into the interior, his knowledge of this area falls far behind that of the lagoon routes.

In his description of the Ijebu political system and, in particular, of the types of chiefs and of military organization, D'Avezac's ac-count has few points of contact with the "ethnographic present" of mid-twentieth-century anthropological research. Here it seems rea-sonable to presume that Osifekunde's knowledge was at fault in spite of his father's high political office. Yet it seems strange that titles as important as *ladeke* should have vanished so completely. In other fields, and especially in his accounts of daily life, Osifekunde seems much more plausible. Yet how far may we trust him on points of de-tail which diverge from what we can see at the present time? It is difficult to find an answer.

Casting doubt on the accuracy of so much of D'Avezac's ethnogra-phy might appear to discredit it entirely as a contribution to our knowledge of Ijebu. It is not my intention, however, to claim greater reliability for the reconstruction of Ijebu society of more than a cen-tury ago from what we can deduce at the present time.[4] Indeed, D'A-vezac's account seems especially valuable in three areas.

First, the life story of Osifekunde stresses the importance of lagoon transport. Today, we see the coastal parts of Yoruba and the creeks of the Niger Delta as areas of relatively poor communications, avoided by modern road systems. Yet compared to a man on foot the canoe provides a superior form of transport. With judicious use of tides, it travels much faster and can bear considerably heavier loads. Before the motor age, travel on the lagoons was far easier than movement through the forests to the north and west of Ijebu Ode. The trade links between Ijebu and Benin were probably far more significant than we imagine today.

Second, the mention of the "Idoko nation" substantiates the im-

4. As, for example, P. C. Lloyd, *Yoruba Land Law* (London, 1962), Chap. VI.

portance of a political unit which otherwise exists only in the myths. (And even here evidence is controversial, for it is obviously in the interest of the rulers in Ijebu Ode to expunge any record of rival or pre-existing dynasties.)

Third, D'Avezac's major contribution may prove to be his linguistic work. Although D'Avezac's extensive vocabulary of Ijebu words is omitted from the present volume because of its specialized field of interest, it is an extremely valuable body of data. Differences between Yoruba dialects are fading in the present century, and many words and phrases peculiar to Ijebu are undoubtedly already lost. While there is no certainty that Osifekunde had not acquired non-Ijebu forms of speech during his twenty years away from Africa, it seems safe to assume that a forty-year-old will remember with fair accuracy the language he spoke for his first twenty years. D'Avezac himself seems to have had a good ear and to have recorded Ijebu words with considerable finesse.[5]

THE LAND AND PEOPLE OF IJEBU

D'Avezac-Macaya's account of Ijebu on the basis of information from Osife-kunde has the external appearance of a short monograph rather than a personal narrative. Even though Osifekunde was responsible for most of the data on Ijebu itself, D'Avezac tried to make the most of the literary sources on neighboring regions and to provide full scholarly annotation. Some of this apparatus is now out of date, but D'Avezac was one of the first European scholars to consider the methodological problems of using African oral data —in his case mainly for ethnology and geography. His small treatise is therefore reproduced with only a few brief omissions, indicated and summarized at the appropriate point in the text. D'Avezac's notes have been retained, and are marked with an asterisk.

The text itself is a translation by Philip D. Curtin from "Notice sur le pays et le peuple des Yébous, en Afrique," by M. d'Avezac, as published in the *Mémoires de la Société Ethnologique*, 2(2): 1–10; 13–27, 30–46, 53–105 (1845). An appendix entitled "Esquisse grammaticale de la langue Yébous" (pp. 106–96 of the original) is omitted here. Vernacular words are given as D'Avezac wrote them, though without his diacritical marks; place names are given in D'Avezac's spelling at their first occurrence, with modern spelling

5. The sections of his work dealing with language are to be found in *Mémoires de la Société Ethnologique*, 2(2):47–53, 106–96 (1845).

in brackets. Subsequent references to identifiable names, however, are given in the modern spelling only. Unidentified or doubtful place names are shown in quotation marks. All interpolations within brackets, either in the text or in the footnotes, are by the present editor.

INTRODUCTION

I. Sources of Information

1. The use of oral information for the investigation of African peoples

It is not only through long and rigorous exploration, aided by all the resources of science, still less through reconnaissance expeditions (however intelligent and accurate), that one may ask for results worthy of being registered in the great book of knowledge about the countries and peoples of the world.

Vast continents streaked at great intervals by the infrequent paths of explorers would still be almost unknown if those narrow and widely scattered lines that record the passage of the European traveller had not been joined to data of another dimension, collected on the spot from the mouths of the natives. Africa in particular offers an unlimited field for enquiries of this kind. Seetzen, Burckhardt, Rüppell, Browne, Hornemann, Lyon, Bowdich, Dupuis, Clapperton,[6*]

6* U. J. Seetzen, "Nachrichten von dem Negerlande Fur," "Nachrichten von dem Negerlande Mobba und einigen Nachbarlaendern," "Ueber das grosse Afrikanische Reich Bornu und dessen Nebenlaendern, und ueber die Sprache von Assadeh." These three pieces, prepared in Cairo in October and November, 1808, appeared in Baron von Zach's *Monatliche Correspondenz*, XIX, 429–446 (May 1809); XXI, 137–155 (February 1810); XXII, 269–275 and 328–341 (October 1810). A French translation is found in Malte-Brun's *Annales des Voyages*, XXI, 143–179 and XIX 164–184 [*sic*, reversal of volume numbers].

J. L. Burckhardt, *Travels in Nubia*, London, 1819, in-4°. In the appendix are found: "Itinerary from the frontiers of Bornou by Bahr el Ghazal and Darfour to Shendi," pp. 477–483; "Some Notices on the Countries of the Soudan West of Darfour, with Vocabularies of the Borgo and Bornou Languages; Collected at Cairo from Negro Pilgrims in the Winter of 1816–1817," pp. 484–492.

Ed. Rueppell, "Notice sur Mehemet-Beg et sa carte du Kordoufan," appeared in Baron von Zach's *Correspondance astronomique*, XI, 359–370 (October 1821), reprinted in Messrs. Eyriès and Malte-Brun's *Nouvelles Annales des Voyages*, XXIV, 409–422 (December 1824) and in M. Verneur's *Journal des Voyages*, XXIV, 263–282 (December 1824).

and many others[7]* have shown what services they can render to geography by relying with care and wisdom on such sources of plentiful and select information about countries hitherto unexplored.

Still bolder efforts have been made in the interest of science. Who can ignore the rich harvest of light that Ludolf gathered at Gotha

---

W. C. Browne, *Travels in Africa, Egypt, and Syria, from the Year 1792 to 1798*, London, 1799, in-4°. See the appendices: "Illustrations of the Maps," pp. 445–450, and "Itineraries," pp. 451–473.

F. Hornemann, *The Journal of Frederick Hornemann's Travels from Cairo to Mourzouk, the Capital of the Kingdom of Fezzan in Africa, in the Years 1797–98*, London, 1802, in-4°. See appendix: "A Memoir Containing Various Information Respecting the Interior of Africa, Transmitted from Mourzouk in 1799 by F. Hornemann," pp. 105–119.

Captain J. F. Lyon, R.N., *A Narrative of Travels in Northern Africa in the Years of 1818, 19 and 20, Accompanied by Geographical Notices of Soudan and the Course of the Niger*, London, 1819, in-4°. *Passim*, but especially pp. 121–151.

T. E. Bowdich, *Mission from Cape Coast Castle to Ashantee, with a Statistical Account of that Kingdom, and Geographical Notices of Other Parts of the Interior of Africa*, London, 1819, in-4°, pp. 161–227 and 422–432.

J. Dupuis, *Journal of a Residence in Ashantee, Comprising Notes and Researches Relative to the Gold Coast and the Interior of Western Africa, Chiefly Collected from Arabic Mss. and Information Communicated by the Moslems of Guinea*, London, 1820, in-4°, pp. 1–115, and appendix, pp. 124–135.

Denham and Clapperton, *Narrative of Travels and Discoveries in Northern and Central Africa, in the Years 1822, 1823 and 1824*, London, 1826, in-4°. Appendix No. 12: "Geographical and Historical Account of the Kingdom of Takroor," pp. 158–167. Clapperton, *Journal of a Second Expedition into the Interior of Africa from the Bight of Benin to Soccatoo*, London, 1829, in-4°, or Philadelphia, 1829, in-8°. Appendix, "The Late Captain Clapperton's Arabic Papers," Translated by Mr. A. V. Saleme, pp. 389–403.

7*. Such as Niebuhr, *Deutsche Museum*, issue of October 1790, pp. 963–1004; A. Von Einsiedel, "Nachricht von den innern Landern von Afrika," in Cuhn's collection, *Reisen in das innere von Afrika*, Leipzig, 1791, in-8°, III, 433–447; V. Denon, *Voyage dans la basse et la haute Egypte*, Paris, 1803, in-12, I, 307–310); M. J. Lapanouze, "Caravanes du Darfuth et du Sennaar," in *Mémoires sur l'Egypte*, Paris, An XI, IV, 77–124; Ledyard and Lucas, in *Proceedings of the African Association, passim;* Mungo Park, *The Journal of a Mission to the Interior of Africa in the Year 1803*, London, 1815, in-4°, pp. 281–284; [James] Grey Jackson, *Account of Morocco*, London, 1814, in-4°, pp. 282–314; *Account of Timbuctoo and Houssa*, London, 1820, in-8°, pp. 1–54; Riley *An Authentic Narrative of the Loss of the American Brig Commerce*, Hartford, 1817, in-8°, pp. 266–295; Fitz-Clarence, *Journal of a Route across India through Egypt to England*, London, 1819, in-4°, pp. 486–498; Cochelet, *Naufrage du brick français la Sophie*, Paris 1821, in-8°, II, 1–26 and 330–334; Koenig, "Renseignements sur diverses contrées à l'ouest du Darfour," in *Bulletin de la Société de Géographie*, VI, 169–175 (October 1826); Lander, *Journal of an Expedition to Explore the Course and Termination of the Niger*, London, 1832, in-18, II, 53–64, 116, 133–138; W. B. Hodgson, "Notice sur les Foulahs," *Bulletin de la Société de Géographie*, IX, 49–52 (January 1838), as well as in *Partington's British Cyclopedia*, I, 918–919; etc.

from his contact in Paris with the Abyssinian, Abba Gorgoryos?[8]* In Paris as well, Guillaume de l'Isle gathered rare data on the states of central Africa from a Tripolitanian envoy.[9]* In London, the African Association, through Beaufoy's agency, received interesting reports on the great routes of communication across the Sahara from the Moor, Ibn Ali.[10]* Still more has been done: Negro slaves who have not lost all memory of their countries have been interrogated at a distance. Thus in the Antilles toward the end of the last century, the Danish missionary, Christian Oldendorp[11]* and the English publicist Bryan Edwards[12]* assembled geographic data, vocabularies, and ethnographic information in regard to the principal nations of western Nigritia, and James MacQueen[13]* found occasional data there to explain and fill out the reports of Mungo Park. It was still before the time of Clapperton's two expeditions that M. d'Andrada[14]* gathered some enlightenment in Brazil about the countries later visited by that explorer, and M. Rugendas[15]* in Brazil also wrote out small vocabularies of certain East African languages. And I can demonstrate the degree of usefulness investigations of this kind can offer, by mentioning the fact that one of these vocabularies made possible an important linguistic discovery by Klaproth—that of the affinity between the language of the Negroes of the east coast and those of the

8*. Job Ludolf, *Historia Aethiopica* and *Commentarius,* Frankfurt, 1681–1691, in-folio.

9*. De l'Isle, *Carte d'Afrique dressée pour l'usage du Roy,* Paris, 1722. One sheet. A series of points are indicated, departing from Tripoli and extending in one direction as far as Bornou and "Courourfa," and in the other as far as "Téloué" and the "Gonge." Intermediate distances are marked in days' travel by caravan, with various other indications based on the manuscript notes of this great geographer, which are preserved at the Ministère de la Marine.

10*. [Henry] Beaufoy, *Proceedings of the Association for Promoting the Discovery of the Interior of Africa,* London, 1790, in-40°, pp. 62, 80, 81.

11*. Oldendorp, "Geographische und Politische Nachrichten von Afrikanischen Nationen," in his *Geschechte der Mission der Evangelischen Brueder auf den Caraibischen Inseln,* 2 vols. Barby, 1777, in-8°. Published by J. J. Brossart. [In fact, Oldendorp was not Danish, but German, though his research was conducted in the Danish West Indies.]

12*. Bryan Edwards, *History of the British West Indies,* 3 vols. London, 1801, in-4°.

13*. James MacQueen, *Geographical and Commercial View of Northern Central Africa,* Edinburgh, 1821, in-8°.

14*. Menèzes de Drumond, "Lettres sur l'Afrique ancienne et moderne," in *Journal des Voyages,* XXXII, 190–321 (December 1826) [sic, should be pp. 190–224].

15*. [Adriano] Balbi, "Introduction" to *Atlas ethnographique du globe,* Paris, 1826, in-8°, pp. 224–227, and in *Nouvelle Annales des Voyages,* I, 133–136 (July 1826).

Congo.[16]* I will say nothing at this point about the samples of various African languages, or the Eyo vocabulary, for which Mrs. Hannah Kilham and Rev. John Raban respectively collected their data in Sierra Leone: I shall have the occasion to return specifically to these two works. More recently, Rev. G. C. Renouard[17]* in London collected the travel accounts of the Negro, Abu Bakr of Timbuktu, and Captain Washington[18]* took down those of the Mandingo, Mohammed Sisei of Niani-Maro; while in the United States of America, Mr. Theodore Dwight[19]* received from the Soninke, Lamine Kebe, a small vocabulary of his language and scarce information on the instruction given to the children of that nation in its schools.[20]*

2. The opportunity to gather information about the Ijebu people

I come in my turn to bring forward a similar offering: I also interrogated, here in Paris, an African uprooted some twenty years ago from his native land and forced to endure a long period of slavery in another hemisphere. When his Brazilian master brought him here three years ago, he became free on touching French soil, but later he

16*. [Heinrich Julius von] Klaproth, "Sur les langues de l'Afrique méridionale," in *Nouvelles Annales des Voyages*, I, 219–224 and 357–368 (September 1826). [In fact, these affinities within the Bantu language-family were recognized by the Portuguese as early as the seventeenth century and were rediscovered and published in England in the late eighteenth century by William Marsden.]

17*. G. C. Renouard, "Routes in North Africa by Abu Bakr es-Siddik," in *Journal of the Royal Geographical Society*, VI, 100–113 (1836). [See above, Chap. 5.]

18*. Capt. J. Washington, R.N., "Some Account of Mohammedu Sisei, a Mandingo of Nyani-Maru on the Gambia," in *Journal of the Royal Geographical Society*, VIII, 448–454 (1838).

19*. T. Dwight, "Remarks on the Sereculehs, an African Nation, Accompanied by a Vocabulary of their Language," in *American Annals of Education and Instruction*, V, 451–456 (October 1835).

20*. Even since the present notice was first communicated to the Société de Géographie, M. Jomard collected some interesting information on the country of Limmou from a young Galla of that nation, who unfortunately died on 5 July 1841. And while the present work is in press, Mr. [W. B.] Hodgson sends word from New York that he intends to take advantage of the presence in the United States of a literate Foulah [Pulo], with whom he has already begun a correspondence in Arabic, in order to obtain the elements of an ethnological introduction, a vocabulary and an essay on grammar. [This account by Ṣāliḥ Bilāli of Massina was first printed in Hodgson's *Notes on Northern Africa, the Sahara, and the Soudan* (New York, 1844), pp. 68–75. It is reprinted above, Chap. 4.]

left secretly and of his own free will for that second fatherland whose warm climate he had always regretted leaving.

Chance brought this man to me, and a few questions about his origin revealed a memory of his homeland that aroused my interest. It showed that he belonged to a considerable nation, whose name is barely mentioned in the most voluminous descriptions of Africa and is generally unknown to the best works on geography. It occurs only in the accounts of a few travellers, and even there the total information is no more than a few lines—without a single word of the language, or about the physical characteristics of the people, with nothing that could aid in determining the ethnological classification of this people within the great human family.

The country is no better known. It is barely indicated on the best maps of Africa. Even the coast, neglected by modern hydrographers, is traced on the basis of bearings taken many years ago.

Let us examine the inner part of the Gulf of Guinea, so rich in gold and slaves, and there, between the entrance to the port commonly called Lagos and the river which the Portuguese explorers formerly called Rio-Fermoso [Rio Formoso, now Benin River], there is a gap of 60 nautical miles in the hydrographic explorations of the great Owen expedition.[21] For this region, it is necessary to go back to the old chart by Dalzel, which dates from 1785 [see illustration facing p. 277]. And generally, all the authors to whom we are indebted for the little information we have about this country (and it is almost nothing, as I have said) have, without exception, gathered it prior to the captivity of my informant. The report I am about to give, imperfect and garbled though it may be, is thus both extensive and new in comparison with what we had before.

I owe a word of explanation about the manner in which I obtained these data, since problems of more than one order of difficulty usually go with this kind of scientific inquiry. The Negro, Joaquim (his baptismal name, received in Brazil), could make himself understood in a formless language composed of Portuguese creole and barely recognizable French words, but this was not the whole solution. The questions themselves had to be put in a thousand different forms, in order to be clearly understood by the man with whom I was speaking. It was necessary carefully to prevent the slightest influence on his an-

21. A British naval expedition under Captain W. F. Owen, which conducted extensive surveys of the African coasts in the later 1820's and early 1830's.

swers from the construction of the questions. I gave the greatest attention to avoiding this dangerous pitfall by taking care not to systematize my questions in a preconceived order of ideas, leaving till a later phase the job of drawing out and coordinating the information gathered as though by chance at the whim of a rambling conversation without apparent object.

But whatever care I may have taken to render my questions perfectly intelligible to the idle mind of my informant, however alert I had to be to grasp the meaning of his words, so badly articulated, combined, and distorted, it is still to be feared that more than one misunderstanding may have occurred on one side or the other of these difficult interviews. On many points, no doubt, initially imperfect information was filled out or corrected by later developments. But how many other points have remained without sufficient cross-checking!

I present my work, then, as a kind of challenge. I call on the enthusiasts for African exploration, more numerous each day, to verify, correct, and complete this imperfect essay when the opportunity presents itself.

II. Retrospective Review

1. Earlier notions about the country of Ijebu from charts and other geographic documents

[A section of the original dealing with early exploration is omitted here.][22]

The most recent reports have been those of the English. At first they copied the Dutch and French, but then they explored the coasts themselves for the express purpose of making maritime surveys. Captain Archibald Dalzel aboard the vessel *Tartar* made a reconnaissance in November 1785, which was later combined with the independent work of Captains Joseph Matthews and Clemisson, and finally completed, for the western section, by a special plan of the mouth of the Lagos River made in 1789 by Captain Horseley of Liverpool. The completed chart was inserted in Laurie's *African Pi-*

22. See *Mémoires de la Société Ethnologique*, 2(2):10–12.

lot,[23]* and it must be considered to be the best we have of the region that presently concerns us. The islands off the coast appear as a long and straight tongue of land, cut at certain points by inconsiderable creeks. [Earlier charts showed the towns of "Oddy" and "Curamo" at either end of the lagoon protected by this spit of land.] Oddy [Ode Omi] and a few nameless towns are again indicated, but Curamo [Kuramo] does not reappear. The name of Eco [Eko],[24] or Ichoo (following the Dutch spelling) is restricted to the town of Lagos. The great lagoon is called the Lake of Cradoo [Ikorodu], and a town of the same name is marked near a river on the north shore of the lagoon, along with the village of Quassee [Ikosi] beside the mouth of another small river. At some distance to the north, on the mainland, the name of Jaboo [Ijebu] appears in large capital letters.

There, in their entirety, are the cartographic notions gleaned about this country over four centuries. Let us hasten to add the information of a small number of travellers, all of them English as well, who have said a few words on our subject.

2. Sketch of information about the Ijebu people gathered by travellers

Snelgrave was the first traveller to mention the Ijebu. News from Dahomey, which came to him after his return to England, told how the king, Truro-Audati,[25] taking advantage of the peace he had just concluded with the Joes [Oyo], had turned his arms against the "Yabous," a people of the interior.[26] He carried out his attack

23*. See chart entitled "A new survey of that part of the coast of Africa comprised between Cape Verga and Cape Formoso" in three sheets, first edition 25 May 1789, and reproduced many times since. Near the name, "Jaboo," it carried the following annotation: "N.B. The coast between river Lagos and river Benin, with the soundings, etc., is laid down according to observations made by Capt. Arch. Dalzel in the ship *Tartar*, in November 1783, compared with those of Capt. Joseph Matthews and Capt. Clemisson."

24. Eko is still used by all Yoruba as their name for Lagos.

25. Agadja, ruler of Abomey, 1708–32, sometimes called Guadja Troudo, meaning untiring or incessant in war. See R. Cornevin, *Histoire du Dahomey* (Paris, 1962), pp. 101–3; I. A. Akinjogbin, "Agaja and the Conquest of the Coastal Aja States, 1724–1730," *Journal of the Historical Society of Nigeria*, 2:545–66 (December 1963).

26. Snelgrave refers at some length to the "J-oes," a powerful nation living far to the northeast of Dahomey and armed with cavalry forces. This has been identified with the kingdom of Oyo. His references to "Yahoo" (in the English text) are slight: they live, he

against them in the first months of 1731 and met a vigorous resistance, during which the first rains of the wet season arrived. Then, making a last effort, the king of Dahomey succeeded in driving the Ijebu from their entrenchments, but without being in a condition to pursue them in their retreat. He was forced to return after having lost the better part of his troops and compromised his great military reputation.[27]*

Captain John Adams, whose voyage to Guinea took place in the year 1803 (though his account was not published until twenty years later), made a stop at Lagos, which he reported as belonging to an absolute chief whose domination extended over two or three populous villages on the north bank of the Ikorodu lagoon, which in turn touched on the fertile kingdom of Ijebu, inhabited by an agricultural and manufacturing people. The author described Ikorodu lagoon from his own experience: It is, he said,

a fine piece of water, and of great extent; but the country surrounding it being very low, and but little elevated above the surface, renders it tame and uninteresting. . . . The colour of its water during the wet season, is that of clay, but when dry weather prevails, it is deeply tinged with decomposed vegetable matter. Fish is very abundant in it, particularly mullet, of a large size and flavour; but the atmosphere so quickly decomposes animal matter after life has become extinct, that in four hours after fish has been taken from the lake, it becomes putrid; so that to render it available, as food for Europeans, it must be taken very near the hour of dinner. As for Africans, they are great epicures in fish, as our gourmands are in game; for the nearer it attains the true epicurean flavour in smell, taste, and consistency (which is that of well digested food), the more suitable it is to their palates.

During the rainy season, hippopotami frequent some marshy islands nearly opposite to Lagos;[28] but they are seldom, if

---

says, far inland in a mountainous and forested area. To identify them with the Ijebu seems to be stretching evidence rather too far.

27*. William Snelgrave, *Nouvelle relation de quelques endroits de Guinée, et du commerce d'esclaves qu'on y fait,* Amsterdam 1735, in-12; pp. 174, 175 [originally, *A New Account of Guinea and the Slave Trade* (London, 1734)].

28. No hippopotami are found in the lagoon today.

ever, taken by the natives, although the teeth of these animals are sometimes offered for sale, but which are brought from the towns of Ikorodu and Ikosi, on the north-east margin of the Lake. Alligators are numerous, and infest the ponds from which water is taken for the use of shipping.

The sailors killed one of them measuring thirty feet. "The Ijebu," he added,

inhabit a country situated between Hio [Oyo] and Benin, are a fine looking people, and always seem as if they came from a land of plenty, being stout, healthy, and full of vigour. They are a very industrious people, and manufacture for sale an immense number of common Guinea cloths:[29] besides raising cattle, sheep, poultry, corn, and calavacies, with which they supply their neighbours.[30]*

Closer by twelve to fifteen years to our own time, even though his *Notes on Africa* had been published four years before Adams' *Remarks,* George Robertson also speaks of Ijebu, having seen several merchants from that country in Lagos. He considered it to be a viceroyalty of Benin,[31] situated between Lagos and the Benin River and he represented the inhabitants as active and industrious, very much

29. Cloth is made, almost throughout Yoruba country, by women using the vertical loom. Strips of a width of 20 inches are woven nowadays, two being sufficient for a woman's wrapper, three for a man's covering cloth; or the same amount can be sewn into a vest and trousers, a man's work clothes. The common cloth is woven in white or with indigo blue and white stripes. Cotton and silk embroidery embellishes cloths used by the wealthy men and titled chiefs. The weaving of narrow strips of cloth four inches wide on the horizontal loom, done by men, seems to have spread through Yoruba country in recent years from Oyo.

30*. Capt. John Adams, *Remarks on the Country Extending from Cape Palmas to the River Congo, Including Observations on the Manners and Customs of the Inhabitants,* London, 1823; in-8°; pp. 96 to 98. [The actual location of these quotations is pp. 105–8 of the edition cited.] The date of Adams' voyage is not perceived by the majority of his readers. This date is implicitly indicated by the traveller (p. 56), where he mentions the breaking of the peace of Amiens a little before his arrival in Whydah. He was there while Lionel Absom, commander of the English fort in Whydah was still alive (p. 52 and 55), and it is known from MacLeod (*A Voyage to Africa,* London, 1820, in-12. p. 77) that Absom died at the beginning of July 1803. [The Peace of Amiens was broken on 16 May 1803.]

31. It seems unlikely that Ijebu was tributary to Benin at this period.

superior to their neighbors, making excellent cotton textiles, twelve to fourteen inches wide and very much sought after. Some were white, others of a very stable blue, still others of different colors, quite well dyed, except the yellows. These people wore, he said, a very short kind of trousers (which they called *choocatoo* [Yoruba: *sokoto*]) and a large piece of cloth which served as a covering, and as a mosquito-net during the night.[32]*

In 1817, Bowdich talked at Cape Coast with a mulatto who had been to Ikosi, from whom he received a report which led him (as a result of a misunderstanding either on his own part, or on that of his informant) to transform the Ijebu town of Ikosi on the shore of the lagoon into a capital of a kingdom on the east bank of the Lagos River, about sixty miles from the mouth. Another error on his part was to mistake another people he found mentioned under the name of "Joos" [Oyo] in the anonymous observations added to the account by Robert Adams, the sailor, for the "Jaboos" [Ijebu]. In fact these [Oyo] were the "Joes" of Snelgrave, the "Hios" of John Adams and of Bowdich himself, the "Ayoes," "Eyoes" or "Eyeos" of Dalzel, Norris, and Robertson, and a people whom it is more exact to call "Eyos."

". . . The Ijebu," he added, "are about 40 miles westward of Ikosi, and not behind Ikorodu, as in Norris's map" (the same as that of Dalzel). "They are celebrated for the cloths of their name, of which the Portuguese have shipped such large quantities."[33]*

Dupuis as well named Ijebu and Ikosi among the states of the second rank included along with Benin in the eastern part of the great region of Ouanqarah [Wangara], according to information he received in 1820 from Muslim merchants at Cape Coast; but that was all he had to say.[34]* The Negroes, Bernard and Francis, while enumerating to M. d'Andrada in Brazil in 1819 the places they had passed in coming from the interior of Africa to the factories on the coast where they were sold, named "Dhiabuh" or "Ghebuh" [Ijebu] as one of their last stops.[35]* That is all the books have been able to

32.* G. Robertson, *Notes on Africa, Particularly those Parts which are Situated between Cape Verde and the River Congo,* London 1819, in-8°; pp. 287, 290, 301 to 303.

33*. E. Bowdich, *Voyage dans le pays d'Aschantis,* pp. 317 to 319 of the French translation. [The passage quoted is from the original, *Mission from Cape Coast Castle to Ashantee . . .* (London, 1819), p. 226.]

34.* J. Dupuis, *Journal of a Residence in Ashantee,* p. lii of the 2nd part.

35*. *Journal des voyages,* XXXII, pp. 209, 213.

teach us up to this moment about the country and people of Ijebu, to which the Negro, Joaquim, whom I interrogated, belonged.

Let us come now to the information I received from his own mouth, but first let us say a word about the man himself.

III. The New Informant

Summary history of the Negro, Ochi-Fekoue De [Osifekunde],[36] a native of Ijebu, baptized in Brazil with the name of Joaquim, and known in Paris under that of Joseph

Being about forty-two to forty-four years old, he must have been born about 1798. His birthplace was the village of Omakou [Makun], opposite Ode Omi, and a dependency of the canton of Ekpe [Epe] of which the capital, unknown to our maps, is situated at two days' journey (or sixteen hours) by water to the east of Ikoro-du, on the north shore of the lagoon. However doubtful may be the practice of placing full faith in the magnificent accounts Negroes usually give of the high rank and power of their families, the slightly obtuse simplicity of my informant, his precise notions of the political organization and administrative mechanism of his country, the precision of the detail he gave me about his origins, which he always repeated in the same way whatever the context—these various considerations lead me to accept it as very probable that he belonged (as he says he did) to a numerous and powerful family allied to that of the kings of Ijebu (in which, furthermore, he only claims a very modest rank for himself).

His grandfather, Ochi-Wo, held the office of *ladeke*[37] or treasurer. The first of this great man's fifteen wives was Ogoua Ade, sister of the king Ochi Gade. Two sons were born of this union: the first,

36. "Ochi-Fekoue De," as D'Avezac wrote it, is not clearly identifiable with any modern Yoruba name, and Yoruba scholars disagree as to the best modern usage. It suggests Osifekode, but while Osifeko, meaning "Osi (a deity) commiserates," is well known, Osifekode is not. Another possibility might be Osifekunde, meaning "Osi has appeared in the midst of tears," but the nearest name generally known today is Osifekunwe, or "Osi has washed himself in the tears (of the suppliant mother)." While it remains uncertain, Osifekunde has been adopted as the most likely, mainly because D'Avezac was generally very careful with his orthography, and he appears to be attempting to reproduce the unusual Yoruban nasal sound in the syllable "kun."

37. The title is no longer in use.

Ochi Nande, was carried away by a premature death, leaving three children, two boys named Ogouti and Ogouti Mouyou, and a daughter named Ouroyou. The second, who also died before his father, was Adde Sounlou, whose bravery and prowess in battle added a series of honorific titles to his name, and these had to be repeated to me frequently before I could comprehend their nature and significance. Here they are in full: *Adde Sounlou, okara, agouagoua omale okbo tagoua tagoua, odi olorogou modi,* which is to say, Adde Sounlou, the brave, the faithful watchdog crying "forward, forward," he who captured the enemy chief by cornering him against a wall.

He in turn had a first wife related to the king, who gave him six children, three boys and three girls. The fifth child, who was second among the male children, received the double name of Ochi-Fekoue, to which the patronymic De was added—thus the full name of Ochi-Fekoue De,[38] which the Negro known today as Joaquim bore in his home country. Of his father's other six wives, the last four had no children; the second had one daughter; the third, a daughter and a son. In the over-all birth order of Adde Sounlou's nine children, Osifekunde was seventh.[39]

Here is a small table of names of the wives and children of Adde Sounlou:

First wife: Egghi Ade, mother of six children:
   Erougoul, daughter
   Ogou-Soya, son (father of many children already grown up before Ochi-Fekoue's departure)
   Otoula, daughter
   Okouyi-Mire, daughter
   Ochi-Fekoue, son (my informant)
   Ochi-Noouo, son (six years younger than Ochi-Fekoue)

38. This explanation does not fit modern Ijebu practice, but Ade (meaning "crown") is the first syllable of several Yoruba personal names and a common nickname among the Yoruba. It is therefore conceivable that the informant's name was Osifeko, followed by his father's nickname, Ade. As indicated in n. 36, however, the form Osifekunde has been preferred, though with some uncertainty.

39. The Yoruba are polygynous. The seven wives of Adesounlou indicate that he was a relatively prosperous man. Today, the number of wives per married man is most commonly two. Women bear children throughout their productive years, and age differences of twenty years between the eldest and youngest child are not uncommon.

Second wife: Loubeko, mother of one child:
   Edenounga, daughter (born before Ochi-Fekoue)
Third wife: Lousoumi, mother of two children:
   Outein, daughter (born before Ochi-Fekoue)
   Ogou Sachou, son (younger than Ochi-Fekoue by only three
   and a quarter months)
Fourth wife: Ibousi, without children
Fifth wife: Okouao, without children
Sixth wife: Oulechou, without children
Seventh wife: Ade Gami, without children

Osifekunde followed the calling of his father, which was that of a merchant. They made many trips together in his youth, which he later repeated on his own account. These were most often by water. The most extended reached eastward as far as Gato [Gwatto or Ughoton], where he disembarked in order to reach the capital of Benin (where, at the age of twelve, he remained for three consecutive months). To the southeast, he travelled as far as the town of Ower [Warri], the surroundings of which are infested with Ouyo [Ijo] pirates (those that Landolphe called *Jos*,[40]* and that David de Nyendaal called the *corsaires d'Usa*).[41] To the west, he went no farther than the factory at Lagos. In his journeys by land, he went to the markets of Ijebu's northern neighbors. He thus knew from his own experience the true extent of his native country.[42]

He continued the active life of the travelling merchant till he

---

40*. *Mémoires du capitaine Landolphe,* Paris 1823, in-8°; I, 134, 173; II, 40, 46.

41. The Ijo were primarily a fishing people living in the swamps of the Niger Delta and the lagoon areas to the north of the Benin River. While the eastern Ijo were organized in substantial trading states, the western Ijo were not. For a few, piracy was a remunerative occupation. They seized canoes, selling the occupants as slaves to the Itsekiri, who in turn sold them to the European slave dealers. The western Ijo do not seem to have traded directly with the Europeans. Pirates were the scourge of the Benin River until the middle of the nineteenth century, raiding the Itsekiri canoes as they travelled down the river to the European factories, and also the launches travelling between the factories and the ships anchored beyond the bar of the river. See P. C. Lloyd, "The Itsekiri in the Nineteenth Century: An Outline Social History," *Journal of African History,* 4:207–31 (1963); E. J. Alagoa, "The Settlement of the Niger Delta: Ijo Oral Traditions" (unpublished Ph.D. thesis, University of Wisconsin, 1965).

42. Osifekunde's activities demonstrate the importance of the lagoon routes at this period and probably earlier. Road transport has tended to render them obsolete today, but it must be remembered that, with judicious use of tides, a canoe can travel faster than a man walking and can transport a much greater load.

reached the age of twenty-two. One day in the month of June 1820, he was going in his boat to the town of Omahe [Mahin] (the easternmost town in Ijebu)[43] having bought a rich assortment of European merchandise in Lagos, when he fell into an ambush of Ijo pirates at five o'clock in the morning. They took him to Warri where they kept him four days, after which he was sold to a slaver and transported to Brazil.

Having become the property of a Frenchman established in Rio de Janeiro,[44]* he was brought to Paris in 1836 or 1837 and thus became free by law, according to the ancient maxim that no slavery can exist in the land of the Franks. When his master returned to Brazil, Joaquim remained in Paris under the name of Joseph and served as a domestic in various establishments. He was employed in this capacity in the rooming house where he had stayed earlier with his Brazilian master, when he became homesick and was brought to me on 21 March 1839 in the hope that I might find means to help him return to Brazil. I dissuaded him from running the risk of being treated on arrival as an escaped slave. I found him a better place, with a kind and benevolent master,[45]* and promised to take the first opportunity to send him home. This opportunity occurred in September 1839; but he was then content with his position, and he declined to take advantage of my offer. Winter brought back his homesickness. He returned and asked again for his repatriation, but a new opportunity was a long time coming. The English Niger Expedition having no use for him as an interpreter, my friend Captain Washington offered to have him sent to Sierra Leone, with which the poor Negro seemed very satisfied. Then I suddenly learned that he had left secretly for Le Havre in order to return to his chains in Rio de Janeiro, having given way to his affection for his old master, promises of good treatment, and above all to the memory of the smiling climate of Brazil and a son he had left there.

He was old enough to have gained an accurate and thoughtful knowledge of his environment, and in the slave country where he

43. Mahin, and its neighbor, Ugbo, are today regarded as independent kingdoms: their culture is not similar to that of the Ijebu. These two towns lie at the only break in the line of seacoast between Lagos and the Benin River. They never developed into trading states, however, perhaps because their hinterland, the forest of southern Ondo, was so scantily populated.

44*. M. Navarre.

45*. M. Vendryès, the elder, of Sablonville.

had already spent seventeen years of his life, he had found enough of his fellow countrymen to make it possible for them to recall their homeland, which they often talked of together, in all its force and clarity—though no doubt it was already deeply engraved on his memory.

The accounts he gave me from time to time after we met are far from providing the elements necessary to a complete essay about his country and people. Our conversations were neither frequent enough, nor sufficiently at ease, for me to be able to assemble a great body of factual information. He was a mine of information, but excavation had barely begun and I can only offer a sample of the ore.

Let me at least set down the results in a synthetic order. But make no mistake, I hasten to repeat: this order is entirely my own, and the outline I am about to give has no organizational resemblance to the wandering and broken conversations, so diffuse and ingenuous, from which I have drawn the essentials.

These elements were gathered almost exclusively during the second quarter of 1839. They were then reviewed and checked in September of that year. The linguistic section was once again reviewed and developed in August and September of 1840, in Sablonville.

FIRST PART: THE COUNTRY

I. Topography

1. Reconciliation, discussion, and use of old and new geographical information on the country of Ijebu

The country of Yebou[46]* [Ijebu] is placed in a general way between Dahomey on the west, Benin on the east, the Gulf of Guinea on the south, and on the north the country of Oyo.[47]* I can make

46*. This name, like other African words inserted into the text, is written in a manner designed to represent the native pronunciation as well as possible to a French reader. I have tried in the small work on grammar which forms an appendix [not included in the present edition] to use a more exact and rigorous orthography, which I have not thought necessary to use in the body of the essay where a simple approximation seemed more convenient and therefore preferable.

47*. Capt. Clapperton, *Journal of a Second Expedition*, Philadelphia 1829, p. 87.

these limits more precise along the coast. The town of Lagos is the boundary in the west. Lagos is the common name given by the Europeans. If we may believe Robertson, Awani [Awori] is the local designation, written "Onis" by Denys Bonnaventure and by most of the earlier navigators, "Aunis" by Palissot de Beauvois and Landolphe, and "Ahony" by De Flotte.[48*] Captain Horseley called it "Eco,"[49*] and so do the Ijebu, but it is not within their domain: it belongs to Benin, whose people call it "Korame" [Kuramo], which is easily recognized as the "Curamo" of the early Portuguese, just as "Eco" represents the "Ichoo" of the Dutch chart-makers. Formerly, Kuramo was joined to its metropolis by the spit of land confined between the great lagoon and the sea, but the Ijebu have long since seized control of this tongue of land, and the eastern extremity was invaded by the Ijo pirates. Kuramo has remained isolated at the end of the long lagoon, still receiving its governor or political chief from Benin. Robertson's designation, "Awanee," belongs to neighboring country to the west, pronounced "Agouani" by Osifekunde, and included with Arada [Allada], Agbadaghi (the Badagry of the English charts), Vida [Ouidah] ("Whidah" of the English, "Juida" of the old French traders), and other more distant places among the possessions of the Igou [Adja] nation, to which both the Dagome (vulgarly, Dahomey) and the Mahi belong.[50]

The eastern border of Ijebu on the ocean is the town of Mahin,

---

48*. Robertson, *Notes on Africa*, p. 287; Denys Bonnaventure, in La Barthe, *Voyage à la côte de Guinée*, Paris 1803, in-8°, p. 101; and De Flotte, *ibidem*, p. 171. The name, as printed there, is *Ahouy* for *Ahony*. Palissot de Beauvois, *Flore d'Oware et de Benin*, Paris 1804–21, in-folio, I, 7, 17; II, 22 and 42; *Mémoires du capitaine Landolphe*, I, 94; II, 98 ff.; *Carte de tout le bas de la Côte-d'Or, et du golfe du Benin*, 1786, by Captain Baugin, among the manuscript charts of the Dépôt de la Marine (portef. 113, chem. 25, no. 8).

49*. The map, "Lagos and its channels," by Capt. Horseley of Liverpool, 1789, in *African Pilot*, as a supplement, on the chart already cited [n. 23*].

50. The name Eko properly refers to the kingdom of Lagos, a Yoruba-speaking state, whose royal dynasty is believed to derive from Benin. Lagos was probably subordinate to Benin in earlier centuries. The capital, or Eko town, was situated at the western end of the coastal island lying between the lagoon and the sea. Its territory included some mainland villages, but it seems unlikely that the kingdom was ever large in extent.

To the west of Lagos lived the Awori, primarily engaged in fishing and piracy. Farther west lived the Egun, a people more closely related to the Fon of Dahomey than to the Yoruba. Badagry is today peopled by groups of both Egun and Yoruba descent. It seems unlikely that either the Awori or the Egun ever controlled a powerful state.

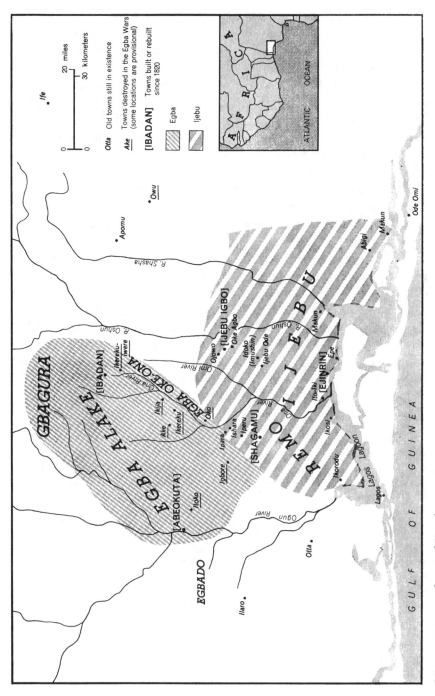

Map 14. Lagos and part of Yoruba, *ca.* 1820.

shown by position but without a place-name on Dalzel's chart[51]* in Laurie's *African Pilot*. It is located at the point where the Ijebu Creek flows into the sea. Only the words, "a town," mark this place on the chart.

[*A section of the original dealing with hydrographic surveys is omitted here.*][52]

Between Lagos and Ode Omi, following the seashore, Osifekunde indicated six hamlets by name: "Okou Ibeoy," "Okou Oblaze," "Okou Ochoro," "Okou Leke" [Lekki], "Okou Chirion," "Okou Eze."[53] The first five names apply quite naturally to five positions of villages determined by Captain Bouët in a recent survey and communicated to me directly by that officer. The fourth will also be seen to coincide with the position marked "town" on Dalzel's chart. The sixth can be placed without difficulty to the east of the fifth, at the point where Dalzel indicates "straggling houses" a few miles to the west of Oddy [Ode Omi] (which should be written "Ode" to conform to Osifekunde's pronunciation).[54]

Neither town nor village is encountered from Ode Omi to Mahin

51*. Or, more accurately, on the chart edited by Norris from material furnished by Dalzel. It is the same that accompanies the *Voyage au pays de Dahomé*, by Robert Norris, Paris, 1700, in-8°, and *The History of Dahomy*, by Archibald Dalzel, London 1793, in-4°. The part of this chart relating to Dahomey belongs exclusively to Norris. Mahin is probably the "Mongyee" of Captain James Fawckner, *Narrative of Travels on the Coast of Benin*, London 1837, in-12; pp. 4, 23, etc.

52. See *Mémoires de la Société Ethnologique*, 2(2):27–29. The section consists entirely of a critique of the European hydrographic surveys of the 1820's and 1830's, with the aim of establishing accurate latitude and longitude for Lagos and other coastal points. D'Avezac compares the positions for Lagos, Ijebu Ode, and the Benin River and gives his own preferences. In general, the latitude of these places was correctly estimated, but they were usually placed about 2° 30′ west of the true position—a measure of the inaccuracy of the nineteenth-century chronometers.

53. Of the six villages, the only one to appear on modern maps is Lekki. The prefix, *okon*, indicates that these were farm hamlets and, in all probability, not permanent settlements, politically organized. Though perhaps living here most of the year, the inhabitants would have had their compounds in one of the Ijebu towns. Lekki became a slave post in the nineteenth century, since, at this point, the island is only a few hundred yards wide, and slaves and goods could easily be carried between the ships lying offshore and the canoes in the lagoon

54. Confusion can arise between Ijebu Ode and Ode Omi, a town on the lagoon east of Lekki. The term *Ode* denotes a capital; thus Ijebu Ode means the capital of Ijebu. Some legends relate that the founder of the present dynasty of Ijebu Ode and that of Ode Omi were brothers migrating from Benin. These versions are current in the lagoon area, but not in Ijebu Ode, where their acceptance would counter claims to overlordship in the lagoon area. Culturally Ode Omi is Ijebu.

which is, as we have seen, the easternmost maritime town in Ijebu territory and should be placed on Dalzel's chart at 6° 4′ N. and 2° 32′ E. of Paris. It takes two days by sea to go from Kuramo to Ode Omi, and, leaving Ode Omi at five o'clock in the morning, one can arrive at Mahin about two o'clock in the afternoon. Passing on, one enters the domain of Warri ("Owere," "Owyhere," "Ouarre," or "Awerri" in various charts and accounts). This is the country of the Ichekri[55]* people [Itsekiri].[56] One comes first to a little hamlet called "Echein," with only eight inhabitants. A little farther on is Yakwa [Jakpa], with about fifty, and then quite close, Oubabi [Bobi], with thirty. Sad memories have engraved these three names in Osifekunde's memory. It was close to "Echein" that he was surprised by the Ijo pirates, who landed him in front of that miserable village and then took him to Jakpa, where he was kept bound for four days, while (without his knowledge) they bargained with the Brazilian slaver whose property he was soon to become. And it was at Bobi[57]* that he was delivered to his purchaser and embarked, never to see his native land again.[58]

55*. Clapperton writes *Chekerie* or *Warrie*, after the Yoruba informants he interrogated. See *Second Expedition*, p. 55.

56. The Itsekiri are a people speaking a Yoruba dialect. The ruling dynasty which established the capital at Warri originated from Benin. The kingdom (known as Warri) was probably at first subordinate to Benin, but later became independent. Missionaries here found a ready acceptance of their proselyting, and spasmodic Christian influence spanned the period from the late sixteenth to the end of the eighteenth century. Itsekiri influence rested on their position as middlemen between the European traders visiting the Benin River, and the interior. See P. C. Lloyd, "The Itsekiri," *in* R. E. Bradbury and P. C. Lloyd, *Ethnographic Survey of Africa: Western Africa, Part XIII* (London, 1957), pp. 172–205.

57*. This village is called *Bobi* or *Boby* by Captain Landolphe (*Mémoires*, I, 160, and II, 30, 122, 343, 346). It was situated only a cannonshot from the establishment founded at the entrance of the River Formoso on behalf of Messrs. Marion de la Brillantais of Saint Malo, which was destroyed in 1782 by an infamous act of piracy. This was at the straits indicated by the name "Salt Town" on Dalzel's chart, and the village of Bobi or Boby seems to be the same as the one called "Lobou" on that same chart. It is carried over, under the name "Boobie Town," to the small chart by Mr. John Arrowsmith, which accompanies Captain Beecroft's note on his journeys to the Benin and Quorah [Niger] rivers in the *Journal of the Royal Geographical Society of London*, XI, 184. The same chart also gives our village of Yakwa under the name of Jacqua Town. Captain Fawckner calls these town Bowbee (pp. 67, 108) and Wackow's Town (p. 107).

58. Jakpa and Bobi are Itsekiri settlements founded probably at the end of the eighteenth century. At this period the European ships ceased to enter the Benin River to visit Ughoton or anchor at Eghoro but anchored outside the difficult bar; see Landolphe's accounts, in J. S. Quesne (ed.), *Mémoires du Capitaine Landolphe* (Paris, 1823). The Itsekiri responded by settling along the banks of the river inside the estuary, from which

The distance from Ode Omi to the factory at Lagos is two days by water. To go from Ode Omi to Mahin, one leaves at five o'clock in the morning and arrives at two o'clock in the afternoon. It takes another day and a half to reach Bobi.

All these inhabited places are spread out along the sea on the elongated spit of land which the Ijebu call "Ikbekou," and which is cut up into islands by several transverse creeks. On the mainland, at two hours' distance across from Ode Omi (itself a half hour from the shore) is found Makun, capital of a small district inhabited by the Idoko nation (which has another town called Ebighi [Abigi]).[59] This is the eastern extremity of Ijebu territory. Stretching eastwards of it is "Issobo,"[60]* a dependency of Benin,[61] while off to the southeast toward Warri are the vague territories where the Ijo pirates carry on their raids.

We have already seen that these pirates are the *corsaires d'Usa* mentioned by David de Nyendaal. Perhaps their name comes from "Osa," which is the Ijebu name for the Ikorodu lagoon of our charts. This lagoon extends, from west to east, from Lagos or Kuramo to a point beyond Makun. On the northern bank a number of towns and villages are scattered along to the eastward of Lagos. Of these, the principal ones are Ikorodu, Ikosi, and Epe.[62] We see on Dalzel's

villages they were able to dominate the trade of the area; see Lloyd, "The Itsekiri." "Echein" probably lies on the lagoon running north from the Benin River.

59. Two towns named Makun are marked on present maps. One is near the mouth of the Shasha River. The other is near Abigi and thus very close to Ode Omi. It is apparently the latter to which D'Avezac refers at this point, though the Idoko are today identified more with the former. The "Idoko nation" have today almost become forgotten, submerged within the Ijebu kingdom. Legends, however, suggest that Idoko was a powerful kingdom, with a capital near the present town of Imushin, six miles east of Ijebu Ode. It antedated the founding of the present dynasty of Ijebu Ode (perhaps in the fourteenth century—there have been over fifty recorded rulers in the dynasty to date). In the decline of the Idoko kingdom its capital apparently moved to Makun, on the lagoon, and much farther from Ijebu Ode. D'Avezac's later account of Osifekunde's father taking sanctuary at Makun suggests that the authority of the ruler of Ijebu did not reach thus far and that the Idoko were at least quasi-independent.

60*. Called *Sooba* by Beecroft ([*J. Roy. Geog. Soc.*, XI] p. 185): "Extensive plains open to the view, upon which, however, neither inhabitants nor symptoms of population of any sort are to be discerned. The Sooba country is the name given to this district by the natives lower down the river, who represent it as forming part of the kingdom of Benin."

61. This refers to the Sobo plains, the country of the Urhobo people, lying southeast of Benin between the River Ethiope and the Niger. Generally flat, the southern part is also much less forested than the remainder.

62. These are still the principal lagoonside towns. The only newcomer is Ejinrin, founded in the early nineteenth century as a market for Ijebu Ode when routes farther

chart the names of "Cradoo" and "Quassee," which correspond without doubt to Ikorodu and Ikosi; but it appears from the relative distances given me by Osifekunde that these names are misplaced on Dalzel's chart from their true positions. One can, in fact, go by water in one day from Kuramo to Ikorodu, leaving at five o'clock in the morning and arriving at three or four o'clock in the afternoon. A half-day is enough to get from Ikorodu to Ikosi (leaving at five in the morning one can arrive at noon), and if one continues without stopping, Epe is reached at around ten at night. Even spending the afternoon in Ikosi and leaving there at six in the evening, one will reach Epe at three o'clock the next morning. Finally, leaving Epe at four in the afternoon, one can arrive at three the next morning in Makun, taking care to watch the tide so as not to sail against the current. This information provides a small table of distances:

From Kuramo to:

Ikorodu = 10 hours or about 17 miles [actually 11 miles]
Ikosi   = 7 hours or about 11 miles [actually 24 miles]
Epe   = 10 hours or about 17 miles [actually 20 miles]
Makun = 11 hours or about 19 miles [actually 34 miles][63]

Carrying these relative distances over onto the Dalzel chart, it appears that Ikosi falls exactly on the position that is attributed to Ikorodu, and Epe on the position of Ikosi, from which it follows that Dalzel has transposed these names, and a correction is necessary.

It is possible to go from Epe to Mahin, by way of Makun, by following the inner channels. This route requires three days, and four days more to reach Olu Warri, the capital of Itsekiri to the southwest —and similarly four days eastward from Mahin to arrive in Gwatto. From there, Edo, capital of Benin, is reached in two days overland.[64]

---

west were threatened by the Egba armies. From Ito Iki (D'Avezac's *Ike*, perhaps) it was possible, in the early years of the present century to travel by canoe to a point only five miles from Ijebu Ode. From Ejinrin and Epe the routes to Ijebu Ode run along the elevated watershed.

63. Or fourteen miles to the closer Makun. The distances and times given by D'Avezac on succeeding pages do not always accord with one another.

64. Warri being the name both of the kingdom and of its capital, the latter may be precisely denoted by adding the title of the ruler, the *Olu*. This is a frequent practice in Yoruba country. Edo is the local name for Benin City. It is also the word used to denote the whole people and their language. Gwatto (or Ughoton), the port of Benin, is only eighteen miles from the capital.

Osifekunde himself followed this latter route on a trip he made in 1810 accompanied by his brother, Ogou Soya. Benin is a great kingdom, to which the provinces of Issobo [Urhobo] and "Eonre" belong. Beyond is the country of "Ekbon" or "Ikbon" (so called in Benin, but called "Ikolobe" by the Ijebu and "Ekalapa" by the Itsekiri).[65] The capital is the large town of Ogoton [Oguta] which must not be confused with Gwatto in Benin.[66*]

Apart from the series of villages I have mentioned on the seaward shore of Ikbekou, there are several others on the northern shore and even some in the interior of the islands. Thus the village of "Sabouko" appears opposite the large town of Epe, and on the creek opposite Ikosi is the village of "Boughiye,"[67] famous throughout the country for the superiority of the vessels that come from its boatyards.[68*]

Let me now try to estimate the extent of the Ijebu country toward the north. The only indications in this respect from my conversations with Osifekunde were the names of two frontier villages, "Oyogwo" and Ikrekou [Ikereku], beyond which lies the territory of "Inongo." Let me say here, first of all, that "Inongo"[69*] is a great nation which includes the country of Oyo (of which [the city of] Oyo is the capital)[70] as well as the country of Ibomno [Igbomina],[71]

65. Ekbon or Ikbon may refer to the Ibo or Igbo. Oguta is a large market town on a river flowing into the Niger Delta.

66*. Bowdich distinguished clearly between the two towns. while placing them incorrectly on his large "Map of North Western Africa Dedicated to the African Association," 1820.

67. "Sabouku" and "Boughiye" are not marked on modern maps; but these maps show only a few hamlets, and their names are perhaps more liable to change than are those of larger towns.

68*. It may be conjectured that this is the place known to the Portuguese as *Aldea das Almadias,* or boat town.

69*. Robertson [*Notes on Africa*] writes "Anagoo" (pp. 209 and 286) and "Inago" (p. 287); it is called "Nagots" in Pruneau de Pommegorge, *Description de la Nigritie,* Paris 1789, in-8°, p. 236, and in La Barthe, *Voyage à la côte de Guinée,* p. 163, following the information of Captain Denys Bonnaventure. Both distinguish them from the "Ayeots" or "Alliots," who are none other than the "Eyeos" of Clapperton and Lander. That is, they are the Oyo themselves. Such double appearances are almost inevitable, given the oral source of the travellers' information.

70. The terms *Anago, Inongo,* and *Nago* puzzle contemporary observers: they are no longer in use. I have heard *Nago* used in Ondo to refer to Yoruba language. D'Avezac used it to refer to the Oyo people, including perhaps not only members of the Oyo kingdom but also of kingdoms tributary to it, and it is still used in Brazil in this sense.

71. The Igbomina are Yoruba-speaking people, living to the east of the old kingdom of Oyo, around the town of Offa.

called Kakanda by the Hausa.[72]* Beyond "Inongo" is Filani [Fulani or Fulbe],[73] then Takpwa[74]* [Nupe] which is Niffe or Noufi of the Hausa;[75] then finally Hausa, a large country where the geographical knowledge of my informant came to an end.

Leaving Ikorodu toward the northeast, Igan [Igaun] is reached in a short day's journey. From there, at three days' distance is the district of "Oukbo." The capital, "Ouke Akbo," is a large town three days from Epe. "Oyogwo" is hardly an hour farther along, and from there, it is one day to "Akbele," belonging to the nation of Ekba Ikeya [Egba Ikija], a dependency of Oyo.[76]

On the other side, leaving Ikorodu for the north, a very long day's journey brings one to Eremo [Remo], a dependency of Ijebu. Its first town is Ikbore [Igbore], then two long days' march to Oko, and two more long days to Ikrekou [Ikereku], still in the territory of Remo. Still farther, four or five hours are enough to reach Ekomoso [Ogbomosho], an Oyo town three days from "Oukbo." Three days beyond Ogbomosho is Ekboumou [Apomu?], an important market town which belongs to the brother of the king of Ijebu.[77]

72*. Oldfield tells us that Kakanda is also called "Ibbodo" or "Ibbodah" and "Mogay" by the natives, whose language is called "Shabbee." See Laird and Oldfield, *Narratives of an Expedition into the Interior of Africa by the River Niger,* London 1837, in-8°; I, 320, 375; II, 25, 298. [They are usually considered a subgroup of the Nupe.]

73. Today there are some settled Fulbe living in the northern parts of the Oyo kingdom, but their main habitat is much farther north. At the time of Osifekunde's capture, Fulbe armies were active in the northern part of Oyo, as Ali Eisami and Samuel Crowther reported (see Chaps. 7 and 9).

74*. Clapperton [*Journal of a Second Expedition*] writes "Tappa" (pp. 33, 140, etc.); Robertson, "Takpa" (*Notes on Africa*, p. 268).

75. Tapa is the Yoruba term for Nupe, then in process of conquest by the Fulbe, who deposed their former kings in favor of a new dynasty of emirs, responsible to Sokoto.

76. D'Avezac's account of the routes into the interior is difficult to elucidate. Perhaps Osifekunde, whose fixing of town sites along the lagoon seems accurate, knew far less about the interior; and D'Avezac is evidently trying to depend on other hearsay information picked up by European explorers. The Egba wars were also beginning about the time Osifekunde was enslaved, with consequent destruction of the towns and massive population movements to the west and south. It would appear, however, from D'Avezac's description of distances and from his map, that "Akbele," "Oyogwo," and "Ouke Akbo" were in the vicinity of modern Ibadan. One would not be surprised at the disappearance of towns in this region. On the other hand, the two last-named may be Ojowo and Ake Agbo, villages which have now merged with three others to form the modern town of Ijebu Igbo, eleven miles north of Ijebu Ode.

77. Today, the Remo people, culturally similar to the Ijebu, are grouped in a number of small kingdoms, which have only recently won administrative independence from Ijebu

If an average value of 15 nautical miles in a straight line is taken to be equal to a day's journey on foot, it may be concluded that the frontier line on the side of "Akbele" is about 70 miles from Ikorodu and 55 miles from Epe, and that on the side of Ogbomosho it is about 85 miles from Ikorodu and an equal distance from Epe. One can deduce from these data a total area for the country of about 500 square leagues, at the maximum.

I have not yet spoken of the capital, Ode Yebou [Ijebu Ode]: its position is given by its distance of one day and a half from Ikorodu and a short day of six hours from Epe. At two and a half miles per hour, these times translate into 35 miles and 15 miles respectively, and yield an approximate position for Ijebu Ode of 6° 48′ north latitude and 1° 54′ longitude east of Paris.[78]

Osifekunde names still other towns whose position I had neither leisure nor opportunity to establish by further enquiry. Among these are "Oke Ako" (the birthplace of his grandfather), "Odomila," "Ipi," "Atou," Erounwo [Erunwon?], "Ichove," "Noforiya," "Iloko," "One," "Oroubo," and "Ike." This last town, however, I found to be two or three hours' walk east of Ikosi.[79]

Among the dependencies of Ijebu, there remains the district of Owwou [Owu], which belongs to the Egba nation. A six-year war, ending just at the time Osifekunde was taken prisoner, was fought between Ijebu and Owu for the possession of a district lying between the two states. At the end, the *oba* of Owu was made prisoner and taken to Ijebu Ode and his territory was annexed to Ijebu. Has this state of affairs continued? We have no information on the subject,

Ode. But Igbore, Oko, and two different towns named Ikereku are regarded as having been Egba and not Remo towns. A third Ikereku is now a hamlet situated between Ibadan and Oyo, but its location appears not to be identical with either Ikereku-Iwere, where Samuel Crowther stopped on his way to the coast, or the larger Ikereku-Idan in the Oke-Ona region. Apomu is halfway between Ijebu Ode and Ogbomosho: though not an important town, its market was famed throughout Yoruba as a meeting place for people from Oyo, Ijebu, and Owu in the period before the Egba Wars.

78. The actual distance from Ikorodu to Ijebu Ode is thirty-five miles; from Epe to Ijebu Ode, seventeen miles; and the actual position of Ijebu Ode is 6° 50′ N. and 3° 55′ E. of Greenwich.

79. These villages, with the possible exception of Ike, probably lie within a few miles of Ijebu Ode. Villages of the same name today exist in this area. Unlike most Yoruba towns, which are surrounded by hamlets or temporary settlements, Ijebu Ode was surrounded by more than a hundred small villages of permanent settlement; see P. C. Lloyd, *Yoruba Land Law* (London, 1962), pp. 136–50.

and my conversations with Osifekunde did not tell me where the district of Owu was located.[80]

The name, however, is not unknown in Europe, nor is that of the Egba nation.[81] In the third part of his small *Eyo Vocabulary,* based on data he collected in Sierra Leone, the missionary John Raban gave the following piece of geographical information: "Yoruba is the general denomination for a large country containing the five following divisions, arranged in order of their importance: 1. Oyo; 2. Egba; 3. Ibarupwa [Ibarapa]; 4. Ijebu; 5. Ijeca [Ijesha] (pronounced Ijetcha). Owu is a large town in Yoruba."[82]* But this calls for clarification. It is well known through Clapperton[83]* that Yoruba is the name given by the Arabs and Hausa to the country and people of Oyo. Osifekunde was not acquainted with this general term. For him, Oyo was the name of the country occupied by the "Inongo" nation, having the *Oba Oyo* as king, and the town of Oyo as its capital. Egba was the nation, having country and capital alike called Owu. Ibarapa was unknown to him in this form; he thought it should be "Gwaroupa." Ijebu is his own country, which we write down, following his pronunciation, as "Yebou." Finally, Ijesha for him is

80. The once powerful kingdom of Owu lay to the northeast of Ijebu. It is unlikely that it was politically dependent on Ijebu, still less on the Egba kingdoms, though it may have shared cultural traits with both peoples. The defeat of Owu, which would appear from Osifekunde's account to have taken place before 1820, probably occurred in 1825 (judging from evidence discussed below, in Chap. 10, in connection with the narrative of Joseph Wright). The probable explanation of the discrepancy is that Osifekunde learned about the fall of Owu from other Yoruba in Brazil, rather than before his departure from Africa. A major military event of this kind would have been widely reported by newly arrived slaves. See Samuel Johnson, *The History of the Yorubas* (Lagos, 1921), pp. 206–10; I. A. Akinjogbin, "The Prelude to the Yoruba Civil Wars of the Nineteenth Century," *Odu,* 1(new ser.):24–46 (1965).

81. The term Egba is now applied to the numerous small kingdoms, traditionally as many as 144 independent towns, which lay between the kingdom of Oyo to the north, Ijebu to the south, and Owu to the east. It is not certain whether these Egba kingdoms were politically related in any way, but it seems likely that they were not. Designating a congeries of culturally similar kingdoms with a single term, like Egba, is analogous to the similar usage of *Ekiti* for the Yoruba kingdoms lying on the outer limits of Benin. After the Egba people settled as refugees in the vicinity of Abeokuta from 1830 onwards, a federal form of government emerged, with the ruler of Ake, one of the constituent towns, becoming paramount ruler of a new Egba kingdom.

82*. *The Eyo Vocabulary compiled by the Rev. John Raban, one of the missionaries of the Church Missionary Society in Sierra Leone;* 3 parts, London, 1830–32; in-18; Part Three, p. 10.

83*. *Second Expedition,* p. 29.

"Iyesa,"[84] which he mentioned several times before Raban's little book came into his hands.[85]*

But where is the physical location of Owu? We still do not know. Perhaps we are permitted to guess that this town is the same Richard Lander spoke of under the name of "Wow" at the beginning of his second journey. According to Clapperton's account of the boundaries of Yoruba toward Badagry, "Wow" certainly belongs to Yoruba,[86]* and its similarity to Owu is striking. But, in still another case, is not Egba Ikija in the direction of "Akbele" identical with Egba? I remain uncertain.

However that may be, after all the information we have just examined, it appears that we can at least form a general impression of the geographical structure of the Ijebu country, with its territorial core bearing the name Ijebu, surrounded on the east by Idoko with its capital at Makun, on the north by Remo with its capital at Igbore, and perhaps on the northeast by Egba with a capital at Owu.

II. Physical Geography and Natural History

1. Land forms and geology, hydrography, plants and animals

The countryside is extremely flat near the coast, and real mountains appear only in the interior. The spit of land the natives call Ikbekou nevertheless has a number of dunes, notably around Sabouko and Boughiye, where they are called "Oke" or mountains. As for those of the interior, they are part of the great granitic chain of hills, which Clapperton crossed farther west. He discovered that they begin in Borghou [Borgu] and continue across Ijebu into Benin. They are, according to the traveller's description, a gray granite out-

---

84. Ibarapa is a term now given to the independent towns to the north of the Egba and to the west of Ibadan. As with Egba, it is unlikely that these towns were ever united politically, but they were at this period individually subject to Oyo. Samuel Crowther came from one of the Ibarapa towns. Ijesha is the Yoruba kingdom to the east of Ile Ife, its capital now being Ilesha—that is, Ile-Ijesha, or home of the Ijesha.

85*. It was brought to my attention by my friend, Captain John Washington, of the Royal Navy, former Secretary of the Royal Geographical Society of London and one of the most active and enlightened members of the African Civilization Society. He is now directing hydrographic research in the North Sea.

86*. Lander, *Journal of an Expedition to Explore the Niger*, I, 58; Clapperton, *Second Expedition*, pp. 29 and 87.

crop through a red clay soil, covered by a black topsoil mixed with sand in the sections that border on the sea.[87]* According to Osifekunde many rich mineral deposits are found there, with gold occurring in the form of large nuggets,[88]* and silver in abundance, but without value or utility in the eyes of the natives.[89] They value iron deposits much more, and they will pay for copper, which is scarce, as dearly as for gold itself.[90]*

Many but inconsiderable rivers water and fertilize this territory. The most important is the Ochou [Oshun], which comes from a great distance in the Oyo country, where it is called "Ichery." It is already a large stream at Ogbomosho and too large to be forded at "Oukbo." It crosses Remo and empties into the lagoon at Ikorodu. Another is the Ome [Omi], which comes from "Akbele," passes One [Oni] and Idoko (where it takes its name) and then ends at Epe. Between these two, a third and smaller stream passes near "Oroubo" and enters the lagoon at Ito-Iki.[91]

All these various watercourses end in the body of water the geographers formerly called Kuramo Lake (now called Ikorodu Lake), but which the Ijebu call only *osa,* or lagoon, as opposed to the sea

87*. Clapperton, *Second Expedition,* pp. 48, 52, 87.

88*. It is unnecessary to insist on this point, when even the name of the country is derived from its fame for an abundance of gold: it is enough to read Villault de Bellefond, *Relation de costes d'Afrique appelées Guinés,* Paris 1669, in-12, pp. 387–397.

89. Most of the Yoruba country lies on granite rocks of the Basement Complex which makes for undulating country with the highest points lying along the watershed between rivers draining towards the Niger and towards the sea. Gold is today found in streams in the vicinity of Ile Ife and Ilesha. Silver is not found, nor are copper ores known to exist. South of a line passing approximately through Abeokuta and a point three miles north of Ijebu Ode the granite rocks lie below sedimentary strata. Iron is found both in the weathered soils of the granite areas and in the soils from sedimentary rocks as a result of processes of laterization; only in a few areas, however, does the ore have a sufficient iron content to justify smelting.

The island between the lagoon and the sea has been formed by the coastwise drift of sand. It is this process which has prevented most of the rivers from directly entering the sea and has resulted in offshore bars occluding the estuaries of those which do reach the sea—as at Lagos, Mahin, and the Benin River.

90*. As Pruneau de Pommegorge remarks of the Sérères of the Senegambia (*Description de la Nigritie,* p. 123).

91. This description of the courses of major rivers is very muddled. It is the Ogun which rises in Oyo and merges into the lagoon near Ikorodu. The Oshun rises beyond Oshogbo, passing twenty miles east of Ibadan to reach the lagoon near Epe. The Oni rises beyond Ilesha to reach the lagoon near Makun. The third stream is probably the Ona, which passes Ito Iki a few miles from the lagoon; the Omi is a tributary of this river, with headwaters southeast of Ibadan. The river Shasha is omitted from the description.

which they call *moloukou* [Yoruba: *okun,* the sea] and rivers which they call *outo* [Yoruba: *ito,* a creek]. A little way beyond the town of Makun, the lagoon becomes so narrow that three boats cannot pass abreast. From this point it becomes a real river, and its special name is Efra [Ofara Creek]. Perhaps the same name reappears to the west of the lagoon, applied to the river which communicates with Ardra, incorrectly called Lagos on Dalzel's map, while D'Anville calls it the "Eufrat," and Denys Bonnaventure, too much in the classical mode, "the Euphrates."[92*]

Other rivers cross Ikbekou to connect the lagoon with the sea, as can be seen on Dalzel's chart, and the best known of these is the "Outo-Boughiye."[93] With the rain and floods of the summer solstice, the waters of the Osa flow in a vast sheet over the lowlands of Ikbekou. The depth of the channel in the middle of the lagoon is fourteen to fifteen fathoms, according to the old charts. Soundings are shallow along the seacoast. The water has an olive green color. The bottom is sand—white, red, and brown in succession as it moves away from the shore to the distance of four, five, six, eight, and ten fathoms. The bottom then becomes a black mud, which also appears immediately at the entrance of the transversal creeks between Ode Omi and Mahin.[94*]

All along the shores runs a steep sandy bank covered with stunted mangroves, above which the red tops of the higher trees can be seen in the distance, especially between Epe and Makun. There are still other attractive forests in the country, and the soil is fertile elsewhere, since maize and calabashes are exported for the use of neighboring peoples.

My conversations with Osifekunde made me realize that his native land produces an abundance of bananas and plantains,[95*] coconuts, palmettos, orange trees, lemon trees, sugar cane, pineapples, pota-

92*. D'Anville's map, "Guinée entre Serre-Lione et la passage de la ligne," 1775; and *Eufrate* on his map of the coast of Guinea, 1729. Denys Bonnaventure, in La Barthe, *Voyage à la côte de Guinée,* pp. 102–103.

93. Today there are no outlets of the lagoon between Lagos and Mahin.

94*. MSS chart by Captain Baugin, cited above. [The depth of the lagoon varies considerably. West of Epe it is quite deep; but in the Lekki lagoon, a wide expanse of water, it is only about three feet deep. The Ofara Creek is likewise shallow and is today often blocked with water-weed.]

95*. The *Musa paradisica* of the botanists, locally *okbo ibroin.* Ordinary bananas are the *Musa sapientum,* locally called *okbo oghede.*

toes, manioc, yams, pimentos, malaguetta[96]* peppers, *obis* (which are nothing less than the famous kola nuts or *gourous* of the European travellers),[97]* indigo, cotton, and many other useful vegetable products about which I have not been able to gather more precise information.[98]*

As to the animal kingdom, he mentioned, among the mammals, numerous hippopotami, the lion, the leopard, the elephant, monkeys and baboons of various species (notably a kind of orangutan which he called *inoki*),[99] anteaters, hedgehogs, porcupines, and rats in large numbers. Among the domestic animals there were horses (though rare except in the province of Idoko), donkeys, dogs, cats, pigs, great herds of cattle, sheep, and goats.[100] Among the reptiles he mentioned monstrous crocodiles, sea and land turtles, toads, frogs, and snakes of several species, of which the most remarkable was called *ere* by the natives and must be a python of the largest size.[101]* (There is another, known in Brazil under the name of *surucúcu*,[102]* and still another smaller one, black with a yellow throat.) Among the birds he mentioned the ostrich, stork, flamingo, heron, gray parrot, pigeon, chicken, duck, spoonbill, and pelican.[103]* Among the insects, bees

96*. Guinea pepper or grains of paradise, the fruit of the *Uvaria aethiopica* and the *Amomum melegueta.*

97*. The *Sterculia tomentosa* of Perrottet (*Florae Senegambiae tentamen*, Paris 1843, gr. in-4°; I, 81, table 16). It is probably the same as the *Sterculia acuminata* of Palissot de Beauvois (*Flore d'Oware*, I, 4, table 24). [Gourou is the word for kola nut in West Atlantic languages like Wolof and Pular, hence familiar to Europeans whose principal contact was with the Senegambia.]

98*. Cf. the similar enumeration given for the vicinity of Accra by Monrad, in Walckenaer, *Histoire générale des voyages*, Paris 1827, XII, 479, and by Bosman, *Voyage de Guinée*, sixteenth letter, for the coast in general.

99. The *inoki* is a baboon or chimpanzee.

100. It is not clear why horses should be more numerous in the low-lying Idoko area, rather than on the high land around Ijebu Ode. Donkeys are now rarely seen in Yoruba country, though they are common beasts of burden in northern Nigeria.

101*. Osifekunde's description of this snake raises doubts that it is the same species as that indicated by Monrad under the name of *serpent royal* (Walckenaer, *Histoire générale des voyages*, XXI, 458). Bosman (*Voyage de Guinée*, pp. 282 and 326) also discusses it. [But D'Avezac is generally correct. The *ere* is the python or boa.]

102*. The name of *surucúcu* and the explanation given me by M. le Chevalier de Lisboa of Rio de Janeiro make possible the identification of this snake as the same described under the name *daboué* in La Barthe (*Voyage à la côte de Guinée*, p. 131n). It appears to belong to the species *eryx.*

103*. Osifekunde identified each animal, sometimes by its Brazilian name if he knew it, sometimes by a description of its most striking features, and sometimes by showing me the picture in Barbot's plates.

(which make the wax sold to the European factories by the natives, and honey for their food), uncomfortable mosquitos, poisonous scorpions, industrious termites, and innumerable red and black ants both large and small. Among the fish he described very precisely the fearful shark,[104]* and among shellfish, the oysters which teem in the lagoon, though the shoreside people have no idea of using them as a food.

That is nearly all I was able to gather from the mouth of Osifekunde about the most common animals of Ijebu.

SECOND PART: THE PEOPLE

I. Fundamentals of Ethnological Classification

1. Moral and physical characteristics

As to man in Ijebu, I can add to the vague but favorable remarks of Robertson and John Adams as an eyewitness, taking my informant as typical of his nation.

On this basis, I should say that the Ijebu is of medium height, well built, brownish black in color, with large and protruding lips, forward sloping upper teeth, and prominent cheek bones. But the most remarkable characteristic of his face is the forehead, divided vertically into three sections, of which one is more withdrawn than the other two. Better stated, the two temple bones protrude markedly beyond the frontal bone, above which they form a bulge eight or nine millimeters thick. His hair is curled and woolly like most of the Negro race. The facial angle seems to me to be extremely sharp.[105]

As to the rest (as the Société Ethnologique points out in its general instructions to guide researchers in the distinctions between human races), the aid of the graphic arts is indispensable in giving a

---

104*. By its Portuguese name, *tuberão.*

105. The facial angle was a measurement first developed in the eighteenth century by Pieter Camper. A more acute angle was supposed to be an indication of mental inferiority, and it should be remembered that D'Avezac was writing at a period when racist modes of thought were increasingly common (see Curtin, *Image of Africa,* esp. pp. 39–40). For a more modern account of the comparative physical anthropology of the Ijebu and neighboring peoples, see P. Amaury Talbot and H. Mulhall, *The Physical Anthropology of Southern Nigeria* (London, 1962).

precise idea of a physical type. My first concern was to draw a double portrait of Osifekunde to accompany this study, but I did not stop there. With the cooperation of M. de Blainville, a life mask of my informant was made at the Muséum Royal d'Histoire Naturelle. A copy can be seen there, as well as in the headquarters of the Société Ethnologique and in my own office.

The moral characteristics of my informant appear to be gentle, and, while his intelligence may be only slightly developed, the information he furnished me shows a degree of aptitude and activity among his compatriots which confirms the travellers' reports on the industrious habits and well-being of his people. The provisions they supply to their neighbors and the textiles they manufacture in such large quantities indicate a degree of perfection in the arts of spinning, weaving, and dyeing which demonstrates their relative superiority over nearby peoples. Ijebu resistance to Truro Audati, the great Dahomean conqueror, and their seizure of the littoral that formerly belonged to Benin are dual proofs of their bravery in war.

[*A section of the original dealing with the Ijebu dialect of Yoruba is omitted here.*][106]

II. Life Cycle

1. Birth, infancy, and early education

However great the diversity of human races, distributed by Providence from one end of the globe to the other, the same laws rule the physical existence of each particle in this vast whole. Under the equatorial fire, as on the polar ice, man is born, grows, matures, fades, and dies. He moves through a succession of burdens and accidents which, seen in perspective, offer only the most insignificant differences; rather, the differences we see are, in a manner of speaking, only the insignia placed on our physical life by our social life.

Let me set down the forms among the Ijebu which govern those actions which all nations agree in celebrating, insofar as my informant's memory permits. The Ijebu, like all other men, are born in

---

106. See *Mémoires de la Société Ethnologique*, 2(2):47–53. This section is not without interest for the history of linguistic studies in West Africa. It properly belongs, however, in the whole context of the grammatical study which D'Avezac included in an appendix (also omitted here).

pain, but the pain is perhaps less, and less prolonged, than in our own climates. The mother is attended during her labor by the women of the family or of the neighborhood who receive the newborn child and knot the umbilical cord, very much as the midwives do in our civilized Europe. But, in great distinction to our own customs, the mother remains for six days on her mat, covered by the same cloths, and having her infant beside her, without having any care as to its cleanliness, and taking none herself. Finally, on the seventh day, the room is cleaned from top to bottom. Even the cinders of the hearth are taken away and thrown in the river. An *alase,* or priest, is called to perform the ceremony of naming the newborn child. The *alase* first rubs a little palm oil on the head of the child. The container in which the cinders were removed is used briefly as a bath, and the infant is rubbed down with enough water to clean him, after which he is returned to his mother. The *alase* then dissolves a few grains of salt in his mouth, takes up the child, and, blowing a few drops of saline saliva on his forehead, calls aloud the name the child's father has told him in advance.

The nursing period lasts at least a year, and often to the age of three.[107] The mother sometimes carries her infant on her arm like nursing mothers in Europe, but sometimes it is tied to her back, its arms around her neck and its limbs fastened to her sides by means of a knotted cloth. When the time comes for weaning, she substitutes a clear maize broth for her milk, and soon after a kind of bread or cake of maize, called *ouri* [Yoruba: *eko*]. The child has no separate cradle; it sleeps by the mother, covered with cloths. Children of both sexes remain absolutely nude to the age of fifteen years, which is that of puberty.

2. Circumcision and scarification

At the age of six or seven, the Ijebu undergo a double operation of scarification and circumcision. The first, called *ella* [Yoruba: *ila*] is common to both sexes.[108] The second, *oufon,* is only practiced on men, with no analogous operation for women.[109]*

107. From eighteen months to two years of nursing is now common.

108. The tattooing or scarification referred to here is the cutting of facial and body marks. Today, facial marking is carried out when a child is about one year of age.

109*. David de Nyendaal (in Bosman [*Voyage de Guinée*], p. 472) says that in Benin a small portion of the woman's clitoris is excised.

Both are done for a fee by an artist of a special professional group, called *alakila*. He uses an instrument with a short, wide, double-edged blade kept very sharp and shaped very much like an eraser knife. The blade is seated in a delicate, rounded wooden handle, which the artist holds in his right hand between the thumb and the middle finger, much as we hold a pen.

Circumcision is usually a religious function, accompanied by ceremonies and the intervention of a priest, but nothing of the kind takes place among the Ijebu.[110] No *alase* presides at the operation, and it is left entirely to the artist.

It is recognized that scarification is a kind of insignia, a national badge, uniform for all individuals of the same group and different from one people to another so as to give each one a distinctive characteristic. It consists of a certain number of more or less deep incisions in a distinct order and in definite locations. Marks of this kind have an ethnological importance to which travellers generally have not paid enough attention. A work of synthesis on this subject would be both rare and interesting, but before it can be undertaken, it will first be necessary to gather the essential data.

Here is the information I have from Osifekunde on the characteristic marks among the various African peoples he knew, either from having visited their countries or from having seen them in his own country or in the market at Lagos.

First, for Ijebu itself (and its dependency, Remo) the national scarification is made up of six vertical lines beginning from the lower stomach and coming up to the breast, where the two middle lines stop, while the others spread out symmetrically and turn under the armpits.

Idoko, a tributary of Ijebu, has a double row of small oblique nicks made around the neck, those of each row being parallel with one another, but inclined in the opposite directions in alternate rows.

"Eggwa," another tributary of Ijebu, is distinguished by five or six long vertical incisions on each cheek from the temple to the lower jaw.

Benin (along with "Eonre") has four to eight vertical nicks in the middle of the forehead, plus a long stroke from the hollow of the stomach to the lower abdomen.

110. Throughout Yoruba country circumcision is purely secular; it is now performed at a much earlier age, often soon after birth.

Urhobo, a tributary of Benin, and Ijo, which seems to be nothing but an independent section of this same people, make three cuts from the corner of the eye, spreading out across the temple.

Ibo, still another Benin dependency, has the forehead marked with a horizontal line, under which are tiny perpendicular cuts, short and closely spaced.

The people of Kuramo have no scars, but they are recognized from their shaved heads, at the top of which they leave a tuft of hair.

Itsekiri has no tattooing.

The badge of the great Oyo nation is four horizontal cuts on either side of the mouth.

Igbomina (or "Kakanda"), which is a dependency of Oyo, has the same marks, but deeper and prolonged to the ear.

The warlike Fulbe people have adopted the same set of incisions, but with them they are only fine light strokes. Their skin color is not black but a reddish brown comparable to our mahogany furniture.

The Nupe, who live beyond Oyo, wear a double diagonal cut from the ear to the mouth, crossed by vertical incisions from the nose to the ear.

The Hausa, still farther away than Nupe, wear five or six horizontal cuts in front of each ear, each one successively longer until the last bends around to reach the corner of the mouth.

Returning to the west, there is the great nation of the Adja, whose marks consist of three small vertical incisions, one on each cheekbone and one in the middle of the forehead.

Such are the various national marks in and around Ijebu.[111]* My

111*. Details of the same kind about these peoples can be found in Mr. Oldfield's journal (Narrative of an Expedition into the Interior of Africa, I, 320, and II, 136, 323 ff.), but there are notable differences between his information and that of Osifekunde. According to Oldfield, the national mark of Idoma is a longitudinal incision from the outside corner of the eye to the mouth. In another place, he says that there are six or seven curved lines from the outer corner of the eye to the lower lip. Those of the Nonfanchis [Nupe] are made up of three curved lines on each cheek, and generally two others under the left shoulder blade. The people of Hausa, like those of Bornu, wear several lines, sometimes eight or nine, drawn from the cheekbone to the chin. Yoruba and the country of the Niger tributary called "Ado" have lines which radiate from the mouth across the cheeks. The Fulbe do not scar themselves and consider the scarified nations to be inferior.

It is noteworthy that one finds in Denham and Clapperton a portrait of a Nupe woman whose scarification resembles Osifekunde's description better than Mr. Oldfield's.

informant told me of still others he met within the land of slavery, but there is no need to take account of them here.

3. Marriage

Marriage is often the result of engagements made at a very early age, at about seven or eight years. An alliance between two families having been negotiated by mutual friends, the boy's parents make a formal request of the girl's parents for her hand in marriage, stipulating the dowry (or rather bride-price) the young man will bring to his fiancée. When these arrangements are set and the day fixed for the ceremony, they meet again at the girl's home in the presence of an *alase* bringing an *obbi* [kola nut] to sanctify the permanence of the engagement. To unite them, he takes the hand of the boy and the girl in succession, saying to one: *"Wirobirewi onrayare"* (this woman will be your wife) and to the other *"Wirokunewi onrokore"* (this man will be your husband). And, having cut the kola in two, he gives each of them a half, which they eat. The *alase* departs and the two families separate. From then on, the boy's mother often goes to visit his little fiancée carrying gifts, and the two children often play together.

When the engaged pair reach fifteen or twenty years of age, or if

---

Adams ([*Remarks on the Country Extending from Cape Palmas to the River Congo*] pp. 75, 116 and 133) shows the scarification of Dahomey, that of Benin, and that of the Ibos, in a manner that does not conform completely to Osifekunde's memory. Dahomey, according to Adams, has only one single vertical line on the forehead. Benin wears the design of a tripartite leaf on each temple, and three long lines on the stomach above the naval. The Ibos have a great number of perpendicular incisions on both temples.

Dapper ([*Description de l'Afrique*], p. 314) says that the inhabitants of Warri are marked by three incisions, one on the forehead and the other two on the temples. This, according to Osifekunde, is the tattooing of the Adja nation.

The portrait of a girl from Ouidah (for which I am obliged to Captain Bouët), however, shows only one vertical incision on the forehead.

David de Nyendaal (in Bosman, pp. 472, 473) speaks of scarification in Benin as pure fantasy, with no other rules than the caprice of the artist; which is evidently quite mistaken. The study of these curious national distinctions is still one of the most important and most neglected aspects of African ethnology.

[The facial and body marks described here by D'Avezac are at variance with those given by Johnson, *History of the Yorubas*, pp. 104–9, which is probably a more reliable source. In general, the marks described by Johnson as being usual in the late nineteenth century are those seen today.]

a marriage is between adults, the young man visits the girl's parents to ask for her, since it is then only a question of arrangements—if, indeed, they had not already been made at the time of engagement. With her parents' consent, he returns with all his relatives to the home of his future wife, to which an *alase* has meanwhile been summoned, and they begin to eat, drink, dance, and play until the moment for retiring comes. Then the *alase* takes some water in which he soaks a sprig of *orounou*, or basil,[112*] and scrubs the foreheads of the couple. He takes their hands, joins them together, and says to them alternately: *"Ayakbo, ayato, onrayare, onrokore"* (husband, this is your wife; wife, this is your husband). And the husband then takes his wife to his father's house, or to his own if he has one. The next day the whole family and their friends come together at the husband's home and enjoy the pleasures of eating, dancing, and playing, as in all their festivals.

Polygyny being allowed by their laws and customs, the same ceremonies are repeated at each marriage. The expense of these festivities and especially the obligation to give a bride-price for each wife clearly keep the multiplicity of wives within proper limits, contrary to the monstrous example of some neighboring countries.[113*] In Ijebu the king has only about fifty wives, and the greatest personages have hardly more than a third that number. Most ordinary people are limited to one or two.

Divorce is also permitted among the Ijebu. It entails the refund of the bride-price and repayment to the family of the repudiated woman for all their expenses with the engagement and the wedding. This constitutes a restriction on abuses. Nevertheless, in spite of this barrier, divorce is frequent, at least among the rich.[114]

112*. Osifekunde led me to recognize this through the Brazilian synonym, *majiricão*, which (for lack of dictionaries) was explained to me by the Chevalier de Lisboa, of Rio de Janeiro.

113*. See Bosman ([*Voyage de Guinée*] p. 362), who cites four to five thousand for the king of Ouidah, and King ("Extrait de la relation inédite d'un voyage fait en 1820 aux royaumes de Benin et de Waree," in *Journal des Voyages*, XIII, 316 and 318, Paris, 1822), who attributes four thousand each to the kings of Benin and Warri. Dapper ([*Description de l'Afrique*], p. 311) gives only a thousand to the king of Benin, which is perhaps closer to the truth, though it hardly seems credible.

114. This comment is interesting in view of the frequent allegations among contemporary Yoruba that a high divorce rate is correlated with present-day social change. The annual rate of divorce in Ijebu in the past decade seems to have been approximately 3 divorces per 100 extant marriages, a rate seven times as high as that of the United States.

4. Diseases and remedies

The Ijebu have doctors of their own called *olouchigou* [Yoruba: *on-isegun*], according to whose orders they take certain *ekboghi* [Yoruba: *egbogi*], or medicines.[115]*

The most frequent serious diseases among them are:

a. Ayano parako or smallpox, which is treated with hot medicated compresses. This treatment is generally successful, provided it is applied at an early stage in the disease.

b. Eba [Yoruba: *iba*], or pneumonia, recognizable by a dry cough, frequently accompanied by the spitting of blood.[116] It is essential to give certain relaxing medicines immediately, otherwise the symptoms become aggravated, a gradual emaciation sets in with a prostration of the life forces and finally death. An ordinary cough from the common cold is called *okko* [Yoruba: *iko*] and is not confused with this dangerous disease.

c. Elougo, or fever, is more frequent among women than among men. It is treated by building a large fire and drinking hot infusions of a plant called *Ewe eloukeze,* for which my informant found no analogy among the plants he has seen in Brazil or in Europe.

d. Oyanou [Yoruba: *isuna, iyana*], or dysentery. Counteracted by eating bananas cooked on hot coals and soaked in a sauce composed of palm oil and the burned and ground-up skin of the banana itself.

e. Olokouroun [Yoruba: *olokunrun*], or dropsy, against which there is no remedy.[117]

In addition to these diseases, the Ijebu, being subject to more or less serious accidental wounds, are familiar with the use of surgical techniques. Suction-cup blisters are frequently employed. For this, small hollowed out calabashes are applied over a wick made of old calabash fiber soaked in oil and lighted. The *olouchigou* also practice surgical operations which require a certain skill and special instru-

---

115*. Landolphe ([*Mémoires*] I, 66, 121) is full of praise for the abilities of the doctors of Warri and Benin. Tedlie (in Bowdich [*Voyage dans le pays d'Aschantis*], pp. 477–484) gives a quite extensive list of the vegetable remedies used by the Negroes of the Gold Coast. It is probable that the knowledge of these is spread among all the people in the vicinity.

116. *Iba* today refers to fever, not pneumonia.

117. *Olokunrun* is a person in perpetual poor health.

ments, which Europe alone can furnish. Armed with a very well sharpened knife and a fine saw, they are not afraid of making amputations, and success ordinarily justifies their courage.

In ordinary cases, they heal wounds by the simple application of a paste formed by dissolving gunpowder in lemon [or citron] juice. It is a form of true cauterization, and the result is both prompt and assured.

5. Longevity, death, and funerals

Having only memory to keep track of their years, the Ijebu generally do not know their precise ages. Nevertheless, insofar as my informant could judge, the mean life span of his fellow countrymen was quite long, and examples of extreme longevity are not rare. He believed that his grandfather died at about one hundred and forty or one hundred and fifty years of age, and without considering this age to be extraordinary.[118]* But with them blindness ordinarily accompanies great age.[119]

When someone dies, his parents and friends gather at his house,

118*. However extraordinary this assertion may appear, I must state it here without modification. In general, Osifekunde's accounts did not lean toward exaggeration, and one can only distrust his means of ascertaining such a great age. However that may be, I will observe that there are many examples of longevity among the Negroes transplanted to America, as is mentioned by Bryan Edwards, *Histoire des colonies anglaises dans les Indes occidentales*, p. 223 [originally, *The History Civil and Commercial of the British Colonies in the West Indies* (2 vols., London, 1794)]. A Negress has even been mentioned who lived to the age of 175 years (London *Chronicle*, 5 October 1780, cited in Virey, *Histoire naturelle du genre humain*, Paris 1801, in-8°, p. 409).

Is it not believable that, if Negroes transplanted to a country not their own have such a long life, so much more are they likely to reach a very old age in their native land? Back at the beginning of the sixteenth century, the Portuguese pilot whose account Ramusio printed following that of Cadamosto (*Navigazzioni e viaggi*, I (1553), in-folio, fol. 125, D.) remarks expressly that the Negroes of Guinea and Benin "anchor che nel mangiar siano disordinati, vivono lungamente, la maggior parte da 100 anni, sempre gagliardi." In a country where *most* men live to a hundred a more advanced age should not be surprising

Doctor Prichard, in his latest work (*Histoire naturelle de l'homme*, Paris, 1843, in-8°, II-218) [originally, *The Natural History of Man*, London, 1843] brought together quite a large number of examples of longevity among Negroes.

119. A very old man is usually said, by contemporary Yoruba, to have been 140 years old at death. An age of 90–100 years is more realistic in these cases—this age being calculated with reference to known events.

along with an *agoune,* or royal servant in charge of taxation, and an *odogo* who offers sacrifices. The body is first washed in a solution of *olosun* leaves from a kind of coconut tree (*jaca* in Brazil). Afterward, it is wrapped in white cloth rolled like the bandages wound around Egyptian mummies. The arms are laid alongside the body and then brought forward so that the two hands are joined with the thumbs fastened together.[120]* Cloth after cloth is wound around the body until it takes on a size proportionate to the wealth and power of the individual. They place it on a bed in this condition. Those present cry aloud and remain in attendance until the end of the funeral, which may last from three to four days for ordinary people, and up to eight days for the rich. Each evening and each morning many musket shots are fired from the doorway of the house, and mourners pass their time eating and drinking around the body. Finally the time of burial comes. The *alase,* or priest, is called and they begin the dance of death. A large grave is dug in the reception room, the body is put in a bier or large wooden coffin and lowered into the grave, where it is immediately covered with earth if it is a poor commoner. But if the dead person was rich there are further ceremonies, and the grave remains open for as long as three more days during which they keep up the feasting, dancing, and firing of salvoes. The last day is that of the sacrifices, and for a man of high rank the victims are slaves: the *odogo* kills them. Two were sacrificed at the funeral of the *ladeke,* Ochi Wo, the grandfather of my informant. Their graves were dug at the threshold of the two doors that led into the room from the court and from the garden, each grave being just outside the doorway and laid crosswise to it. Funerals are ended with the covering of the open graves. The *alase* then takes a goat for himself, the *agoune* takes a second, and the *ogodo* is entitled to a male goat. The family slaughters an ox to entertain those present. After this final meal, they dance once more, passing through the town, and finally separate to return to their own homes.

The same ceremonies take place for women, in proportion to their fortunes and the rank of their families.

120*. Clapperton (*Second Expedition,* pp. 79, 183, 184) describes, for two nearby peoples of the same language group, a form of burial in which the body is placed in a squatting position, as among the ancient Nasamonians (Herodotus, IV, 190) and certain savage nations of America. This peculiarity is found, according to Landolphe (*Mémoires,* II, 52) in the kingdom of Benin.

III. Material Culture

1. Clothing

Among all peoples, but especially among those that are partly civilized, costume is a subject worthy of very serious attention from observers. A whole body of important data is associated with costume —the nature, production, and workmanship of textiles, dye stuffs, leather, precious stones and metals; agriculture and the pastoral and manufacturing industries, commerce, the social make-up of the political hierarchy—all these are revealed by man's external appearance, the study of which may seem at first to be solely a matter of curiosity.

In the simple exposition of the little I have gathered from my conversations with Osifekunde, I make no pretense of giving an exact answer to so many important questions. I have just barely been able to bring together enough general information to satisfy the most commonplace curiosity. It is left to intelligent minds to deduce, after the fashion of Voltaire's Zadig, the subtle and wise interpretations that will come naturally to thoughtful people.

The Ijebu dress themselves, by and large, in textiles which they make themselves. These are cotton cloths whose raw material is furnished by the soil. In each family, the harvest, spinning, weaving, and dyeing are the customary occupations of the women, and it is known that a considerable quantity of textiles is manufactured and exported, not merely to nearby countries but even to Brazil, whence ships come to Lagos in search of this merchandise so highly esteemed by the peoples of African origin transplanted to those distant lands.[121]* The most common colors, after white and blue, are yellow, red, crimson, and green, some in solid colors, others multicolored. A simple cloth wrapper, knotted at the waist, is the usual costume for men in the interior of their homes. Outdoors, they wear a kind of wide, short pantaloons, called *choukotou* [Yoruba: *sokoto*]. And the rich replace the knotted cloth of the common people with a large

---

121*. Clapperton (*Second Expedition,* p. 177), in speaking of the commerce of the African interior and of the commodities involved, especially mentions the Ijebu textiles, which are used as clothing for slaves and the poorer classes. He says they are sold by the piece, six yards long and about the same width as sailcloth, with one or two blue selvages.

open gown.[122] Women wear a cloth wrapper as well, but larger, rolled around the body, and held in place below the bust by a knotted kerchief in the form of a belt.

Linen cloth imported from Europe is valued by the Ijebu as having the same superiority over cotton that we ourselves recognize.

Ordinary or embroidered silk textiles, even our most luxurious, are not unknown to these people, and the rich wear these magnificent clothes on special occasions. Velvet, satin, and brocade are used in the costume of the sovereign.[123*]

Footwear is not worn by the common people, but restricted to those of the higher orders. There is a kind of sandal or slipper called *lagolago;* and a more distinguished form of shoe, which looks like our clogs, is called *saka.* It is these that the monarch wears for ceremonies, at which times they are made so massively of gold and of such weight that they force the prince to walk with a solemnity suitable to the etiquette of such occasions.[124*]

Headdress is highly variable. The common people go bareheaded, or at the most content themselves with the *botiboti,* a simple cap made in the country. The more well-to-do prefer the *akode* or brimless hat, or the straw hat, called *akoro,* both of them native to the country. Distinguished men require a red wool hat; and the rich, a felt hat with a wide brim, imported from Europe.[125] The chief priest wears a kind of brimless cloth hat similar to our toque. As for the king, his headdress is raised up in the form of a tiara of great rich-

122. It is not clear whether the "open gown" refers to the voluminous gown and trousers—the *agbada* and *sokoto*—made from narrow strips of cloth woven by men on the horizontal loom. It seems to have been diffused throughout Yoruba country from Oyo, perhaps within the past century. The official clothing of priests and ambassadors, described below, seems to consist of large cloths draped around the body but not tailored into gowns.

123*. Everyone knows that these rich fabrics are commodities found on all the lists of merchandise destined for the Guinea coast. See, among others, Dapper [*Description de l'Afrique*], p. 310.

124*. Villault de Bellefond [*Relation de costes d'Afrique*] pp. 393, 394) mentions the ability of the Negro craftsmen of Guinea to make various articles of adornment in gold, and he assures us that in their festivals, rich women may be wearing ten to twelve pounds of gold and the men fourteen to twenty. And these are only private individuals: kings must have carried enormous weights.

125. The red woolen cap is no longer seen in Yoruba country. It remains a mark of chieftaincy among some Ibo and other peoples to the east and north of them. The wide-brimmed hat is still worn by chiefs in Lagos and Abeokuta.

ness. It is made of coral beads mounted close together on a background of crimson leather; at the crest is a tuft or tassel of gold braid.[126*]

Coral is one of the most sought after adornments. The size and quality of the beads are a sign of rank and wealth among the Ijebu, as diamonds are in Europe.[127*] The important people wear up to four strings of coral beads, hanging down to the navel, and the king wears a great number.

The monarch even has apparel of coral for his legs, called *schaba* and similar to the greaves of the ancients.

In addition to their usual clothing, the Ijebu have official costumes of set form and color for certain professions or certain functions. Thus the dress of priests is white and consists of two large cloths, one wrapped around the chest and the other draped over the head. That of ambassadors is made up of a white wrapper, called *ebbo,* bordered in blue and knotted at the hip with a tasseled cord, and a second white cloth passed over the shoulder like a sling. On the head they wear an *akode,* or native rimless hat in white, and in the hand they carry an *illaghe,* or leather whisk, the special symbol of office.[128] The soldier's uniform is characterized by a white sling passed around the neck and crossed over the chest like the crossed belting of our own soldiers, and by a red cloth or kerchief rolled like a turban around the head.

2. Food

With the Ijebu, as with any other people in the world, food is coarser and less plentiful for the poor classes, more abundant and refined for the rich. Without wishing to present either the *Royal Cookbook* or the *Middleclass Cookbook* of the Ijebu Negroes, it must be noted that the menu of the well-to-do is always used to describe the cu-

126*. Lt. John King (*Journal des voyages,* XIII, 318) describes the crown of the king of Warri, which is very similar but much higher, being three feet high.

127*. This high esteem for coral is widely distributed in the region, and in Warri and Benin coral necklaces have a well-known official significance. See, among others David de Nyendaal in Bosman [*Voyage de Guinée*], pp. 463, 466, and Landolphe [*Mémoires*], I, 113, and II, 37, 53.

128. It is not clear who these ambassadors were; they have no modern counterpart and their special dress is no longer used by anyone.

linary resources of any nation, however barbarous or civilized.[129*]

The food of the Ijebu is composed of meat, fish, roots, and various fruits. Palm oil plays an important role in the recipes I have been told about; yams and potatoes are used a great deal, whether they are served alone or as part of the main dish, as a simple accessory to fowl, fish, a piece of beef, mutton, or goat. Both bananas and plantains are left to ripen for five or six days until they are completely yellow and ready for cooking. They are then crushed to a pulpy consistency, providing what our restaurants would call a sweet. Finally, oranges, bananas, sugar cane, and honey make pleasant desserts. The lime is too acid to be eaten; it is used medically as I have had occasion to mention above. I shall say nothing here about the various kinds of pepper, pimento, and kolas which serve as condiments and even as appetizers.

But I must not leave out the essential article of bread, or that which takes its place. Maize fulfills that function, not that they reduce it to flour as in neighboring countries, they only soak it in water for five days, after which they reduce it to a uniform paste by cooking; then they wrap small portions in banana leaves; they heap these loaves under a woolen cover, and the next day they are ready to be eaten. This paste is called *ouri*. The small loaf made out of it is *eyori*. A double-sized loaf is called *eyaroun*, and the quadruple loaf is *arigochou*.[180]

As for manioc, that great food resource of so many Negro peoples, it is scorned completely and used to feed pigs.[131]

As for beverages, European wine and brandy or American rum offer an exceptional treat, as rare as it is sought after, so that I need not mention them further. The usual beverage is palm wine, sometimes sweet (*emou*), more often fermented (*okko*), and it is drunk in great quantities at all parties and festivals, which are frequent.

129*. My information may be compared with the nomenclature given by Monrad (in Walckenaer, *Histoire générale des voyages*, XII, 411, 412) for the dishes which make up the ordinary food of the Negroes on the Guinea coast. David de Nyendaal (in Bosman, *Voyage de Guinée*, p. 467) provides similar information for Benin, and Richard Lander (in Clapperton, *Second Expedition*, p. 383) for Yoruba, as well as Clapperton himself (p. 181) for Nupe.

130. This maize bread is today known by the Yoruba as *eko*.

131. Manioc or cassava is today the prime staple of the Ijebu. Yam cultivation is small. Manioc seems to have spread rapidly during the present century, perhaps because of the discovery of new modes of preparation.

3. Shelter

Ijebu houses, whether isolated in the countryside or grouped in hamlets, in villages, or in cities, are generally laid out on a uniform plan except for differences in size and comfort proportional to differences in income. A single exterior doorway leads into a walled-in compound or large courtyard, where all the huts or houses of all the individuals united under the authority of a single head of family are lined up as though in a street. The principal building, belonging to the head of the family, is always placed beside the gateway of the compound wall. The whole of the structure is called *oga* [Yoruba: *iga*]; the compound wall is *odi,* and the houses inside are *oule* [Yoruba: *ile*].[132*]

The houses never have a second story, even the royal palace.[133*] The walls are of adobe or swish, about a yard thick; the roof is thatch, supported by joists, held up in turn by pillars within the house.[134*] The houses of the rich have several rooms lighted by windows and used for set purposes, such as the reception room, the kitchen, or the bedroom. This elegance, strictly limited to the principal structure, does not recur with the more or less numerous huts attached to it, which serve for the lodging of women, children, and slaves. For the lower classes, the principal house itself is nothing but a simple hut, lighted only through the doorway.

As for the furnishings, they are arranged to suit the rooms. A bed always consists of a stand on which mats and cattle hides are stretched. Mats also cover the earthen floor in the homes of the rich: European tapestries are reserved for the king. Seats are usually

132*. Clapperton (*Second Expedition,* p. 128) gives the plan of a house in Wawa, which may help to clarify Osifekunde's description. [D'Avezac seems to infer that the descendants' compound is formed of a number of detached houses facing one another along a short street court. A few instances of such a pattern can still be seen in Ijebu Ode. He does not, however, tell us of the plan of the individual buildings, or if the rooms were built around an enclosed courtyard. Today, such courtyards are of small dimensions—often only fifteen feet square, contrasting with the larger courtyards of northern Yoruba, but similar to those of Ondo or Benin.]

133*. It is known that in Hausa the dwellings often have two stories. Clapperton (*Second Expedition,* p. 209) even speaks of a three-story house in "Babagie" near Kano.

134*. The description of Benin houses given by Landolphe (*Mémoires,* I, 111, 123) and by King (*Journal des voyages,* XIII, 314) agrees with Osifekunde's statement about those of his country.

wooden stools made in the country: the important people, however, would not refuse a European armchair, but its use is restricted by custom to a very small number of men who are invested with the most eminent responsibilities of the state.

Household utensils are few and simple: some iron and earthen pots, large and small drinking cups of wood or pottery, a large wooden mortar with its pestle, some plates, baskets of different shapes, bottles, goblets, and knives—these suffice for the kitchen and the service of food. Chests and boxes take the place of wardrobes and drawers. The import trade supplies locks and fittings, but local industry also produces very ingenious locks and keys made of wood.

In paying a call, the visitor first announces himself by knocking on the compound door. A slave comes to open it and escorts the visitors (who may be of either sex) into the reception room. The master of the house always offers his guests some sweet palm wine. They greet one another by shaking hands, both on arrival and on departure, and it is the custom to accompany the departing guests as far as the doorway. Candles made of wax and tallow in imitation of those from Europe provide interior lighting.[135]

IV. Industry

1. Household occupations and the specialized professions

The usual occupations of the Ijebu people are agriculture and gardening, using nothing but a hoe; raising herds of large and small cattle and domestic flocks;[136] the fabrication of cotton textiles with very simple looms; gold mining, either by washing alluvium or in excavated mines;[137] fishing with hook and line, nets, and even har-

135. The usual lamp is a coarse cotton wick lying in a small basin of palm oil.

136. It is not clear what D'Avezac means by "large and small cattle." The former may refer to the humped Zebu cattle, kept by the Fulbe and today driven to the coast for immediate slaughter. These cattle are liable to trypanosomiasis and cannot be kept in Yoruba country for long periods. The small *muturu* cattle are more resistant to fly-borne diseases and are today kept in small numbers in Ekiti, Ondo, and Warri. Few are now seen in Ijebu country.

137. Gold exists in the crystalline rocks of the Basement Complex; it can probably be panned from streams passing through the areas of sedimentary rocks, though in very small quantities. It could not be mined in these rocks.

poons; and hunting with traps, but also with military weapons such as bows and arrows, lances, javelins, and even muskets.

The specialized professions show none of the variety which increases in step with the increasing needs of a more refined civilization. There, where each family supplies its own labor for work too unskilled to require special training, it is hardly necessary to call on professional workmen. Thus the houses are built by the owner himself, or by slaves and servants working under his direction. It is the same with agricultural work. I have already shown that making cloth is the usual task of women. Each household also makes a black soap, or rather a detergent made of ashes without the use of oil, for washing clothes and other domestic uses.[138]

There are nevertheless some separate trades, such as those of the carpenters, woodworkers, and of smiths who work with many different metals. There are also leather-workers, and perhaps some other craftsmen making everyday objects for sale.[139]

As for the liberal professions, I have already mentioned medical men and tattoo artists. I hardly dare mention in the same breath the diviners and sorcerers who make it their business to profit from the credulity and superstition of their fellow citizens.

2. Commerce, money, and transportation

What I have said about industry applies naturally to commerce as well: self-sufficient households rarely need to go shopping. Nevertheless, butchers, palm wine sellers, and others are found in Ijebu. The retail sale of European imports is another important branch of internal trade. But foreign trade is the main commercial occupation: native textiles, salt, cattle, and vegetables are exported; the imports

138. D'Avezac's original is: "On fait aussi dans chaque ménage un savon noir, ou plutôt une lessive rapprochée au feu sans mélange d'huile, pour servir au blanchissage et autres usages domestiques" (pp. 76–77). I am uncertain of the meaning he intends.

139. Each metal—iron, brass, gold—is worked by specialist craftsmen. Iron smelting is an occupation distinguished from blacksmithing. Today the Ijebu predominate among the goldsmiths of Yoruba country. One would have expected this craft to have originated in the late nineteenth century, for almost all the gold now used is imported. D'Avezac's information, however, seems to imply a much older craft. It is still difficult to believe that the gold was obtained from local sources. Johnson asserted that there were no goldsmiths in Yoruba country (*History of the Yorubas*, p. 118).

consist either directly in European goods or in African products destined for exchange against goods from Europe.[140]

Barter, or the exchange of goods for goods, is hardly ever carried on except at wholesale. Markets, where goods are bought and sold and find their relative values, operate through the medium of a currency, which is both an effective money and a currency of account and is based on the cowrie shell, called *owwo* [Yoruba: *owo*]. A *string* of forty cowries is called *ogoji*. A *bunch* of five strings is given the name of *ogwao* [Yoruba: *igba owo*]; a *head* of ten bunches takes that of *egwegwa* [Yoruba: *egbawa*], and ten of these heads forms an *oke,* or *bag,* which becomes in turn a unit of account.

To summarize this series of monetary multiples in tabular form:[141]

Oke	Egwegwa	Ogwao	Ogoji	Owwo
—	—	—	1	40
—	—	1	5	200
—	1	10	50	2,000
1	10	100	500	20,000

As to the value of this money, compared with other monetary systems within our range of knowledge, I will confine myself to Osifekunde's observation that 2 *oke,* or 40,000 cowries, represent the price of an ordinary slave, and that 5 *ogwao,* or 1,000 cowries, are the value of an *ochouon* of gold dust.[142]

The *ochouon* is a small measure of quantity, which my informant says is comparable to the dimensions of a sewing thimble. It is used by the *eddomoo,* or gold merchants, and it is not without interest to mention in this context that this is the only fixed measure the Ijebu use. They have nothing more, not even for weight, and every other judgment as to the quantity of goods or produce is by eye or by the piece.

140. It is not clear why salt should be listed among Ijebu's exports. It is not found locally, though some waterside villages may have obtained it from sea water or from burning the branches of the mangrove.

141. See also Johnson, *Yorubas,* pp. lii, 118–19.

142. Sir Richard Burton, *Abeokuta and the Camaroons Mountains* (2 vols., London, 1863), 1:318–22, gives some cowrie equivalents and prices.

To return to the evaluation of Ijebu money, according to Robertson's information on the value of cowries in Lagos market, they should be put at 5 shillings the thousand.[143*] Following European methods of calculation, 16,000 cowries would then represent an ounce of gold, or about 100 francs. But on the other hand, it should be noted that the *ochouon* of gold dust cannot be reasonably set at less than 50 grams in weight, or 150 francs in intrinsic value for us. Sixteen thousand cowries would suffice to buy 16 *ochouons* of gold, or the value of 2,400 francs, which is forty-eight times the cost price of cowries calculated by Robertson. In other words, European merchandise valued at 100 francs brings the seller in Lagos market a return of 16,000 cowries currency; and with this sum he can buy about eight hectograms of gold, which will have an intrinsic value of more than 2,400 francs in Europe.

It is difficult to discover in all this a fixed value analogous to *value at par* in our money: gold in this case is a commodity, on the purchase of which enormous profits are to be made. On the other side, to bring the hundred francs worth of merchandise from Europe entails new costs, and the sale of this merchandise should bring a profit well above cost price. By estimating these new costs and profits together at 60 per cent of the original French value, the value of the French goods in Lagos would be 160 francs. We can then conclude with a crudely approximate but very convenient evaluation of Ijebu money. Since the 16,000 cowries will have a sale value of 160 francs, therefore one cowrie is worth .01 franc; one *ogoji*, .40 franc; one *ogwao*, 2 francs; one *egwegwa*, 20 francs; and one *oke*, 200 francs.

Goods in Ijebu are transported by land on the backs of donkeys or camels, according to the distance travelled, or by boat when it is possible to take advantage of water routes. The boats used in such cases are small. They are sometimes sailed, but they are more often rowed, paddled, or poled.[144]

143*. Robertson, *Notes on Africa*, p. 292. Cf. Dalzel, *The History of Dahomey*, London 1793, in-4°, p. 135, note signed J. F. [James Ferguson?].

144. It is most improbable that Osifekunde ever saw a camel in any of his travels. Trans-Saharan camel caravans usually ended at Kano. Sails are today used on canoes, but only to run with the wind; they cannot be used to tack into the wind.

V. Intellectual Life

1. Calendar

The Ijebu calendar is worthy of special attention. Their means of measuring time is not based on the week but, as with the Malays and the Mexicans, on a short period of only five days, called *oyose*.[145] The names of the days are as follows: first day, *eni;* second day, *ola;* third day, *otounla;* fourth day, *iyere;* fifth day, *oyose.*

Six *oyose* make a month of thirty days, or *okbon* [Yoruba: *ogbon*]; and a series of twelve months makes the year, *oddou* [Yoruba: *odun*], which is divided, as in ancient Egypt (and, it must be added among most African peoples), into three seasons related to changing patterns of weather. These are the rainy season, *oyyo* [Yoruba: *ojo*]; the harvest season, *ougbe,* and the dry season, *erounou* [Yoruba: *erun*].

Each of these seasons invariably has four set months, as shown on the following table (along with some indications of the weather each month):

First season: *Oyyo*

1st month: *Ochou ogou* (showers and storms)
2nd month: *Ochou osoro* (heavy showers and big storms)
3rd month: *Ochou koudou* (storms and intermittent rains)
4th month: *Ochou gheghe* (heavy and continous rain)

Second season: *Ougbe*

5th month: *Ochou ibe* (cooling and foggy)
6th month: *Ochou* (harvest time, important festival)
7th month: *Ochou ereno* (fair weather)
8th month: *Ochou abibi* (some storms toward end of month)

Third season: *Erounou*

9th month: *Ochou oyoko* (storms, preparing the land)
10th month: *Ochou ogme* (hot season, planting)
11th month: *Ochou roko* (weeding)
12th month: *Ochou kadi* (lightning storms)

145. The Ijebu today, in common with other Yoruba, use a four-day week for market cycles and the like. The names given to the second and third days by D'Avezac simply denote "tomorrow" and "the day after tomorrow." *Ojo ose* (*oyose*) now designates Sunday, the first day of the seven-day week.

The tropical rainy season in the northern hemisphere is known to begin at the precise moment of the summer solstice: this is therefore the fixed beginning of the Ijebu year and shows that it is a solar year, although the name of each month repeats the word *ochou* [Yoruba: *osu*], meaning moon. But this latter circumstance is without doubt merely of etymological interest, as it is with us in regard to the word *month*.[146]

However that may be, the months are uniformly thirty days long, or six complete *oyose*, so that the twelve months only make up a total of 360 days, unless an additional *oyose* is added somewhere to make a rough year of 365 days. But I was not able to learn from my informant how this interpolation is carried out. He naïvely claimed absolute ignorance on this point, and I myself held back from attempting a solution that could only be a conjectural choice between the various interpolations one can imagine, such as the simple addition of an extra *oyose* at the end of the year, or the insertion at certain intervals of extra days between one *oyose* and the next.

The year begins with a three-day ceremony, during which the Ijebu speak to no one and abstain from sexual intercourse. These three days are called *oyo ogou, oyo warou,* and *oyo orifo*.[147]* Each month also has its own festival, from which it is named and which usually falls in the last *oyose* of the month. Nevertheless, the greatest of these monthly festivals, that of the moon, is movable and is celebrated at the full moon during the month simply called *ochou*.

These festivals are celebrated by public and private rejoicing, dances, and feasting.

2. Religion and worship

A deeper study of the so-called fetishism[148]* of the Negroes would no doubt lessen our disdain for the religious principles of these peo-

146. Cf. the list of Ijebu months cited in R. C. Abraham, *Dictionary of Modern Yoruba* (London, 1958), p. 492: *sere, erele, erenon, igbe, ebibi, okundu, agemon, ogun, owewe, owara, belu, ope.*

Some of these names, e.g. *agemon* and *ogun*, refer to religious festivals celebrated during the month. Some names recur in the lists of both D'Avezac and Abraham, though the order is changed. D'Avezac's first season is that of the rains, his first month presumably being March; his third season is the dry season, ending in February.

147*. This festival answers to one spoken of by Isert (*Voyage en Guinée*, p. 190).

148*. Various travellers have expressed their difficulty in defining a fetish: they have forgotten that it is a word imported from Europe, the Portuguese *feitico*, that is, charm,

ple, whose ideas we assume too easily to be unworthy of attention or interest. My conversations with Osifekunde, touching lightly on this matter, revealed beliefs in the paganism he remembered which seem less opposed to the adoption of the dogmas of a purer religion than we ordinarily believe.

They have knowledge of a single God, superior to all the rest and called *Obba Oloroun,* or king of heaven.[149]* They raise neither statues nor temples for him; he is an immaterial being, invisible, eternal, the supreme will which created and governs all things.[150]*

There are secondary gods in great number, called *orisa.* They are a kind of private genie, male or female, which are represented by wooden images placed in sacred compounds (each with an *alase* in attendance), to which the faithful are called for prayer by bells. At Epe, capital of the district where my informant was born, there are two of the *oule orisa* [Yoruba: *ile orisha*], or temples—one for the goddess *Alaro*[151]* inside the town, another outside for the god *Ogoumoude* [Yoruba: *Ogun mode*]. In the capital there are also two temples, one dedicated to *Batala* [Yoruba: *Obatala*] and the other to *Aye.*[152]

Each town thus has its patrons, but the greater belief in Obba Oloroun dominates everywhere, and the priesthood which serves such a numerous assemblage of inferior gods forms a single body under the authority of a sole chief, whose title is *okbo alase* [Yoruba: *agbo alase?*].

The belief in an evil genie exists alongside the adoration of the gods: *Elegwa* [Yoruba: *Elegba* or *Esu*][153]* has neither priests nor

---

spell, potion; and the superstition of many of our uneducated women cannot yield a candle to that of the Negroes in this respect. This small observation is enough to explain how fetishes coexist in Africa with a religion that seems bound to exclude them.

149*. Or simply *oloroun,* that is, *olou-oroun* or master of the sky.

150*. It is the same in Yoruba, according to Clapperton (*Second Expedition,* p. 82). Cf. Bosman (*Voyage de Guinée,* p. 147), David de Nyendaal (in Bosman, p. 482), Father Loyer (*Relation du voyage du royaume d'Issiny,* Paris, 1714, in-12, pp. 242 ff.), Des Marchais (*Voyage en Guinée,* Paris, 1730, in-12, II, 160, 269), Isert (*Voyage en Guinée,* p. 187 ff.), Monrad (in Walckenaer, *Histoire générale des voyages,* XII, 272 ff.), etc. etc.

151*. She is the goddess of rain. Perhaps she is the same goddess to whom Adams (*Remarks,* p. 98) saw a young Negress sacrificed in Lagos. Travel between Epe and Lagos is common.

152. The roles of Olorun and of the *orisha* of the Yoruba pantheon are described in E. Bolaji Idowu, *Olodumare: God in Yoruba Belief* (London, 1962).

153*. This name resembles *Lolcou,* the devil of Benin, mentioned by Landolphe

temples, but in certain cursed spots, marked by an ugly figure in wood or by some other sign, the passer-by throws down a small loaf which he has soaked in palm oil and circled twice around his head while averting his eyes: it is a sort of expiatory offering which becomes food for the neighborhood dogs.

Offerings to the *orisa* are made up (according to means) of chickens, a sheep, or an ox, and are divided after the ceremony between the priest and the participants.[154] Human sacrifices, so frequent and horrible in Dahomey and Benin, are unknown among the Ijebu.[155]

The religious ceremonies which give rise to these offerings are repeated quite frequently: there are usually two each month, one at the beginning and the other toward the middle of the month. They are accompanied by chants. I have recorded, as an example, a kind of hymn in praise of *Batala,* one of the patrons of the capital of the country. Unfortunately, I lacked the time to note down the music, which my concern with the words led me to neglect at first, and I had no opportunity to have it repeated later on. The movement was slow and soft, and the modulations were analogous to those of our church music. I will record only the first line, from memory:

Ni − − si o − li − lé   ri − bé O'ri − − sa.

As for the words of the entire hymn, here they are in the rough form in which I wrote them down, divided into lines according to the rhythm of the chant, which may not always be in conformity with the sense of the phrases. I was unable to get a sufficiently good explanation of the whole text to give a full translation:

> Nisi olile ribe orisa
> Onrolile
> I Batala onrolile
> Ribe orisa eu 'yirikbo

(*Mémoires*, I, 118), while *orisa* seems to be the same word that Dapper ([*Description de l'Afrique*], p. 313) writes *orifa* in speaking of Benin.

154. The sacrifice of animals depends partly on the specific requirements of each *orisha.*

155. D'Avezac has already mentioned above that slaves were sacrificed on the death of a rich man.

Onrolile
Nisi olile ribe orisa
Eu 'yirikbo
Ouon Batala onrolile
Ribe orisa onrolile.

The general sense of these words is that the god Batala is the master and patron of the town, and that none other than he can claim any right to it. They are chanted by the assemblage, which stands up in front of the hut where the statue of the god appears.

There are, in addition to hymns of this sort, prayers which are recited while prostrate on the ground, but, as far as I can make it out, these are addressed exclusively to the great Obba Oloroun. I recorded one, which seemed the most common, and the way in which I came by it makes me think that it is for the Ijebu what the *Pater* is for Christians. My informant knew the *Pater* quite well in Portuguese, and I had him recite it in order to make certain, wishing to obtain the Ijebu version. When I thought my dull informant understood completely what I wanted him to do, I wrote down his words with care as he dictated them, but not without some surprise at the ease with which he seemed to make the translation. Returning later on, as I usually do, to the first rough transcription in order to clean up the orthography and the division into words, I looked in vain for a correlation between the Portuguese text and the supposed Ijebu translation. I finally recognized that Osifekunde had dictated an Ijebu text with which he was familiar, not a version of the *Pater,* which he was never able to recite in his own language. His explanation then made clear that it was a form of prayer which all his countrymen knew and repeated daily, prostrate on the ground, as he was himself in front of me while reciting it anew. Here it is:

Obba olorun ebba hono
Ko ma 'yi mi ku
Ko ma 'yi mi ku
Orisa! ko fu ogo ri mi
Oriwo me ko chu orire.

In a free translation: "O God, who are in heaven, preserve me from sickness and death. God, give me wisdom and good fortune."

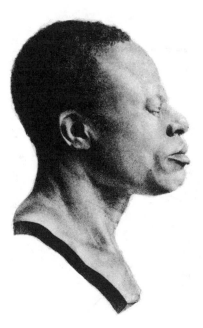

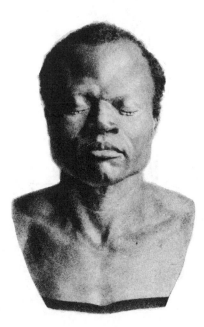

Osifekunde, from a life mask
made in Paris, *ca.* 1838.
From D'Avezac, "Notice sur le
pays et le peuple des Yébous,"
*Mémoires de la Société
Ethnologique*, 2 (1845).

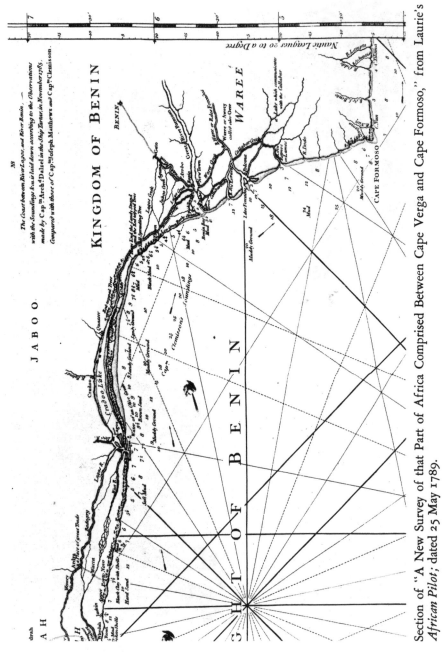

Section of "A New Survey of that Part of Africa Comprised Between Cape Verga and Cape Formoso," from Laurie's *African Pilot*; dated 25 May 1789.

Reflecting on the beliefs of these people, on the forms of their worship, on the organization of the clergy, and even on the form of prayer I have just reported, is one not tempted to suppose that European Christianity must already have penetrated by now-forgotten channels to the Ijebu, who have unknowingly derived from it all these institutions whose analogy to Christianity is so striking[156]—including the bells in their temples?[157]*

3. Music

It is known that Negro instrumental music in general is, to European ears, nothing but a deafening noise, in which one tries in vain to discover something resembling melody or harmony. For the Negroes themselves, this music is nothing more than the accompaniment of their chants: the songs must take first place if we are to understand their musical abilities.

Among the Ijebu as among their neighbors, there are songs for every circumstance of life, for every daily event. By singing, they show joy; by singing they express sorrow; they sing to encourage work; and they even sing to make rest seem sweeter. Songs are mixed in religious ceremonies and in public celebrations. They are a continual expression of a lively and careless spirit, which dislikes silence and isolation.

I collected only a few Ijebu songs. They emerged during my conversations with Osifekunde only as a sidelight to a story or a description, and it was only thanks to their usual brevity that I was able to snatch them from the midst of other matter in which they were embedded. A Negro song, in fact, is hardly more than a phrase, being repeated again and again for hours on end.

I will relate, for example, how two of these songs are presented in their official character within the pattern of a solemn procession made by the king at certain times on the great square of his capital.

---

156. Ijebu legends relate that Portuguese priests once lived in Ijada, a quarter of Ijebu Ode, but no documentary corroboration of this story has come to light. The forms of worship described by D'Avezac are, however, fairly typical of the Yoruba, and it seems unnecessary to postulate a European origin.

157*. Landolphe (*Mémoires,* II, 38), Adams (*Remarks,* p. 125), and King (*Journal des voyages,* XIII, 318) have found incontestable traces of certain Catholic ceremonies introduced by Portuguese or Brazilian missionaries in Warri, bordering Ijebu.

On such occasions, as the king's *ofonkpwe,* or trumpeters, place their *oukpwe,* or great horns made of hollowed elephant tusks, to their mouths, his servants are busy covering the ground he is to walk on with tanned cowhides, and they all sound forth as from a powerful megaphone with this song, repeated a hundred times.

The words mean: "We are all slaves of the king our sovereign." It is a call heard to the ends of the town. The nobles, the chiefs of every rank, the entire people, hasten toward the square to do homage to their prince and follow after him. As for the monarch, his head is covered by a high crown of coral; from his shoulders floats a mantle of gold brocade; over his chest hang many necklaces; his bosom is covered by a tunic of silk; in place of the wide and short *choucatou* of his subjects, he wears narrow trousers of red velvet, called *schaka,* which come down below the knee where they hold the coral greaves that cover his lower legs; he is shod in his heavy clogs of massive gold and carries in his hand a fly-whisk (*iya*) made of horse hair attached to a gilded handle; in the other hand he carries a circular goatskin fan (*ejoujou*), also mounted on a gilded handle. He walks with a slow and measured step, while the musicians (*oukbedou,* and one of the essential attributes of sovereignty) play a piece in which the *ofonkpwe* sing the words while the other musicians accompany them on a single great drum, each one drumming a special beat so as to perform a concert of indefinite duration repeating the same phrase without end. I have tried to write out the parts for the benefit of the readers:[158]*

158*. In order not to write all the parts uniformly with one single note, I have given a series of notes in perfect harmony, although the difference in intonation cannot be considered to represent the difference in intensity in the sounds—the only difference clearly distinguishable between the various parts.

The meaning of these words is: "Here is the bravest of the brave. Follow his example."

I must explain how the parts I have just written down are performed. The drum is in the form of a cylinder about three feet in diameter and two feet high and covered by a strong hide. It is hung from the neck of one of the musicians by a double sling so that without touching the ground the upper surface is not raised above the breast of the carrier, whose hands beat out near the rim of the drum head the part marked above by the word *aya*. A second musician armed with two short drumsticks is given the part marked *afere*. A third, with longer sticks, plays the part marked *agwako*. Two others with very long heavy drumsticks take the bass, called *ogwo*. Finally, the whole ensemble is controlled by a musical director, bearing the title of *omono*, who takes the *agwako* jointly with the musician who plays that alone.[159]

It is clear that the instrumental equipment for the royal music is remarkably simple.[160]* To accompany songs without the official character of those I have just told about, the Ijebu have various other instruments. I have information only in regard to a few of these, such as the *agogo*, a drum in the shape of a very long and slightly truncated inverted cone, covered by a skin on which the musician beats with a single short and heavy stick. The *akasa* are small dried gourds in which a few fragments of metal are shaken in time to the music; they are played in pairs like the castanets of southern Europe.

There is still another kind of drum, called *ouji*, which is a war drum. It is in the shape of a flat cylinder, open at the bottom. It is used for military drumming and may be used to accompany war songs. These, it must be added, completely lack the intoxicating force which makes our own *Marseillaise* a weapon fearful in itself, but they have their local merit, and I hope it will not be held against me if I insert here the only one I can recall:

O-'yo kueñu ma-ka - lè   o-' yo minkba

tè- run a- -ya - rè   kue-ñu ma-ka- -lè

o - 'yo mink-ba   tè - run a - ya - - rè.

159. The drums used at present in Yoruba country have been described by Laoye I, Timi of Ede, "Yoruba Drums," *Odu*, 7:5–14 (March 1959). D'Avezac does not mention "talking drums," in which the tone may be varied by pressure on the lateral strings.

160*. One can judge from the account of David de Nyendaal (in Bosman [*Voyage*

These words mean: "Only the coward stays home, kept there by the advice of his wives."

VI. Political Organization

1. The monarchy and the legislature

The political organization of the Ijebu, like that of several neighboring states, is a kind of tempered monarchy, in which the monarch bears the title of *obba,* common to all sovereigns of that region.[161]* These various *obba* are sometimes distinguished from one another by their proper names, such as *obba* Ade Yoko, the reigning king of Ijebu at the time of Osifekunde's enslavement, *obba* Ouve, the king then reigning at "Ekboumou" and brother of *obba* Ade Yoko—or *obba* Avon 'ya oloudou Oghereya, the king reigning at that time over Oyo, etc. Sometimes, and more frequently, they are known by the indication of their kingdom, such as *obba* Ijebu, *obba* Oyo, *obba* Benin, or *obba* Itsekiri. Finally, they are sometimes known by a title sanctioned by international practice, which, for the king of Ijebu, is *obba* Obrogolouda, for the king of Oyo, *obba* Oyo, and for the king of Itsekiri, *obba* Warri. Something similar happens in our own Europe when we speak of His Most Christian Majesty, His Catholic Majesty, His Most Loyal Majesty, and other such titles.[162]

Is the legislative distinguished from the executive power? Without

---

de Guinée], p. 481) that the royal music of Benin is nearly as simple. Nevertheless, Landolphe (*Mémoires,* I, 115) gives trumpets a more prominent role there.

161*. Cf. Bowdich (*Voyage dans le pays d'Aschantis,* pp. 356 ff.) for Ashanti; Norris (*Voyage au pays de Dahomé,* Paris 1790, in-8°, pp. 97, 98 [originally, *Memoirs of the Reign of Bossa Ahadee, King of Dahomey,* London, 1789]) for Dahomey; David de Nyendaal (in Bosman [*Voyage de Guinée*], pp. 464, 465, 477) and Landolphe (*Mémoires,* I, 112, II, 66, 95) for Benin and Warri.

162. The terms "*obba* Oyo" and "*obba* Benin" simply refer to the kingdom or town ruled: these are not, as D'Avezac suggests, honorifics. Thus the *oba* of Warri is also the *oba* of Itsekiri.

The names of rulers cited in present-day king-lists are rarely those used in the rulers' lifetimes. Thus it is not possible to identify most of the rulers named. Does "*obba* Avon 'ya oloudou Oghereya" stand for the ruler of Oyo? And, if so, does the name "Avon 'ya" refer to Afonja, who was not king but a rebel war leader who established his own state at Ilorin?

D'Avezac names "Ekboumou" as a town ruled by a brother of the king of Ijebu. It is probable that the two rulers were not full brothers but that early rulers of the two dynasties were so related—or so the legends tell—and that a type of perpetual kinship emerged.

being able to cast a precise light on this question, it may be conjectured that the distinction exists from the fact that, perhaps unknown to those who obey the force of custom, it at least appears certain that no important action is taken without having been submitted to the examination, if not to the regular deliberation, of a senate or council of elders, the members of which are called *akamore,* and its meeting place, *nechirouga.* It is an assembly of learned men, most of them former provincial magistrates whom the king and his ministers wish to consult, and in their deliberations both internal and external political questions are debated. They are the keepers of legal tradition and of national history, and those wishing knowledge must go to them for instruction. Without writing and books, some such institution is necessary in order to preserve the memory of the past.[163]

In the midst of a society at a rudimentary stage of civilization, one cannot expect to find powers perfectly defined in the make-up and usages of such a body. The public appears to be admitted to the *nechirouga.* Does it also mix in the discussion of public affairs, and is there a firm distinction between casual get-togethers and official sessions? These are points which the conversations of Osifekunde did not illuminate. But at least the presence of the king gives more solemnity to the assembly; the *akamore* are more numerous then, up to the full number of one hundred; and the public is no doubt excluded from the council, or allowed to be present only as spectators.[164*]

2. The executive

The executive power is not exclusively in the hands of the monarch: he is obeyed only on condition that he exercise it collectively with four princes or ministers, all bearing the title of *odi* along with other designations showing their hierarchic rank, in this order: (1) *odi,* (2) *oukabake 'yi odi,* (3) *oukbaketa odi,* (4) *okbenoudi.*[165]

163. The description of the personnel and processes of government as outlined by D'Avezac seems to bear no relation to what is deduced today as being the traditional system. The terms *akamore* and *nechirouga* are not recognized. For present-day analysis see Lloyd, *Yoruba Land Law,* pp. 146–50.

164*. Judging by analogy from what happened in Benin in a similar case, according to Landolphe (*Mémoires,* I, 113, II, 95) these councils carry on their affairs with great dignity.

165. The *odi* are today senior palace servants and close advisers to the king. The title of *Ogbeni odi* (*okbenoudi*) is now held by one of the titled associations (though not necessarily by a former *odi*), and it is one of the most senior titles in the kingdom.

The numbers two, three, and four—in Ijebu *e'yi, eta,* and *ene*—are easily recognized in these titles, with the addition perhaps of the word *ekbaeka,* arm. Thus, these would be the first, second, third, and fourth arms of the government, the head of which is the *obba.* The latter can do nothing except with their consent and through their agency. The Ijebu truly follow the maxim of utopian constitutionalists, that the king should reign but not govern.

The entire royal family is lodged in the same palace, except the young princes, who are secretly sent far away to be raised beyond the range of the ambitions and the influence of courtiers until the deposition or death of the reigning king opens access to the throne for one of these princes;[166*] he is then recalled, recognized, and proclaimed by the *odi.* His brothers are given provincial governments.

Thus the disposition of the throne itself is in the hands of these four great dignitaries, since they can depose their sovereign and name his successor, who should, according to Osifekunde, be the eldest son of the preceding *obba.* But the series of monarchs he could remember proved that this order of succession is not always rigorously observed. Ade Yoko, the *obba* in 1820, was the brother and not the son of his predecessor, Beleboua, who himself had succeeded Ochi Gade (the maternal great-uncle of my informant) though he was not his son but that of Ladegay, Ochi Gade's predecessor. Osifekunde's memory goes no further back. Only the *akamore* can recite the long list of *obba* who have reigned in Ijebu since the foundation of the monarchy.[167]

One cannot fail to be struck by the immense power with which the four *odi* are seized, and anxious to discover its source. Is this an aristocratic usurpation? or, on the contrary, a delegation from the people? I do not know whether Osifekunde might have enlightened me in that regard. Being pressed to ascertain the more immediate facts, I

166*. Something similar happened in Benin, according to Landolphe (*Mémoires,* II, 57 ff.). It recalls Amba Geshen in Abyssinia. [Amba Geshen was one of several mountains that have figured in Ethiopian history as a place of exile or imprisonment for all the male line of the royal house with the exception of the king's immediate descendants.]

167. Primogeniture is not now held to have operated in Ijebu. For the past century and a half the title is believed to have rotated among four ruling houses. In each of these, however, a man may only succeed to the throne if he was "born in the purple," i.e. to a reigning king. Beleboua (Gbelegbuwa) is today remembered as a ruler of the late eighteenth century; none of his own children reigned and his line became defunct, to be revived in 1933.

always put off such difficult questions till some later time, and he left Paris before I could ask him.

After the four *odi,* the most important personage in the state was the *ladeke,* or treasurer, into whose hands flowed all revenue and all judicial fines, and who was himself the paymaster of all expenditures and dispenser of all rewards granted by the sovereign. He had the special responsibility of putting into effect the measures passed by the *odi,* and he shared with them the privilege of sitting on a European armchair at state occasions, a distinction reserved, like the curule chair of the Romans, for the most important dignitaries. It was this important office of *ladeke* that was vested in Ochi Wo, the grandfather of my informant.

3. Civil and criminal justice

The administration of justice is closely allied to political government. Ultimately it devolves upon the supreme court of the *odi,* and in the first instance, on the chiefs of villages and districts, without distinction between civil and criminal cases. The sentence of the first judge is put into effect without further proceedings, if there is no complaint from the condemned party. If he appeals, the case is taken to the supreme court of the *odi,* who listen to the litigants, confirm or reverse the judgment, and have it executed directly without further recourse.[168]*

The execution of the commands of justice is vested by the inferior courts in the *omodogwa,* a permanent urban militia comparable to our police force.[169] The supreme court uses for the same purpose the *agoune,* a kind of palace force or royal guard composed of crown slaves. Either group hunts out, arrests, and executes the criminals.

We have hardly any data on the civil or criminal law that governs the tribunals. Equality before the law appears certain among the Ijebu, even for women, whose ability to inherit, own, and dispose of property is unlimited. The division of inheritance is made in equal portions between all children, whatever their sex.[170]

168*. Cf. David de Nyendaal (in Bosman [*Voyage de Guinée*], pp. 477–481) for Benin.

169. The *omodogwa* (*omode owa*) are more likely to have been servants of the king— this being the transliteration of the term. The *agoune* are today unknown.

170. Present-day succession in Ijebu follows the general Yoruba pattern; a man's

Repressive justice calls for two distinct kinds of punishment, like our former barbarous laws. There is a role for the state and a role for civil complainants: the first consists of a fine for the treasury, while the second is resolved by a settlement. The settlement is not a fixed indemnity imposed directly by the judge and graduated according to the nature of the crime, but rather an indeterminate right allowed to the civil claimant to compromise with the guilty party for the remission of the corporal punishment the latter has incurred, and the sum of this transaction, argued and arranged in a friendly way, is always proportional to the power of the offended party and the wealth of the guilty.

The history of Osifekunde's family provides two examples for the elucidation of these customs, which he told me with candor and I shall report in my turn in all their simplicity.

Adde Sounlou, his father and one of the bravest and most renowned warriors of his time, seems to have had a hot temper and a quick hand. In a quarrel at Epe he beat to death Otou-Noyo, another soldier of high rank. Otou-Noyo had a brother, Olou-Yanjou, a rich and powerful figure, who put such anger and stubbornness into the pursuit of the murderer that the death of the guilty party seemed the inevitable outcome. Adde Sounlou was forced to run away. He took refuge on the frontier among the Idoko in the town of Makun, where he lived four whole years. It was during his exile that his wife, Egghi Ade, gave birth to Osifekunde. Finally, after a time he was able to return to Epe, his father, Ochi-Wo, having been able to pacify Olou-Yanjou by paying him a settlement of more than 200 *oke*, or more than 4,000,000 cowries, representing the value of 40,000 francs.

Six or eight years later, Adde Sounlou again had the ill fortune to kill, in a fit of anger, an important person named Ourekou. He was then forced to flee to Eda [Edo], the capital of Benin, until this second affair could be satisfied by the same means as the first.

Thus, all crimes may be redeemed for money, but the price is high; besides, agreement to a settlement is not always easy to get, and the guilty party is obliged to attend to his personal safety while waiting, by looking for an asylum where he cannot be reached. Such customs

---

property is divided into as many equal shares as there are wives with children. See Lloyd, *Yoruba Land Law*, Chap. IX.

must necessarily lead to the acknowledgment of certain towns as places of refuge: we have already seen that Makun enjoyed this privilege, and it was the same with Mahin and no doubt with other places.[171]

4. Military organization

War is a sad necessity of the political existence of nations, and in all states of the world, whatever their form, a military organization permeates the country so as to have armies ready for the day of combat.

In Ijebu, all the able-bodied population of the kingdom is divided among the *olorogou* [Yoruba: *olorogun*], or captains, whose family, slaves, and clients form a military company varying in size from fifty to two hundred men. These are the elements of a temporary army, where service is not obligatory, but which rises spontaneously with the impetus of war songs exalting courage and denouncing cowardice, encouraging rivalry by the promises of rewards held out to the brave.

In addition, I have already mentioned a twofold permanent militia[172*]—the *agoune* constituting the military establishment of the king and marching with him, and the *omodogwa*, a kind of *gendarmerie* established in each village or canton for local security and police. In the capital, the body of *omodogwa* comes to a thousand soldiers. Here is the core and the real power of the military.

Three commanding generals, with rank just below that of the *ladeke*, live at court, along with the majority of the *olorogou*. The hierarchic titles of these three chiefs are: *oloukongbon* for the first, *ade chegou* for the second, *ade kola* for the third. In case war breaks out unexpectedly, they immediately take the field at the head of the thousand *omodogwa*, who are always assembled near them and ready to march. The *olorogou* go to their respective cantons to assemble their companies. An *omodogwa*, seizing an *ouji* or drum, walks

171. It seems more probable that Makun, Mahin, and Edo (Benin City) were cities of refuge for the Ijebu because they lay beyond the frontiers of the kingdom of Ijebu and the writ of its rulers. One does, however, find within Yoruba towns that certain compounds are recognized as sanctuaries for fugitives from local justice.

172*. A small permanent army also existed in much the same way in Dahomey, according to the report of Pruneau de Pommegorge (*Description de la Nigritie,* pp. 164, 165).

through the town and the countryside beating a special signal whose meaning is: "Whoever wishes to march to war, come!" Everyone takes up his arms and, in an instant, the companies are formed[173]* and the captains go to place themselves under the orders of the three generals, dividing the army into three separate bodies of troops, each of which takes on the rank-order of its chief.[174]

The native arms are the bow and arrow (*ageya, ova*), the javelin (*echi*), the lance (*afoloko*), and the cutlass or machete (*oda*). European civilization has brought them our sabers (*oda einho*), muskets (*ibon*) with gunpower (*etou ibon*), pistols (*olewo*), and even cannon (*akba*); that is, small bronze pivot guns which they aim from behind the palisades of their fortified towns.

Cavalry is inconsiderable for lack of horses, which are only numerous in the province of Idoko. Their harness is very simple: a saddle on the order of our pack saddles (*ogogo*), wooden stirrups (*okasiko*), an iron bit (*orokbo*), held by a cord replacing a bridle (*okou eroun echi*), finally a whip (*ochouchou*). Such is the complete equipment of the rider and his mount.[175]

In a country cut by rivers, lagoons, and creeks, naval expeditions play a major role. The boatyards of Boughiye produce many war canoes, which I need not describe: it is enough to recall the picture published by the Lander brothers of the ones they saw on the Quora [Niger]. I had barely shown them to Osifekunde when he recognized with a burst of joy the *oko* of his native land, with their paddles (*aye, aye akoako*). He also talked of the pole or quant (*echo*), the rigging (*okou*), and the sails (*bokou*), but I am uncertain whether he applied all these terms to the Ijebu vessels or to the European ships which frequent the factories on the coast of these countries.

Let me bring these disconnected pages to a close, a hasty collection of incomplete data drawn from an unexpected source and one that

173*. In Benin, where a parallel organization existed, the king could, according to Dapper (*Description de l'Afrique*, p. 311), raise an army of twenty thousand soldiers in a single day, and in a short time he could form an army of eighty or a hundred thousand men.

174. The traditional method of recruiting an army, as today remembered, lies through the age-set system. The titled leaders of the age-sets are now the *agbon, kakanfo*, and *lapoekun*.

175. See J. F. Ade Ajayi and R. S. Smith, *Yoruba Warfare in the Nineteenth Century* (Cambridge, 1964), for a description of Yoruba arms and methods of warfare.

too soon became silent. Especially during my work of coordination I have become conscious of many important gaps that remain to be filled; but I no longer have Osifekunde to answer my questions, and I can only offer the results of our long and often fruitless conversations. I like to hope that the form in which I have presented these data will be excused by the interest of their source, and above all by the indulgence of my readers.

CHAPTER 9

SAMUEL AJAYI CROWTHER OF OYO

J. F. Ade Ajayi

Samuel Ajayi Crowther is probably the most celebrated of all the authors represented in this volume. His unusual qualities had begun to attract attention when he wrote the story of his capture and travels to the coast. The narrative not only throws light on the Yoruba Wars, it is also a preface to one of the greatest success stories of all time. Rescued from slavery, he became an Anglican bishop well known throughout West Africa, and a household name in many Christian homes in Britain and North America. He was a tireless traveller and scholar who founded churches, reduced his own Yoruba and other languages to writing, translated the Bible, and established schools and training colleges. He is now recognized as one of the most important of the nineteenth-century architects of modern Nigeria.

Crowther's journeys as a slave boy in the Yoruba country took place in 1821 and 1822. He claimed that he was about thirteen years of age at the time of his capture,[1] but the tradition of his family has usually modified this to about fifteen, and 1806 is generally accepted as the most likely date of his birth.[2] After being loaded in Lagos for

1. Crowther to Commander Bird Allen, 1841, MS in Cape Town Diocesan Archives (hereafter cited as CTM); this recently discovered manuscript was the subject of a brief note by C. T. Wood, "A Crowther Manuscript in Cape Town," *Bulletin of the Society for African Church History,* 1:99–100 (December 1964), and is to be published in a future number of the *Bulletin.* I am grateful to Rev. A. F. Walls, editor of the *Bulletin* and Secretary of the Society, for advance copy of the manuscript.

2. See H. Macaulay, "The Romantic Story of the Life of a Little Yoruba Boy Named Adjai," *Nigeria Magazine,* No. 24, pp. 169–79 (1946).

shipment to Brazil, he was captured at sea by two vessels of the British antislavery squadron and landed in Freetown on 17 June 1822. He quickly learned to read and write, was baptized in 1825, and spent a few months in 1826–27 at school in Islington, London. In 1827, he was the first student to register at Fourah Bay College in Freetown, now the oldest institution of higher learning in West Africa. He left to get married in 1829, was appointed a government school teacher in 1830, and returned to Fourah Bay as a tutor in 1834.[3]

Later he accompanied the British Niger Expedition of 1841–42 as a cathechist. His published journal[4] was only one of many works written by the members of the expedition, but it much impressed his employers, the Church Missionary Society. They sent him back to the Training College at Islington in 1842. He was then ordained deacon and later priest in 1843, after which he returned, first to Sierra Leone and then to the Yoruba country, where he served as a missionary in Badagry in 1845 and Abeokuta in 1846. He again accompanied Niger expeditions in 1854 and 1857, with still another published work of geographical discovery resulting. Meanwhile, he had also published a study of the Yoruba language in 1843, followed by an augmented edition in 1852.[5]

His most important work, however, was the Niger Mission, which he founded for the Church Missionary Society in 1857 with an all-African staff. In 1864, he was consecrated bishop, and in the following decade and a half he played a crucial role in opening the lower Niger Valley to British enterprise and the Christian religion. With the 1880's, however, he began to face a more hostile attitude on the part of Sir George Goldie and other British traders. They were gradually displacing African traders, and they therefore demanded European missionaries as well. Crowther was forced to resign in August 1890, and he died on New Year's Eve, 1891, at well over eighty years of age.

3. For Crowther's career in general, see Jesse Page, *The Black Bishop: Samuel Adjai Crowther* (London, 1910), J. F. Ade Ajayi, *Christian Missions in Nigeria: The Making of a New Elite, 1841–91* (London, 1965).

4. *Journals of the Rev. James Frederick Schön and Mr. Samuel Crowther, who with the Sanction of Her Majesty's Government Accompanied the Expedition to the Niger in 1841* (London, 1842)

5. *Journal of an Expedition up the Niger and Tshada . . . in 1854* (London, 1855); *Vocabulary of the Yoruba Language* (London, 1843; augmented edition with introduction by O. E. Vidal, 1852).

Crowther's account of his early life therefore has a real importance for understanding the character and later career of an unusual man. It is the main source we have for the first twenty years of his life. Through it we catch glimpses not only of his domestic background, but also something of his developing character. He was always a very affectionate man. His character was nurtured on love, and the keynote of his later ministry and episcopate was charity. He was once described as "a little man with nerves of steel, whom incessant work did not seem to wear," and he later won a gold medal from the Royal Geographical Society for his journeys and explorations on the Niger. Yet his real bent was towards quiet study and intellectual pursuits. He was shy and retiring, but he never lacked courage or, on occasion, the kind of daring which he showed when he struck his old Brazilian master, on board the British man-of-war.

Furthermore, Crowther's narrative is an important document on the early stages of the Yoruba Wars of the nineteenth century. It is in fact surprising that, while so much has been made of the accounts of the journeys of Clapperton and Lander through western Yoruba, so little attention has been paid to this account of a journey through the central part in 1821–22.

This journey began at Osogun, Crowther's home town in the Ibarapa district, some five miles off the modern motor road from Abeokuta to Iseyin and Saki.[6] The ruins that remain today are extensive, covering an area some three miles from east to west and two miles from north to south. On the western fringe, there is now a small village resettled in 1912 with the encouragement of members of Crowther's family, the settlers being descendants of the original inhabitants brought from surrounding areas, especially Lanlate and Old Eruwa.[7]

6. The motor road probably follows the course of older path and trade routes, and Osogun is reached by a track leaving it a few miles beyond Lanlate.

7. In the village of Osogun there is an 1888 edition of Jesse Page's *Black Bishop* which is held in very great esteem. It is kept locked up in a box in the possession of the direct descendants of the first *bale* of the new settlement. On the flyleaf of the book, there is a memo in Abigail Crowther's hand which reads as follows:

"Abigail Crowther Macaulay. The last surviving daughter of the late Bishop Crowther. For the last 20 years I have been praying for the rebuilding of the town of my father's birth-place Oshogun, and as Nehemiah prayed and went to have Jerusalem rebuilt so we went in January 1912 took possession of the ruins of Oshogun. The Lord helping us.

"Be it known to all, to whom it may concern, that we the descendants of The

According to traditions recorded by Jesse Page, Crowther's biographer, Osogun was originally founded by a number of princes from Old Oyo (Oyo Ile) as a breakaway settlement from Iba-Agbakin, probably in the eighteenth century. Such settlements by unsuccessful candidates for the throne were not unusual, and there is in the village of Osogun today a strong tradition of a direct connection with the Oyo royal lineage. Apart from the settlers from Old Oyo, others came from Ketu and the Popo country to the south. Farming, weaving, and dyeing seem to have been the principal occupations. The ruins also show evidence of considerable iron-working, and it is said that iron was smelted in the neighborhood.

Dominating a central position of the ruins is a huge tree, which marks the central shrine of Obatala (goddess of purity), the town's most important deity, known more affectionately as Iyalode (the first Lady). Even today in spite of the inroads of Islam and Christianity, Iyalode retains a special place in the beliefs and religious affiliations of the villagers.[8]

According to the tradition of the Crowther family, Samuel's father was named Aiyemi.[9] He was a descendant of one of the leading migrants from Ketu, and the family was well known for the peculiar type of cloth they wove (*aso elerin*),[10] probably with an elephant design in the pattern. Crowther himself wrote: "I am the son of a weav-

---

Great King Abiodun have taken full possession of the ruins of the old town Oshogun (the birthplace of the late Bishop Samuel Adjai Crowther, Bishop of the Niger Territory), according to the rites of the Yoruba country. In January 16th 1912, Frank Gurney Venn Macaulay, grandson of the late Bishop Crowther, Olatufe the brother of the Bale of Lalete, whose mother was a native of Oshogun, the Bale's priest and doctor, with 25 men, went to the ruins of Oshogun and took full possession of it with the forest palm trees etc. and all that pertaineth to it for our *Heirs*.

"I am encouraged and quote a passage in a letter in the Book of the Black Bishop Samuel Adjai Crowther, in writing to Salsbury Square (my kind respects to all who care for the Africans, and I would comfort them that they need not be in despair that shall not return etc. etc.). We are a small band returning to Oshogun. I pray, trust and hope for great things. We are under the Alafin of Oyo.

"Yours truly,

"Abigail Crowther Macaulay with all others, relations, friends, from the town of Oshogun.

"God helping us."

8. This opinion is based on field work carried out in Osogun during February to April, 1964, with Mr. Wande Abimbola of the Institute of African Studies, University of Ibadan.

9. Macaulay, "A Yoruba Boy Named Adjai."

10. Page, *Black Bishop*, pp. 2–3.

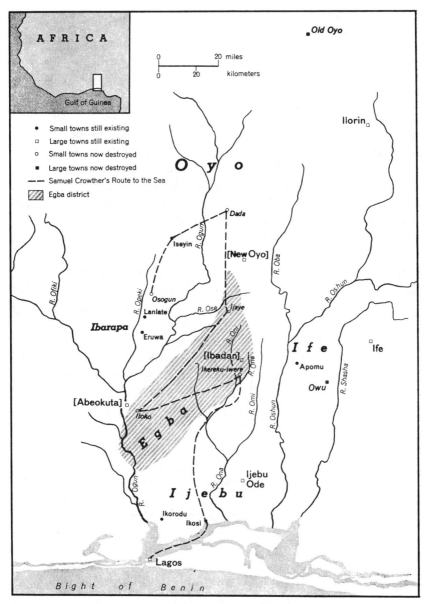

Map 15. Samuel Crowther's route to the coast.

er, . . . My father gradually introduced me into the trade of weaving the country cloth as well, as all his relations were of that trade. He also occasionally attended to agriculture" (CTM).

His mother's family was even more distinguished. Her grandmother was said to have been a daughter of *Alafin* Abiodun (1770–89), the last great ruler at Old Oyo. Her father was said by Crowther himself to have been the "eldest" (perhaps the most senior) councillor to the *bale* of Osogun.[11] She herself, Afala, was an important priestess of Obatala. She had four children, first Bola, a girl, then Ajayi, followed by two other daughters, Lanre and Amosha. Also living with them in the same household was a cousin of Crowther's, and an adopted son. The household therefore was still relatively young and small when it was disrupted by war. It is not clear, however, whether it was self-contained or part of a larger family compound, with other wives and other brothers of Aiyemi. Later references mention Crowther's half-brother, which seems to imply that Aiyemi had a second wife.

In any event, this household was caught up in the Yoruba Wars at the point in time when Afonja and his Fulbe allies made their bid for power in Oyo. And on this phase of the disorder, Crowther's own account provides some useful evidence. Some writers have been eager to see in the Afonja revolt only an extension of Usuman dan Fodio's jihad in Hausa. But Crowther reports: "The enemies who carried on these wars were principally the Eyo [Oyo] Mahomedans —with whom my country abounds—with the Foulahs [Fulbe], and such foreign slaves as had escaped from their owners, joined together, making a formidable force of about 20,000 who annoyed the whole country."[12]

Insofar as the impressions of an intelligent boy of thirteen (or fifteen) are reliable, this evidence of a significant role played by Oyo Muslims in the Afonja revolt—and of the spread of Islam in Oyo even before the Fulbe jihad—tends to corroborate hints in the oral traditions collected by Samuel Johnson.[13] These traditions mention a certain Solagberu as leader of the Oyo Muslims, whose quarter in the city of Ilorin was named Oke Suna. It is further supported by the number of Yoruba slaves professing Islam who arrived in Brazil and Sierra Leone in the early nineteenth century.[14]

11. "Journal of an overland route journey, December 1871—February 1872," Archives of the Church Missionary Society, London, CA 3/04 (cited hereafter as CMS).

12. Excerpt from text; see below.

13. *The History of the Yorubas* (Lagos, 1921), pp. 190, 193–94.

14. Gilberto Freyre, *The Masters and the Slaves* (New York, 1946), pp. 313–15; C. Fyfe, *A History of Sierra Leone* (London, 1962), p. 186.

But the presence of a large Islamic population is not proof that the disorders in Oyo were necessarily connected with the Fulbe jihad at a very early date. Afonja, as a military leader seeking to increase his power, sought and received valuable support from Solagberu, the leading Muslim of Ilorin. But the alliance was not necessarily based on religion: Solagberu supported Afonja for the same reasons that others throughout Oyo supported him—friendship, political conviction, or convenience. Solagberu's support, however, made it possible for Afonja to appeal to discontented Hausa slaves. From these and other discontented Muslims, he constituted bands of war boys, called *Jama'a,* or followers. They brought in new military techniques, and the defection of the Hausa slaves in particular weakened the cavalry force that remained loyal to the *Alafin.*[15]

It may also have been Solagberu who was instrumental in inviting Alimi, an important Fulbe *mallam,* to come to Ilorin (though it was not unusual for important warriors to employ itinerant Muslim *mallams* as makers of charms and consultants on military, political, and other matters). In any case, Alimi had no official connection with the Fulbe jihad. He did not arrive until the early 1820's, and the jihad had begun long since, in 1804. He also lacked an official appointment to act as "flagbearer" for the Sokoto government—otherwise, he would have become the emir after the victory. But Alimi brought the Fulbe jihad to Yoruba in a more indirect manner. At Afonja's urging, he invited his sons to come down from Sokoto. Their arrival just before 1821 brought a new stage in the revolution. Where the father was a pious, shy, and humble cleric, the sons, and particularly Abdulsalam, were fighting statesmen who finally did convert Afonja's secession into an outpost of the movement directed from Sokoto.

Afonja soon began to find the Fulbe and the *Jama'a* too powerful, and he became suspicious of their intentions. Before he could act against them, however, he was captured and killed.[16] The movement then became clearly religious, though a further struggle for power ensued between Abdulsalam and Solagberu, with Abdulsalam emerging victorious. Much later, in about 1829 or 1830, Abdulsalam

15. This reconstruction of the Afonja revolt owes a good deal to information received from Mr. P. G. Gbadamosi, research student in the History Department, University of Ibadan, who is writing a Ph.D. thesis on the rise of Islam in western Nigeria.

16. Johnson, *Yorubas,* pp. 197–99.

finally received a symbolic flag from the caliph and assumed the title of emir. Ilorin then became part of the Fulbe empire.[17]

It is thus possible (though not certain) that this second phase of the Afonja movement began in the opening months of 1821, just at the time of Crowther's capture. Crowther's account makes it clear that the particular contingent which destroyed Osogun was made up mainly of Oyo Muslims, operating from a base in Iseyin, but under conditions of great rivalry between the Yoruba and their Fulbe allies for the larger share of the booty. It may also be significant that the people of Osogun did not expect to be attacked that day, since Crowther remarks that the Muslim army "used to pass over [our] town before without doing any harm" (CTM).

It would seem, therefore, that Oyo had been more than twenty-five years in crisis before Crowther's journey began, and the collapse of the Oyo empire was well under way. It was only to be expected that the anarchy in the metropolitan province to the north of Crowther's Ibarapa would have its impact on this part of southern Oyo. The

17. The Landers were among the rare European visitors to Old Oyo at this period. Talking of the growth of Fulbe influence, they reported in 1829:

"Another town of prodigious size has lately sprung into being, which already far surpasses Katunga [Old Oyo] in wealth, population, and extent. It was at first resorted to by a party of Falatahs [Fulbe] who named it Alorie [Ilorin], and encouraged all the slaves in the country to flee from the oppression of their masters, and join their standard. They reminded the slaves of the constraint under which they laboured, and tempted them by an offer of freedom and protection, and other promises of the most extravagant nature, to declare themselves independent of Yarriba [Yoruba, that is, Oyo]. Accordingly the discontented many miles round eagerly flocked to Alorie in considerable numbers, where they were well received. This took place as far back as forty years, since which other Falatahs have joined their countrymen from Soccatoo [Sokoto] and Rabba . . ." (R. and J. Lander, *Journal of an Expedition to Explore the Course and Termination of the Niger* [2 vols., London, 1832], 1:176–90).

The reference to the movement beginning some forty years before is reasonably consonant with the present view that anarchy began in Oyo during the 1790's. The Landers' further statement that the Fulbe had "recently" forced from the *Alafin* "a declaration of independence" probably refers to the time when Afonja lost control of the movement, not to his initial revolt. Afonja's first revolt is usually dated 1817 on evidence from Ilorin, which is further supported by the evidence of Ali Eisami (see S. J. Hogben, *The Muhammedan Emirates of Nigeria* [London, 1930], pp. 151–54; K. V. Elphinstone, *Gazetteer of Ilorin Province* [London, 1921], p. 15). Furthermore, Afonja's second step of defection to the Fulbe took place while the Owu War was still in progress; that is, *ca.* 1818 or 1820 to 1825 (see I. A. Akinjogbin, "The Prelude to the Yoruba Civil Wars of the Nineteenth Century," *Odu*, 1 [new ser.] :24–46 [1965]). Crowther's information that the Yoruba still dominated among his attackers in 1821, though relations were beginning to be strained, suggests that Afonja's loss of control took place at about that time, or between 1821 and 1825.

spread of disorder to other parts of Yoruba to the south of Oyo, on the other hand, had only begun with the siege of Owu. But Owu had not yet fallen by 1821, and the Egba and Ijebu towns and villages through which Crowther passed were still intact. In this way, Crowther's account of his passage southward helps to confirm our chronology for the beginning of the Egba wars.

It also shows us something of the slave trade and trade routes carrying Oyo prisoners southward to the coast before these routes through Egba and Ijebu were disrupted in their turn. Accepting Crowther's estimates of the length of time spent in each place, and working backward from April 1822, when he was put on board the Brazilian ship at Lagos, it is possible to reconstruct the chronology of his journey.

In March 1821 he was captured at Osogun and taken to Iseyin. There, he was allotted to the chief of the captors, who bartered him for a horse; that is, he was captured by warriors and sold for war munitions. Then, for two months (March to May 1821) he served as a domestic slave to the horse merchant in Iseyin. At the beginning of the rainy season (perhaps May 1821), the war chief decided he did not like the horse, and he took his slave back. When the chief left the war base at Iseyin for his home in Dada, Crowther went with him and remained as a domestic slave during all of the early rainy season, when little long-distance trade was possible. With the usual August break in the rains, the chief decided to sell him again—either for weapons, for cowries to buy arms, or for profit. He was sold to Ijaye, a central market, and bought by an Oyo woman trader, who took him to Itoko. During the later rains (August-November 1821), the woman trader took to weaving while waiting for the dry season, and Crowther stayed with her for three months as a domestic slave. In November he was sold for cowries, perhaps for the first time into the professional and more impersonal slave trade. His buyers become nameless, and he gives less information about his stopping places. He was taken first to the Ikereku-iwere slave market; but this was just a clearing house, and he stayed only a short time. From November to December he remained in an unnamed town, and in isolation. Probably this was a collecting station for slaves, or perhaps slaves were also kept there pending satisfactory arrangements for a rapid passage to the lagoon port of Ikosi. In December the passage took place. Crowther was taken across the lagoon to Lagos, where the

Portuguese had regular customers and enjoyed political protection which allowed them to choose their time for embarkation. Crowther stayed there four to five months. Finally, on 7 April 1822, the Portuguese chose to dispatch their cargo. They were unlucky.

THE NARRATIVE OF SAMUEL AJAYI CROWTHER

Crowther's account of his capture and travels was originally prepared in 1837, after his unusual abilities attracted the attention of missionaries in Sierra Leone. In response to their request he produced the letter which constitutes the text below, the original manuscript of which is now in the archives of the Church Missionary Society, London. The letter was first published, with very little editing, in the *Church Missionary Record*, 8:217–23 (October 1837); was later reprinted as an appendix to the *Journals of Rev. James Frederick Schön and Mr. Samuel Crowther* (London, 1842), pp. 371–85; and appeared again, somewhat condensed, in the 1910 edition of Jesse Page, *The Black Bishop* (London), pp. 9–17.

A second manuscript, already mentioned here (see n. 1, above), contains the account of his early life which Crowther prepared in 1841 at the request of Commander Bird Allen, on whose ship, H.M.S. *Soudan,* Crowther travelled as a member of the Niger Expedition. Allen later gave the manuscript to Captain H. D. Trotter, the leader of the expedition, and eventually, after passing through several more hands, it came into the possession of Archdeacon Lightfoot of the Cape Town diocese. This later manuscript provides a useful supplement to the original; the source of the present text, however, is the version published in the Schön-Crowther *Journals*. It is printed here without omissions or changes, other than the modernizing of identifiable place names, after giving them in Crowther's spelling at first occurrence.

Letter of Mr. Samuel Crowther to the
Rev. William Jowett, in 1837, then Secretary of
the Church Missionary Society, Detailing
the Circumstances Connected
with His Being Sold as a Slave

Fourah Bay, Feb. 22, 1837

Rev. and Dear Sir,

As I think it will be interesting to you to know something of the conduct of Providence in my being brought to this Colony, where I have the happiness to enjoy the privilege of the Gospel, I give you a short account of it; hoping I may be excused if I should prove rather tedious in some particulars.

I suppose some time about the commencement of the year 1821,[18] I was in my native country, enjoying the comforts of father and mother, and the affectionate love of brothers and sisters. From this period I must date the unhappy, but which I am now taught, in other respects, to call blessed day, which I shall never forget in my life. I call it unhappy day, because it was the day in which I was violently turned out of my father's house, and separated from relations; and in which I was made to experience what is called to be in slavery—with regard to its being called blessed, it being the day which Providence had marked out for me to set out on my journey from the land of heathenism, superstition, and vice, to a place where His Gospel is preached.

For some years, war had been carried on in my Eyò [Oyo][19] Country, which was always attended with much devastation and bloodshed; the women, such men as had surrendered or were caught, with the children, were taken captives. The enemies who carried on these wars were principally the Oyo Mahomedans, with whom my country abounds—with the Foulahs [Fulbe], and such foreign slaves as had escaped from their owners, joined together, making a formidable force of about 20,000, who annoyed the whole country.[20]

18. The usual time for the conduct of wars and raids was from January to April, in the dry season, when the floods began to subside and the rivers could be easily forded, and while there were still crops in the fields and warriors could live on the land.

19. Eyò is a variant of Oyọ. (In early Yoruba orthography, it was for a while suggested that diacritical marks might be better above, rather than below letters.) The Oyo were the largest subgroup of the Yoruba. Other subgroups were Ife, Ijebu, Egba, Egbado, Ijesha, Ekiti, Ondo, Owo, and Akoko, each with its own dialect. At the beginning of the nineteenth century, there seems to have been no common name for all the subgroups. Yoruba (Yarriba) was the dialect of the Oyo people. Largely owing to the influence of Crowther, it was a modified version of this dialect that was popularized by the missionaries as the standard written form of the language of all the subgroups. In this and other ways the term Yoruba came to describe the language, country, and people of all the subgroups. (See J. F. Ade Ajayi and R. S. Smith, *Yoruba Warfare in the Nineteenth Century* [Cambridge, 1964], pp. 1–2; J. A. B. Horton, *West African Countries and Peoples* [London, 1868], p. 159, quoted in T. Hodgkin, *Nigerian Perspectives* [London, 1960], p. 285.)

20. In describing the "enemies," CTM puts the Fulbe before the Oyo Muslims: "The army was composed of Foulahs, Yorriba Mahommedans and slaves of every description who had run away from their masters. These collected together into an army of about 20,000 having strong swift horses, they became a plague to the kingdom of Yorriba." The military might of the Old Oyo empire depended very much on its cavalry force.

They had no other employment but selling slaves to the Spaniards and Portuguese on the coast.

The morning in which my town, Ocho-gu [Osogun],[21] shared the same fate which many others had experienced, was fair and delightful; and most of the inhabitants were engaged in their respective occupations. We were preparing breakfast without any apprehension;[22] when, about 9 o'clock A.M., a rumour was spread in the town, that the enemies had approached with intentions of hostility. It was not long after when they had almost surrounded the town, to prevent any escape of the inhabitants; the town being rudely fortified with a wooden fence, about four miles in circumference, containing about 12,000 inhabitants, which would produce 3,000 fighting men. The inhabitants not being duly prepared, some not being at home;[23] those who were, having about six gates to defend, as well as many weak places about the fence to guard against, and, to say in a few words, the men being surprised, and therefore confounded—the enemies entered the town after about three or four hours' resistance.[24] Here a most sor-

---

This necessitated the regular importation of horses from the north. It also became established that those who knew how to care for horses best were Hausa, and the slave trade was used, in this as in other cases, as a means of recruiting the required skilled labor from outside one's own ethnic group. For this reason, Hausa slaves were very prominent in the Old Oyo empire. Their defection to join Afonja's secessionist movement as well as the Fulbe hegemony at Ilorin quickly weakened the importance of cavalry in the Yoruba country. With the shift of population southwards into the forest region, new techniques of warfare were developed, and by 1840, cavalry had ceased to play any important part in Yoruba wars (Ajayi and Smith, *Yoruba Warfare*, pp. 15–16).

21. Or *Oshogun*. As with many Yoruba place names, it is difficult to find out what *Osogun* means. Jesse Page records an ingenious explanation, presumably from Crowther himself, that it means "it is not like medicine, that is, wisdom being the gift of the gods, unlike medicine, is freely imported from man to man." It is now generally taken to mean *O-se-Oogun*, the ones that make medicine, being a shortened form of *Osoogun-senu eye*, the ones that make medicine with birds' beaks.

22. CTM adds: "as they used to pass over [our] town before without doing any harm, we thought they would do so at this time also."

23. CTM adds: "The day being fine as was above mentioned, several of the men went to their farms. Those who were at home being confused by the sudden approach and having four or five gates to defend and many decayed places about the town to guard against, they could not resist the approach of their enemies into the town."

24. CTM adds: "After some skirmishes, they entered the town, and set the houses on fire so that the inhabitants fled. There was not much slaughter as the aim was to capture as many as they could."

The tradition in the village of Osogun today is that the town was surprised early in the morning while the people slept; that the town was riddled with arrows, remnants of

rowful scene imaginable was to be witnessed!—women, some with three, four, or six children clinging to their arms, with the infants on their backs, and such baggage as they could carry on their heads, running as fast as they could through prickly shrubs, which, hooking their blies[25] and other loads, drew them down from the heads of the bearers. While they found it impossible to go along with their loads, they endeavoured only to save themselves and their children: even this was impracticable with those who had many children to care for. While they were endeavouring to disentangle themselves from the ropy shrubs, they were overtaken and caught by the enemies with a noose of rope thrown over the neck of every individual, to be led in the manner of goats tied together, under the drove of one man. In many cases a family was violently divided between three or four enemies, who each led his away, to see one another no more. Your humble servant was thus caught—with his mother, two sisters (one an infant about ten months old), and a cousin—while endeavouring to escape in the manner above described. My load consisted in nothing else than my bow, and five arrows in the quiver;[26] the bow I had lost in the shrub, while I was extricating myself, before I could think of making any use of it against my enemies. The last view I had of my father was when he came from the fight, to give us the signal to flee: he entered into our house, which was burnt some time back for some offence[27]

---

which were picked up in large quantities by the early resettlers. This differs from the Crowther story, but is more in line with the usual Fulbe tactics of attacking towns early in the morning, sometimes sending a flight of doves with lighted tapers onto the roofs of houses, and then frightening the people into mass surrender by blocking exits with skilled bowmen.

25. Probably intended to be the plural of the Australian word "bluey," meaning a bushman's load.

26. It is indicative of the place of archery in Yoruba warfare of the time that a boy in his early teens should have his own bow and quiver of arrows. Old people in Ibarapa remember from their childhood days the game of *elego* in which children learned to shoot at objects with improvised bows and arrows. Muskets were rare in early nineteenth-century Yoruba warfare.

27. This is an allusion to the cult of Shango, the Yoruba god of thunder. If lightning struck a house, it was believed that the owner had done evil, and he was required to propitiate Shango. Similarly, if someone were caught in a crime offensive to Shango, his house could be burnt down, partly as punishment, partly to prevent the god from bringing worse calamity.

The fourth *Alafin* of Oyo had been named Shango; when he was later deified he took on the attributes of an older deity called Jakuta who represented the wrath of the gods and chastised evil-doing, especially lying and dishonesty, with lightning. Worship of

given by my father's adopted son.[28] Hence I never saw him more.—
Here I must take thy leave, unhappy, comfortless father!—I learned,
some time afterward, that he was killed in another battle.

Our conquerors were Oyo Mahomedans, who led us away through
the town.[29] On our way, we met a man sadly wounded on the head,
struggling between life and death. Before we got half way through
the town, some Foulahs [Fulbe], among the enemies themselves,
hostilely separated my cousin from our number. Here also I must
take thy leave, my fellow captive cousin! His mother was living in
another village. The town on fire—the houses being built with mud,
some about twelve feet from the ground with high roofs, in square
forms, of different dimensions and spacious areas: several of these
belonged to one man, adjoined to, with passages communicating
with each other.[30] The flame was very high. We were led by my
grandfather's house,[31] already desolate; and in a few minutes after,

Shango became the imperial cult of Oyo, and as the empire spread the cult spread with it.
(See E. B. Idowu, *Olodumare: God in Yoruba Belief* [London, 1962], pp. 89–95.)

28. The practice of adopting children (usually those of friends or relatives) was not
uncommon in Yoruba country. A wealthy and indulgent parent might give someone
else a child to bring up, partly for fear of spoiling the child and partly as a mark of
courtesy. A girl would usually be given to a female friend or relation, and a boy to a male
friend. If the arrangement worked well, the child might live with the adopted parent till
he became an adult, married, and was ready to establish his own household. This type
of adoption was in line with the extended family system, which encouraged a less personal and more communal form of family relationship.

29. The CTM version is more explicit. "In attempting to escape in the crowd with
my mother, two sisters and a cousin, we were taken by two Yorriba [Yoruba] Mahommedans who immediately threw nooses of cords around our necks and led us away as
their prey. . . . Scarcely had we got to the middle of the town when two Foulah [Fulbe]
men attacked our captors and contended with them about dividing their prey as they had
not gone in time to get any. My cousin was violently held on both sides; and my mother
hearing the threats from the Foulahs to cut the poor fellow to pieces if our captors did
not let him go; she entreated them rather to give him over to the Foulahs instead of
having him killed; our captors having some feelings of humanity, left the boy to them
with whom they ran off with the fury of a tiger. We four now remaining, great care
was taken lest we should also be lost in like manner, as the soldiers were no little robbers
among themselves."

30. The traditional Yoruba compound (*agbole*—"where the males and their wives
and unmarried children live," in R. C. Abraham, *Dictionary of Modern Yoruba* [London,
1958]) consisted of a number of houses with common verandas, grouped around an
open space for cooking and recreation. The size varied from place to place, depending
not only on the size of the particular extended family, but also on how quickly the
lineage segmented. Usually, brothers continued to live together with their wives and
children in the same compound, but by the time the sons began to marry, the older
brothers would tend to move out and establish their own compounds.

31. CTM makes clear that this was the maternal grandfather. Presumably, Crowther's

we left the town to the mercy of the flame, never to enter or see it any more. Farewell, place of my birth, the play-ground of my child-hood, and the place which I thought would be the repository of my mortal body in its old age![32] We were now out of Osogun, going into a town called Isehi [Iseyin],[33] the rendezvous of the enemies, about twenty miles from our town.[34] On the way, we saw our grand-mother at a distance, with about three or four of my other cousins taken with her, for a few minutes: she was missed through the crowd,[35] to see her no more. Several other captives were held in the same manner as we were: grandmothers, mothers, children, and cousins, were all led captives. O sorrowful prospect! The aged women were to be greatly pitied, not being able to walk so fast as their children and grandchildren: they were often threatened with being put to death upon the spot,[36] to get rid of them, if they would not go as fast as others; and they were often as wicked in their prac-tice as in their words. O pitiful sight! whose heart would not bleed to have seen this? Yes, such is the state of barbarity in the heathen land. Evening came on; and coming to a spring of water,[37] we drank a great quantity; which served us for breakfast,[38] with a little

own house was near to, or perhaps was part of, the paternal grandfather's family compound.

32. For the Yoruba, to die abroad is a hard lot. Even today there remains a longing to retire, die, and be buried at home near the bones of the ancestors.

33. Sometimes spelled Isehin. By 1837, Crowther was already grappling with the problems of Yoruba orthography, particularly with the nasal sounds. Four years later, in CTM, he spells the name "Isehing." See J. F. Ade Ajayi, "How Yoruba Was Reduced to Writing," *Odu*, No. 8, pp. 49–58 (October 1960).

34. The distance by bush path would have been a little more than twenty-five miles, but in the circumstances, this was a good estimate.

35. In CTM, Crowther describes the crowd. He says they left the town "in company with thousands of our fellow townsmen, companions in affliction, in the midst of wicked men, extending in the plain before and behind, beyond the reach of the eye, marching to the large and populous town of Isehing."

36. CTM says: "Think how hard it must have been for many children who were younger than myself and for these women who were bowed with age: go they must or be killed on the spot."

37. CTM says this stream was about seven or eight miles from Osogun. The normal walking rate was about four miles an hour, but with the crowd it probably took some three hours to reach the stream. Crowther said the attack came about 9 A.M.; there was resistance for three or four hours. The taking of captives, the burning of the town, and the departure must have taken another hour or two, so that it would have been near evening when they reached the stream, which was probably part of the headwaters of the Opeki River.

38. Both manuscripts speak of "breakfast" here, although it was evening. Hours earlier, when the town was invaded, the victims had been about to eat breakfast.

parched corn and dried meat[39] previously prepared by our victors for themselves.

During our march to Iseyin, we passed several towns and villages which had been reduced to ashes. It was almost midnight before we reached the town,[40] where we passed our doleful first night in bondage. It was not perhaps a mile from the wall of Iseyin when an old woman of about sixty was threatened in the manner above described.[41] What had become of her I could not learn.

On the next morning, our cords being taken off our necks, we were brought to the Chief of our captors—for there were many other Chiefs[42]—as trophies at his feet. In a little while, a separation took place, when my sister and I fell to the share of the Chief, and my mother and the infant to the victors. We dared not vent our grief by loud cries, but by very heavy sobs. My mother, with the infant, was led away, comforted with the promise that she should see us again, when we should leave Iseyin for Dah'dah [Dada],[43] the town of the Chief. In a few hours after, it was soon agreed upon that I should be bartered for a horse in Iseyin, that very day. Thus was I separated from my mother and sister for the first time in my life; and the latter not to be seen more in this world. Thus, in the space of twenty-four hours, being deprived of liberty and all other comforts, I

39. CTM says "parched corn and preserved dried meat, both well seasoned with pepper." This was the usual traveller's diet, especially for warriors; women traders travelling in caravans might have had *agidi* (steamed corn pudding) and bean cakes, specially prepared to last two or three days.

40. They had travelled about twenty-five miles in something like ten hours, which for a crowd including old women and children was a fast pace. CTM adds that they "had occasionally to rest."

41. The treatment of the old woman left a clear impression on Crowther. Four years later, in CTM, he gave more detail: "I heard an aged woman of about 60 who had kept up as far as fifty yards of the wall of Isehing threatened in this manner: she was worn out with the long march; poor fellow, she was staggering from one side of the road to the other like a drunken person."

42. The army apparently consisted of different contingents supplied by a number of Yoruba chiefs and their Fulbe allies. Each contingent reported to their chief with the bulk of their booty.

43. CTM spells it Dadda. The ruins of Dada lie a few miles from the village marked on the maps as Iporin Owo. As at Osogun, there is now only a hamlet beside the old ruins. It is not clear at what point in the Yoruba Wars the town was destroyed. There is, however, evidence to suggest that it was a town of considerable importance, with a crowned head as ruler. The present ruler, a queen, attempts to keep up the tradition. The surrounding district has been opened for cultivation, and there is now an important market for yams and cocoa.

was made the property of three different persons. About the space of two months, when the Chief was to leave Iseyin for his own town, the horse, which was then only taken on trial, not being approved of, I was restored to the Chief, who took me to Dada, where I had the happiness to meet my mother and infant sister again with joy, which could be described by nothing else but tears of love and affection; and on the part of my infant sister, with leaps of joy in every manner possible.[44] Here I lived for about three months, going for grass for horses with my fellow captives. I now and then visited my mother and sister in our captor's house, without any fears or thoughts of being separated any more. My mother told me that she had heard of my sister; but I never saw her more.

At last, an unhappy evening arrived, when I was sent with a man to get some money at a neighbouring house. I went; but with some fears, for which I could not account; and, to my great astonishment, in a few minutes I was added to the number of many other captives, enfettered, to be led to the market-town early the next morning. My sleep went from me; I spent almost the whole night in thinking of my doleful situation, with tears and sobs, especially as my mother was in the same town, whom I had not visited for a day or two. There was another boy in the same situation with me: his mother was in Dada. Being sleepless, I heard the first cock-crow. Scarcely the signal was given, when the traders arose, and loaded the men slaves with baggage. With one hand chained to the neck, we left the town. My little companion in affliction cried and begged much to be permitted to see his mother, but was soon silenced by punishment. Seeing this, I dared not speak, although I thought we passed by the very house my mother was in. Thus was I separated from my mother and sister, my then only comforts, to meet no more in this world of misery.[45] After a few days' travel, we came to the market-town, I-

44. This was Amosha. CTM has: "Tears of joy flowed from our eyes; and on the part of my infant sister, she expressed her joy at seeing me again with such a leap on me, the rememberance of which time shall never erase from my memory."

45. Little did Crowther think when he wrote this that he would again find his mother, Afala, or his sisters, Lanre and Amosha. But they were living near Abeokuta when Crowther arrived there in August 1846. After Crowther had been taken away to the coast, a half-brother ransomed the mother and the two girls. The girls grew up and married. Later on, Afala and Lanre were once again kidnapped, on the way to market. Lanre was ransomed by her husband, and later she was able to buy freedom for Afala as well.

jah'i [Ijaye].⁴⁶ Here I saw many who had escaped in our town to this place; or those who were in search of their relations, to set at liberty as many as they had the means of redeeming. Here we were under very close inspection, as there were many persons in search of their relations; and through that, many had escaped from their owners. In a few days I was sold to a Mahomedan woman, with whom I travelled to many towns in our way to the Popo country,⁴⁷ on the coast, much resorted to by the Portuguese, to buy slaves. When we left Ijaye, after many halts, we came to a town called To-ko [Itoko].⁴⁸

On arriving in Abeokuta, Crowther heard about them and sent for them. He later described the reunion:

"The text for today in the Christian Almanac is 'Thou art the Helper of the fatherless.' I have never felt the force of this text more than I did this day, as I have to relate that my mother, from whom I was torn away five and twenty years ago, came with my brother in quest of me. When she saw me she trembled. She could not believe her own eyes. We grasped one another, looking at one another in silence and great astonishment, while the big tears rolled down her emaciated cheeks. She trembled as she held me by the hand and called me by the familiar names which I well remember I used to be called by my grandmother who has since died in slavery. We could not say much, but sat still, casting many an affectionate look towards each other, a look which violence and oppression had long checked, an affection which twenty-five years had not extinguished. My two sisters, who were captured with me, and their children are all residing with my mother. I cannot describe my feelings. I had given up all hope, and now, after a separation of twenty-five years, without any plan or device of mine, we were brought together again."

Afala then came to live with her son, and some eighteen months later she was converted to Christianity and baptized Hannah. She continued to live with Crowther until she was nearly 100 years old, dying in Lagos, 13 October 1883 (Page, *Black Bishop*, pp. 94–97, 349–50; see also Macaulay, "A Yoruba Boy Named Adjai").

46. CTM uses the modern spelling. Ijaye in 1821 was on the northern fringe of the Egba forest. It was a town of the Egba Gbagura, one of the three main subdivisions of the Egba people, and an important route center. It apparently had a central market, where the Oyo brought slaves and other goods to exchange with the Egba for goods from the coast. Sometime before 1830, Ijaye was captured by Oyo warriors and the Egba were pushed southward. The new Ijaye was in turn destroyed by Ibadan forces in 1862. Like Osogun and Dada, it was later resettled toward the end of the nineteenth century, and the present village is at the center of the old ruins.

47. The Popo, also known as Egun or Gun, inhabit the coastal region from Badagry to west of Porto Novo (called Ajase by the Yoruba). Porto Novo in particular was the outlet of Oyo trade in the seventeenth and eighteenth centuries. Crowther's new mistress, the "Mahomedan woman," was Oyo-speaking. She seemed to have made Itoko her home, and apart from trading, she did some weaving (CTM). She obviously traded to the coast toward Badagry, rather than toward the Ijebu country.

48. An Egba town located near the site of the present Abeokuta. In fact, the Itoko people claim that Abeokuta was founded on land they used to farm (E. C. Irving, "The Ijebu Country," *Church Missionary Intelligencer*, 7:65–72, 93–96, and 117–20 [March-

From Ijaye to Itoko all spoke the Ebwah [Egba] dialect,[49] but my mistress Oyo, my own dialect. Here I was a perfect stranger, having left the Oyo country far behind. I lived in Itoko about three months; walked about with my owner's son with some degree of freedom, it being a place where my feet had never trod: and could I possibly have made my way out through many a ruinous town and village we had passed, I should have soon become a prey to some others, who would have gladly taken the advantage of me. Besides, I could not think of going a mile out of the town alone at night, as there were many enormous devil-houses[50] along the highway; and a woman had been lately publicly executed (fired at), being accused of bewitching her husband, who had died of a long tedious sickness. Five or six heads, of such persons as were never wanting to be nailed on the large trees in the market-places, to terrify others.

Now and then my mistress would speak with me and her son, that we should by-and-bye go to the Popo country, where we should buy tobacco, and other fine things, to sell at our return.[51] Now, thought I, this was the signal of my being sold to the Portuguese; who, they often told me during our journey, were to be seen in that country. Being very thoughtful of this, my appetite forsook me, and in a few weeks I got the dysentery, which greatly preyed on me. I determined with myself that I would not go to the Popo country; but would make an end of myself, one way or another. In several nights I attempted strangling myself with my band; but had not courage enough to close the noose tight, so as to effect my purpose. May the

May 1856], p. 72; R. S. Smith, "Ijaye, the Western Palatinate of the Yoruba," *Journal of the Historical Society of Nigeria*, 2:329–49 [December 1962]).

49. This is one of the last recorded journeys through the Egba country before it was disrupted by wars which pushed them southward and westward to their present location based on Abeokuta. These wars took place between 1825 and 1830 and resulted in the enslavement of Joseph Wright (see Chap. 10).

50. Sacred shrines and groves of the polytheists.

51. Perhaps the woman trader took a liking to her sharp and intelligent slave. Crowther became a companion to her son. He was a domestic slave, probably sleeping on the same mat as the son, and eating from the same plate. The longer this continued the more would Crowther have become a regular member of the household, with less and less likelihood of being sold. Or perhaps, as Crowther suspected, the woman was only waiting for a favorable opportunity to take him down to Badagry for sale. However, she does not appear to have been essentially a slave trader. She seems to have regarded the slave trade as a means of recruiting domestic labor, rather than as providing the principal article of trade.

Lord forgive me this sin! I determined, next, that I would leap out of the canoe into the river, when we should cross it in our way to that country. Thus was I thinking, when my owner, perceiving the great alteration which took place in me, sold me to some persons. Thus the Lord, while I knew Him not, led me not into temptation and delivered me from evil. After my price had been counted before my own eyes, I was delivered up to my new owners, with great grief and dejection of spirit, not knowing where I was now to be led. About the first cock-crowing, which was the usual time to set out with the slaves, to prevent their being much acquainted with the way, for fear an escape should be made, we set out for Jabbo [Ijebu], the third dialect from mine.

After having arrived at Ik-ke-ku Ye-re [Ikereku-iwere],[52] another town, we halted. In this place I renewed my attempt of strangling, several times at night; but could not effect my purpose. It was very singular, that no thought of making use of a knife ever entered my mind. However, it was not long before I was bartered, for tobacco, rum, and other articles.[53] I remained here, in fetters, alone, for some time, before my owner could get as many slaves as he wanted. He feigned to treat us more civilly, by allowing us to sip a few drops of White Man's liquor, rum; which was so estimable an article, that none but Chiefs could pay for a jar or glass vessel of four or five gallons: so much dreaded it was, that no one should take breath before he swallowed every sip, for fear of having the string of his throat cut by the spirit of the liquor. This made it so much more valuable.

---

52. The previous sentence seems to suggest that this was an Ijebu town, and that from Itoko Crowther travelled directly south out of Egba country toward Ijebu. But in fact he traversed the Egba country toward the east. CTM makes this clearer: "From Ijaye to Ikekuyere, about four or five days journey, the people speak the Egba dialect." Crowther was sold for money (that is, for cowrie shells, as CTM explicitly states), but he tells us nothing about his buyers. They might have been Egba traders who thought they could make a profit if they bought slaves from the Oyo at Itoko and sold them to the Ijebu at Ikereku-iwere.

I have not been able to locate the precise physical site of Ikereku-iwere (or Small Ikereku), but it is clear from the later journal of the missionary, Hinderer (15 December 1854, CMS, CA 2049) and from Irving ("The Ijebu Country," p. 224) that it was within an hour's walk of Ibadan on the road to the south. It should not be confused with Ikereku-idan (or Great Ikereku) near the Asa River in the Oke-Ona region.

53. Crowther was bought by a trader, in this case an Ijebu trader, bringing tobacco, rum, and other articles from the coast in exchange for slaves which he intended to sell there.

Bishop Samuel Adjai Crowther in 1888. From Jesse Page, *Samuel Crowther.*

Tree marking the shrine of Obatala in the ruins of Osogun, Samuel Crowther's original home. Photograph by J. F. A. Ajayi.

Freetown in the 1840's. From W. Fox, *Wesleyan Missions on the Western Coast of Africa.*

I had to remain alone, again, in another town in Ijebu,[54] the name of which I do not now remember, for about two months. From hence I was brought, after a few days' walk, to a slave-market, called I'-ko-sy [Ikosi], on the coast, on the bank of a large river, which very probably was the Lagos on which we were afterwards captured. The sight of the river terrified me exceedingly, for I had never seen any thing like it in my life. The people on the opposite bank are called E'-ko.[55] Before sun-set, being bartered again for tobacco, I became another owner's. Nothing now terrified me more than the river, and the thought of going into another world. Crying was nothing now, to vent out my sorrow: my whole body became stiff. I was now bade to enter the river, to ford it to the canoe. Being fearful at my entering this extensive water, and being so cautious in every step I took, as if the next would bring me to the bottom, my motion was very awkward indeed. Night coming on, and the men having very little time to spare, soon carried me into the canoe, and placed me among the corn-bags, and supplied me with an *Ab-alah* [*abala*][56] for my dinner. Almost in the same position I was placed I remained, with my *abala* in my hand quite confused in my thoughts, waiting only every moment our arrival at the new world; which we did not reach till about 4 o'clock in the morning.[57] Here I got once more into another dialect, the fourth from mine; if I may not call it altogether another language, on account of now and then, in some words, there being a faint shadow of my own.[58] Here I must remark that during the

54. Perhaps Offin or Makun, in central Ijebu-Remo. Crowther was now in the hands of professional slave traders. He was no longer a domestic slave, but a slave in transit pending departure overseas.

55. The Yoruba name for the town of Lagos, not for the people. The journey from Ikosi to Lagos involved a crossing to the southern side of the lagoon, but it was even more an east-west coastal trip down the lagoon. There seems to be a slight confusion here. CTM explains that he was "sold to the people from a town on the opposite shore or rather an island in the Lagos River." This is therefore not necessarily a reference to Lagos (though it is indeed an island in the lagoon), but to the traders who handled the traffic between Ikosi and Lagos.

56. Defined by R. C. Abrahams in *Dictionary of Modern Yoruba* as "Yoruba rice-pudding." More likely it was a steamed pudding made from maize or plantains, often used by travellers because it kept better than bean pudding, but I have nowhere found this called *abala*. In Oyo is it *sanpala;* in Ekiti, *abari.*

57. It is not clear why the traders chose to travel at night. It might have been because of the tides, or to avoid pirates and kidnappers. But it could have been out of fear of British antislavery patrols.

58. There is little evidence about the Lagos dialect at this period, but it is remarkable that Crowther found only faint echoes of Yoruba. A strong influence from Benin and

whole night's voyage in the canoe, not a single thought of leaping into the river had entered my mind; but, on the contrary, the fear of the river occupied my thoughts.

Having now entered E'ko [Lagos], I was permitted to go any way I pleased; there being no way of escape, on account of the river.[59] In this place I met my two nephews,[60] belonging to different masters. One part of the town was occupied by the Portuguese and Spaniards, who had come to buy slaves. Although I was in Lagos more than three months, I never once saw a White Man;[61] until one evening, when they took a walk, in company of about six, and came to the street of the house in which I was living. Even then I had not the boldness to appear distinctly to look at them, being always suspicious that they had come for me: and my suspicion was not a fanciful one; for, in a few days after, I was made the eighth in number of the slaves of the Portuguese. Being a veteran in slavery, if I may be allowed the expression, and having no more hope of ever going to my country again, I patiently took whatever came; although it was not without a great fear and trembling that I received, for the first time, the touch of a White Man, who examined me whether I was sound or not. Men and boys were at first chained together, with a chain of about six fathoms in length, thrust through an iron fetter on the neck of every individual, and fastened at both ends with padlocks. In this situation the boys suffered the most: the men sometimes, getting angry, would draw the chain so violently, as seldom went without bruises on their poor little necks; especially the time to sleep, when they drew the chain so close to ease themselves of its weight, in order to be able to lie more conveniently, that we were almost suffocated,

Gun would be expected, and perhaps also from Portuguese. After 1851, the strong invasion of literary Yoruba has reduced the foreign element in the dialect.

59. It is remarkable that although the Ijebu slave traders seemed to have felt so unsafe on the Lagos lagoon that they chose to travel by night, at Lagos itself, protected by the solid political backing of the Lagos monarchy, the Portuguese traders were completely at their ease. Their only problem was to choose the right time to elude the squadron until they were on the high seas.

60. These were likely to be sons of half-brothers or half-sisters much older than himself. Thus although Crowther nowhere mentions other wives of his father, there must have been at least one other, probably senior to Afala.

61. The main residential area of Lagos was at the time what is now called Isale-Eko, around the palace. The European—or more likely Brazilian and Cuban—traders probably lived on the Marina or what later became the Brazilian quarter around the Holy Cross Cathedral.

or bruised to death, in a room with one door, which was fastened as soon as we entered in, with no other passage for communicating the air than the openings under the eaves-drop. Very often at night, when two or three individuals quarrelled or fought, the whole drove suffered punishment, without any distinction. At last, we boys had the happiness to be separated from the men, when their number was increased, and no more chain to spare: we were corded together, by ourselves. Thus we were going in and out, bathing together, and so on. The female sex fared not much better. Thus we were for nearly the space of four months.[62]

About this time, intelligence was given that the English were cruising the coast.[63] This was another subject of sorrow with us—that there must be war also on the sea as well as on land—a thing never heard of before, or imagined practicable. This delayed our embarkation. In the meanwhile, the other slaves which were collected in Popo, and were intended to be conveyed into the vessel the nearest way from that place, were brought into Lagos, among us. Among this number was Joseph Bartholomew, my Brother in the service of the Church Missionary Society.

After a few weeks' delay, we were embarked, at night in canoes, from Lagos to the beach; and on the following morning were put on

62. It would appear from this that Crowther spent about seven months altogether in Lagos—more than three months at Isale-Eko, nearly four months in chains—but this was probably an exaggeration, especially as to the time spent in chains awaiting embarkation. In 1821 when the vigilance of the British squadron was still so inadequate, it was unlikely that no opportunity considered favorable for eluding them should turn up in four months. CTM mentions only about three months "in this factory called by the natives Eko," before he was sold to the Portuguese, and says nothing about the period spent in chains. In my calculations, I have allowed only four to five months for the stay in Lagos.

63. By this time, the British anti-slave-trade squadron had been reinforced to a normal strength of six ships, and they were enjoying a period of relative success in capturing slavers. Between 21 February and 9 April 1822, they captured nine vessels, five of them on the same day; and in June, Commodore Sir Robert Mends wrote to the Admiralty: "Within a very short period, the ships of war on this coast have boarded forty-five vessels engaged in the Slave Trade of which sixteen were captured having on board 2,481 slaves. . . . [These captures] show beyond the possibility of doubt or contradiction, the preponderance of France (19) and Portugal (19) in this traffic" (Mends to Admiralty, 17 April and 20 June 1822, Public Record Office, London, ADM 1/2188). But the chance of capture was still slight; since the Royal Navy was not yet permitted to seize vessels unless slaves were actually found on board, and it was limited by treaty in its operations south of the equator (see C. Lloyd, *The Navy and the Slave Trade* [London, 1949]).

board the vessel, which immediately sailed away.[64] The crew being busy embarking us, 187 in number, had no time to give us either breakfast or supper; and we, being unaccustomed to the motion of the vessel, employed the whole of this day in sea-sickness,[65] which rendered the greater part of us less fit to take any food whatever. On the very same evening, we were surprised by two English men-of-war;[66] and on the next morning found ourselves in the hands of new conquerors, whom we at first very much dreaded,[67] they being armed with long swords. In the morning, being called up from the hold, we were astonished to find ourselves among two very large men-of-war and several other brigs. The men-of-war were, His Majesty's ships *Myrmidon*, Captain H. J. Leeke, and *Iphigenia*, Captain Sir Robert

64. Crowther and his companions left the Marina by canoe on the evening of 6 April 1822. They were loaded early next morning on board the *Esperanza Felix,* a polacre schooner belonging to Manuel Jose Freire of Bahia in Brazil and commanded by Joaquim de Britto Lima. The *Esperanza Felix* was a vessel of 142 tons, mounting four guns, and carrying a crew of 24 men. She was 112 days out of Bahia at the time of capture, and in this instance she carried a cargo of 187 slaves, as Crowther reports correctly (Mends to Admiralty, 17 April 1822, ADM 1/2188).

The slaver was thus a Brazilian, rather than a Portuguese ship. But the distinction was not yet one of law, only of nationality. The Portuguese Court had been transferred to Rio de Janeiro from Lisbon between 1808 and 1821. The formal declaration of Brazilian independence did not come until some months after these events, in September 1822. The *Esperanza Felix* therefore flew the Portuguese flag and came under the provisions of the Anglo-Portuguese Anti-Slave-Trade Treaty.

On the night of Crowther's embarkation, H.M.S. *Iphigenia* and *Myrmidon* were cruising eastward along the coast, accompanied by a captured slaver with a prize crew. Several times, off Ouidah and Badagry, they gave chase to possible slavers, but without success (logs of *Myrmidon* and *Iphigenia,* ADM 52/4545 and 51/3231).

65. As well they might: the *Esperanza Felix* was at anchor in the open sea outside the Lagos bar, which then blocked the entrance into the present harbor. The day was marked by squalls accompanied by thunder and lightning, common weather at that time of year off the West African coast.

66. When the British ships appeared, the *Esperanza Felix* was still at anchor. The *Myrmidon's* Master's Log reads: "At 4 Commodore and Prize in Co. At 5 saw 2 sail ahead. Made all sail. Observed the Prize fire at a Brigantine and bring her too. . . . One of the strangers found to be Esperanza Felix with 181 slaves on Board. Sent two boats manned and armed to bring the vessels off the River to the Commodore" (ADM 52/4545). But the capture in this case was credited to a prize crew under Lt. Mildway from the *Iphigenia,* sailing a Portuguese schooner captured a few days earlier with only three slaves on board.

67. CTM adds: "We used to entertain very good opinions of our Portuguese masters; they called the English sea robbers. We could not tell where our miseries would end, especially as we thought there was no safety in the land nor on the sea, particularly at sea where we thought war was totally impracticable."

Mends, who captured us on the 7th of April 1822, on the river Lagos.

Our owner was bound with his sailors; except the cook, who was preparing our breakfast. Hunger rendered us bold; and not being threatened at first attempts to get some fruits from the stern, we in a short time took the liberty of ranging about the vessel, in search of plunder of every kind. Now we began to entertain a good opinion of our conquerors. Very soon after breakfast, we were divided into several of the vessels around us. This was now cause of new fears, not knowing where our misery would end. Being now, as it were, one family, we began to take leave of those who were first transshipped, not knowing what would become of them and ourselves. About this time, six of us, friends in affliction, among whom was my Brother Joseph Bartholomew, kept very close together, that we might be carried away at the same time. It was not long before we six were conveyed into the *Myrmidon,* in which we discovered not any trace of those who were transshipped before us. We soon came to a conclusion of what had become of them, when we saw parts of a hog hanging, the skin of which was white—a thing we never saw before; for a hog was always roasted on fire, to clear it of the hair, in my country; and a number of cannonshots were arranged along the deck. The former we supposed to be the flesh, and the latter the heads of the individuals who had been killed for meat. But we were soon undeceived, by a close examination of the flesh with cloven foot, which resembled that of a hog; and, by a cautious approach to the shot, that they were iron.

In a few days we were quite at home in the man-of-war: being only six in number, we were selected by the sailors, for their boys; and were soon furnished with clothes. Our Portuguese owner and his son were brought over into the same vessel, bound in fetters; and, thinking that I should no more get into his hand, I had the boldness to strike him on the head, while he was shaving by his son—an act, however, very wicked and unkind in its nature. His vessel was towed along by the man-of-war, with the remainder of the slaves therein. But after a few weeks, the slaves being transshipped from her, and being stripped of her rigging, the schooner was left alone on the ocean—"Destroyed at sea by captors, being found unseaworthy, in consequence of being a dull sailer."

One of the brigs, which contained a part of the slaves, was

wrecked on a sand-bank: happily, another vessel was near,[68] and all the lives were saved. It was not long before another brig sunk, during a tempest, with all the slaves and sailors, with the exception of about five of the latter, who were found in a boat after four or five days, reduced almost to mere skeletons, and were so feeble, that they could not stand on their feet. One hundred and two of our number were lost on this occasion.

After nearly two months and a half cruising on the coast, we were landed at Sierra Leone, on the 17th of June 1822. The same day we were sent to Bathurst, formerly Leopold, under the care of Mr. [Thomas] Davey.[69] Here we had the pleasure of meeting many of our country people, but none were known before. They assured us of our liberty and freedom; and we very soon believed them. But a few days after our arrival at Bathurst, we had the mortification of being sent for at Freetown, to testify against our Portuguese owner. It being hinted to us that we should be delivered up to him again,[70] notwithstanding all the persuasion of Mr. Davey that we should return, we entirely refused to go ourselves, unless we were carried. I could not but think of my ill-conduct to our owner in the man-of-war. But as time was passing away, and our consent could not be got, we were compelled to go by being whipped; and it was not a small joy to us to return to Bathurst again, in the evening, to our friends.

From this period I have been under the care of the Church Missionary Society; and in about six months after my arrival at Sierra Leone, I was able to read the New Testament with some degree of freedom; and was made a Monitor, for which I was rewarded with sevenpence-halfpenny per month. The Lord was pleased to open my heart to hearken to those things which were spoken by His servants;

68. The multiplicity of vessels which appears in Crowther's account at this point is explained by the fact that the *Iphigenia* and the *Myrmidon* continued their cruise to the eastward. On 15 April 1822, they came on five loaded slavers in the Bonny River of the Niger Delta, all of which were captured "after a sharp action" (Mends to Admiralty, 17 April 1822, ADM 1/2188). The *Myrmidon* thus continued to take other recaptives on board, until Crowther's original group had grown to some seventy-three before the ship finally reached Freetown in June.

69. That is, to the same town to which Ali Eisami had been assigned four years earlier.

70. In the event that the Court of Mixed Commission did not condemn the *Esperanza Felix* and confiscate the cargo. Slaves were usually left on board until the judicial process was completed; but in this case the vessel had been abandoned at sea, and the recaptives had arrived in Sierra Leone aboard a variety of different ships.

and being convinced that I was a sinner, and desired to obtain pardon through Jesus Christ, I was baptized on the 11th of December, 1825, by the Rev. J. Raban.[71] I had the short privilege of visiting your happy and favoured land in the year 1826.[72] It was my desire to remain for a good while, to be qualified as a Teacher to my fellow-creatures; but Providence ordered it so, that, at my return, I had the wished-for instruction under the tuition of the Rev. C. L. F. Haensel, who landed in Sierra Leone in 1827;[73] through whose instrumentality I have been qualified so far, as to be able to render some help, in the service of the Church Missionary Society, to my fellow-creatures. May I ever have a fresh desire to be engaged in the service of Christ, for it is perfect freedom!

Thus much I think necessary to acquaint you of the kindness of Providence concerning me. Thus the day of my captivity was to me a blessed day, when considered in this respect; though certainly it must be unhappy also, in my being deprived on it of my father, mother, sisters, and all other relations. I must also remark, that I could not as yet find a dozen Osogun people among the inhabitants of Sierra Leone.

I was married to a Christian woman[74] on the 21st of September 1829. She was captured by His Majesty's Ship *Bann*, Capt. Charles

71. The name Samuel Crowther, which he took at this time, was chosen to honor an English benefactor of the Church Missionary Society (Fyfe, *Sierra Leone*, p. 172).

72. He accompanied Rev. and Mrs. Thomas Davey, his first guardians at Bathurst, to Britain in 1826 and for a few months attended the parish school at Liverpool Street, Islington, North London.

73. Haensel was a Bavarian who had formerly worked for the Basel Missionary Institution. He was sent out to revive the C.M.S. training college and to alter its character from a trade school to a seminary. To this end, the college was transferred from the village of Regent to Fourah Bay, then just outside Freetown. It was designed to be a nursery for the C.M.S. Training Institution in Islington, but at the same time it offered a liberal education in English, the classics, and Arabic. When it opened in its new quarters on 3 April 1827, Crowther was the first student enrolled. He was also the only one adequately prepared. Three others were accepted on probation. See D. L. Summer, *Education in Sierra Leone* (Freetown, 1963); T. J. Thompson, *The Jubilee and Centenary Volume of Fourah Bay College, Freetown* (Freetown, 1930), pp. 9–10; Fyfe, *Sierra Leone*, p. 172

74. Susan Asano Crowther, née Thompson. There is a tradition that she was a grand-daughter of *Alafin* Atiba, the first *Alafin* at present-day Oyo (through her mother, Siye). Samuel and Susan grew up together under the Daveys. Susan was a trained schoolmistress, and she later opened schools for girls in Abeokuta and Lagos. She died 19 October 1880 (Macaulay, "A Yoruba Boy Named Adjai"; Page, *Black Bishop*, pp. 348–49).

Phillips, on the 31st October 1822. Since, the Lord has blessed us with three children—a son, and two daughters.[75]

That the time may come when the Heathen shall be fully given to Christ for His inheritance, and the uttermost part of the earth for His possession, is the earnest prayer of

Your humble, thankful, and obedient Servant,

Samuel Crowther

75. Samuel Crowther, Jr., had some medical training in England and for a time operated a dispensary in Abeokuta. Later, he took to trade and then became an architect and draftsman of some note.

Abigail Crowther was also educated in England. In 1854, she married Rev. T. B. Macaulay, who later founded and became the first principal of the Lagos C.M.S. Grammar School. She was the mother of Herbert Macaulay, the prominent Nigerian political leader of the early twentieth century.

Susan Crowther married Rev. G. C. Nicol, for a time government chaplain at Bathurst in Gambia.

Crowther later had three other children: Josiah, who became a businessman; Julianah, who married Thompson, another businessman; and Dandeson, who became an archdeacon in the Niger Delta Pastorate.

CHAPTER 10

JOSEPH WRIGHT OF THE EGBA

Philip D. Curtin

Joseph Wright was the latest-born and latest-enslaved of the four Nigerian narrators. Nevertheless he was captured at the earliest phase of the crisis as it affected his particular city and his family, since Egba was only drawn into the general Yoruba collapse at a late date. Wright's narrative therefore has a special charm, as he looks back on the relatively stable world of his early years. It is also one of the few that have survived in manuscript form, written in what is presumably his own hand and free of editorial corrections by European friends. It was also written within a dozen years after his capture, and before his period of education in England. Wright later became a thoroughly educated man, whose letters during his career as a missionary for the Wesleyan-Methodist Missionary Society read like those of the European missionaries, but this narrative is recounted by a man not yet fully within the Western tradition, though he was already on his way to prominence in Sierra Leone.

Wright belonged to the Egba Alake, one of the three major subdivisions of the Egba people, along with Gbagura and Oke-Ona. The Egba Alake were essentially a forest people, north of the more open land of Ijebu and well south of the savanna. Their many walled towns were apparently virtually independent of one another, serving as small centers whose inhabitants worked at crafts or went out to hunt or practice shifting cultivation. Whatever political unity they enjoyed was a loose confederation under the leadership of the *alake*, or ruler, of the town of Ake, who was chosen in turn by an inner circle of five towns—Ake, Ijeun, Iporo, Kemta, and Itoku—though the total number of Egba Alake towns was about twenty.[1]

The Egba met their crisis in the 1820's. It was then that the Ijebu began to arm themselves with firearms purchased from European slave traders on the coast, and the weakening of Oyo removed the stabilizing influence over their international relations to the north.[2] The immediate background was the Owu War (1818 or 1820, to 1825),[3] and the Owu War was a direct result of the spreading slave trade from Ijebu. The quarrel developed as people from Ife began to capture Owu travellers, selling them through Ijebu to the European slave dealers, Owu retaliated by attacking outlying Ife towns, to which Ife responded by forming an alliance with Ijebu as the core of a broader anti-Owu coalition. Firearms now began to be used extensively for the first time, since the coalition could obtain muskets from Lagos.[4] The allied armies formed a war camp not far from Owu and laid siege to the city for a period of five to seven years.

During all this time the Egba towns did nothing, and later historians have sometimes been critical of their blindness to their own danger. They had rather tenuous traditional ties with Owu, but they

1. See S. O. Biobaku, *The Egba and Their Neighbours, 1842–1872* (Oxford, 1957), pp. 1–4, and *passim*, as the most authoritative recent Egba history. A. K. Ajisafe, *A History of Abeokuta* (London, 1924), p. 19, gives a list of nineteen towns considered to have belonged to the Egba Alake.

2. Biobaku, *The Egba*, pp. 12–13.

3. The dates of the Owu War are given variously by different authorities, with 1821–28 and 1820–27 being most common. These estimates are apparently based on the traditional seven-year length of the war, which agrees with Wright's mention of seven years from the beginning of the wars to the destruction of his city. However, Samuel Johnson (*The History of the Yorubas* [Lagos, 1921], p. 109) allows only five years for the siege of Owu, though preliminary fighting may well have occupied another two years. Whatever the beginning of the war or the siege, 1825 appears to be the most likely date for the destruction of Owu. It is suggested by the information of another recaptive, named Barbour, who had been to Sierra Leone and returned to Abeokuta where he was interrogated by Dr. E. C. Irving in the 1850's. Barbour was certain of the date of his liberation in Sierra Leone, which was 1827. And he was certain that the city of Ikereku was captured and destroyed one year earlier, in 1826. Accounts agree that Ikereku fell after Owu, with a lapse of less than a year between the two events (E. C. Irving, "The Ijebu Country," *Church Missionary Intelligencer*, 7:65–72, 93–96, and 117–20 [March-May 1856], pp. 70–71). This would place the fall of Owu in 1825 or early in 1826. Biobaku (*The Egba*, p. 14) also gives 1825 as the date of the fall of Owu, but without showing the evidence on which the estimate was based.

4. Johnson, *Yorubas*, pp. 206–8; Ajisafe, *Abeokuta*, p. 49; Biobaku, *The Egba*, p. 13; I. A. Akinjogbin, "The Prelude to the Yoruba Civil Wars of the Nineteenth Century," *Odu* 1 (new ser.):24–46 (1965), esp. pp. 43–46.

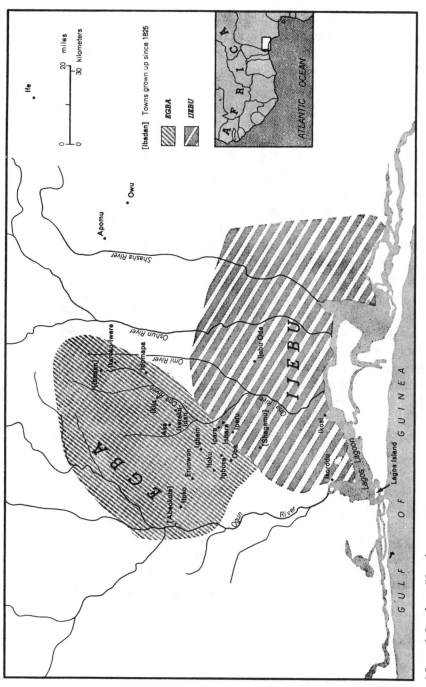

Map 16. Southern Yoruba, *ca.* 1825.

also had certain ties of self-interest. They were Owu's nearest neighbors to the west, and even nearer neighbors to the growing Ijebu power south of their own frontiers. They were also probably damaged to some extent by the rise of Ijebu slave trading. The failure to unite behind Owu has been accounted for in various ways—the rise of Islamic influence in Egba itself, petty jealousies, or sheer blindness to their own danger.[5] Whatever the cause, Owu was allowed to fight alone and was captured and destroyed in 1825.

After the fall of Owu the coalition armies turned westward against the Egba towns. First they captured and destroyed Ikija, which was accused of having supplied Owu with food during the siege. Then they moved the war camp into northern Ijebu, to Ipara immediately south of the Egba Alake. This was too close for comfort. The three Egba towns of Igbore, Imo, and Igbein formed an alliance and tried to drive the coalition armies from the new stronghold. This effort failed, and the Ife-Ijebu coalition retaliated by destroying Igbore, Imo, and Igbein.[6] From this point, the aftermath of the Owu War turned into a general, if piecemeal, attack on the disunited Egba. Ikereku was the next to fall, but before its capture it enlisted the help of Itoku, Oba, and Erunwon. These three were therefore the next target, and all three were captured in a single day. Joseph Wright was captured at the fall of Oba.

The attack then spread through the other Egba Alake towns and farther north to those of the Gbagura as well. The Egba were thus reduced to a succession of small groups of refugees and dispersed bands of fighting men. Some deserted their fellow countrymen and even joined the coalition against the remaining Egba towns. By 1829, this pro-coalition Egba force was the only remaining center of concentrated Egba power. In that year, the main army of the coalition moved its war camp again, this time from Ipara in Ijebu northward to Ibadan, one of the Gbagura towns that was still relatively undamaged. The pro-coalition Egba troops moved with it. Ibadan began to grow from a war camp into a city, as it absorbed refugees and recruits from a broad area. Within a few decades it was to become the largest of all the Yoruba cities.[7]

5. Johnson, *Yorubas,* pp. 209–10; Biobaku, *The Egba,* pp. 13–14; Irving, "The Ijebu Country," pp. 71–72.

6. Irving, "The Ijebu Country," p. 71.

7. Biobaku, *The Egba,* pp. 14–15; Irving, "The Ijebu Country," pp. 71–72.

Meanwhile, most of the Egba refugees had scattered toward the west, away from the region of violence. In about 1830, the Egba units of the Ibadan coalition quarreled with the other leaders and withdrew to the west as well, where they established themselves at Abeokuta, a fortified site near the Ogun River. This settlement soon became a general center of refuge for Egba from all groups and towns, and for refugees from Owu as well. People from the various townships settled in separate wards of the new city, so that Abeokuta kept some of the old Egba confederated structure of government. It was nevertheless far more united than the Egba had ever been in the past, and it provided an established center to which many of Wright's fellow recaptives were to return from Sierra Leone in later decades.

Joseph Wright himself, however, was gone from Yoruba before the foundation of either Abeokuta or Ibadan. Although he does not give the name of his own town, his report that it fell on the same day the enemy captured two other towns indicates that it was either Itoku, Erunwon, or Oba.[8] This is finally confirmed by the fact that he identifies Korowa as the principal deity of his city, and the descendants of the Oba refugees to Abeokuta still refer to themselves as the "children of Korowa."[9]

Wright's later shipment south to the commercial center at Ikorodu, his sale to the Portuguese in Lagos, and his capture at sea by the British cruisers were all routine—except that far more of his compatriots found themselves in Brazil or Cuba than in Sierra Leone. Once liberated, Wright also followed the normal course for recaptives. After judicial condemnation of the slave ship and its cargo, the recaptives were either apprenticed for a time to the black settlers of Sierra Leone, or else distributed among the agricultural villages scattered about the peninsula. Wright's career in York village, together with his opportunity for Western-style education, is obscure, though the Methodists maintained the King Tom Institution in Freetown for postprimary education, and Wright undoubtedly went there. It is clear that he became a Methodist in 1834, and a class leader by 1839. Only a little later, he was selected by the Wesleyan-Methodist Missionary Society for two years of training in England, returning in 1844 to become a Native Assistant Missionary for the society. In

8. Irving, "The Ijebu Country," p. 71.
9. Personal communication from Dr. A. B. Aderibigbe, University of Lagos.

1848, Wright and another recaptive named Charles Knight became the first native Africans to be ordained as full ministers in the Wesleyan Church of Sierra Leone. Unlike Crowther and others who followed the returning recaptives back to their homes in Nigeria during the 1840's and 1850's, Wright remained in the mission field of Sierra Leone itself, working mainly in the villages with the newly arrived recaptives. For a time he was in charge of the Wesleyan missionary station in York, where he himself had been sent some twenty years earlier. He died in the later 1850's still less than fifty years of age.[10]

THE NARRATIVE OF JOSEPH WRIGHT

The original of this text is a small bound notebook, to be found in the box labeled "Sierra Leone, 1835–1840" in the Archives of the Methodist Missionary Society, 25 Marylebone Road, London. It is apparently in the author's hand, with grammar and punctuation uncorrected, but otherwise a fair copy. Its original title was "The Life of Joseph Wright: A Native of Ackoo,"[11] dated June 1839. The present version contains some corrections of punctuation, grammar, and spelling but otherwise adheres closely to the original. Another printed version was included in John Beecham, *Ashantee and the Gold Coast* (London, 1841), pp. 349–58, again in a corrected version. Beecham produced some variant spellings of proper names, which are given below in brackets with the initial *B*. The editor wishes to express his appreciation to the Methodist Missionary Society for permission to reproduce this text, and to Mr. Christopher Fyfe, of Edinburgh University, for calling it to his attention.

I was born a heathen in a heathen Land, and was trained up in my youth to the fashion and customs of that heathenish Country, but the Lord, who would not have me to live to be old in that unhappy Country, brought among us war and confusion as the wages of our sins.

10. Christopher Fyfe, *A History of Sierra Leone* (London, 1962), pp. 254 and 289; Wesleyan-Methodist Missionary Society, *Reports* (annual), *passim*. Rev. Joseph Wright should be distinguished from the other prominent Creole, Joseph G. Wright, a younger contemporary, born in Sierra Leone in 1840, who left a manuscript diary. There is no apparent relationship between the two Wrights. See J. E. Peterson, "Freetown: A Study of the Dynamics of Liberated African Society, 1807–1870" (unpublished Ph.D. thesis, Northwestern University, 1963), p. 347.

11. *Ackoo* or *Aku* was the usual Sierra Leone term for the Yoruba as a whole, derived from the Yoruba greeting, *Eku*.

I was born of respectable parents, but they were not very rich. My father was a member of Council,[12] and he had two wives, besides those of his father which he left to him at his death according to the law of our country.[13] My mother was the first wife my father had, and she bore us five children unto my father. We were all boys except one girl—and we all were with our parents until this last tumultuous war which was the cause of our separations. . . . The war had been heard of long before, but our fathers know not how to repent of the impending Wrath of God. . . . All the time we heard of that war in a far distant land, we confidently thought they will not come to us. Alas, in the space of about seven years after [the wars began][14] they came to us unexpectedly. To our surprise, they came and besieged us round about. These people that raised up this war they are not another nation. We are all one nation speaking one language.[15]

The war shut us from all business. They fought us with all their strength, and we fought against them with all our might, but not with hope of escape. In this miserable state we lived for about seven months, destitute of all food. We had nothing to eat in order to have strength to fight our enemies. In this hard case of ours, we had no real God to go to for help, but we constantly sacrificed to our gods. There is a god which we call public god. It is god of man, and not

12. The Ogboni council, which dominated the government of the Egba towns before the dispersal and reconcentration in Abeokuta. It was associated with the worship of the god Oro, but the council also met periodically to perform functions similar to those of a court of law, a town council, and an electoral college for choosing the ruler, or *oba*. Some powers were executed directly by the members of the Ogboni society, particularly in criminal cases. After the foundation of Abeokuta, each town maintained its Ogboni council which shared power with three other councils or societies—the Olorogun council for military affairs, the Parakoyi council for commerce, and the Ode council of hunters. See Biobaku, *The Egba*, pp. 3–5; Ajisafe, *Abeokuta*, pp. 27–30; R. C. Abraham, *Dictionary of Modern Yoruba* (London, 1958), pp. 484–85; G. Parrinder, *West African Religion* (2d ed., London, 1962), pp. 130–32; and J. O. Lucas, *The Religion of the Yorubas* (Lagos, 1948), pp. 120–28.

13. Widows were inherited. That is, marital rights passed to a successor of the deceased. A women had some choice, however, as to the new husband. But if she did not like the man selected, she had to get a divorce, repaying the bride-wealth. All the wives need not go to one successor; a distribution was more likely (see Johnson, *Yorubas,* p. 115).

14. Reference is probably to the outbreak of fighting before the siege of Owu began about 1820.

15. That is, they were all Yoruba-speaking, though there were dialectical differences between Egba and other varieties of Yoruba.

of woman. No woman is ever allowed to go or pass by the Mountain[16] where they place that god. The name of that god was Carowah [Korowa].[17] To this we all looking for help—and to another by name of Sarbertaroo [*B:* Turbertaru]. This is woman's god, the females often killing pigeons, fowl, and sometimes bullock as a sacrifice for their god.

And these were to overcome in the war which had besieged our city (besides thousands of private gods the people kept in their houses), but all this was in vain. At last the famine overcame us, so that the chosen men of war could not forbear. One night, about seven months after the war had besieged us, all the mighty men of war consulted together to go to another Country in order to buy us some food to preserve us children of the land. And so they did; and in this band were my father and mother. They went to get us some food too, for they pitied us when they saw us perishing with hunger. At the time they left me and all my brethren, they knew not that they would never see us again in the flesh, or else they would never have left us, or they would have given us a final kiss, as dear children; but they knew not what would take place after they left us. A short time after, they were gone, with all the mighty men of war for fear the enemies would break upon them on the way. Maybe the enemies knew that all the chosen men of war had gone for food to a foreign country; so they got ready to take the city before the people who had gone for food should come back. The town had become very poor for want of people to fight; because when my countrymen knew the men of war were going for food, the most part of the people determined to go, knowing they would be safe if the enemy's scouts should break upon them on the way.

The city was in danger of being taken every day, because there remained but women and young men and boys in the town. In a night, before the city was taken, people were trying to make their escape, and many had escaped. When I heard of this, I took my brethren with me, and we come to the gate of the city,[18] to make our escape if

16. Egba religious ceremonies, especially those for the god Oro, were often performed outside the town walls in *Igboro,* or Oro groves, and the deities were often associated with the main hill overlooking the town. Women and the uninitiated were excluded from these ceremonies on pain of death (Ajisafe, *Abeokuta,* p. 34; Lucas, *Religion of the Yorubas,* pp. 120–28).

17. The particular deity of the town of Oba.

18. The Yoruba fortifications of this period sometimes were merely a breastwork, but

The Life of Joseph Wright
A Native of Ackoo

I was born heathen in a heathen
Land, and was trained up in my youth to
the fashion and customs of that heathenish
Country, but the Lord who will not have me
to live, to be old in that unhappy Country,
hast brought among us war and confusion
as the wages of our sins—
I was born of a respectable parents but
they are not very rich, my father is
a member of Council and he have two
wives, besides, those of his fathers
which he left to him at his death,
according to the law of our Country,
my mother is the first wife my father
have, and she has bear us five children
unto my father, we were all boy except
one girl— and we all were with our
parents until this last tumultuous war

The beginning of Joseph Wright's diary.

possible. The gate was quite crowded, so that the strong trod upon the feeble. Doubtless there were many dead from being trodden upon. Had I and my brethren attempted to go over the wall, we would have been trodden upon and would have died. The wall we built round the City was so high and strong, and had beside a large and very deep ditch dug round behind [outside] the wall; there was no way to pass except through the gate, and we were obliged to come back to our father's house, there to remain to see what would take place in the morning.

Oh sorrowful, sorrowful morning! When the morning came, I and my brethren took a walk about in the town to see what the people were doing. We found the city in sorrowful silence, for many had fled and many of the aged men had put an end to their lives. Among these, was one in our house, my father's near and very dear relation. He was full of morality. He had put an end to his life too. His name is Ahkarlah,[19] but since he became the Chief Priest of Carowah [Korowa], the public god of man, his name was changed to Abborreh,[20] for so they call the chief priest of the city. His manner of dressing was remarkable. The day when he was going to officiate, he would put on all white, white garment, white cap; he would put on all white. He would be attended by all the other ministers, and all those whose office was to attend the ministers of the said god; and when they were about to come out from the closet of the priest, warning would be given to the women in the yards to hide. And also warning would be given to the market women, to hide themselves, or bow down their heads beneath their knees, or cover their faces with their handkerchiefs; for they are not allowed to see the priest in his ministerial dress—or if they do, they die for it.[21] They always re-

---

major towns had broad walls of sun-dried earth, often as much as twenty feet in height, with a ditch of similar depth on the outside and occasionally a ditch within as well. The ditches were planted with thorn bushes to make them more difficult to cross. Gateways through the walls were usually elaborate structures, especially fortified to defend the bridge or causeway that crossed the external ditch at this point (see J. F. Ade Ajayi and R. S. Smith, *Yoruba Warfare in the Nineteenth Century* [Cambridge, 1964], pp. 23–26).

19. Probably the present-day name, Akala.

20. Abore Oro, the chief priest of Oro. This seems to imply that Korowa may have been considered a local version of Oro.

21. The ceremony described is clearly an Oro ceremony, conducted by the Oshugbo or Ogboni society, which organized the worship of this god. Oro worship was most common among the Egba towns, where it was closely tied to municipal government

mained very long, when they carried a bull to sacrifice. When they came in the night someone would stand before, hailing, giving warning [lest] perhaps maybe some women yet remain in the streets.

And when this aged relation of our father, to whom we should have looked for some guidance, had put an end to his life, of course there remained no hope for ourselves. I brought my brethren back home. The enemies had fully taken the city. When I saw none of them pass by my father's house to take us for slaves, I then took my brethren with me. We came out in the street, and when we walked about 50 fathoms from our house, we saw the city on fire, and before us the enemies coming in the street. We met with them, and they caught us separately. [They] separated me from all my brethren, except one of my father's children born to him by his second wife. I and this were caught together by one man. By the time we left the house of our father, I saw my father's mother pass the other gate. She, I had no hope of seeing again in the flesh, because she was an old woman. Doubtless they would kill her. Many were killed. They killed our Captain, Jurgoonor [*B:* Jargunor][22] (for so they called the Captain) by the river side, and they killed Barlah[23] in his gate. He was second to the king. He was a very high man in the city. Nothing could be decided without his presence.

The city was taken about nine o'clock in the morning. There were two cities (beside our own) that this enemy had besieged on the same day. Our city was taken in the morning and the other two were taken in the afternoon about two o'clock.[24]

The enemies satisfied themselves with little children, little girls, young men, and young women; and so they did not care about the aged and old people. They killed them without mercy. Father knew not the son, and the son knew not the father. Pity had departed from

---

through the Ogboni council. This fact, along with the membership of Wright's father on the council and his kinship ties to the Abore Oro, tends to confirm the high status of his family in local society.

22. *Jaguna,* or *ajagun,* a military title carried by the commander-in-chief of the forces of any of the Egba towns before the dispersal. Later, when the Egba were united in Abeokuta, the *jaguna* of Igbein became the *jaguna* of the new city. *Jaguna* was also a lesser title in the corporation of the *Ode,* or hunters, but Wright's reference appears to be to the military commander (see Ajisafe, *Abeokuta,* pp. 29–30).

23. *Bala,* a title; in Wright's town apparently the most senior Ogboni title.

24. The three cities taken in one day were Itoku, Oba, and Erunwon (Irving, "The Ijebu Country," p. 71; see also Johnson, *Yorubas,* p. 223).

the face of mothers. Abundant heaps of dead bodies were in the streets, and there were none to bury them. Suckling babies were crying at the point of death, and there were none to pick them up. Mothers looked upon them with contempt—a lamentable day!

These three Cities were consumed in one day, and many of the inhabitants were taken as slaves by the enemies, among whom was one of our chief men of war they punished severely. His name is Offersopuh [B: Ofersapu]. In this manner they punished him. They first [cut] his private [parts]. After that, they put rope on his neck. Then they dragged him about a quarter of a mile. Thus they put an end to his life. They took revenge on him because he was valiant in fighting them. Very many of the chief men of war they punished more severely than I can mention, especially Kings. When they caught any of the king [king's counselors?] they punished them severely and unmercifully, and when they met with any of the Chief men they treated them with contempt, and after that they killed them, and thus they continued, picking [up] those people who had escaped to the mountains and in the bushes.

I was brought the same day the city was taken to Imodo, that is, the place where they made their residence when they besieged us, or rather in the camp.[25] When I came to that place, the man who took me in the city took me and made a present to the chief man of war who commanded the band which he belonged to; for the custom was when any of their company went with bands of war, if he catch slaves, half of the slaves he would give to his Captain. I was with them in the camp about ten days, during which time they used to send me for fire wood. In one of the Cities they took the same day they took our own, there I saw some people burned in the city.

They dug out many dead bodies from their graves. They dug them out in order to take off the grave clothes to sell for money; for the manner of dressing the dead in that part of the world quite differs from that of this country [Sierra Leone]. In this manner they dress the dead.[26] If the dead had been a man of fortune, he would be dressed by the Council. They would take all his valuable clothes and dress him carefully, with all costly apparel. The dress will make him

25. There is an Imodo a few miles northwest of Ijebu Ode, but this was probably too far from Oba to be the place intended here.

26. See the narrative of Osifekunde (Chap. 8, above) for similar customs in Ijebu; see also Johnson, *Yorubas*, pp. 137–40, for Oyo.

about four feet high from the ground. Perhaps there would be twenty large pieces of costly cloth, besides those with which they lined the wall where the dead man lay. And then they would make a large coffin about five feet high and about four feet wide and properly dressed with all fine and costly cloths. After that, they would send for king's drum (or band). About twelve or fourteen men would take up the coffin upon their shoulders, and one would stand before giving out country hymns; and, followed by thousands of people singing after them, they would go round the city with this beautiful coffin. And when they had gone round they would come back to the place where the dead person lay. After all these amusements, the relations of the dead would give warning to the Councils when the body should be buried, and in the night when the body was to be buried the Council drum would beat. The market would be broken about eight o'clock in the evening and they would come to the place where the body lay, and abundant apparel would be perfumed to line the bottom of the tomb, and plenty of money would be laid at the bottom of the grave. Then they would lay the body of the dead upon these things, and then cover him over with dust. This is the way they bury the dead. We do not bury the dead out of the house as they do in this country. We bury a person in his own room, but if the person be a slave, we bury him in the piazza. The house where the dead person is buried is not to be forsaken, but to be taken possession of by another person. So a dead body may remain many years and not spoil. This is the cause why the enemy dug out the dead bodies in order to take the money and fine clothes with which the dead bodies were dressed. But this cannot be done unless the city is taken by the enemies.

While I was with these enemies in the camp I saw many wonderful instances, all which I cannot now mention. I saw a child of about eighteen months old cast out of the camp because the child was so young that nobody would buy him. That poor orphan was there crying at the point of death for about two days, and none [took] pity to pick him up. Another time I took a walk about in the camp. I saw my own brother. I was not allowed to speak to him, although they knew him to be my own brother. Few days after this, the person who I then belonged to sent me home to his wife for sale, and I was with his wife one day and a half. She sent for a trade man to examine me. They stripped me naked. The man examined me all over.

They went aside from me to make a bargain. In few hours after that, the man came again. My mistress told me to go with the man and fetch some rum. Just as I went out of her sight, the man stripped me of my clothes and sent it to my mistress. Then I knew that they only deceived me by saying go with the man to fetch me some rum.

Then I went along with this man who had bought me from my mistress. The man tried to feed me and make me clean as possible for the next market day: for one day out of six is general market day.[27] One morning at the cock crow the man started [out with] me, for next day would be market day. We walked mournfully, and when we came to the village near the place where the market was to be held the day after, we slept. It was then a late hour. Early in the morning we came to the market. Many hundreds of slaves, we were put in rows, so that we all could be seen at one view by the buyers; and in about five hours another trade man came and bought me. He put me in a canoe at once and we sailed all that night. Next morning, we came to another slaves market by name Krodoo [Ikorodu],[28] and there we remained the whole day, for the man wanted to buy more slaves. At the time of evening, the canoe was quite loaded with slaves and we sailed for his home directly. We arrived about twelve o'clock in the night. The town where we had just arrived, by name of Ikko [Lagos], is the place where the Portuguese traded. Early in the morning we were brought to a white Portuguese for sale. After strict examination, the white man put me and some others aside. After that, they then made a bargain, how much he would take for each one of us. After they were well agreed, the white man sent us to the slave fold. When we entered into the slave fold, the slaves shouted for joy for having seen another of their countrymen in the fold. These are the articles the Portuguese paid

27. It is not clear whether this would have been an Egba or Ijebu market cycle of six days, but it is clearly in contrast both to the present-day Yoruba market cycle of four days and to the five-day cycle reported by Osifekunde.

28. It is impossible to trace Wright's movements from his capture to his mention of Ikorodu, which was then, as now, an important trading center on the northern shore of the lagoon, opposite Lagos. Conjecturally, however, the first move from the camp was probably southward to Ipara, which was the principal base of the coalition armies. Ipara was just within the Ijebu frontier, and Wright's first move from Ipara was apparently to a market near the Ona, the Ibu, or the Ogun River. All three were within a day's march from Ipara, and any one of them provided a canoe route by which it would have been possible to reach Ikorodu in twelve to twenty-four hours. From there, the next transfer to Lagos was merely an evening's sail across the lagoon.

for slaves: tobacco, rum, clothes, powder, gun, cutlasses, brass, iron rods, and jackey [jaki][29] which is our country money.

The inhabitants of Ikko are very cruel people. They would even sell the children of their own bosom. May God almighty make bare his holy arm in sending the gospel to this benighted land.

I was there in the fold for about two months, with a rope on my neck. All the young boys had ropes on their necks in a row, and all the men with chains in a long row, for about fifty person in a row, so that no one could escape without the others. At one time, the town took fire, and about fifty slaves were consumed because the entry was crowded—so that these slaves were burnt.

During the time I was in that cruel place, their king was very sick. Then the business of his attendants was to ask the diviner, [and] whatsoever he commanded to be done for the recovery of the king's health [was] immediately attended to. During the time of the king's sickness, the slaves often met with goat or sheep sacrifices and money put on the top of the sacrificed beasts, to appease the god of their land. This money the slaves always took as good luck, for the money generally amounted to 2000 half pennies, £4 3s. 4d. This large sum of jakays they used to put upon the top of the sacrificed beasts, and one jakay is worth as much as an English half penny. Alas, the worthless prophets with all their Ododowor[30] and Obbahtahlah[31] (for so they call their god) were not able to do any good for the king in regard to his recovery. . . . This king of Ikko . . . never recovered from his disease; for he died.[32] Three days after his death we came away over the river to prepare for shipping; for their custom was, when the king died, to sacrifice about one thousand

29. If cowries are meant here, *jaki* is not the ordinary Yoruba word for them.

30. Oduduwa: deified ancestor figure of all Yoruba, variously interpreted in myth and theology, sometimes as a god and sometimes as a goddess, but with the common theme of his or her leadership of the Yoruba people in their migration to Ile-Ife from some distant place of origin—or, in some versions, a progenitor of all Yoruba in their creation story. See E. B. Idowu, *Olodumare: God in Yoruba Belief* (London, 1962), pp. 22–29; Parrinder, *West African Religion*, p. 27.

31. Obatala, or Orisha-nla: the senior god of the Yoruba pantheon, standing above all others except Olodumare, the creator. Obatala means "the king who is great" or "king in white clothing" (Idowu, *Olodumare*, pp. 71–75).

32. If the conjectural date of Wright's recapture on 17 March is correct, this would be about 12 March 1827. Wright spent two months in Lagos awaiting shipment, having arrived there perhaps two weeks to one month after the fall of Oba. This would place the fall of Oba in January 1827 or December 1826, a dating which accords with other calculations (above).

slaves for the celebration of the king's death; for we supposed at that time, if we still remained in that cruel town, and if the king's slaves should not be enough for the celebration of the king's death, doubtless they would ask our master for some slaves to make up the number. We all believed this was what induced our master to bring us over the river in haste for shipping. The place that they brought us to, it is Igaye, and we were all naked both men and women; so that we hardly had any rest in the night for we were very cold. Next day, early in the morning, we were all brought down close to salt water for to be put in canoes. We all were heavy and sorrowful in heart, because we were going to leave our land for another which we never knew; and not only so, but when we saw the waves of the salt water on which we were just to enter, it discouraged us the more, for we had heard that the Portuguese were going to eat us when we got to their country. This put [us] more to despair, and when they began to put us in canoes to bring us to the Brig, one of the canoes drowned and half of the slaves died. After they had done with loading the brig, they stowed all the men under the deck; the boys and women were left on the deck. The Brig sailed in the evening. Next day we saw an English man-of-war coming. When the Portuguese saw this, it put them to disquietness and confusion. They then told us that these were the people which will eat us, if we suffered them to prize us; and they also enticed us, if they should ask us how long since we sailed, we must say it was more than a month; and they also gave us long oars and set us to pull. About ten men were set on one oar, and we tried to pull as far as we are able, but it is of no avail. Next day the English vessel overtook us and they took charge of the slaves.[33] We were very poor for water. We were only allowed one

33. By 1827, there were six ships attached to the West African station under Commodore Bullen, and the number of recaptives that year reached a total of 5,393 from nineteen ships, the largest number of recaptives in a single year up to this time and a total exceeded in only two other years in the whole history of the antislavery blockade (C. Lloyd, *The Navy and the Slave Trade* [London, 1949], pp. 275–76, 281). It is difficult to identify Wright's carrier beyond doubt, but it appears to have been the *Velas*, a Brazilian vessel sighted twelve miles from Lagos at 12:30 P.M. on 16 March 1827, by Bullen's flagship, H.M.S. *Maidstone*. After a twelve-hour chase, she was captured, but no notice appears in the log of there having been slaves on board, nor of her subsequent disposition. Since ships without slaves were not subject to condemnation until after 1835, even if they were obviously fitted out for the slave trade, it would be hard to account for the prolonged chase unless the *Velas* were indeed a slaver with a cargo on board; nor were logs at this period always models of efficient record-keeping. See Master's Log of H.M.S. *Maidstone*, Public Record Office, London, ADM 52/4178.

glass of water a day and we were allowed only breakfast, no dinner. Many of the slaves had died for want of water, and many men died for crowdedness.

One day as I sat by the fireside where they were cooking, boiling water was thrown on my head, and my head became all peeled and sore, and this pained me very much. All the slaves thought I would have died, but the Lord nourished me in that painful time and I am not dead. Glory be to his name for his Tender care over a poor wretch like me.

We landed to Sierra Leone in about a month after we sailed from Igaye. It was great joy among the slave that day, for we supposed we should never see land anymore.

After we were landed at Freetown, they sent us boys to Mr. [William] B[enjamin] Pratt, manager of York, in order that we may be instructed.[34] There, we were placed in school. We begin at once to learn to read English book, which book I have cause to praise God for while I have life and breath. Through the reading of these books I came to know that High and Glorious name of Jesus Christ the Saviour. I have to acknowledge that although I read these books which teach me to know Jesus Christ the Saviour, I did not believe in him as I ought to have believed. Although I did not embrace or believe from my heart when first I read the word of God, I had great love to it. I liked to hear reading, and I liked to hear the minister preach to me Jesus. In five or six years after I came to this country, I began to learn to pray morning and evening, although I did it not from the heart; for I did not know the nature of prayer at the time. In the year 1834 . . . I began to attend Methodist Chapel. I praise God and I have to praise him if I be faithful to the end that I have joined Methodist Society, for they are not careless about my soul. They do not only tell me that the heaven is happy place, but they do teach me the ways to it. May God Bless this Sect or body. May the

34. Under the procedures established at this time by the Liberated African Department in Sierra Leone, the recaptured slaves were first landed in Freetown and then assigned to villages in the vicinity, each of them under a European manager who acted as magistrate, schoolmaster, and occasionally as a missionary as well. Recaptives were subsidized at first from government funds, then allowed to fend for themselves. See Fyfe, *Sierra Leone,* and Peterson "Freetown," esp. pp. 98–109. Most of the recaptives took European names shortly after their arrival in the colony, often those of missionaries or managers they admired, or those of the earlier settlers to whom they were apprenticed. Wright was probably named after a member of the Wright family of Negro American settlers who had come from Nova Scotia in the 1790's among the earliest settlers.

work of God prosper in their Land. From the day I met in class, I begin to seek the peace of God. That was from 15th June 1834. Bless be God! On 25th of December 1834, I obtained peace of God. From that blessed day I went among my friends, telling them that the Lord is Good, inviting them to come and taste for themselves. . . .

INDEX

Abazee, Nigeria, 177
'Abd al-Karīm (Abū Bakr's maternal uncle), 160
'Abdallah (Abū Bakr's brother), 160
'Abdallah ibn al-Ḥājj Muḥammad al-Watarāwi (scholar of Bouna), 153, 157
'Abdallāh Tafsīr aṣ-Ṣifā (Abū Bakr's maternal uncle), 159
'Abd al-Qādir (ancestor of Abū Bakr), 152
'Abd al-Qādir Kaba, 164
'Abd al-Qādir Mōr (Abū Bakr's ancestor), 160
'Abd al-Qādir Sankari (of Futa Jallon), 157
'Abd al-Salam Shabīnī, 174
'Abd ar-Rahmān (Abū Bakr's brother), 160
'Abd ar-Rahmān (Abū Bakr's uncle), 157–58
'Abd ar-Rahmān (of Kong), 153
'Abd ar-Rahman al-Sa'di: 26n, 153n, 174; reference, 148, 186
Abderrahman al-Sa'di. See 'Abd ar-Rahmān al-Sa'di
Abdolah (Abdullaye Ayuba Diallo, son of Ayuba Diallo), 39
Abdoul-Rahhahman (of Mississippi), 4n
Abdu (Armenian sea captain), 175

Abdullahi (brother of Usuman dan Fodio), 146
Abdulsalam, in Oyo, 295–96
Abdur, Biyi. See Biyi Abdur
Abeokuta, Nigeria: foundation of, 198, 307n, 321; political structure of, 248n; Samuel Crowther in, 290, 305n–6n; mentioned, 250n, 264, 291, 306n, 323n
Abigi, Nigeria, 243
Abimbola, Wande, 292n
Abiodun (Alafin of Oyo), 292n, 294
Aboh (division), Nigeria, 64, 68
Aboh, Nigeria, trade routes to, 61
Abomey, Dahomey, 230
Abraham, R. C., reference, 273, 309, 323
Abraham (the patriarch), 82
Absom, Lionel, 232n
Abū Bakr (ruler of Diawara), 158
Abū Bakr (sultan of Timbuktu), 173n, 185
Abū Bakr (uncle of Abū Bakr al-Ṣiddīq), 158
Abū Bakr al-Ṣiddīq: languages used by, 7; career of, 143–44; introduction to narrative of, 152–56; narrative of, 156–63; in Jamaica, 163–66; trade routes described by, 166–69; mentioned, 8, 35n, 145, 147, 184n, 187n, 189n, 227